POLAND AND THE COMING
OF THE SECOND WORLD WAR

Anthony J. Drexel Biddle, Jr.

POLAND AND THE COMING OF THE SECOND WORLD WAR

The Diplomatic Papers of

A. J. Drexel Biddle, Jr.

United States Ambassador to Poland

1937–1939

Edited with an Introduction by

Philip V. Cannistraro

Edward D. Wynot, Jr.

Theodore P. Kovaleff

OHIO STATE UNIVERSITY : COLUMBUS

Quotations from the Papers of Anthony Drexel Biddle, Jr., Box 1937, deposited with the Historical Society of Pennsylvania, are used by permission of Nicholas Biddle. Document 10 was previously published in *Foreign Relations of the United States, 1938* and Document 30 was previously published in *Foreign Relations of the United States, 1939.* Both are reproduced here by permission of the publisher.

Library of Congress Cataloging in Publication Data

Biddle, Anthony Joseph Drexel, 1896–1961.
    Poland and the coming of the Second World War: the diplomatic papers of A. J. Drexel Biddle, Jr., United States Ambassador to Poland, 1937–1939.

    Includes index.
    1. United States—Foreign relations—Poland—Sources. 2. Poland—Foreign relations—United States—Sources. 3. World War, 1939–1945—Diplomatic history—Sources. I. Title.
E183.8.P7B5   327.73'0438   75-45433
ISBN 0-8142-0237-3

TO THE MEN AND WOMEN OF ALL NATIONS
WHO STRUGGLED AGAINST FACISM
AND THOSE WHO CONTINUE THE TRADITION

CONTENTS

A map depicting the principal events and locals described in this narrative is presented on page 114.

One of the last telegrams sent by American Ambassador A. J. Drexel Biddle, Jr. from Poland during that fateful September, 1939, was composed on my portable typewriter placed upon a tree stump in the park at Zaleszczyki. The ambassador and his reduced staff had just arrived by motorcade at Zaleszczyki on the Romanian frontier. Together with key personnel of the Polish Foreign Office and other members of the diplomatic corps we had fled from Krzemieniec, which had been ruthlessly bombed and strafed by the German Luftwaffe.

While I do not remember the details of that telegram nor do I know whether it ever reached the State Department, its concluding sentence has remained clearly imprinted in my mind. Ambassador Biddle asked, "Why do England and France continue to drop propaganda leaflets when it has been shown what havoc can be wrought by dropping bombs?"

The question was rhetorical. The introductory essay and the documents published in this book reveal that Ambassador Biddle knew the answer: England and France were simply not prepared for armed conflict despite their declaration of war on September 3, 1939.

Zaleszczyki represented, so to speak, "the end of the line" for me in Poland. We crossed the bridge over the Dniester River on Friday, September 15, into neutral Romania. As a Kosciuszko Foundation scholar, I had been in Poland since July, 1938, doing research on a doctoral dissertation in history. During the fifteen months of my sojourn in Poland I had witnessed the numerous international crises that preceded the outbreak of World War II. Munich occurred in the fall of 1938 and Czechoslovakia surrendered the Sudentenland to the Nazis. In Warsaw, the atmosphere was tense as the Poles demonstrated for Teschen Silesia and appeared ready to make war upon the Czechs if their demands were not met. In the spring of 1939 Nazi Germany overran the whole of Czechoslovakia and annexed the Lithuanian city of Memel; Poland reacted by calling up certain age groups for military service and by rushing troops to the frontiers.

The summer of 1939, when I joined the staff of the American Embassy in Warsaw, was the deceptive calm before the storm. Then suddenly on August 23, 1939, came the explosion of a diplomatic bombshell: the signing of the Nazi-Soviet Non-Aggression Pact. We all knew war was close at hand.

As a resident scholar in Poland and then a staff member in the American Embassy, I was merely an observer of those momentous events. The American ambassador, on the other hand, was in close personal contact with Polish political leaders who played a major role in them. That is why his "Report" and communiqués to Washington are so revealing and so valuable to the historian. Our government was indeed fortunate to be represented in Poland by a person of Ambassador Biddle's caliber. Probably no other foreign official had such intimate relations with Polish government leaders. He and Mrs. Biddle entertained frequently and lavishly. He often played tennis and golf with Polish dignitaries. He spent many weekends on the Potocki estate at Łancut (a member of the Potocki family was the Polish ambassador in Washington). Thus he had more than the ordinary number of opportunities to engage in confidential conversations with the highest Polish authorities.

The Poles did not hesitate to confide in the American ambassador. His engaging personality, his frankness and honesty, his concern for Poland's problems and its difficult international position—all served to convince the Poles that he was a sincere friend of their homeland. Moreover, he represented a friendly nation that had assisted in the reestablishment of Poland, that had given generous economic support to the new state, and that included within its borders millions of citizens of Polish descent. Through the ambassador, the Poles hoped to inform America of their plight and their needs.

Tony Biddle, as he was known to his intimates, was certainly the right man at the right time and place. He possessed an uncanny understanding of international diplomacy and military strategy. Thanks to his simple, cogent literary style, his eyewitness account of Poland's fateful days is an absorbing and exciting narrative. Readers of this volume will be grateful to its editors for making his "Report" on the fall of Poland available to them.

Charles Morley

Columbus, Ohio
November, 1974

In the final years prior to the Second World War and during the initial phase of the conflict itself, Poland occupied a leading role in the tension-filled drama unfolding in international affairs. Diplomats were preoccupied with speculation regarding the posture Poland would actually adopt once the pressure of Hitler's Germany was applied fully to Warsaw, which seemed to vacillate between allegiance to the Western democracies and an apparent partnership with the Reich. Moreover, interested observers voiced concern about the strength of the Polish internal political system, economy, and social structure, and wondered about the state's ability to support a major war effort. Simultaneously, pointed questions were raised about the domestic political position of President Franklin D. Roosevelt and the directions that he would select for United States foreign policy, especially regarding the danger zone of East Central Europe.

The diplomatic papers of the last American ambassador to interwar Poland provide important new contributions to both discussions. A. J. Drexel "Tony" Biddle, Jr. served in Warsaw from the summer of 1937 until the outbreak of war, and then accompanied the Polish government on its flight from Poland through Romania to France and, ultimately, London. During his prewar tenure, Biddle supplied Washington regularly with detailed, perceptive analytical reports; then, while serving in France, he wrote a lengthy involved account of the final days of peace and the first phase of war, drawing upon his own notes, recollections, and private papers as well as his official documents. Not only are these materials of great interest per se but, considered in the context of the time in which they were written, they shed significant light on the attitude and role of the United States in the events that led to the Second World War. The Biddle reports furnished the American government with indisputable evidence of the nature, intent, and tactics of Nazi aggression in Europe. It is clear from these documents that Roosevelt and his foreign policy advisers were given a clear assessment of the crucial circumstances surrounding the fall of Poland, as well as a remarkably accurate judgment on Hitler's long-range goals and ambitions. Moreover, Biddle's dispatches to Washington also kept the administration abreast of domestic political and economic developments inside Poland, and of the entire range of extremely difficult external pressures under which Poland struggled for survival.

For purposes of clarity and cohesion, the book is divided into three main parts. The first contains an introductory essay, based on Polish as well as Western sources, that discusses Biddle's role and the atmosphere in which he worked. Next follows the lengthy report that Biddle began writing shortly after his arrival in Paris in October, 1939. This document is of particular interest, since it not only provides the most authoritative eyewitness account of the collapse of the Polish Republic, but also draws definite conclusions about the lessons to be learned for Western defense and foreign policies. In fact, Biddle apparently intended the report to have a pedagogical value, and accordingly wrote it as an official diplomatic document, with a subjective summary part. Thus, it is more than a mere memoir of his personal involvement in events of historical significance.

The materials presented in this book were originally written under trying circumstances without regard for the fine points of literary style; moreover, they were intended for a highly select group of key American political figures, and not for mass public consumption. Therefore, in preparing them for a general audience nearly forty years after their production, the editors have followed generally accepted editorial procedure, in an effort to make the account more comprehensible and readable without altering Biddle's own words or meanings. The numbers at the beginning of each paragraph have been eliminated, and many of the short paragraphs have been consolidated to give ideas and descriptions greater unity. The titles for each chapter are those of the original. Those occasional vague or confusing references made by Biddle have been clarified in editorial footnotes. In instances where Biddle misspelled Polish personal or geographical names, the editors have corrected the errors in line with accepted Polish usage by noting the proper forms in footnotes at their first appearance. Finally, where a word or phrase has been added for clarity, the editorial insertions have been placed within brackets. Otherwise, all spellings and punctuation forms, as well as grammatical and stylistic nuances, are exactly as Biddle wrote them in those tempestuous years.

The same observations apply to the third section of the book, which contains a selective yet representative collection of Biddle's important diplomatic correspondence with both the United States Department of State and President Roosevelt himself prior to the war. The report and his dispatches all reveal Biddle as an extremely perceptive observer with broad, varied contacts in Polish diplomatic and political circles, and the keen understanding essential to a correct analysis of the events and personalities on which he reported.

The editors gratefully acknowledge the cooperation and assistance of several individuals and institutions in the preparation of this book. The directors and staff of the Franklin D. Roosevelt Library in Hyde Park, New York, where the unpublished materials are deposited; The Historical Society of Pennsylvania, which houses the private papers of Biddle; and the libraries of Warsaw University, Florida State University, and Columbia University all greatly facilitated the research for this project. Mr. Nicholas Biddle, son of the late ambassador, kindly provided the editors with much useful information, as well as permission to consult his father's private papers. Several colleagues were extremely helpful during the preparation of the manuscript. Professors George Alexander Lensen and Ralph V. Turner of Florida State University, and John C. Rule of Ohio State University, offered considerable encouragement in undertaking this project, while Professors Thomas Campbell of Florida State University and W. W. Kulski of Duke University read the manuscript and contributed many valuable suggestions. A special word of gratitude belongs to Professor Charles Morley of Ohio State University, who accompanied the Biddles out of Poland and thus participated in the events described herein. He not only offered numerous helpful comments on the manuscript but also kindly consented to write the foreword to the book. Thanks also to Mr. William Johnson for drawing the excellent map of Poland printed in this volume, and to Mrs. Kathy Wynot and Mr. Charles C. Moore, Jr., who devoted considerable time and effort to preparing the manuscript for finished publication. Finally, the authors would like to express their appreciation for the superb editorial work performed upon the manuscript by the staff of the Ohio State University Press, especially Assistant Editor Sarah T. Millett.

Just as whatever merits the editorial contributions possess are due in large part to the above-named individuals, we alone are completely responsible for any deficiencies in this regard. Of course, the opinions and conclusions expressed herein are totally those of A. J. Drexel Biddle, Jr.

P. V. C.
E. D. W.
T. P. K.

Tallahassee, Florida
November, 1974

PART ONE

Introduction

Introduction

Anthony Joseph Drexel Biddle, Jr. was appointed United
States Ambassador to the Republic of Poland in May, 1937.
Biddle's credentials for the post were exceptionally good; for
in addition to close personal and political ties to the Roosevelt
administration, which afforded him the full confidence of the
president, Biddle was equipped with a first-rate diplomatic
mind and an engaging personality. His ability to gather and
absorb detailed information, as well as to grasp the broad implications of complex diplomatic maneuvers, provided Roosevelt and the Department of State with a clear, accurate, and
uncompromising analysis of the course of European diplomacy.[1] The selection of Biddle to represent the American government in a crucial and sensitive diplomatic center like Warsaw,
suggested a significant increase in American interest in East
Central Europe on the eve of the European crisis.

Biddle's excellent record as ambassador to Poland was especially remarkable since he had no professional training in the
foreign service. Yet, his background, personality, and social
position reinforced his innate talent for formal and informal
diplomacy. He was born on December 17, 1896, in Philadel-
phia, the son of Anthony Drexel Biddle and Cornelia Rundell
Bradley. The future diplomat was descended from a prominent
and wealthy Pennsylvania family; his father had been a well-

4	INTRODUCTION

known lecturer, author, and explorer, who once had taught for the Bureau of Investigation at the Department of Justice Training School.

Biddle was educated at St. Paul's School in Concord, New Hampshire, but never attended college. At the age of twenty he enlisted in the United States Army and fought in France from 1917 to 1918, rising to the rank of captain. With the end of the First World War, Biddle entered private business and quickly became involved in a wide range of interests. Between 1922 and 1934 he was, among other pursuits, director of a realty company, shipping line executive, an officer in the Acoustic Products Corporation, chairman of the De Forest Radio Corporation, and member of a South African mining company. Biddle married Mary L. Duke, heiress to the Duke tobacco fortune, and became a prominent social figure admired for his trim, well-dressed appearance and personal charm, his athletic skill, and a genuine capacity for human compassion. Moreover, he was equally known in European social and political circles, where he spent considerable time, and kept a house in Austria. In 1931 Biddle was divorced and married Margaret Thompson Schulze.[2]

Returning to the United States after a tour of Germany in the fall of 1930, Biddle threw himself into domestic politics as an early and active participant in Franklin D. Roosevelt's campaign. He contributed heavily in money and support to the Pennsylvania Democratic Party during the 1932 presidential election, and in 1934 campaigned extensively for George H. Earle, the first Democratic governor of Pennsylvania elected in more than one hundred years. In January, 1935, Governor Earle (who had been American minister to Austria in 1933) introduced Biddle to Secretary of State Cordell Hull, and in July Roosevelt appointed Biddle ambassador to Norway, where he remained until his transfer to Warsaw in 1937.

Biddle assumed his first diplomatic post at a tense moment in European history. Hitler, who had already startled the world by his brutal consolidation of power in Germany and his attempted coup against Austria in the summer of 1934, had recently announced the rearmament of the Reich, and Mussolini was preparing his final plans for the invasion of Ethiopia. In the two years preceding Biddle's appointment to Warsaw, the Italo-Ethiopian War would be fought and won by Mussolini, the Rhineland reoccupied by Nazi troops, and Spain would become the battlefield of a bloody civil war. As a result, both the League of Nations and the principle of collective security were wrecked by the success of Fascist and Nazi aggression. Throughout this critical period, the United States stood stead-fastly behind its isolationist shield, responding to European events by passing neutrality legislation designed to keep America out of foreign entanglements. Despite the efforts from many quarters to make Roosevelt aware of the dangers that threatened world peace, he took no decisive action. This lethargy resulted not only from his fear of domestic political repercussions but also from his own personal isolationism. Consequently, the foreign policy of the United States lapsed into "amoral drift."[3] In the face of this abandonment of responsibility, Europeans began to call upon the United States to exercise its leadership as a world power in order to counterbalance the actions of the aggressors. One French observer noted that despite his rigorous domestic programs, Roosevelt lacked a clear policy toward Europe and that "in these troubled times . . . which may lead to imminent catastrophe, the action of the United States may be decisive."[4]

By 1937, Roosevelt's attitude toward the rapidly deteriorating situation in Europe had matured and the administration began to assume a more decisive stance in foreign affairs. The 1936 election victory had given the president a renewed confidence in his leadership, whereas his defeat over the Supreme Court and other domestic issues in 1937 and 1938 led Roosevelt to subordinate questions of internal reform to the problem of foreign policy.[5] Moreover, alarming reports on Hitler's preparations for war were being sent to Washington from American diplomatic representatives abroad, so that both Roosevelt and Hull should have been more than ever convinced of the dangers of inaction. Ambassador William E. Dodd's dispatches from Berlin revealed the extent of Hitler's efforts to prepare Germany for war and clearly informed the State Department of Nazi designs in Central and Eastern Europe.[6] Similar opinions were expressed and driven home by John Cudahy, United States ambassador to Poland, whose optimistic views had undergone a sharp reversal since his arrival in Warsaw in 1933. In March, 1936, at the time of the Rhineland crisis, Cudahy wrote to the White House that "the past week has demonstrated very clearly that . . . the League of Nations and collective action are all illusory. . . . If the Hitler Government is not overthrown, a war in Europe is as certain as the rising sun. This certainty of war we must recognize and accept as an established fact."[7] In December Cudahy told Roosevelt flatly that "Germany is the outstanding threat. The whole impulse of the country is war preparation," and he warned that Hitler's plans inevitably would include Czechoslovakia and Danzig.[8] Nonetheless, in his letters to Roosevelt and in public speeches Cudahy argued strongly for a reinforcement of American neutrality in the impending conflict.

Biddle, closely in touch with European diplomacy from his post in Oslo, wrote to Roosevelt in equally urgent terms. In a letter of February, 1936, Biddle gave a brief but cogent analysis of Poland's position in the rapidly changing power shifts:

> General Picture. Realignment of major Powers taking place. At the present moment, the scene on this side of the Atlantic may be described as a mad scramble for position, in view of the major regroupings. In order to forestall further ambitious attempts on the part of the expansionists, Germany, Japan, and Italy, it would appear, for the time being at any rate, that England and France might look to Russia for the balance of power. Pending such re-groupings taking definite form, Poland is on the fence as regards definite position. In her desire to take a position in the realignments from which she can derive the greatest advantages, she has remained, to date, noncommittal. It is considered that, so far she has been able to maintain, so-to-speak, an even balance between Russia and Germany. Though it is felt by foes of the Soviet here that Poland would naturally join the Italo-German group, were it to take definite form, nevertheless, the keenest, and less prejudiced observers believe that Poland must eventually fall in line with the British-French-Soviet combination.[9]

Although Biddle's dispatches from Norway were cognizant of

the dangers of war, they were always marked by a careful analysis of conditions and events that was the product of calm and controlled study rather than bleak despair. To Biddle's portrayal of the European situation Roosevelt replied in April that "the general situation on the other side seems not only chaotic but much in need of some new plan and new leadership. Perhaps the time is not ripe but it is at least worthwhile pointing towards it."[10]

In April, 1937, on the eve of the congressional debates over the extension of the Neutrality Act, Roosevelt announced Biddle's appointment as ambassador to Poland.[11] After confirmation by the Senate, Biddle and his wife arrived in Warsaw on June 2, having left a most favorable impression on official circles in Oslo. On his departure from Norway the important labor daily *Arbeider Bladet* had high praise for Biddle, characterizing him as an example of the "younger and more attractive type of diplomat," conscientious and lacking in the "stiff formality of the older generation."[12] Biddle's transfer to Poland was not a sudden decision. As early as April, 1935, Cudahy had let it be known to William C. Bullitt, then ambassador in Moscow, that he was "anxious to get out of Poland as he has had enough of the physical disorder of Eastern Europe." Bullitt cautioned the president that "the man you send to Warsaw . . . should also be very much of a gentleman and acutely intelligent," and he immediately proposed Biddle for the post, although Cudahy could not be transferred to Dublin for another two years. It is clear, however, that Biddle's appointment to Norway was meant only as a temporary measure until a more important position could be found for him.[13]

Cudahy's pessimism over events in Central Europe and Poland must have contributed to Roosevelt's decision to send Biddle to Warsaw. Shortly before the latter's appointment, Cudahy wrote a despairing letter to the president in which he concluded that "Poland is the poorest country in Europe and I must tell you very confidentially that I will be surprised if it can survive economically another ten years. The country is without natural resources, is over-populated, [and] has no definite economic or political policy."[14] On the other hand, Biddle was enthusiastic about his move to Warsaw, where he felt important diplomatic events were rapidly converging, and he quickly set about "acquiring a clear picture of Poland in terms both of domestic and foreign policy."[15] He rapidly won the confidence and friendship of Polish leaders, particularly of Foreign Minister Józef Beck and President Ignacy Mościcki. Indeed, Biddle was so successful in obtaining the trust and confidence of key Polish and foreign diplomatic, political, and economic officials that his opinions and views were highly prized by Polish leaders as well; Jan Szembek, the Polish under-secretary of foreign affairs, praised Biddle as being "customarily well-informed."[16] The impact of the change in ambassadors became evident within a few months after Biddle's arrival. His appraisals of the Polish scene drew high praise from Roosevelt, who, after being informed by the State Department that Biddle had begun immediately to send Washington first-rate and highly interesting reports, paid particular attention to them.[17]

The Polish government, equally delighted with the new ambassador, welcomed Biddle warmly and impressed upon him their "utmost interest" in Roosevelt's efforts to preserve world peace.[18] Taking Biddle's arrival as a sign of renewed American concern for European affairs, the Polish ambassador in Washington, Jerzy Potocki, told Hull that "Poland . . . is looking to the United States for leadership in Europe as well as throughout the world." The Polish statesman also expressed his confidence that "such leadership with a program will be forthcoming when the time is ripe."[19]

Biddle brought a fresh perspective to the American view of Poland as a result both of his intensive energy and a genuine sense of compassion for the Poles. Sincerely convinced of the need to foster closer ties between America and Poland, Biddle immediately immersed himself in efforts to remove any obstacles to the attainment of that positive relationship. He therefore devoted considerable attention to the less glamorous but equally vital area of financial affairs, and was largely responsible for the relative ease with which Polish-American relations were regulated. His efforts were particularly evident in such delicate matters as arranging loans and debt cancellation.[20] He also moved swiftly to avoid any embarrassment that might arise from occasional incidents involving illegal or indiscreet actions by American citizens visiting the country.[21] His diligent and concerned involvement with such mundane affairs, together with his record of overall success, earned Biddle the respect and gratitude of Polish officials.

This proved to be extremely fortunate, for Biddle arrived in Warsaw at a time when the country was undergoing a fundamental political transformation from within and experiencing mounting pressure from Nazi Germany. The death of Marshal Józef Piłsudski in May, 1935, deprived Poland of the only source of effective leadership it had known since 1926. The power vacuum was all the more serious because of the widespread domestic unrest over worsening economic conditions and the rising protest of antigovernment German and Ukrainian minorities. In the power struggle that erupted in 1935, Piłsudski's self-appointed heirs formed a supraparty coalition, known as the Camp of National Unity, whose structure and ideology were designed to forge an authoritarian regime capable of rallying all sections of the population around the slogan of "National Defense." The regime rested on Marshal Edward Śmigły-Rydz as inspector general of the armed forces, Ignacy Mościcki as president, and Józef Beck as foreign minister. Although Poland was technically still a constitutional republic with a parliament (*Sejm*) representing a wide range of socioeconomic interests and ideologies, the leaders of the camp appeared intent on pushing the country rapidly toward a fascist-like dictatorship. They argued that this was necessary to consolidate internal authority and bolster national strength in the face of increasing domestic and foreign difficulties.[22]

Cudahy's appraisal of the domestic situation five months after Piłsudski's death revealed little comprehension of the basic forces at work. "Here in Poland," he told Roosevelt, "there are no radical changes to record and the government continues under President Mościcki much as it did under Marshal Piłsudski."[23] Biddle, on the other hand, quickly grasped the real trend in Polish politics and its relationship to the country's foreign policy problems. In his first lengthy report from Warsaw, he advised Roosevelt that the new leadership "appreciates the importance of maintaining a democratic facade during this *still formative* period of Poland's regeneration. Accordingly, they recognize the importance of maintaining a Parliament despite the decidedly centralized character of the present Government. The keynote of Government policy, therefore, is: 'a conducted democracy'—that is to say, 'a democracy conducted under an authority'. . . . Moreover, the Government feels that until the masses become more enlightened they will continue to be subject to the sway of subversive influences of the 3rd Internationale as well as the continued existence of cross currents and the play of other externally inspired forces. . . . I now look for Government inner circles to exert a quiet but definite effort to strengthen in every way possible the Government front [the Camp of National Unity] in their aim to exercise a firm check against communistic and other disturbances."[24]

Biddle's assessment of internal Polish politics was considerably more optimistic and tolerant than that held by other elements of American opinion—a fact that was not lost upon Polish leaders. From the first appearance of the government bloc, the *New York Times* greeted it and the emerging political orientation it represented with a distaste that soon ripened into open hostility.[25] In June, 1937, *Times* writer-editor Otto Tolischus visited Poland for a firsthand view of the situation, and reported that it was increasingly evident that the regime was adopting a form of Polish fascism that focused on alienating the non-Polish ethnic and religious minorities in order to gain support from the Polish middle and lower classes.[26] Prompted by these revelations, the paper devoted an editorial to the Camp of National Unity, angrily calling it "not only strongly nationalist and authoritarian, but also more and more racial and exclusivist." The *Times* concluded by warning that "Poland, the oppressed land freed in the name of liberty and self-determination, is being remade in a spirit and on a pattern terribly like that of Nazi Germany," a trend that would certainly alienate from Poland "the world sympathy which more than anything else won the Poles their independence."[27] British public and private appraisals of domestic Polish affairs were equally critical. Both the London *Times* and the British ambassador to Poland, Sir Howard Kennard, bemoaned the thinly disguised authoritarian nature and program of the Camp of National Unity, and later ridiculed it as the farcical attempt of nonpoliticians to find a political solution to Poland's myriad problems.[28] The French press, however, was more restrained in discussing these developments. It generally accepted the political evolution within Poland as a necessary evil given the country's geopolitical situation.[29]

Biddle, too, was aware that, in a larger sense, Poland's domestic development was a reflection of her extremely unstable international position. Traditionally, one constant factor overshadowed Polish diplomacy: the dangerous geopolitical position of Poland between Germany to the west and Russia to the east. Piłsudski had long since laid down the fundamental precept that if Poland were to survive as an independent state, she would have to pursue a policy of "equilibrium" between her two great neighbors. As practiced by Colonel Beck, this policy meant good relations with both powers but no formal alliance with either. Poland, Piłsudski argued, must steer a middle course of her own, while building up the defensive alliance with France. Although sound in conception, the policy of equilibrium was fraught with new dangers as a result of Hitler's seizure of power in 1933. Thereafter, Poland became a potential battleground, in both the military and ideological sense, in the struggle between Nazi Germany and Soviet Russia. Consequently, the pressures for Poland to go the totalitarian route of her two powerful neighbors became increasingly greater during the later 1930s.[30] Biddle's dispatches made it painfully clear that Poland's fate would be a crucial test of Europe's future, not only in terms of that country's ability to escape Nazi aggression but also to the extent that the country was able to maintain its remaining democratic institutions intact in the face of the totalitarian wave that appeared to be engulfing the continent.

Roosevelt's search for a solution to the deteriorating situation in Europe and the Far East first emerged in his famous

"Quarantine" speech, delivered in Chicago on October 5, 1937. Breaking openly for the first time with his earlier isolationist stance, Roosevelt condemned those aggressors who jeopardized the freedom and security of the world, and hinted at the need for collective action to guarantee international peace. The speech provoked both applause and violent isolationist reaction in the United States, while the European response was equally varied. The German government immediately assumed that the combined influence of Roosevelt and Hull had begun to have its effect on American foreign policy. The Nazi ambassador in Washington cabled Berlin that henceforth "we must not count on American isolationism as an axiom," although he suggested that the United States would intervene actively in European affairs only if Great Britain were directly involved in a world conflict.[31] Biddle informed Roosevelt later that month that Polish leaders welcomed the new American position, but he stressed that Poland could do very little by itself to oppose German aggression in East Central Europe.[32] Moreover, on October 7 *Gazeta Polska*, the official organ for the Polish government, lauded the Quarantine speech as the signal for a dramatic switch from American isolationism to a more active role in world affairs. The Poles, however, apparently realized that Washington was more concerned with Asia than Europe. Several days later, a lead editorial in the same newspaper speculated that although isolationism was deeply rooted in American tradition, nevertheless Japanese aggression in the Far East would enable Roosevelt to change American opinion.[33]

In his letter to Biddle on November 10, four days after Italy joined Germany and Japan in the Anti-Comintern Pact, Roosevelt revealed his growing concern over Poland's difficulties and the worsening European situation in general: "I am glad that the Chicago speech has apparently made a real dent in government thinking in Europe even though it is heartily disliked by some of the 'powers that be.' Since you wrote, the general situation seems to have got worse instead of better and there is no question that the German-Italian-Japanese combination is being amazingly successful—bluff, power, accomplishment or whatever it may be." He underscored the importance of alerting the entire world to the expansionist nature of fascism, for "we cannot stop the spread of Fascism unless world opinion realizes its ultimate dangers." The president concluded by assuring Biddle that he was "awfully glad to have you . . . in Warsaw where you are literally on the firing line—more so in many ways than if you were in Paris or Berlin or Moscow. If things get worse, Warsaw and Prague and Vienna will, one or all, become focal points."[34]

From his vantage point in Warsaw, Biddle eagerly agreed with the president's views, but presented a somewhat more realistic appraisal of the forces operating in Poland. He noted that in East Central Europe, an area "constantly subjected to the cross currents of various conflicting ideologies," an observer did not have to be "supersensitive to feel the terrific pressures which the advocates of totalitarian doctrine constantly bring to bear on the leading statesmen, both here and in the neighboring states." In this context, Biddle voiced his belief that the political attitudes of the East European leaderships served as "barometers" of the Western democracies' desire and willingness to enforce the spirit and letter of the League of Nations system. With regard to Poland, he offered the following analysis of the domestic political scene: "So far, the predominant leading element of the present Polish regime has evinced its adherence to Piłsudski's idea of advancing during this regenerative interval along the lines of 'democracy conducted under the idea of authority,' a condition which from a Western viewpoint would appear to be inconsistent with pursuance of a strictly democratic concept. However, in terms of Eastern European viewpoints, such a course is accepted as an evolutionary process compatible with their forward looking program." In this situation, Biddle assured Roosevelt, he was doing his best to advance the cause of democracy in Poland by developing his daily contacts to the point where he could "discreetly offer constructive suggestions whenever the opportunity might psychologically present itself."[35]

These observations on the state of Polish democracy provoked some interest in Washington, but Roosevelt and the

State Department naturally focused their attention on Biddle's reports concerning Nazi activity. His day to day, exhaustive analysis of German policy toward Poland, with its careful recording of the alternating degrees of German pressure, was an accurate gauge by which the American government could measure the broader aspects of Hitler's tactics and strategy in Europe. Biddle had a keen awareness of the Nazi danger in Europe from both personal and professional experience. In July, 1934, a few days after the murder of Austrian Chancellor Engelbert Dollfuss by Nazi agents, Biddle—who was entertaining a group of friends and relatives at his hunting lodge in Strecken—decided to journey to Vienna to attend the funeral of the dead statesman. On the way there, his party was caught in the cross fire during an engagement between armed Nazi party "militia" and the Austrian *Heimwehr* in a small village outside Vienna, and several of those present were arrested for a short while and treated rather harshly by Nazi bullies.[36] This demonstration of Nazi brutality left a strong impression on Biddle that greatly influenced his subsequent attitudes toward Germany.[37]

Biddle confirmed this firsthand impression of the National Socialist movement during the following two years by a conscientious study of European politics and diplomacy, especially after he had access to classified information as American representative in Oslo. Consequently, when he arrived in Warsaw in June, 1937, Biddle was prepared not only to lend a sympathetic ear to a country that he knew was high on the list of Hitler's ambitions but also to keep his own government well informed of real or anticipated Nazi moves against Poland. Accordingly, he developed a close working arrangement with Ambassador William C. Bullitt, then in Paris. Since Bullitt was a major proponent of American involvement in Europe, Biddle was able to gain a clear perspective regarding the impact of Polish-German relations in France and England and, indirectly, on United States policy toward Europe. Through the use of personal correspondence as well as occasional visits, Biddle developed an information network that he used to update both American and Polish official circles on the nuances of each other's diplomacy. For example, in July, 1938, when the Czechoslovak question had emerged as the key issue of international affairs, he informed Bullitt of how a personal animosity of long standing between Beck and the under-secretary of the French Foreign Office, Alexis Léger, had entered into the delicate equation of Franco-Czech-Polish relations.[38] Conversely, on numerous occasions Biddle passed along to Polish diplomats the information he had received from his American counterparts in London, Berlin, and Moscow as well as Paris, and became highly prized by Warsaw as an important source of knowledge on Western outlooks.[39] Beck also utilized Biddle as a conduit for transmitting Polish views to the Western powers, especially France, on the correct assumption that the American would promptly pass them on to Bullitt.[40]

The major Polish personality with whom Biddle had the closest contact was Colonel Beck, a long-time associate of Piłsudski and minister of foreign affairs since 1932. With Piłsudski's death, Beck's position within the Polish regime had grown steadily stronger, particularly after Hitler's seizure of power began to affect Poland's foreign relations. In an attempt to adjust Polish foreign policy to the new circumstances, it appeared to many that Beck had brought Poland closer to Germany through the conclusion of a ten-year Declaration of Non-Aggression in January, 1934, and by at least outwardly indicating that Polish-German problems could be resolved peacefully and through greater mutual understanding.[41] But although he seemed to be pulling decisively away from Piłsudski's axiom of equilibrium between Germany and Russia, Beck was careful to step evenly between the two great powers and to make no genuine commitment to either side.

At first Biddle, too, misjudged the actual degree to which Beck had tied himself to a pro-German course, even suggesting that official Polish anti-Semitism had been influenced by German pressure.[42] More accurately, in one of his first reports from Warsaw, Biddle speculated that "the reason why Colonel Beck is so strongly pro-German is found in his theory that the Fascist powers in Europe are growing stronger, while the Democratic forces are gradually losing out"; he suggested that as France lost its ability to keep Germany in check, Poland would have to rely increasingly on her own devices.[43] "From my own observations," he informed Roosevelt in August, "Colonel Beck is steadily becoming the leading force in the Polish Government, due mainly to his initiative, his willingness to make decisions, and to shoulder responsibility. I find him a man of courage and intelligence." Biddle noted that during their "frequent conversations," Beck placed "increasing emphasis on what he calls 'voisinage'—or the good neighbor policy," while admitting that "his 'tight-rope walking' role is a difficult one."[44]

Indeed, by 1937 Beck's "tight-rope walking" had become more precarious than ever. In spite of the relatively smooth relations with Germany since the Declaration of Non-Aggression and Hitler's personal assurances that "it would be madness to attempt to seize territories from Poland or . . . to push her away from the Baltic," the Nazi remilitarization of the Rhineland had drastically shaken Poland's position.[45] The abject failure of the French to take decisive action against Hitler's repudiation of the Locarno Pact seriously undermined the entire Eastern and Central European alliance system erected by France in the 1920s. Throughout most of 1937 there was a subtle but obvious increase of German pressure on Poland, including rising tensions in Danzig and German demands for free extraterritorial transit across the Corridor. Roosevelt, who was kept closely informed of these events, wrote to Biddle: "I appreciate the difficult position of Poland, but I hope that the Polish government will not find itself compelled to do things which would be regarded by the democratic nations as yielding to Germany."[46] But Beck, who had never had much faith in the ability or willingness of France to fulfill her commitments to Poland, demanded with a sense of futility that the time had come to demonstrate the "vitality, strength, and permanence" of the Franco-Polish alliance.[47]

Nevertheless, in July, Beck confided to Biddle that he did not believe Hitler wanted war with Poland. Biddle concluded that, for the moment at least, Hitler would "humor" Poland and maintain good relations with her.[48] Although Hitler's

statement of November 5 to the effect that he had no intention
of altering the status of Danzig apparently found some credence among Polish officials, Biddle himself was convinced that
Hitler simply wished to postpone the conflict until a more
favorable moment.[49] In retrospect Biddle's viewpoint proved to
be correct. On the same day that Hitler gave his assurance
about Danzig, the führer also told his generals at a meeting in
the Reich chancellery to prepare Germany for war in the near
future, and on November 6 Italy joined Germany and Japan
in the Anti-Comintern Pact. In December, after six months of
intensive study and observation, Biddle sent the State Department a balanced and accurate summary of Poland's position:

> Although Colonel Beck has been frequently suspected in the
> past (particularly by the French) of leaning towards Germany,
> my own observations convince me that he is first and foremost
> a *Polish patriot* thinking in terms mainly of Poland's own
> interests, and following the precepts of his former chief, the
> late Marshal Piłsudski. . . . Piłsudski had constantly stressed
> the importance not only of maintaining an equilibrium between
> forces on Poland's Eastern and Western frontiers but also the
> importance of building up as good friendship as possible with
> Germany during peace times, as well as of maintaining correct
> normal relations with the Soviet. This formula envisaged Po-
> land's ability both to rehabilitate herself economically, socially,
> and otherwise, and to construct her defenses, militarily, so-
> cially, religiously, and otherwise, against what Colonel Beck
> . . . considers the "unlimited" menace of Bolshevism. In
> contrast to Colonel Beck's regarding *communism as an "un-
> limited" menace* which seeks to penetrate every element in
> the structure of national life, he regards *Germany as a "lim-
> ited" menace*, whose aims are at least ear-marked. To my
> mind, this . . . has been the guiding influence in Colonel
> Beck's direction of Poland's foreign policy. . . . I definitely
> feel Beck, in directing the course of Poland's foreign policy,
> constantly keeps his *eye on Britain's movements*, and that
> his estimate of Britain's future action plays an important role
> in the Minister's formulation of Poland's long-term policy.
> To my mind, in terms of European considerations Beck's
> fondest aspiration is a close tie-in with Britain.[50]

Biddle apparently hoped that by presenting the Polish situation in this light, he could prod Washington into adopting a more forceful stance in European affairs. His frustration at American lethargy in this area was evident in a private memorandum written at the same time as the above-quoted official report. To himself, Biddle observed that in the crucial years of growing international danger "it was always Britain and France who were asked to carry the burden. The United States of America sits happily on the outside and every other nation sighs with hands folded."[51]

The events of 1938 tended to confirm the impression that Beck was acting in ever closer association with Germany. In fact, Beck's analysis of Polish interests, aside from Danzig and the Corridor, was based on his anticipation of Western reactions to German policies in Central Europe. He was fully convinced that the Western Powers would not risk war in order to block Hitler's ambitions in Austria and Czechoslovakia, and that to oppose Berlin on these issues would only serve to endanger Poland's relations with Germany. Consequently, the Nazi takeover of Austria in March was mutely accepted by the Polish government as an internal matter for Austria and Germany.[52] As for Czechoslovakia, Beck was equally sure that Poland should take advantage of the destruction of that country if it came about as a result of its abandonment by the Western Powers. Relations between Prague and Warsaw had been marked by open hostility since 1920, when the Conference of Ambassadors in Paris had ceded parts of Teschen (Cieszyń, Česin) and Austrian Silesia to Czechoslovakia along with 76,000 Poles. Not only would the breakup of the Czech state restore this area to Poland, but the transfer of the equally contested Subcarpathian Ruthenia to Hungary would produce a common Polish-Hungarian frontier. Beck believed this development to be especially desirable, for it would strengthen Poland's position in Central Europe and lead to the formation of an East European bloc to stem further German aggression in this area. During the early months of 1938, therefore, he began to apply pressure on Czechoslovakia on behalf of the Polish minority, a campaign clearly coordinated with similar demands made by Hitler for the Sudeten Germans and by Hungary for Ruthenia.[53] Biddle reported his analysis of Beck's plans to Hull in April:

> Beck's energetic action vis-à-vis the Polish minority in Czechoslovakia comes as no surprise to me, for . . . Beck has informed me that the Polish minority would claim autonomous administration immediately, in the event that German influence led to a like claim by the Sudeten Deutsch. It is now becoming steadily clearer to me that in the light strictly of Poland's own long-range defensive policy, Beck's energetic activities . . . are motivated mainly by an underlying serious apprehension as regards Germany's potential moves. I am aware that Beck is concerned lest through intensified diplomatic and political-economic pressures, the Germans succeed in bringing the Czech government around to making a "deal" with Germany on all of Bohemia, or perhaps even on the whole of Czechoslovakia, before Poland might succeed in her efforts to bring about automony for her own minority in Czechoslovakia. . . . I am, moreover, aware that the Government is also concerned lest Hitler at the back of his mind might visualize the extension of German political and economic hegemony right down the Danubian Valley, to the Black Sea, with an eventual eye to the Ukraine. . . . Beck has not forgotten the late Marshal Piłsudski's long-range dream, which . . . envisaged a neutral wall from the Baltic to the Black Sea, as a means of stiffening the defensive position of each state in such an area, towards resisting, according to Piłsudski's apprehensions, an eventual and inevitable German drive eastwards. In this connection, Piłsudski was hopeful that an eventual direct contact might be resumed between Poland and Hungary.[54]

A few days later, Biddle observed to Roosevelt that "in this part of Europe the atmosphere may be characterized by steadily increasing tension. All States, including Poland, east and south of Germany, live in constant apprehension as to which might be the next victim of Hitler's expansion program." This in turn led Beck to direct Polish foreign policy "even more cautiously than ever," trying "to make friends with Germany at every possible turn, in a play for time, wherein he hopes to strengthen Poland's defensive position against what Piłsudski anticipated, and now he, Colonel Beck anticipates, as an inevitable eventual conflict with Germany."[55]

In the aftermath of the May crisis, during which Czechoslovakia had mobilized its armies along the German frontier in anticipation of a Nazi invasion, Biddle presented the State Department with an important analysis of Beck's policies designed to delineate his motives and clear away the confusing inconsistencies in Polish policy.[56] Biddle explained that Poland felt she could make no firm international commitments in advance of an actual war between Germany and the Western Powers for fear of endangering her policy of equilibrium and, in fact, her very existence; hence, Beck "necessarily plays his diplomatic cards with extreme care." Moreover, Beck had anticipated the failure of London and Paris to support Czechoslovakia, and the realization of his fears only further undermined belief in Polish circles in the sincerity of France's commitments to her East European allies. Nonetheless, Beck realized that Poland could not resist German military or political pressures alone. Accordingly, Biddle believed that once the democracies employed forceful military action against Hitler, "I should look for Poland to strike out vigorously, and even eagerly, on the side of Britain and France."

This lengthy memorandum formed part of a series of reports designed to furnish the American government with a broad survey of major trends in European diplomacy set down on the eve of the Munich crisis. In another paper written at the same time, Biddle sought to calculate the effects of Hitler's Eastern European ambitions on Polish policy in particular, and their more general effect on Poland's relationship with the Western Powers. Ever since the Austrian *Anschluss*, Biddle had been convinced that the direction of Nazi ambition lay to the east, and that Hitler's ultimate goal was the acquisition of the Ukraine with its vast food and mineral resources.[57] From conversations with Beck and other officials in 1938, Biddle gathered that this view was also prevalent among Polish leaders, and that in spite of his apparently pro-German policies, Beck would never accept an alliance with Hitler against the Soviet Union. On the contrary, Beck told Biddle emphatically that Poland would do everything it could to prevent or counter a German move into Russia. "My observations lead me to feel," Biddle informed the State Department, "that the [German] acquisition of any part of the Russian Ukraine would fail to compensate Poland for having Germany on her East and South as well as her West. . . . Beck imparted in the strictest confidence what I consider to be a most enlightening disclosure of his foreign policy in terms of its long-range outlook. In effect he said he felt that someday, in the event that Germany might find an envisaged acquisition of the Ukraine impossible, through Nazi-styled peaceful penetration, Poland might have to fight to prevent passage of German troops over her territory. . . . In such event, Germany would attack Poland, not as the *objective*, but as the means of reaching Germany's envisaged Ukrainian objective."[58]

Beck, in the same conversation, also admitted that he believed Germany's friendship to be only temporary. Danzig and the Corridor would soon become "objectives of German aspirations," and Poland increasingly recognized that "a conflict of German and Polish interests is being led to by events in the making." In the event of a German attack, Beck argued, Poland would resist with all her resources in the hope that she would halt the Nazi war effort. Biddle further observed that although Beck knew that Chamberlain wished to avoid war at any cost, he nevertheless felt that the aid of Britain and France represented Poland's only chance in the event of a war with Germany. Biddle concluded his report with a rather bleak assessment of the policy of appeasement: "In evaluating Beck's policy, I wish to emphasize the importance of bearing in mind not only Poland's potentially black outlook in the event either of continued German military or peaceful infiltration eastwards, but also . . . that Beck . . . was bitterly disappointed over France's refusal to march, subsequent to Hitler's march into the Rhineland. In fact, Beck later told me personally that France had made a great tactical error. To his mind, failure to march at that time would prove costly in terms of the long-run, not only for France, but also for Poland and Britain."[59]

By the end of July, Biddle cautiously noted a somewhat more relaxed atmosphere prevailing in Europe, in view of the possibility of a peaceful settlement of the Czech problem as a result of Lord Runciman's impending trip to Prague. Nevertheless, he informed Roosevelt that although Polish officials were "keeping their fingers crossed . . . the next six weeks may be expected to prove a period characterized by show-downs, back-downs, and critical negotiations."[60] In fact, the pessimism of official circles in Warsaw over the outcome of the Czechoslovakian situation resulted in a direct inquiry by the Polish government as to what role the United States might play should a European war break out. For the first time since his arrival in Warsaw, Biddle was put in the difficult and, evidently for him, frustrating position of having to admit that his government could offer no official encouragement or support to Poland. In talks with a "high ranking Polish official," Biddle could only attempt to allay Polish fears that the United States might supply Germany with war materials, and to suggest that although neutrality sentiment was still wide-spread in America, "Nazidom's neo-pagan policy of extreme anti-Semitism" had caused considerable revulsion there.[61]

Regardless of Biddle's guarded remarks, the impending Czech crisis stirred the administration into action. Alarming dispatches about Hitler's plans from American representatives in Europe, particularly from Bullitt in Paris and Joseph Kennedy in London, began to reach the State Department, and on August 16 Hull announced that the Axis nations "could not count us out in pressing their plans for conquest."[62] While Chamberlain conferred with Hitler at Godesberg on September 22–23, Bullitt urged Roosevelt to intervene as a mediator in the crisis, and Hull told the president that "the evidence we had been receiving was overwhelming that Germany was armed to the teeth and was bent on widespread aggression at all hazards." On September 26 Roosevelt addressed a strongly worded message to Hitler urging a peaceful settlement of the issue, and he instructed Biddle to communicate the same message directly to Beck in order to dissuade Poland from pressing its demands on Czechoslovakia.[63]

But in spite of the peaceful outcome of the Munich settlement, Hull remained skeptical of its long-range results. From Warsaw Biddle cabled him on September 30 that the still unresolved demands of Poland and Hungary for Czech territory continued to make the situation in Central Europe dangerous, and he recommended that Roosevelt suggest an international conference of these states to negotiate the issue. In reply, Roosevelt instructed Biddle to give Beck a personal message to the effect that he hoped Poland would contribute to peace by avoiding the use of force.[64] The seizure of Teschen by Poland on October 2 frustrated Roosevelt's move; for, as Biddle informed him four days later, Beck's determination to settle accounts with Czechoslovakia in the event that country was abandoned by the West, had been unshakable. Biddle's subsequent summary of the Czech crisis reinforced Hull's skepticism: "It is now becoming clear that Hitler's plans envisage (a) a period of internal reconsolidation and 'digestion' for Germany; and (b) a reinvigorated drive Eastward and Southeastward. . . . As for what is left of unfortunate Czechoslovakia, Hitler, as I have long anticipated, is bringing all possible pressure to bear on Prague to fall in line with Berlin. I still perceive no tangible grounds for hopes that the Munich Conference might lead to a general European appeasement and pacification—and I continue to feel that Europe is passing through a period of armed truce."[65] In a similar letter on November 5, Biddle repeated his doubts as to the positive results of Munich, concluding that: "I find it equally difficult at this writing to foresee any development which in final resort will not imply a variable degree of German hegemony over the various individual states east and southeast of Berlin."[66]

Although Beck had gained one of the goals of his policy, the dismemberment of Czechoslovakia seriously weakened Poland's international position and resulted in its further encirclement by Germany. The Munich settlement was hardly completed when Hitler began to apply pressure against Poland in the by then familiar pattern. Nazi strategy focused on Danzig, the area that Beck called the "barometer of German-Polish relations."[67] On October 24, German Foreign Minister

Ribbentrop presented Polish Ambassador to Germany Józef Lipski with a series of "fundamental demands" that included the return of Danzig to the Reich, the construction of a German highway and railroad across the Corridor, and Polish membership in the Anti-Comintern Pact.[68] Beck rejected these demands through a note to Ribbentrop on November 19, and five days later Hitler issued a secret directive ordering preparations for the military occupation of Danzig.[69] The Poles were keenly aware of the growing tension in Polish-German relations, and moved to bolster their international position. Hence, on November 27 Warsaw and Moscow issued a joint Polish-Soviet declaration confirming all existing agreements between the two countries and expressing the determination to resolve calmly any outstanding issues. A major increase in trade between the countries was listed as a major objective.[70]

By December, Biddle, who had received accurate information about these developments from his numerous contacts, reported to Hull in no uncertain terms his views on Hitler's plans for Poland. He felt certain that Germany's ultimate goal was complete European hegemony, and foresaw the establishment of a vassal Ukrainian state as the key to that policy. Although the Soviet Union loomed as the chief obstacle to this program, Biddle felt that Hitler would avoid a direct military confrontation with the Russians until he had gained "complete ascendancy over the area between Germany's eastern and the Soviet's western frontier." Accordingly, Biddle believed that Berlin intended to apply the Czechoslovak "solution" to Poland: dividing the country into several parts through annexation of the Corridor, Danzig, and Upper Silesia to the Reich, outright incitement of the Ukrainian minority to break away from Poland and join up with Ruthenia, and the promise of Vilna to Lithuania. He predicted that Hitler would unleash the heretofore muzzled Nazis in Danzig to agitate against Poland much as the Sudeten Germans had been used to pressure Prague, and concluded pessimistically: "I discern increasing signs that Hitler is fast closing in on Poland."[71]

In the uncertain early months of 1939, Biddle kept Washington closely informed of the rapidly deteriorating relations between Germany and Poland, having already concluded that war between them would be averted only in the unlikely event that Beck made substantial concessions to Hitler regarding Danzig. It was clear to Biddle that the attitude of Britain and France toward Poland's dilemma would be the crucial factor in Beck's negotiations with Hitler, but he judged that, unlike Czechoslovakia, Poland would fight alone if necessary.[72] The American envoy set out to arouse his country's support for the valiant Polish cause, while simultaneously bolstering the resolve of Warsaw. Roosevelt's January 4 speech to the Congress, in which he announced that the United States would adopt "all measures short of war" to halt international aggression, produced a wave of articles in the Polish press greeting this American initiative with overt enthusiasm.[73] Biddle promptly called upon Szembek to express his pleasure at the Polish response, indicating that his own personal satisfaction was shared by the American government.[74] On the following day Beck traveled to Berchtesgaden, and after several days of talks with Hitler and Ribbentrop came away in a very pessimistic mood. Immediately upon his return to Warsaw, he telephoned Biddle to confirm that Roosevelt's speech had made a profound impact on the Polish government and had caused Hitler considerable worry. Beck then arranged to confer with Biddle at length about his talks with the führer. Although Hitler had insisted that Danzig return to Germany, he had assured Beck that all problems were open to negotiation, an assurance in which Beck had little faith. Moreover, the Polish foreign minister was uneasy over what he discerned as a marked departure from Hitler's normal behavior: "When Hitler had greeted him, he was philosophical and pensive in demeanor—and only during his oration wherein he reviewed his accomplishments over the past year did he evince a spirit of boastfulness."[75]

Events began to move rapidly after Beck's meeting with Hitler. Biddle's representations on behalf of Poland appeared to be achieving concrete results when the Export Bank in Washington granted long-term credits for the Polish purchase of American cotton. Toward the end of January, Ribbentrop visited Warsaw and repeated Hitler's earlier demands concerning Danzig and the Corridor. Beck, confiding in Biddle, revealed the substance of the German demands and admitted that they were completely unacceptable. Biddle hazarded the guess that Hitler's apparent willingness to negotiate with Beck was an effort to put England and France off guard as he prepared for his final move against Poland.[76] In March, Biddle reported that he and Beck were in full agreement that Hitler would launch his drive against Poland within six months. Moreover, he wrote to Roosevelt that the American armaments program and the "firmness of attitude" on the president's part with regard to aggression "have served as a 'stop, look and listen' sign to the dictators," and had the effect of "stiffening British and French resistance."[77] But the Nazi seizure of Bohemia and Moravia on March 15, which Biddle had predicted in a dispatch to Hull the previous month,[78] and the similar absorption of Memel on March 23, precipitated a major turnabout in the European situation. On March 26, Lipski in Berlin reaffirmed Poland's refusal to yield to German demands, and two days later Beck bluntly told the German ambassador in Warsaw that any attempt to alter the status of Danzig would be considered a *casus belli*. The Polish position was strengthened considerably on March 31 when Britain declared itself ready to guarantee the independence of Poland.

When the British verbal guarantee received new stature with its conversion on April 6 into an Anglo-Polish statement of intent to sign a formal mutual assistance pact,[79] Hitler resolved to act decisively. The infuriated führer had already drawn up a far-reaching, secret directive for military operations against Poland—the famous "Case White"—which was issued April 3. Now, in a major foreign policy speech before the German Reichstag on April 28, he openly condemned Polish "acts of belligerence" and expressed his keen disappointment with the deterioration of German-Polish relations due to Warsaw's treachery.[80] When Hitler capped this sweeping indictment by declaring that the Anglo-Polish agreements had voided the 1934 German-Polish nonaggression declaration, the situation had become ominous. Beck responded in equally determined fashion on May 5, likewise speaking before a joint session of the Polish legislature. After convincingly exposing as hollow each German charge that Poland had refused to negotiate with Berlin in good faith, the Polish foreign minister closed with a defiant warning to Hitler: "We in Poland do not recognize the conception of peace at any price! There is only one thing in the life of men, nations, and states which is beyond price, and that is honor."[81] Hitler in turn accepted the Polish challenge by concluding the "Pact of Steel" alliance treaty with Mussolini on May 22, amidst much bellicose publicity. Thoroughly alarmed at the mounting threat to Poland, Biddle promptly sent the State Department a lengthy memorandum in which he presented a remarkably accurate survey of the German policy that he had gathered from Polish intelligence sources.[82]

The courageous stance of the Poles strengthened Biddle's resolve to help them as much as possible. Throughout the summer of 1939 he painfully chronicled the evidence of mounting Nazi pressure against Poland, urgently seeking to make the American government aware of the impending danger. His letters to Roosevelt continuously underscored the importance of the British position toward Poland and expressed the hope that the president's attitude would have a bolstering influence on England and France.[83] Simultaneously, Biddle began to espouse openly the Polish cause in messianic tones that revealed the extent of his deeply felt personal involvement in and identity with the destiny of his host country. Szembek noted a conversation with him on April 25, in which he "expressed admiration for the position and conduct of Poland" and asserted that "if Europe succeeded in freeing itself from the totalitarian dictators, it could thank Poland for that."[84] Shortly thereafter, during a dinner at the American Embassy, Biddle went so far as to tell Polish officials that England, France, and the United States should be made to understand that Polish armies represented the advance guard of the European forces against aggression and that consequently Poland deserved the active financial and diplomatic support of those states. He suggested that the Polish government should step up its propaganda in America in order to drum up support for its stance against Germany, and pledged his own active participation in such an undertaking.[85] In June he warned the State Department that the apparent easing of German press attacks against Poland, and Hitler's insistence on his willingness to negotiate with Warsaw, were merely familiar Nazi tactics designed to confuse the Western Powers.[86]

Indeed, by the end of the month Biddle, in an increasingly philosophical mood, had become so pessimistic that he wrote to Roosevelt that he doubted whether war could be averted. After a series of in-depth conversations with a number of Polish officials, Biddle noted that "it would be difficult to liquidate the current conflict of forces in Europe through statesmanship and diplomacy in that the differences at stake did not wholly constitute material problems. Indeed, underlying the conflict were two discernable, basically different conceptions. . . . recognized principles governing international relationships counted for naught in Berlin's view." He felt that the Western democracies could not realistically expect to coexist with "the totalitarian regimes and all they implied." Since Munich had revealed the bankruptcy of appeasement, the only recourse left was to strengthen and maintain "the anti-aggression front [which] might prove an expensive operation, but if it succeeded, . . . it would prove far cheaper than a conflagration."[87]

These observations, as well as some prodding by the Polish embassy in Washington, began to have some effect on the administration. At a lengthy White House conference with Senate leaders on July 18, Hull stressed the urgency of the diplomatic cables and reports from Warsaw and Berlin in a futile effort to have the embargo on arms shipments to Europe lifted.[88] The meeting was especially important because it came on the eve of Poland's requests for an extension of American credit in order to build up and supply her armed forces in preparation for a German attack. The administration had already turned down a Polish request for helium in November of the previous year on the grounds that Poland's military situation, and hence nonbelligerent status as demanded by the Neutrality Act, was too precarious. More recently, in May, 1939, the Polish minister of trade, Antoni Roman, had vainly appealed to Henry Morgenthau that his country would need considerable financial assistance to keep its army mobilized when that step was taken.[89] On August 9, Ambassador Potocki reported to Sumner Welles in the State Department that Germany had begun to station troops along the Polish border, and that Poland was determined to resist an invasion. Potocki added that the refusal of Congress to revise American neutrality laws had encouraged Hitler's plans against his country, and he ended the interview with an appeal for money in order to buy planes, copper, and other raw materials.[90]

The final days of August saw the culmination of hopes for a peaceful resolution of Polish-German disputes and, therewith, the preservation of peace. Near the end of August, both Bullitt and Biddle cabled Hull that Hitler would probably launch an attack against Poland within the next week.[91] On his own initiative Biddle had already drawn up plans for the evacuation of his embassy staff from Warsaw by August 21, and four days later the Polish government released its evacuation plans.[92] Both Chamberlain and Bonnet appealed to Roosevelt to use his influence in order to preserve peace. Accordingly, on August 24, the American president, not wanting to pressure Poland, sent a note to Hitler and Mościcki urging negotiation, a move that Hull argued would have no substantial effect.[93] Meanwhile, the conclusion of the German-Soviet nonaggression pact on August 23 had rendered Poland's situation more desperate than ever. On August 25, when the formal Anglo-Polish Mutual Assistance Treaty was finally concluded, Biddle telegraphed to Hull that Poland had decided to fight if Danzig were invaded, but that the whole issue was still open to possible negotiation.[94] When Berlin ignored Roosevelt's appeal and Mościcki replied by blaming Hitler for the inflammatory situation and stressing the Polish desire to avoid war, the cause of peace seemed doomed.[95] Nonetheless, in Warsaw Biddle continued to offer encouragement to the Polish government while urging them to use restraint.[96] All of these last minute efforts to ward off hostilities ended on September 1, as the German armies suddenly poured across the Polish frontier and Nazi aircraft began to bombard Polish cities.

The outbreak of war thrust Biddle into the center of world attention, and gave him an opportunity to marshal international support for beleaguered Poland. The saturation bombing of Warsaw presented him with the issue upon which he could build his entire case against German aggression and the system that had spawned it. When Luftwaffe pilots also bombed the American Embassy villa at Konstancin, just outside Warsaw, Biddle promptly expressed outrage and indignation at the fact that he personally was considered a military target.[97] He vented his displeasure in a telephone call to Bullitt in Paris, who transmitted reports of the German aerial attacks on Polish civilians to Roosevelt.[98] The president used this eyewitness account as the basis for a message addressed to the leaders of the belligerents, plus Britain, France, and Italy, demanding a halt to further "ruthless bombing from the air of civilians," and ordered additional investigations to confirm the initial reports.[99] With German troops rapidly advancing into Poland, the government withdrew from Warsaw on September 6 and began a retreat across the country to the Romanian border. On the road to the designated temporary government seat of Krzemieniec, Biddle, his wife, and their diplomatic entourage experienced their second brush with German aircraft, which harassed the moving columns continually. Biddle had fastened a large American flag to the roof of his car to emphasize his diplomatic neutrality, but found it only attracted the attention of the pilots. Estimating that there were "about 5,000" German planes involved, he noted that "It seemed impossible to get away from them. My own car . . . was bombed fifteen times and machine-gunned four, forcing me to take refuge in a roadside ditch."[100] Biddle's dispatch of September 8, deliberately published by the State Department a few days later, decisively exposed the hollowness of Hitler's denials that civilians had been bombed by German aircraft, and greatly furthered the growth of world outrage against Berlin.[101]

Biddle was most upset, however, by the vicious air attack

on Krzemieniec, a small, defenseless market village distinguished only for its temporary diplomatic visitors. The town was completely devoid of military or political significance, having as yet neither Polish military nor government leaders in its midst. Nonetheless, on September 12 waves of German dive-bombers struck in late morning, killing about fifty Poles and wounding scores of others. Biddle at once called an "indignation meeting" of the assembled diplomats, who agreed to send messages to their home offices protesting the outrage.[102] Accordingly, Biddle had good reason to wire Hull on September 14 that "in view of what the members of my staff and my family and I have experienced and witnessed, I find it difficult in many cases to ascribe the wanton barbaric aerial bombardment by German planes to anything short of deliberate intention to terrorize the civilian population and to reduce the number of child-producing Poles irrespective of category."[103]

From that point on, collapse of the Polish state was only a matter of time. When Britain and France failed to deliver the massive air assistance they had promised, the Polish civilian and military leadership hastened the push southeastward to the friendly Romanian territory under cover provided by the valiant but outmanned Polish army. The Poles were especially disheartened when the great French land offensive against the German rear, which the French General Staff had guaranteed would take place within fifteen days of a German attack on Poland, likewise did not materialize. The final blow to Polish hopes came on September 17. On that date, the Soviet Union violated its nonaggression treaty with Poland by invading the beleaguered country from the east, in line with the secret protocols of the Nazi-Soviet Pact. Caught between the proverbial hammer and anvil, and abandoned by her allies, Poland faced the inevitable. Her government crossed the Romanian border, arriving in Bucharest on September 18. From there Biddle made his way to Paris, where Hull sent him a telegram commending his work "under conditions of great emergency."[104] On September 30, Mościcki, interned by the Romanian government, resigned as president of Poland, and former cabinet minister Władysław Raczkiewicz assumed the office in

Paris. Hull immediately issued a statement recognizing the Polish government in exile and continuing Biddle in his capacity as ambassador to Poland.

During the course of the war Biddle was subsequently appointed ambassador and minister plenipotentiary to six additional governments in exile (Czechoslovakia, Greece, Luxemberg, Norway, Yugoslavia, and the Netherlands), as well as interim ambassador to France, and conducted crucial negotiations with the Reynaud government immediately prior to the fall of that country in June, 1940. Biddle retired from the State Department in 1944 and was commissioned a lieutenant colonel in the United States Army. After the war, he was attached to the Allied forces headquarters in Europe (SHAPE) and later made a special assistant to the Army Chief of Staff. He died on November 13, 1961, six months after having been appointed ambassador to Spain.

All of the traits attributed to Biddle in the above sketch of his activities—careful attention to all factors that might influence foreign policy decisions, a broad range of personal contacts that opened valuable sources of information to him, an appreciation of both the Polish and the general European international situations, and above all, a concern lest his government not realize the dangers to international order posed by Hitler—are particularly evident in the detailed analytical report of the fall of Poland and selected prewar dispatches and memoranda presented below. They prove decisively that "Tony" Biddle was, indeed, a "diplomat's diplomat," despite his clear lack of any formal training in the art of diplomacy. Moreover, he provided the exceptional example of a "citizen diplomat" rising to the task before him, thus justifying the appointment of men without prior diplomatic experience to key posts.

---

1. Arthur Krock, writing Biddle's obituary for the *New York Times* on November 14, 1961, noted that "his reports of the oncoming Nazi assault on Poland and France remain in the State Department files as models of prescience and accurate information." See also Cordell Hull, *The Memoirs of Cordell Hull*, 2 vols. (New York, 1948), 1: 652–53, and William L. Langer and S. Everett Gleason, *The Challenge to Isola-*

tion, 1937-1940 (New York, 1952), p. 60, for additional recognition of the importance of Biddle's dispatches.

2. The *New York Times*, November 14, 1961, p. 39, contains a good sketch of Biddle's life and career. Various editions of *Who's Who in America* have also been consulted by the authors.

3. Foster R. Dulles, *America's Rise to World Power, 1898-1954* (New York, 1954), pp. 168, 175, 183-84; Langer and Gleason, *The Challenge to Isolation*, p. 32. Robert A. Divine, in his *Roosevelt and World War II* (Baltimore, 1969), makes a strong case for the view that Roosevelt was hampered by his own isolationist convictions. For an analysis of the scholarly literature on American isolationism, see Justus D. Doenecke, "Isolationists of the 1930s and 1940s: An Historiographical Essay," paper presented to the Southeastern Regional Meeting of the Society for Historians of American Foreign Policy (February 24, 1973). -

4. Alexandre Gauthier, "Les États-Unis et l'Europe," *Revue d'Histoire Diplomatique*, 51, no. 2(April-June, 1937): 241-42. See also Firmin Roz, "Le Président Roosevelt et l'Europe," *Revue des Deux Monds* 107, no. 1(January 15, 1937): 399-406; and R. de Roussy de Sales, "L'Amerique et l'Europe," *L'Europe Nouvelle* 20(May 29, 1937): 511-14.

5. Basil Rauch, *Roosevelt from Munich to Pearl Harbor* (New York, 1950), pp. 70-73.

6. Many of Dodd's observations, including a lengthy, detailed report on Nazi foreign policy dated November 28, 1936, are in the Franklin D. Roosevelt Library, Hyde Park, New York (hereafter cited as FDRL), PSF, box 34, "Germany." See also *Ambassador Dodd's Diary, 1933-1938*, ed. William and Martha Dodd (New York, 1941). On Dodd's reports to and relations with the U. S. State Department, see Robert Dallek, *Democrat and Diplomat: The Life of William E. Dodd* (New York, 1968).

7. Cudahy to Roosevelt, March 20, 1936, FDRL-PSF, 50, "Poland."

8. Cudahy to Roosevelt, December 26, 1936, in *F. D. R. His Personal Letters*, 4 vols. (New York, 1950), 3: 577-78.

9. Biddle to Roosevelt, February 27, 1936, in *Franklin D. Roosevelt and Foreign Affairs*, ed. E. B. Nixon, 3 vols. (Cambridge, Mass., 1969), 3:211.

10. Roosevelt to Biddle, April 15, 1936, in *F.D.R. His Personal Letters,* 3:576.

11. *New York Times*, April 7, 1937.

12. A copy of the article, together with an English translation, is among the Papers of Anthony Drexel Biddle, Jr., deposited in The Historical Society of Pennsylvania (hereafter cited as Biddle Papers), box 1937, "Poland and Oslo."

13. Bullitt to Roosevelt, April 12, 1935, in *Franklin D. Roosevelt and Foreign Affairs*, 3:478.

14. Cudahy to Roosevelt, February 6, 1937, FDRL-PSF, 14, "Poland." Cudahy overlooked Poland's impressive coal reserves in making this gloomy, but otherwise accurate, assessment. Both in total known reserves and in production, Poland ranked seventh in the world among the coal-producing countries; in fact, coal was one of her most important export commodities. See *Maly Rocznik Statystyczny 1939* (Warsaw, 1939), p. 125, table 5, and p. 148, table 26.

15. Biddle to Roosevelt, August 28, 1937, FDRL-PSF, 37, "Poland," and ibid., May 18, 1937, 24, "Poland."

16. *Diariusz i teki Jana Szembeka*, ed. J. Zarański, 4 vols. (London, 1964-72), 4:151.

17. Roosevelt to Biddle, August 16, 1937, FDRL-PSF, 37, "Poland."

18. Biddle to Roosevelt, July 26, 1937, FDRL-PSF, 37, "Poland." Printed below in Part 3 as Document 1.

19. Hull memorandum, June 4, 1937, in *Foreign Relations of the United States, 1937* (Washington, 1954), 2:552. A year earlier Cudahy had reported the extreme disappointment of Polish officials over the lack of American leadership in foreign affairs. Cudahy to Roosevelt, January 16, 1936, FDRL-PSF, 37, "Poland."

20. Szembek, *Diariusz i teki*, cites several occasions when Biddle settled some involved financial affairs at his request; see 3:142, 144–45; 4:126–27, 129. Many of Biddle's reports published in the series *Foreign Relations of the United States* deal with financial matters; see vol. 1 for 1938 (Washington, 1953), and vols. 1 and 2 for 1939 (Washington, 1956).

21. For example, in September, 1937, two Polish-Americans, Głowacki and Milewski, were arrested and convicted of trying to export illegally 60,000 Polish złoty. Biddle requested Szembek to speed up the appeal process and to do what he could to reverse the conviction, or at least obtain a suspended sentence, lest Polish-American relations suffer a setback from adverse public opinion in the United States. As a result of this intervention, the two Americans were freed. Szembek, *Diariusz i teki*, 3:145, 151.

22. For a detailed study of these events, see Edward D. Wynot, Jr., *Polish Politics in Transition: The Camp of National Unity and the Struggle for Power, 1935–1939* (Athens, Ga., 1974). For the general domestic political background, see Anthony Polonsky, *Politics in Independent Poland, 1921–1939* (Oxford, 1972), and Hans Roos, *A History of Modern Poland* (New York, 1966).

23. Cudahy to Roosevelt, October 11, 1935, FDRL-PSF, 50, "Poland."

24. Biddle to Roosevelt, report entitled "Outline of Polish Government's Present and Forward Looking Course," December 10, 1937, FDRL-PSF, 37, "Poland."

25. See issues of May 17 and 26, July 16, 1935; September 18, 20, 1936; and February 12, 22, and March 2, 1937.

26. *New York Times*, June 5, 11, 1937.

27. June 12, 1937.

28. For example, see the articles and editorials in the London *Times* of May 29, July 17, October 9, 21, and November 10, 1936; February 23–24, March 23, April 3, 23, 27, and July 21–26, 1937. For Kennard's opinions, see his reports to Foreign Secretary Anthony Eden of February 22, 24, March 10, 24, and November 2, 1937—British Foreign Office (Public Record Office, London), files 371/20759-20760, "Poland."

29. For example, *Le Temps*, February 22–23, March 3, 1937.

30. On Polish foreign policy in this period, see especially Roman Debicki, *The Foreign Policy of Poland, 1919–1939* (New York, 1962); Anna Cienciala, *Poland and the Western Powers, 1938–1939* (Toronto, 1967); and Hans Roos, *Polen und Europa. Studien zur polnischen Aussenpolitik, 1931–1939* (Tübingen, 1957). Invaluable sources for this period are the Szembek diaries cited above, and the memoirs of Polish Foreign Minister Józef Beck, *Final Report* (New York, 1957), as well as those of the French envoys to Warsaw in the 1930s, Jules Laroche, *La Pologne de Piłsudski: Souvenirs d'une ambassade, 1926–1935* (Paris, 1953), and Leon Noël, *L'Agression allemande contre la Pologne* (Paris, 1946).

31. Hans Dieckhoff to German Foreign Ministry, October 9, 1937, *Documents on German Foreign Policy, 1918–1945* (Hereafter cited as *DGFP*), Series D (Washington, D. C., 1949), 1:635–41, and ibid., December 7, 1937, p. 655. For a general discussion of American-German relations during this period, see James V. Compton, *The Swastika and the Eagle: Hitler, the United States, and the Origins of World War II* (Boston, 1967); Saul Friedländer, *Prelude to Downfall: Hitler and the United States, 1939–1941* (New York, 1967); and Arnold A. Offner, *American Appeasement: United States Foreign Policy and Germany, 1933–1938* (Cambridge, Mass., 1969).

32. The contents of Biddle's letters are summarized in *F.D.R. His Personal Letters*, 3:726.

33. *Gazeta Polska*, October 11, 1937.

34. Roosevelt to Biddle, November 10, 1937, FDRL-PSF, 37, "Poland." Also in *F.D.R. His Personal Letters*, 3:725.

35. Biddle to Roosevelt, January 13, 1938, FDRL-PSF, 37, "Poland."

36. *New York Times*, September 5, 1934.

37. Nicholas Biddle to Theodore P. Kovaleff, conversation held on November 28, 1972 in New York City.

38. Biddle to Bullitt, July 25, 1938, FDRL-PSF, 37, "Poland."

39. See the notations on Biddle's information, and Polish comments on it, in Szembek, *Diariusz i teki*, 3:195–97, and 4:80, 183–85, 366, 389, 460, 561, 574, 625.

40. As Beck himself admitted in a conversation with Szembek, *Diariusz i teki*, 4:216.

41. Of the numerous studies of Polish-German relations during this period, see especially Richard Breyer, *Das Deutsche Reich und Polen, 1932–1939* (Würzburg, 1955); Josef Korbel, *Poland between East and West: Soviet and German Diplomacy toward Poland, 1919–1933* (Princeton, N.J., 1963); Józef Krasuski, *Stosunki polsko-niemieckie 1919–1925* (Poznań, 1962), and *Stosunki polsko-niemiecki 1926–1932* (Poznań, 1964); Marian Wojciechowski, *Stosunki polsko-niemieckie 1933–1938* (Poznań, 1965); and Anna Cienciala, "The Significance of the Declaration of Non-Aggression of January 26, 1934, in Polish-German and International Relations: A Reappraisal," *East European Quarterly* 1, no. 1 (March 1967):1–30.

42. Memo of June, 1937, Biddle Papers, Box 1937, "Poland and Oslo." For an analysis of Polish anti-Semitism during this period, see Edward D. Wynot, Jr., " 'A Necessary Cruelty': The Emergence of Official Anti-Semitism in Poland, 1936–1939," *The American Historical Review* 76, no. 4(October 1971): 1035–1058. Biddle quickly changed his mind and came to understand the real causes and issues involved in official Polish policy toward the Jews. For example, see his letters to Roosevelt (November 10, 1938, FDRL-PSF, "Biddle") and to Hull (December 22, 1938, FDRL-PSF, 37, "Poland"). Both are printed below in Part 3 as Documents 9 and 13, respectively.

43. Memo of June, 1937, Biddle Papers, Box 1937, "Poland and Oslo." Reprinted by permission of Nicholas Biddle.

44. Biddle to Roosevelt, August 28, 1937, FDRL-PSF, 37, "Poland."

45. Hitler's remarks, made to Beck on June 3, 1936, are in Szembek, *Diariusz i teki*, 1:330.

46. Roosevelt to Biddle, November 10, 1937, FDRL-PSF, 37, "Poland."

47. Biddle memo of December 6, 1937, Biddle Papers, Box 1937, "Poland and Oslo." Reprinted by permission of Nicholas Biddle.

48. Biddle memo of July 28, 1937, based on his conversation with Beck of July 23, in Biddle Papers, Box 1937, "Poland and Oslo."

49. Biddle memo of December 1, 1937, ibid. Hitler's remarks to Józef Lipski are printed in *DGFP*, D (Washington, D.C., 1953), 6:26–27. See also the recently published selection of Lipski's private papers, *Diplomat in Berlin, 1933–1939: Papers and Memoirs of Józef Lipski, Ambassador of Poland*, ed. Wacław Jędrzejewicz (New York, 1968), pp. 303-5.

50. Biddle to Roosevelt, December 10, 1937, FDRL-PSF, 37, "Poland." Many of the key points in this report were later confirmed by Beck in his memoirs, *Final Report*, esp. pp. 175–76.

51. Biddle memo of December 4, 1937, Biddle Papers, box 1937, "Poland and Oslo." Reprinted by permission of Nicholas Biddle.

52. For specific studies of Polish foreign policy during this period, see Henryk Batowski, *Austria i Sudety 1919–1938* (Poznań, 1969), and *Kryzys dyplomatyczny w Europie, jesień 1938–wiosna 1939* (Warsaw, 1962); and Stefania Stanisławska, *Wielka i mała polityka Józefa Becka* (Warsaw, 1962), plus works cited in note 41 above.

53. Beck, *Final Report*, p. 163. For studies of Polish-Czech relations, see Jerzy Kozeński, *Czechosłowacja w polskiej polityce zagranicznej w latach 1932–1938* (Poznań, 1964), and Michał Pułaski, *Stosunki dyplomatyczne polsko-czechosłowacko-niemieckie od 1933, r. do wiosny 1938* (Poznań, 1967). The most detailed work on Poland and the Munich Conference is by Stefania Stanisławska, *Polska a Monachium* (Warsaw, 1967). For Polish-Hungarian relations during this crucial period, see Maciej Koźmiński, *Polska i Węgry przed drugą wojną światową, październik 1938 - wrzesień 1939* (Wrocław, 1970).

54. Biddle to Hull, April 7, 1938, FDRL-PSF, 37, "Poland."

55. Biddle to Roosevelt, April 10, 1938, ibid.

56. Biddle memo, "Outline of the Salient Features of Poland's Present Role in the Continental Political Arena," June 19, 1938, FDRL-PSF, 37, "Poland." Printed below in Part 3 as Document 4.

57. Biddle memos, "My observations on the Various Aspects of the Current Trend of German Eastward Expansion," and "Observations . . . on the Economic Bloc Resulting from Germany's Annexation of Austria," both of June, 1938, ibid. Printed below in Part 3 as Documents 4 and 5, respectively.

58. "Streamlined Observations on Various Aspects of the Complex Effect of Hitler's Expansion Program . . . ," ibid. Printed below in Part 3 as Document 4.

59. Ibid.

60. Biddle to Roosevelt, July 29, 1938, FDRL-PSF, 37, "Poland."

61. Biddle memo of July 28, 1938, ibid. Printed below in Part 3 as Document 6.

62. *Memoirs of Cordell Hull*, 1:587.

63. Ibid., pp. 591–92.

64. Ibid., p. 596.

65. Biddle to Roosevelt, October 15, 1938, FDRL-PSF, 37, "Poland." Several recent scholarly works have attempted to refute the standard appraisal of Beck's policy during the Munich crisis, represented by Biddle's analysis. According to this thesis, not only did Beck not wish to "settle accounts with Czechoslovakia" but in fact he placed the acquisition of the Teschen territory last on his list of priorities, which were concerned more with general questions of Poland's position in international diplomacy. Moreover, Beck seized Teschen mainly as a form of dramatic "protest" against the exclusion of Poland from such a major diplomatic function involving East Central Europe as the Munich Conference. The major figure in this "rehabilitation" of Beck is Anna Cienciala; in addition to her book cited above, see her article, "Poland and the Munich Crisis, 1938—A Reappraisal," *East European Quarterly* 3, no. 3(June 1969):201–19.

66. Biddle to Roosevelt, November 5, 1938, FDRL-PSF, 37, "Poland." Printed below in Part 3 as Document 8.

67. Beck, *Final Report*, p. 174.

68. *DGFP*, D, 5:104–7.

69. *Trial of the Major War Criminals before the International Military Tribunal, Nuremberg, 14 November 1945–1 October 1946* (Nuremberg, 1948), 20:9–13.

70. For an in-depth discussion of this turn in Polish-Soviet relations, see Bohdan Budurowycz, *Polish-Soviet Relations, 1932–1939* (New York, 1963), pp. 127–33.

71. Biddle to Roosevelt, December 22, 1938, FDRL-PSF, 37, "Poland." Printed below in Part 3 as Document 11.

72. Biddle to Hull, January 5, 1939, ibid. Printed below in Part 3 as Document 16.

73. For example, see *Gazeta Polska* and *Ilustrowany Kurjer Codzienny* of January 6, 1939.

74. Szembek, *Diariusz i teki*, 4:460.

75. Biddle to Hull, January 13, 1939, FDRL-PSF, 37, "Poland." Printed below in Part 3 as Document 17.

76. Biddle to Hull, February 15, 1939, ibid. Printed below in Part 3 as Document 18.

77. Biddle to Roosevelt, March 4, 1939, and Biddle to Hull, March 10, 1939, both in ibid. The former is printed below in Part 3 as Document 21.

78. Biddle to Hull, February 16, 1939, ibid.

79. Text in *The Polish White Book. Official Documents concerning Polish-German and Polish-Soviet Relations, 1933-1939* (New York, 1940)—hereafter cited as *PWB*—no. 71.

80. Ibid., no. 75.

81. Ibid., no. 77.

82. Biddle memo, May 20, 1939, FDRL-PSF, 37, "Poland." Printed below in Part 3 as Document 25.

83. Biddle to Roosevelt, January 12, May 6, 20, and Roosevelt to Biddle, June 6, 1939, all in ibid.

84. Szembek, *Diariusz i teki*, 4:574.

85. Ibid., pp. 577–78.

86. Biddle to Hull, June 9, 1939, FDRL-PSF, 37, "Poland." Printed below in Part 3 as Document 27.

87. Biddle to Roosevelt, June 27, 1939, ibid. Printed below in Part 3 as Document 28.

88. *Memoirs of Cordell Hull*, 1:649–52.

89. See the various entries in the "Morgenthau Diaries" (FDRL), vol. 153, pp. 304–5, November 29, 1938; vol. 190, pp. 139–40, May 17, 1939.

90. Memo by Sumner Wells, August 9, 1939, FDRL-PSF, 37, "Poland." Printed below in Part 3 as Document 30. See also Potocki's interview in the *New York Times*, August 10, 1939. Hull agreed with Potocki's appraisal of the neutrality laws—*Memoirs of Cordell Hull*, 1:653.

91. *Memoirs of Cordell Hull*, 1:660, and Biddle to Hull, August 15, 1939, FDRL-PSF, 37, "Poland."

92. Biddle to Hull, August 21, 25, 1939, *Foreign Relations of the United States, 1939* (Washington, D.C., 1956), 2:669–71.

93. *Memoirs of Cordell Hull*, 1:662. The text of Roosevelt's message is in *The Public Papers and Addresses of Franklin D. Roosevelt*, 13 vols. (New York, 1941), 8:444–48.

94. Biddle to Hull, August 25, 1939, FDRL-PSF, 37, "Poland." Printed below in Part 3 as Document 31. For a superb account of these critical days, see Henryk Batowski, *Ostatni tydzień pokoju* (Poznań, 1964).

95. Mościcki's reply to Roosevelt's letter is in the *Public Papers*, 8:449–50.

96. Szembek, *Diariusz i teki*, 4:697. Biddle assured the Poles that Mościcki's response was perfect and would draw a highly favorable opinion in the United States.

97. In *The War Hitler Won: The Fall of Poland, September 1939* (New York, 1972), p. 4, Nicholas Bethell reports that Biddle phoned Clifford Norton, counsellor at the British Embassy, shortly after the attack began: " 'They're attacking!', he shouted. The bombs were going off closer and closer, until finally one exploded in his garden. His voice by now was one of utter disbelief. 'They're attacking *me*!' he shouted down the telephone." While not wishing his colleague ill, Norton was pleased that the Germans were bombing American property, for he hoped that the enraged Americans would take decisive action against Berlin.

98. Biddle's message, sent via Bullitt, was revealed by Roosevelt in his press conference held on September 1, *Public Papers*, 8:455.

99. For Roosevelt's message to the belligerents and their allies, see ibid., p. 454.

100. As recounted by Biddle in his press conference in the *Times* (London), September 24, 1939.

101. Department of State, *Bulletin* 1, no. 1 (September 16, 1939): 249–50. See also Henryk Batowski, *Pierwsze tygodnie wojny. Dyplomacja zachodnia do połowy września 1939* (Poznań, 1969).

102. See the firsthand account by British journalist Clare Hollingsworth, *The Three Weeks' War in Poland* (London, 1940), p. 66.

103. *Memoirs of Cordell Hull*, 1:678.

104. Ibid., pp. 685–86.

PART TWO

The Biddle Report

CHAPTER ONE

Pivotal Events

Factors and Forces

Which Led to War

From Warsaw I had observed the course of Hitler's machinations and the fulfillment of his aggressive plans [first] vis-à-vis
Austria, then Czechoslovakia and Lithuania.[1] Neither in the
case of Austria nor of Czechoslovakia did I look for support
from the Western powers. At the same time, however, I felt
that when in turn Poland became the object of Nazi appetite,
the Poles could be counted upon to fight, and that by the time
Germany's aggressive attention would have turned vis-à-vis
Poland, the continental picture would have become so changed
as to have prompted the Western powers to lend their support
to the first country willing to resist Herr Hitler's apparent
determination to redraw the map of Europe.

In observing various aspects of Nazi technique vis-à-vis Austria and in turn Czechoslovakia, I discerned the same formula
in the preliminary stage of machinations against the latter as
had been practiced against Austria. Herr Hitler was still playing on the "right of self-determination" as a pressuring instrument, a political pretext for intervention in the internal affairs
of neighboring states. By then he had made it a "racket". In
a later stage, however, he broke even his own moral code, by
deliberately enveloping the Slavs of former Czechoslovakia in
his aggressive drive.

During the course of the foregoing lamentable events,

Nazidom's policy was one of divide and conquer, a policy involving the study of and the play on weakness. The formula, moreover, conceived by Berlin's "political engineers" and applied in the cases of Austria, Czechoslovakia, and eventually Poland, entailed in each case, similar tactics by stages: first demands, then hate propaganda, including insults and pin-pricking, then wild accusations, then inspired border-incidents, and finally leading up to shameless, deliberate aggression.

As regards the policy of "divide and conquer" (a leaf more than likely taken from the Hapsburg's book), I discerned and appraised as significant the fact that while Herr Hitler was engaged in waging his campaign vis-à-vis Vienna (and simultaneously feeling the pulse in London and Paris), his attitude towards Prague was cordial; towards Warsaw unusually friendly. (That Herr Hitler was more friendly towards Warsaw than Prague at this time, augured to my mind that Czechoslovakia was "next" on Herr Hitler's "political menu"). Once Austria was swallowed, Herr Hitler's attitude towards Prague changed from friendly to frigid; thence to ice cycles. Meanwhile, he became even more disarmingly amicable with Warsaw (an attitude which by this time might be likened to the wolf in "Little Red Ridinghood"). When Czechoslovakia had succumbed, Herr Hitler in characteristic fashion "glared" at Warsaw in turn—his next potential victim.

OCTOBER 16, 1938

Polish official circles, shortly after October 16, 1938,[2] informed me confidentially to the following effect:

In conversation with Polish Ambassador [Józef] Lipski on this date, [German Foreign Minister Joachim von] Ribbentrop had alluded significantly to the necessity of an early settlement of the Danzig problem, and to the question of facilitating communications, in terms of an autostrada [highway], between the Reich and East Prussia. On this occasion, however, Herr von Ribbentrop had not mentioned the question of extra-territoriality in connection with the proposed autostrada. Ambassador Lipski had subsequently imparted to his Government his concern over Herr von Ribbentrop's insistence upon an early settlement of these two points.

I was aware, moreover, that the Polish Government had been studying various formulae looking to a solution of the Danzig problem as well as of the question of facilitating German-East Prussian communications across Pomorze.[3] In this connection, I had gained the impression that Minister Beck and his associates were inclined to prefer a non-extra-territorial autostrada to the then existent numerous routes of communication between the Reich and East Prussia. In that they felt these numerous routes served to facilitate anti-Polish espionage activities, they looked upon the establishment of one main route as affording better opportunity to guard against these activities. I furthermore gained the impression that they hoped to trade a Polish-financed non-extra-territorial autostrada for a just and permanent settlement of the Danzig question.

In connection with the foregoing, a leading official of the Foreign Office subsequently told me that in studying Berlin's envisaged plans in connection with the proposed autostrada, his attention was drawn to the fact that not only did each successive plan envisage an extra-territorial highway, but also that each plan in turn specified an increase thereof, ranging from five to twenty-five kilometers, in width. In discussing this point with Minister Beck, he emphasized his opinion that Berlin's specifications on this score only went to show that Berlin regarded the project more as a strategic factor, than one facilitating communications.

JANUARY 5 [1939]

Following Beck's return from his January 5, 1939 visit to Herr Hitler at Berchtesgaden, I asked him whether Herr Hitler was difficult to talk and deal with personally.[4] Minister Beck replied that on occasions previous to January 5, when he had meetings with Herr Hitler, the latter had usually evinced a clear and reasonable attitude and a most cordial manner. During the Minister's aforementioned meeting with Herr Hitler, however, he stated [that] the latter was cordial as usual, but in other respects a different man; a discernible change had taken place. In the course of their lengthy conversation, Herr Hitler seldom looked Minister Beck in the eye as had previously been his custom; instead, he kept his eyes focused on the ceiling. I gained the impression that this conversation took the form more or less of a monologue, wherein Herr Hitler "thought out loud" in a *tour d'horizon* for several hours. This attitude of Herr Hitler's put Minister Beck on guard. The Minister sensed that this was not the man he had known before, and even during the course of the conference, he realized that Poland henceforth had to be more alert than ever before vis-à-vis Germany.

As to whether he thought Herr Hitler was bluffing or meant war, Minister Beck observed that he did not know. Herr Hitler, previous to the close of 1938, had been confident he could gain his objectives without involving Germany in a war. His easy "bloodless" successes had apparently gone to his head, an effect which had in a large measure contributed towards the change which Minister Beck discerned on January 5.

In response to my further inquiry as to whether among the circles around Hitler, there were any individuals possessing the qualities of real leadership, Minister Beck stated in effect the following: when Herr Hitler had surrounded himself with what now composed the inner Nazi circles some of the latter, like [Alfred] Rosenberg and Ribbentrop, acted on their own initiative along lines of their conception.[5] Minister Beck attributed to them the attempt to set up Ruthenia as a center of Ukrainian agitation, for he had been unable to discern Herr Hitler's hand therein. Indeed, Minister Beck felt that von Ribbentrop had become a danger for Herr Hitler's regime in that Minister Beck suspected him of refraining from giving Herr Hitler the correct versions of discussions and communiques. In this connection, Herr Hitler could read only German and was thus at the mercy of translators under von Ribbentrop's direction. Men of the calibre of [former Foreign Minister Konstantin] von Neurath were not whole-souled Nazis, but they carried out Herr Hitler's orders to the letter. Field Marshal [Herman] Goering possessed the qualities of leadership, but his influence on the direction of German foreign policy was apparently eclipsed, for the moment at least, by von Ribbentrop's hold on Herr Hitler. Minister Beck went on to say that during his January 5 meeting with Herr Hitler, the latter revealed for the first time that he regarded Goering as his successor. In this connection, Herr Hitler remarked that he regretted that the necessity to concentrate so much labor on the construction of the Siegfried Line had retarded progress on his construction program for Berlin. However, Field Marshal Goering was thoroughly familiar with his program and could carry on in case anything happened to him.

After his conference with Herr Hitler at Berchtesgaden, Minister Beck and Count Michael Łubieński, his Cabinet Chief, dined with von Ribbentrop in Munich. Minister Beck informed me that during the dinner he told von Ribbentrop that following all previous conferences with Hitler he had left Germany with a feeling of optimism as to the possibility of coming to an arrangement on whatever Polish-German differences happened to have been outstanding at the moment. This time, however, he was leaving with a sense of pessimism as to the future. Minister Beck inferred that he had deliberately made this remark in the hope that von Ribbentrop would repeat it to his chief. Minister Beck felt, however, that von Ribbentrop failed to do so. From the time that Minister Beck returned from Berchtesgaden, I discerned underlying signs of increasing Polish-German dissension.

* * * * * * * * * * * * * * * *

March ushered in a crucial political period, with a series of pivotal events which proved disadvantageous to the security of the Polish state; in brief, they marked Poland's partial encirclement:

Occupation of Prague, March 15

Germany's ultimatum to Lithuania, March 20

Germany's treaty with Slovakia, signed March 23

Germany's treaty in connection with Memel, signed March 24

In sum, this spelled the liquidation of one country, and the partial decomposition of another, all within a period of two weeks. Thenceforth, it became increasingly clearer that the European situation in general was rapidly deteriorating. The Polish-German situation in particular went from bad swiftly to worse. Herr Hitler's action vis-à-vis Czechoslovakia was interpreted by the Polish Government and military circles as a breach of Herr Hitler's avowed code of bringing back with [in] the Reich only people of German nationality. Moreover, these Polish circles felt that this action presaged the possibility of unlimited adventures in Eastern and Central Europe. I became aware, moreover, that the events between the 15th and 24th of March augured added difficulties for future potential negotiations between Poland and Germany, in that through these actions Herr Hitler had destroyed the last vestige of confidence the Polish Government and military circles might otherwise have had in his word. Partly attributable to Germany's unilateral actions between March 15th and 20th, and partly due to Ambassador Lipski's having discerned signs of an early presentation of German demands on Poland, the Polish Government on the night of March 20 undertook a "regroupment" of its armed forces, as well as a secret calling up of certain classes of reserves. No mobilization posters appeared; the police discreetly notified the reservists at night time. Several cleverly conceived black-outs in Warsaw served to cover the movement of men out of the city.

MARCH 21

I was informed by Polish officials that on March 21, von Ribbentrop verbally communicated in behalf of his Government the following "proposal" to the Polish Government:

1. Danzig's return to the Reich.

2. Extra-territorial railway line and autostrada between East Prussia and the Reich.

3. The Reich in exchange was willing to recognize the whole of the Polish Corridor and the whole of Poland's Western frontier.

4. The Reich would recognize the maintenance of Poland's economic interests in Danzig.

5. The Reich would recognize the settlement of the outstanding economic and communications problems arising for Poland out of the union of Danzig with the Reich.

In von Ribbentrop's conversation with Ambassador Lipski on this occasion he stressed the importance of speed in the settlement of these questions as a condition of the Reich's maintaining its proposals in force in their entirety. Minister Beck subsequently told me that his Government was surprised by the urgency with which these proposals were presented and the circumstances under which they were made; however, animated by the desire of maintaining good Polish-German relations, his Government did not refuse conversations, although they considered the German demands unacceptable in the sense in which they were presented.[6]

MARCH 26

Minister Beck informed me that in the interests of a search for an amicable solution of outstanding Polish-German differences in regard to Danzig and the transit roads between the Reich and East Prussia, his Government had that day formulated its point of view in writing to the German Government as follows:

Fully appreciating the importance of maintaining good neighborly relations with Germany, the Polish Government proposed a guarantee by Poland and Germany of the separate entity of the Free City of Danzig, the existence of which would be based upon the complete freedom of the internal life of the local population, and the safeguarding of the respect for the rights and interests of Poland. Moreover, the Polish Government was willing to study together with the German Government all further facilities for travellers in transit, as well as technical facilities in railway and road transit between the Reich and East Prussia.[7]

Minister Beck interjected at this point that his Government was guided by the idea of offering to the citizens of the Reich all possible facilities for them to travel in transit across Polish territory without any difficulties. The Minister went on to say that his Government had stressed that it was its intention to treat German demands with the utmost liberality, with the only reservation that Poland could not surrender her sovereignty over the territory through which the transit roads would pass. Finally, his Government had stated that its attitude in the matter of communications facilities through Pomorze was dependent upon the attitude of the Reich with regard to the question of the Free City of Danzig. Minister Beck emphasized, moreover, that his Government in formulating these proposals was acting in the spirit of the Polish-German Declaration of 1934, which provided for the direct exchange of views in problems concerning both countries, entitling each of them to state its point of view in the course of negotiations. He concluded by stating that on the occasion of Ambassador Lipski's transmitting the Polish Government's reply to von Ribbentrop, the former had told von Ribbentrop that in view of events which had threatened Poland's strategic position, Poland had undertaken as a precautionary measure a regroupment of her armed forces.

MARCH 29

An officer of the President's [Mościcki's] household as well as an official of the Foreign Office divulged in strictest confidence the following broad outline of Poland's plan of defense: (a) to keep the Polish army intact; (b) to resist as long as possible an attempted capture of Warsaw and/or the "Industrial Triangle";[8] (c) withdrawal of the main body of Polish forces under cover of delayed action if and when pressure from a potential German attack made it necessary, to the main defensive position on the line of the strategic Narew, Bug, Vistula and San rivers; (d) to delay the adversary's advance until the advent of rainy and wintry weather and until assistance from Poland's Western Allies might have diverted the full brunt of the German attack from the Polish front. My informants went on to say that while this was the Polish defense plan in terms of the broad sweep, the Government and the General Staff had decided that, in event the capture of Warsaw by the adversary became imminent, the Government and the General Staff would withdraw from Warsaw—the Government reestablishing its seat in Eastern Poland, the General Staff setting up its headquarters at some point between the newly established Government seat and the fighting front. In other words, allowing for unforeseen turns in the course of a potential conflict, the Polish Government and High Command (a) regarded as their paramount aim: to hold the Polish fighting forces intact, awaiting the effects of wet and subsequently wintry weather, and effective action of Poland's Western Allies to alleviate pressure on the Polish front; and (b) had come to feel that they could less afford the loss of any sizeable portion of their first line fighting strength, which would be difficult if not impossible to replace, than the loss of territory and even of their capital, the recapture of which changed conditions and counter attacks in a later stage might permit.[9]

The British Ambassador on numerous occasions between March and the outbreak of war, as well as the French Ambassador and the Belgian Minister, discussed with me the question of evacuating Warsaw in the event the Government decided to move its seat into Eastern Poland. On these occasions we exchanged ideas as to the most practical methods of transporting our respective staffs, and the kind of clothes and equipment which, as well as provisions, our staffs should take along.[10]

MARCH 31

On March 31, Prime Minister Chamberlain announced the assurance of British and French support to Poland "in the event of any action which clearly threatened Polish independence, and which the Polish Government accordingly considered it vital to resist."[11] Between that date and April 4, the date of Minister Beck's departure for London, Berlin directly and indirectly exerted pressure on Poland in an effort to prevent the Minister's London visit. This was done obviously with a view to precluding the signing of any agreement. In connection with Germany's efforts on this score, I noted that Berlin resorted vis-à-vis Danzig and the Ukrainian minorities to what had become its classical pressuring tactics. In fact, I came to consider the condition of [the] political atmosphere in Danzig as a barometer of the state of Polish-German relations. In turn, the state of these relations was reflected in the relations between the Polish Government and the Ukrainian minority.

On April 6, an Anglo-Polish Communique recorded the assurances of mutual support agreed upon by both Governments, pending the completion of a permanent agreement, [ultimately] signed on August 25, 1939.[12] Upon his return from London, the Minister informed me that he had been deeply impressed by the seriousness and earnestness both of Prime Minister Chamberlain and Lord Halifax. He had talked perhaps four hours with each. Their conversations were characterized by a *tour d'horizon* in general and a discussion of Polish-German relations in particular. Minister Beck reminded me of a remark he had made several months previously to the effect that if war were eventually to be declared on Germany, it would be decided in Paris. Now, since his trip to London he said he felt that the point at which it might be decided to declare war on Germany was about "mid-channel."

The Minister concluded his remarks by emphasizing his sense of profound appreciation of London's comprehension of Poland's position in particular and European developments in general. The Anglo-Polish Pact was unique in that it marked Britain's first definite commitment in Eastern Europe. The Pact prescribed that it was for each country to decide when and if the independence were threatened. These provisions placed each contracting country in respect to the other, in a position somewhat similar to the bridge player who watches over the shoulder of his partner while the latter plays the hand. In the current situation it was Britain watching over the shoulder of Poland. In discussing these provisions with me, Minister Beck emphasized that he was profoundly sensible of Poland's responsibility as a partner in the Pact.

In the last days of March, the Belgian Minister imparted to me that he and several others of our colleagues had learned in strictest confidence a general idea of the Government's defense plan. He added he felt that well in advance of any move on the part of the Government and the General Staff to re-establish their seat and headquarters respectively, in Eastern Poland, a train should definitely be reserved for and assigned to the Diplomatic corps in order to avoid last minute confusion. He wondered whether I would make some discreet soundings on this score and apprise him of my findings. In response I said that I understood that the Government's plan provided among other factors for transportation facilities for the Diplomatic corps as well as for the various governmental departments in [the] event [that] the Government decided to move its seat elsewhere.

For over one month, the Polish Government received no formal reply to its counter proposal of March 26, (made in reply to Ribbentrop's verbal proposal of March 21 to Ambassador Lipski). Minister Beck told me at about this time that he had been led to understand that his Government's counter proposals had been treated by Berlin as a refusal of negotiations. On April 28, however, Herr Hitler delivered an address to the Reichstag wherein he announced that he had proposed to the Polish Government the following:

1. Cession of Danzig to the Reich.

2. Extra-territorial railway line and autostrada between East Prussia and the Reich.

3. In exchange, the Reich would recognize the existing Polish-German frontiers.

4. In addition, Herr Hitler said that these proposals had included two other conditions which the Reich was willing to give in exchange, namely: a 25-year non-aggression pact; and a Polish-German-Hungarian condominium of Slovakia.

Moreover, Herr Hitler stated that these proposals, which had been transmitted to the Polish Government on March 21, represented Germany's minimum demands of Poland.[13]

Minister Beck subsequently told me that Herr Hitler's mention of a triple condominium of Slovakia was the first he had heard of that suggestion. He added that in former conversations only allusions had been made that in the event of a general agreement the problem of Slovakia could be discussed. As far as Poland was concerned, however, she had not consented to carry on such conversations, for it was not Poland's custom to make bargains with the interests of others. The Minister also stated that Herr Hitler's mention of an extension of the non-aggression pact to 25 years had not been put forward in any definite form in any of the recent conversations. In this same address as well as in a memorandum handed to the Polish Government on the same day, Herr Hitler unilaterally denounced the Polish-German non-aggression Pact of 1934, on the grounds that it was incompatible with the recent Anglo-Polish Agreement of Mutual Assistance and hence no longer binding. In analyzing the contents of the memorandum and the speech, I was of the opinion that the memorandum represented more or less a translation in diplomatic language of Herr Hitler's speech.

In discussing with Minister Beck, later in the day, his reactions to Herr Hitler's Reichstag address and memorandum, Beck said in effect the following: Herr Hitler had misrepresented facts in suggesting that Poland had become intransigent after the British Prime Minister's announcement on March 31 of British "assurance of support to Poland in the event of any action which clearly threatened Polish independence and which the Polish Government accordingly considered it vital to resist." The Minister emphasized that Poland had been compelled to take precautionary measures for defense in mid-March. Indeed, he was explicit on the date whereon Poland had made its stand vis-à-vis Germany, stressing that these measures had been taken on March 20–21, which was prior to the British Prime Minister's offer of support.

The Minister went on to say that since he regarded Herr Hitler primarily in the light of an Austrian mentality, he thought the latter would still have a flash of reasoning. Moreover, Herr Hitler in his own interests had moved inadvisedly in having changed his methods of diplomacy and his diplomats at the same time. He might have successfully changed one or the other separately, but the simultaneous change had been a major error. Hitler had been confused and off-balance since he had learned of the Anglo-Polish Pact and had not yet collected himself.[14]

It was obvious that Herr Hitler was now trying to create a cleavage between the Western powers and Poland. Minister Beck earnestly hoped Herr Hitler's efforts on this score would not succeed, for if the Western Powers and Poland stood together, they might possibly hold Herr Hitler in check. The greatest danger lay in the possibility that he might be allowed to gain the illusion he could localize a conflict. He might be halted—yet this could not be accepted as a foregone conclusion—for Minister Beck recalled that Herr Hitler had remarked to Admiral Horthy that if matters came to the point whereat he found it necessary to risk war, it was better to have it soon.[15] Minister Beck felt that should this be the mood Herr Hitler might develop in the course of the next few months, it would be dangerous. This, the Minister said, was in line with his own thought that the Austrian mentality knew how to deal with weakness but became undecided when faced with the necessity of dealing with strength.

Herr Hitler had committed a major diplomatic error in having resorted to an open declaration of demands in a public address. Moreover, von Ribbentrop had committed an even greater blunder in permitting his Chief to omit diplomatic channels, after the Anglo-Polish Pact, as a means of exchanging ideas toward ascertaining Poland's position vis-à-vis Herr Hitler's demands. Indeed, by having resorted to an open declaration of demands, Herr Hitler had given Poland its first opportunity to make public her side of the case. The Minister then said that he had previously abstained from making public reference to Polish-German differences in order to avoid risking a challenge to Herr Hitler's prestige in view of the potential dangers involved therein.

Turning to the subject of Herr Hitler's unilateral denunciation of the Polish-German Non-Aggression Pact of 1934, Minister Beck said that his Government could not accept any

interpretation thereof which would amount to a renouncement of the right to conclude political agreements with third
parties—for this would be practically equivalent to the renouncement of the independence of foreign policy. Indeed,
Poland's acceptance of such an interpretation would boil
down to Poland's permitting Germany the right to define
what corresponded to Poland's interests. As far as this point
went, Germany had herself publicly undertaken obligations
towards Italy and the German-Slovak agreement of March
1939. These were clear indications of what interpretation
Germany had placed on the Pact of 1934. Moreover, Minister
Beck rejected as groundless Herr Hitler's objections to the
alleged incompatibility of the Anglo-Polish Pact of Mutual
Assistance with the Polish-German Pact of 1934. The Anglo-
Polish Pact had a purely defensive character and threatened
the Reich no more than did the Polish-French Alliance which
the Reich had recognized as compatible with the Pact of
1934.

The Minister pointed out that the Pact of 1934 stated
clearly in its opening paragraphs that: "the two governments
are determined to base their mutual relations on the principles
contained in the Paris Pact of August 27, 1928." The Paris
Pact, a general renouncement of war as an instrument of state
policy, just as the Pact of 1934 constituted such a renouncement in bilateral Polish-German relations, clearly made the
reservation that "every signatory power which would henceforth seek to promote its state interests through war, will have
to be deprived of the benefits of the present treaty." Germany,
the Minister said, had accepted that principle by signing the
Paris Pact, and confirmed it in the Pact of 1934, along with
the other principles of the Paris Pact. It followed, therefore,
that Poland would be no longer bound by the Pact of 1934 if
Germany had recourse to war in contradiction with the Paris
Pact. Poland's obligations, according to the Polish-British
understanding, would come into operation in the event of
German action threatening the independence of Great Britain
and consequently in the very circumstances wherein the Pact
of 1934 and the Paris Pact had ceased to be binding on Poland
as regards Germany.

Minister Beck added that Herr Hitler had no justification for his unilateral decision to renounce the Pact of 1934. He also stated that the manner in which Herr Hitler had abrogated the Pact was a flagrant violation of the provisions contained in the Pact which called for a 6 months' notice by either Government before denunciation. Moreover, the Minister pointed out that the decision to renounce the 1934 Pact had taken place after the previous refusal of the Reich to accept explanations as to the compatibility of the Anglo-Polish Pact with the 1934 Pact, which the Polish Government had intended to furnish the Reich's representative in Warsaw. Herr Hitler, as indicated by the text of the German memorandum, had apparently made his decision on the strength of press reports without consulting the views either of the British or the Polish Governments as regards the character of the agreement concluded. It would not have been difficult to do so, for immediately upon the Minister's return from London he had expressed his readiness to receive the German Ambassador, who had hitherto not availed himself of the opportunity. Hence, Poland had had no possibility to discuss its viewpoint because since April 6, the Reich had rendered impossible all direct contact.

In reviewing the substance of Herr Hitler's April 28 speech, I was aware that in many respects it was a skillful as well as menacing bit of oratory. Since the occupation of Czechoslovakia and previous to his address, reports had indicated that in terms of home public opinion, Herr Hitler's star had gone into a tail spin. However, by this speech he had succeeded in regaining over night public favor and had started his star again in the ascendency. Indeed, his play up of "encirclement" proved a popular rallying slogan for Germans of all shades of opinion. Moreover, to internal mass opinion, lacking in factual data, he appeared convincing in his claims as to the great value of the country's material gains. I noted furthermore, that his address, though probably primarily designed to meet demands of his internal situation, was at the same time aimed at serving external policy as well.

It seemed to me that Herr Hitler was making a subtle bid to detach the Western powers from Poland, and in line with this a bid for renewed intervention of the "peace at any price" elements in Western Europe. As a matter of fact, as early as May 4 the London *Times*, as I recall it, bluntly stated that Danzig was really not worth a war. One of the leading foreign correspondents in Warsaw informed me the day after the address that London had telephoned him several times asking why the Poles had refused what seemed like reasonable proposals and at the same time adding that in London political circles there was considerable consternation. In my own opinion, I felt that the speech was far from reassuring. As a matter of fact, it served to abrogate two important Pacts: the Anglo-German Naval Accord, and the Polish-German Non-Aggression Pact. Herr Hitler's allusions, moreover, to President Roosevelt's constructive efforts on the side of peace savored of a play to the home galleries at the expense of dignity and statesmanship. To my mind, his "play up" of "Lebensraum" smacked again, as it always had in the past, of long-range war-like intentions. The very word "Lebensraum" implies to me intended aggression, for it indicates a program envisaging the annexation of those resources which the country would require for the conduct of war—otherwise, access of these resources might be acquired through normal commercial channels. I considered the speech as a whole mainly in the light of defensive prestige propaganda for home consumption. As to the potential effect of the address, I was inclined in the first place to consider it not as a "marking time" dissertation, but one presaging events to come. While the door was left open a crack, it had been slammed on the only worthwhile factor—disarmament. Moreover, I felt that it left Europe in a state of iron tension with alliances the only alternative.

Polish official circles "kept their chins up" in the face of Herr Hitler's unilateral abrogation of the Polish-German Non-Aggression Pact of 1934, and did their best to minimize its potential effect. I had the impression, however, that the Polish Government's industrialization program was based, more than they were willing to admit openly, upon the Government's hope of maintaining this Non-Aggression Pact in vigor for another year and a half at the least. As a matter of fact, while a large part of the "Industrial Triangle" had been constructed with a notable degree of efficiency by the time war eventually broke out, the project as a whole required at least six months for completion—and additional time for tuning into volume production schedules.

I was informed by official circles that before industrialization in the so-called "Industrial Triangle," Poland [was] faced with the question as to whether to confine its acquisition of the main part of its armaments' requirements to purchases abroad, or to construct its own industrial base of supply. My informants admitted that in adopting the latter course, the Government's decision was partly attributable to optimism as to the duration of the 10-year Non-Aggression Agreement signed in 1934. They believed they would at least have the "Industrial Triangle" a going concern before encountering a definite challenge from Germany. It appeared, moreover, that the Government's industrialization program envisaged (a) building up a capacity to supply its army with essential arms and ammunition, after as well as before the potential outbreak of war, which the Government felt would immediately cut Poland's access to western sources of supply, and (b) creating industrial balance in a chiefly agricultural state, as well as additional fields of employment as a contribution towards solving the increasing problem of overpopulation. As matters turned out, when the challenge came after only five years of the 10-year Non-Aggression Agreement and war appeared inevitable, construction of the industrial center had progressed too far to permit a turning back. This meant that funds which might otherwise have been available for the large-scale purchase of much needed armaments were tied up in the uncompleted industrial development at the time war broke out.

In a lengthy conversation with Minister of Finance [Eugeniusz] Kwiatkowski, he remarked that previous to Poland's March regroupment of armed forces, Poland had been on her way towards a gradual raising of the living standard of the masses and towards economic rehabilitation. It had long been his dream and the object of his strenuous efforts to witness during his term of office tangible evidence of progress resultant from the combined endeavors of himself and his associates to bring Poland out of "red ink". In a predominantly agricultural state [such] as Poland, benefits from economic and financial ascendency were slower in reflecting themselves in the lives of the masses than in the more industrialized states. However, during the past year he had perceived a noticeable amelioration in the economic structure of the country as a whole. Moreover, he and his associates, realistically facing the problem of over-population with which Poland would be increasingly faced during the ensuing 10 years, had determined to diversify the economic structure of the country through an industrialization program which they aimed, among other factors, as a means of creating openings for employment. Then came the necessity to mobilize, forcing the Government to alter instantly and completely its comprehensive program of economic rehabilitation. Indeed, .in a country with such limited financial means, mobilization to the extent of the present one meant a diversion of the flow of funds from the channels of economic development into purely defense channels. There was no alternative, for there was not enough money to serve both purposes simultaneously. However, under the circumstances, the Government had decided to protect the state which they had helped reconstruct. There was no course but to prepare to defend Poland's independence through sacrifice. Moreover, the Government was profoundly impressed by the whole-hearted and consolidated support of the Polish people, behind their decision. There was a minimum of grumbling, and the mood and capacity of the masses to make sacrifices for the independence of their country was indeed touching. Mobilization was costing Poland at the rate of 2,000,000 złotys per day.[16] The Government was meeting these costs not with an ideal schedule, but in the most practical manner possible.

I was aware that as late as March 7, 1936, Herr Hitler had stated publicly that it would be unreasonable and impossible to deny a state of such a size as Poland an outlet to the sea. However, I had frequently received reports from usually reliable sources to the effect that Herr Hitler's plan vis-à-vis Poland envisaged the diminution of the Polish state by the annexation of Danzig, Pomorze (the Corridor) and Upper Silesia, as well as the decomposition of the rest of Poland (in line with Herr Hitler's further reported plan to set up a chain of small units, dependent upon Germany, as a buffer between Germany and Russia). I felt that if these reports were well-founded, Herr Hitler envisaged a Polish state reduced considerably in terms of territory, and to about 15,000,000 racial Poles in terms of population. The obvious inconsistency between Herr Hitler's statement of March 7, 1936 and his reported plans raised the question in my mind as to whether, if Herr Hitler eventually succeeded in reducing the size of the Polish state, he would still feel morally bound by his March 7, 1936 declaration.

MAY 5

On May 5, Minister Beck delivered an address before the Polish Parliament, elaborating Poland's case in reply to Herr Hitler's address to the Reichstag on April 28.[17] In general Minister Beck said that his Government regarded the proposals of the Reich as a demand for unilateral concessions. He emphasized that his country was prepared to approach objectively and with utmost good will any points raised for discussion by the Reich. However, two conditions were essential if the discussions were to prove of real value; peaceful intentions, and peaceful methods of procedure. The address, moreover, reiterated most of the points which the Minister had previously imparted to me in a discussion following Herr Hitler's speech to the Reichstag of April 28, and which I have recited in substance under date of April 28 of this report. On the same day [May 5], the Polish Government sent a note to the German Government explaining their point of view in reply to the German Government's memorandum of April 28. The Polish Government repeated its counter proposals and refuted the German argument that the Anglo-Polish mutual assistance pact was incompatible with the Polish-German Non-Aggression Pact of 1934. It reminded the German Government that no formal reply to the Polish counter proposal had been received for a month, and that only on April 28 did the Polish Government learn that "the mere fact of the formulation of counter proposals instead of the acceptance of the verbal German suggestions without alteration or reservation had been regarded by the Reich as a refusal of discussions."

In addition the Minister developed his Government's point of view on the question of Danzig along the following lines: in refuting Herr Hitler's description of Danzig as a German city whose contacts with Poland were forced upon it by the dictators of the Peace of Versailles, Minister Beck stated that Danzig was not invented by the Versailles Treaty. It had existed for many centuries. As a result, if one were to set apart the emotional elements, Danzig was a positive cross between Polish and German interests. The German merchants of Danzig had assured the development and prosperity of that time, thanks to the Polish overseas trade. Not only the development but the very reason of Danzig's existence were formerly due to the then decisive fact that it was situated at the mouth of Poland's only great river; now it is also important because of its position on the main waterway and railway line connecting Poland of today with the Baltic. While the population of current-day Danzig was predominantly German, its livelihood and prosperity depended upon the economic potential of Poland.

Poland stood firmly on the ground of its rights and interests in connection with its overseas trade and its maritime policy in Danzig. Seeking reasonable and conciliatory solutions, Poland had purposely notendeavored to exert any influence on the free national ideological and cultural development of the German majority in Danzig. Minister Beck stated that he heard a demand for the annexation of Danzig to the Reich. When he received no reply to his Government's proposal of March 26 of a common guarantee of the existence and rights of Danzig, and when he subsequently learned that this counter proposal had been regarded as a refusal of negotiations, he asked himself what was the real aim of it all. Was it the freedom of the German population of Danzig, which was not menaced, or a matter of prestige—or was it a matter of barring Poland from the Baltic, wherefrom Poland would not let herself be barred? The same considerations concerned the communications across Pomorze (the Corridor). Poland had granted the Reich all railway facilities and had allowed the citizens of the Reich to travel from the Reich to East Prussia without customs or passport formalities. Moreover, the Polish Government had suggested the extension of these facilities to road transport, and again the question appeared as to what was the real aim of it all. Poland had no reason to obstruct the German citizens in their communication with their eastern province. Neither did Poland have any ground whatsoever for restricting its sovereignty on its own territory.

In connection with both questions, the future of Danzig and the communications through Pomorze, it was still a case of one-sided concessions which the Government of the Reich seemed to be demanding from Poland. A self-respecting nation did not make one-sided concessions. Where was reciprocity? It looked rather vague in the German proposals. In Herr Hitler's speech, the Minister continued, he had proposed as a concession the recognition and definite acceptance of the existing frontier between Poland and Germany. In that it would have been a recognition of Poland's property, indispensable, *de jure* and *de facto*, this proposal also could not alter the Minister's point, that the German claims with regard to Danzig and communications across Pomorze remained one-sided demands. In concluding his address the Minister stated that peace was a valuable and desirable thing. His generation which had bled in several wars surely deserved a period of peace. However, peace, like almost all things of this world, had its price, high but definable. He and his countrymen of Poland did not know the conception of peace at any price. There was only one thing in the life of men, nations, and states which was without price—that was honor.

About 20 minutes after I returned to my office from Parliament, the Minister telephoned to ask me whether I thought that he had presented Poland's case in such a way as to be understood clearly by the Anglo-Saxon mentality. He then requested me to call on him later in the afternoon. In the meantime, my inquiries amongst the known experts on all sections of Polish public opinion disclosed that the tempo of public sentiment was considerably in advance of the calm tone of Minister Beck's address.

Later in the day when I called on the Minister he touched on several outstanding points. He said that good neighborly relations with Germany had always been a cornerstone of Polish foreign policy. Hence, the German memorandum would be studied with understanding and attention. He felt that Germany's recent demands for an extra-territorial autostrada and railway had been caused, not by the communications needs of the German citizens so much as by Berlin's desire to disorganize Poland and other countries neighboring on Germany. His envisaged plan vis-à-vis Poland was far more extensive than his stated claims in respect to Danzig. Indeed, strategic and *lebensraum* considerations had played a larger role than racial considerations in Hitler's desire for Danzig's annexation to the Reich.

Just as the cession of the Sudeten area to Germany removed the keystone in the dam in Czechoslovakia, so the cession of Danzig and an extra-territorial passageway across Pomorze to a Germany whose Führer envisaged himself the sovereign of a pan-Germanic Europe, would prove the barring of Poland from the Baltic and Poland's consequent suffocation. This eventual undoing of Poland as an independent state would throw her at the mercy of Germany. In other words, for Poland it was not a question of prestige but of keeping open the national economic windpipe.

While Poland in taking this strong stand was at first motivated by a desire to protect her own interests, she also hoped thereby to instill in other states a spirit of resistance against Germany's boa-constrictor appetite. Hence, Poland's submission to Germany's demands would undermine the physical and moral forces which Poland was trying to foster. Poland felt that were Hitler ever to be stopped, this was the time to do it, and since Germany's aggressive attentions at that moment were turned on her, it was her duty to "halt Hitler". It was essential at this point to draw the line whereat all countries would resist Germany's aggressive intentions. In discussing the more general aspects Minister Beck said that Germany had had recourse to a policy of pressure and faits accomplis in Eastern Europe. Now Germany was no doubt of the opinion that she could employ the same methods against Poland. Poland, however, to all attempts of the kind, would duly answer. No one-sided decisions would ever be accepted by Poland.

It was obvious that Herr Hitler was exerting great efforts towards detaching the Western powers from Poland. Moreover, Herr Hitler had evinced considerable resentment of what he endeavored to make out as Britain's interference in German aims in Eastern Europe. The Minister would also like to rectify one statement which Herr Hitler had made regarding the Non-Aggression Agreement, wherein Herr Hitler had said that he himself had initiated it. The Minister was in a position to know that it was the former Marshal Piłsudski who had actually conceived of the Non-Aggression Pact.[18]

Were Danzig eventually to be militarized under German control, this would spell a German threat to the Port of Gdynia and to all traffic of that Port.[19] It only took a glance at the map to appreciate that Gdynia would come within easy range of any high calibre guns in the Free City. (In connection with Germany's possible eventual militarization of Danzig, one of von Ribbentrop's agents who visited Warsaw about this time remarked to me that Germany would eventually insist upon Danzig's annexation. In fact, von Ribbentrop had been known openly to state that his Government would have to have Danzig by September at the latest. My informant further remarked that in order to satisfy German mass mentality, a triumphal victory march into Danzig would be an essential requisite). With reference to Herr Hitler's demand for an extra-territorial passageway across Pomorze, the Minister said that the Polish General Staff, having studied the effect of the autostrada in Czechoslovakia, stated that from the military viewpoint an autostrada in the width envisaged by the Germans could be made to serve strategically as a barrier almost as formidable as a broad river.

According to British Embassy circles, General [Edmund] Ironside, during his visit to Poland [July 17–21], had denoted his sense of satisfaction over the Polish General Staff's defensive plan envisaging, when circumstances made it advisable, gradual retirement of the main body of Polish troops under cover of delayed action to a main defense position along the line of the Narew, Bug, Vistula and San rivers.[20] Furthermore, while I was unable to acquire confirmation from official circles, I understood from unusually reliable sources that both General Ironside and representatives of the French General Staff had made it clear, in Paris as well as Warsaw, that the Western powers could not be expected to render Poland effective assistance for at least three months from, say, the first of August.[21]

Polish Ambassador to Berlin, Lipski, imparted to me, as an illustration of the increasingly imperialistic attitude of upper Nazi circles, that during a conversation a few days before with a German industrial magnate, he had made an astonishing remark to him. He had said that Poland, as well as other smaller states, had to come under German domination since their economic structures were complementary to that of Germany. This would be only good business—these were no times to consider sentiment and the rights of smaller nations to independence. This remark, the Ambassador felt, typified the increasingly imperialist view that the inner Nazi circles were assuming.

Towards the end of July there arose amongst the diplomatic corps of anti-aggression forces a feeling that further delay in the implementation of the Anglo-Polish Pact with some definite form of financial accommodation, might conceivably serve German diplomacy as an instrument for discrediting London with other anti-aggression forces. Reports were also reaching official and diplomatic circles in Warsaw that Berlin was maintaining close surveillance over Anglo-Polish relations—and particularly negotiations for the extension of financial and military equipment aid to Poland. Further reports indicate that Herr von Ribbentrop continued to tell Herr Hitler that certain political and financial influences in London opposed to Britain's involvement in war over Danzig or Pomorze, were still sufficiently effective to exert a restraining influence upon the leading members of the British Government.

JULY 20

By July 20, I had come to the conclusion that Europe was headed for war some time before the middle of October—that little short of a miracle could prevent it. I was convinced, moreover, that the first stage would be a Polish-German conflict. Accordingly, I felt that we should take at least preliminary steps towards establishing a practical means of evacuating American citizens from Poland in event of an emergency. I discussed this matter with the officers of my staff, and with Consul General John K. Davis. They were all in accord with my foregoing views. Following several further conversations between Mr. Davis, Mr. C. Burke Elbrick, Third Secretary of Embassy, Mr. E. Tomlin Bailey, vice consul, and myself, Mr. Elbrick accompanied by Mr. Bailey and clerk of consulate, Mr. Sadler, proceeded to Brześć (which we considered to be the most practical center for evacuation, due among other reasons, to its geographical position, as well as to its being an important railway junction), to seek a near-by country place which might serve as a suitable concentration center for American citizens in event of hostilities. After careful search, they returned to Warsaw and submitted a well-considered recommendation that an estate belonging to Mr. and Mrs. W. Vierzbicki[22] be leased for the purpose in view. They found it possible to rent the second floor of the rather large manor house, the chapel, and other premises. This place was 10 kilometers northwest of the Brześć railway. As a result we took an option on this estate, pending (a) further developments in the international and political arena, and (b) authorization from the State Department to accomplish a formal lease.

In conversation with Beck in the latter days of July, he told me that Poland did not want war. However, if war came, Poland would fight. He felt, nevertheless, that peace could still be preserved, but not at the price of unilateral concessions. At this point he said that at a recent meeting of the Council of Ministers it was decided Poland had a line beyond which she would not permit German infringements. While on that occasion the Minister refrained from divulging what constituted the line, it later became clear that Poland would not tolerate any arbitrary alteration in the political status of Danzig as a Free State. Moreover, Poland would not tolerate interference either with the Polish-Danzig customs union or Polish rights and interests in the Free City. He referred then to Herr Hitler's renunciation of the Non-Aggression Pact, stating that he had asked himself how and why could a new non-aggression pact be expected to give assurance when the Pact of 1934 had been denounced out of hand.

By this time, I was aware that while Minister Beck felt that peace could still be preserved, he had not shut his eyes to signs indicating that an eventual German attack was almost unavoidable. I knew, however, that he was striving in every way to postpone the hour of a potential clash as long as possible. I recall his having stated on several occasions that if it had to come eventually, he earnestly hoped he could put it off as long as possible—at least until the winter weather set in. He emphasized that the Poles would fight if necessary and if an attack came in the wet and wintry weather, Poland could defend herself more effectively against the type of warfare to which the German fighting machine was attuned. On each of these occasions he would add that the prospect of another war was lamentable—grim. Two wars for one generation were more than enough.[23] What Poland needed and what he had always hoped to see were at least 15 more years of peace wherein to rehabilitate herself. He would then add that if there were no way to prevent the threatened conflict honorably, then he for his part would do his utmost to gain time for his country and his allies.

In conversation with Economic Counselor of the Foreign

Office, Mr. Jan Wrszlacki,[24] on July 31, I asked him what was the attitude of Polish officialdom and the "man in the street" in Poland towards the United States, in connection with the prospect of war in Europe. He replied that neither official circles nor the "man in the street" looked to the United States for active intervention. While both elements regarded the United States as a great moral force on the side of peace and of the maintenance of the international codes of law and order, they felt the United States was too remote from the scene of European difficulties to assume other than a neutral role at least during the preliminary stage of European conflict. In a subsequent conversation with Beck, he expressed similar observations. Towards the end of July the Polish financial delegation, who for some weeks had been negotiating in London for financial accommodation in implementation of the Anglo-Polish Pact, returned to Warsaw. They were disappointed over the results of their negotiations, which had yielded them export credits only. These they were unable to translate into purchases other than in England, where they could not get an immediate delivery in essential military requirements in time to meet a rapidly approaching German challenge. By this time the Polish Government realized that if they were to acquire the necessities in terms of military equipment before the threatened outbreak of war, they would need cash with which to purchase in the open market planes and anti-aircraft guns and ammunition, and other vital necessities of war. Marshal [Edward] Śmigły-Rydz bore out this thought in his remarks which are recounted in a later part of this report under the date of August 10.

1. The original version of this report, written in October, 1939, is deposited in the Franklin D. Roosevelt Library (Hyde Park, New York), under the file listing PSF 38, "Poland."

2. Biddle undoubtedly meant October 24, 1938, when German Foreign Minister Ribbentrop held a lengthy conversation with Polish Ambassador to Germany Józef Lipski at the latter's request. For the German minutes of this talk, see *DGFP*, D, 5:104–7; the Polish version is in Lipski, *Diplomat in Berlin*, pp. 454–58. For a discussion of the significance of this conversation for the future of German-Polish relations, see M. Wojciechowski, *Stosunki polsko-niemieckie 1933–1938*, pp. 520–30.

3. Known as "Pomerania" or the "Corridor" to English-language readers.

4. For Biddle's official report to Washington on the Polish appraisal of this conversation, see Document 17 printed in Part 3 below. The German report on the Hitler-Beck talk of January 5 is in *DGFP*, D, 5:152–58; Beck's version is in *PWB*, no. 48. See also Lipski, *Diplomat in Berlin*, pp. 482–94.

5. The rival, often competing, concepts of Germany's international destiny within the hierarchy of the Nazi regime are well treated in Klaus Hildebrand's *The Foreign Policy of the Third Reich* (Berkeley, Cal., 1973), esp. pp. 12–32.

6. Ribbentrop's report on the March 21 conversation with Lipski is in *DGFP*, D, 6:70–72. See also *PWB*, no. 61.

7. Lipski's memorandum to Germany and Ribbentrop's report on the talks of March 26 are in *DGFP*, D, 6:121–24. Lipski's account is in *PWB*, no. 63.

8. Biddle here refers to the *Centralny Okręg Przemysłowy*, or "Central Industrial Zone," frequently known by its initials COP. The COP was designed to serve two main ends: (1) to convert the Sandomierz region in the heart of the backward southeastern part of Poland into a major industrial zone that could alleviate the serious Polish unemployment problem by providing many new job openings in a densely populated area, and (2) to develop an industrial complex that could turn out the sorely needed mechanical aids for the Polish manufacturing, communication, and agricultural sectors, but at a moment's notice convert to armaments production, far from the vulnerable borders. For contemporary views of the COP, see W. Kowieradzki, *Plan Centralnego Okręgu Przemysłowego* (Warsaw, 1937), and J. Rakowski, *Rola Centralnego Okręgu Przemysłowego* (Warsaw, 1938).

9. Full details of the Polish Operational Plan "Zachód" (West), as the plan for military action against the Germans was called, are in the official publication of the Historical Commission of the Polish General Staff in London, *Polskie Siły Zbrojne w drugiej wojnie światowej*, vol. 1: *Kampania Wrześniowa 1939*, part I (London, 1951), pp. 257–420. That portion of the General Staff charged with operational planning was understaffed, and hence could only concentrate on one potential target area at a time. Accordingly, convinced that the primary danger to Poland lay in the Soviet Union, they had worked out a complete operational plan "East" by March, 1939. As it became increasingly apparent that Germany would be the more likely foe, the Polish planners worked furiously to develop a coherent operational plan for a western front, but they were unable to advance beyond detailed planning for the first stage of what would be essentially a defensive action against the Germans (as Biddle reported). But such crucial questions as how the additional succeeding steps of the campaign, especially the actual route of withdrawal across Poland to Romania, would be conducted, were never answered in detail. Hence, as the campaign rapidly passed through its initial phase, Polish actions appeared to be increasingly based on impromptu calculations and improvisations rather than solid preparatory planning.

10. Assuming that the provisional government seat would be somewhere east of the Vistula River, perhaps in the Pripet Marshes, the British began to prepare for their escape. During the summer the wife of Clifford Norton, counsellor to the British Embassy, hid a cache of skis and foodstuffs in the mountains near the border, and also purchased a medium-sized truck, which was kept ready for evacuation use at a moment's notice. Bethell, *The War Hitler Won*, p. 102.

11. The text of Chamberlain's statement of guarantee is in *Documents on British Foreign Policy 1919–1939*, Third Series (London, 1951), 4:552 (hereafter cited as *DBFP*). See also Edward Raczyński, *In Allied London* (London, 1962), pp. 13–14.

12. The text of the April 6 communiqué is in *DBFP*, Third Series (London, 1952), 5:47–49. See also Raczyński, *In Allied London*, pp. 16, 342.

13. See N. H. Baynes, ed., *The Speeches of Adolf Hitler* (London, 1942), 2:1631.

14. The reader should keep in mind that no firm obligation, in the form of a binding treaty, existed between Britain and Poland on the date mentioned by Biddle. What in fact had been signed by the two states—as Biddle himself noted—was a temporary, provisional agreement outlining the basic principles upon which the permanent mutual assistance pact would be formulated later; this was finally arranged and signed on August 25, the day before Hitler's originally scheduled assault on Poland. Thus, when Biddle refers to an "Anglo-Polish Pact" prior to that date, he means the earlier provisional agreement to conclude such a treaty.

15. Miklos Horthy, regent (and hence head of state) for Hungary. His relationship with Hitler has been spotlighted in the collection of Horthy's personal documents, *The Confidential Papers of Admiral Horthy*, ed. M. Szinai and L. Szucs (Budapest, 1965). See also the recent studies by M. Adam, *Allianz Hitler-Horthy-Mussolini* (Budapest, 1966), and M. D. Fenyo, *Hitler, Horthy, and Hungary: German-Hungarian Relations, 1941-1944* (New Haven, 1972).

16. In 1939, the internationally accepted value of the Polish *złoty* was 5.26 units to one American dollar.

17. *PWB*, no. 77.

18. For a discussion of the Polish-German Non-Aggression Pact, see K. Lapter, *Pakt Piłsudski-Hitler* (Warsaw, 1962), and A. M. Cienciala, "The Significance of the Declaration of Nonaggression of January 26, 1934, in Polish-German and International Relations: A Reappraisal," *East European Quarterly* 1 (1967):1-34.

19. The development of the port of Gdynia began in 1923 as a result of Polish difficulties with Danzig, and owed much to the interests and energy of Eugeniusz Kwiatkowski (minister of trade and commerce in 1926-1930, deputy premier and minister of finances from October, 1935 to September, 1939). It was located 21 kilometers west of Danzig, on Polish territory. From a tiny fishing village of 15,000 in 1923, it grew into a city of 150,000 in 1939 and was then the second largest Baltic port after Copenhagen.

20. General Ironside noted, however, that the Polish defense plan was based on "too low an opinion of the German army's value." See Roderick Macleod and Denis Kelly, eds., *Time Unguarded: The Ironside Diaries 1937-1940* (New York, 1962), p. 80. The British summary of Ironside's visit is in *DBFP*, Third Series, 6:415-19.

21. Anglo-French and Anglo-Polish staff talks in April and May, 1939, clearly indicated that Britain and France would offer only limited and indirect help to the Poles. See Sidney Aster, *1939: The Making of the Second World War* (London, 1973), pp. 146-47. See also the *Ironside Diaries*, pp. 80-81, 185.

22. The name is correctly spelled "Wierzbicki." In this case, as in all instances of spelling or typographical errors in the original report, the corrected version will be footnoted only at the first occurrence.

23. Beck here undoubtedly referred to the First World War and the Russo-Polish War of 1919-1921, both of which exacted a heavy toll of Poland's human and material resources.

24. The name is correctly spelled "Wszelaki."

CHAPTER TWO

Final Steps of the Crisis: A
Prelude to the German Onslaught

By the beginning of August the situation in Danzig had rapidly deteriorated. It appeared that German diplomacy was exercising all the chicanery at its command to build up a case on an envisaged aggression. The swift march of events in connection with Danzig and the German minority in Poland were drifting towards a situation wherein it was likely that neither side would be in a position to "climb down". German accusations in the persecution campaign inspired by Nazi propaganda increased in tempo and volume. Minister Beck in regard thereto remarked to me that Herr Hitler's technique entailed making a statement and then repeating it a sufficient number of times to force the reader to believe it. Gradually, the familiar Nazi technique came into full play, reminding one of the days preceding the violation of Czechoslovakia: pin-pricking and baiting incidents along the frontier increased.

As over the past 18 years, the Free City had frequently been looked upon as Europe's powder magazine, so now it was rapidly taking its place at the head of the list of "high explosives".[1] I recall that during my visit to Danzig during the first week in August, my conversation with a leading official of the Danzig Senate revealed the rapidly growing imperialistic attitude on the part of Danzig statesmen, reflecting no doubt the attitude in Berlin. This official said to me that Danzig and the

Corridor represented only a part of the question in Germany's mind vis-à-vis Poland—there was Upper Silesia as well, and even the matter of Poznań. He personally liked some of the Poles and realized they saw the question from their own standpoint. However, since the question at issue was a matter of German policy, it would have to be settled on German terms.

AUGUST 9

On August 9th, the German Government made a démarche in the form of a Note Verbale to the Polish Government, through the Polish Chargé d'Affaires in Berlin, which marked Germany's first direct intervention in differences between the Polish Government and the Danzig Senate. In brief, this démarche took issue with the Polish Government over the tenor of the latter's then recent Note to the Danzig Senate. Moreover, the German Government made itself clear in no uncertain terms that it regarded Danzig as a German question.[2]

I recall that before sending their reply to this Note, Minister Beck and his associates weighed the question with utmost care. After consideration of all aspects (and in step with current Polish public opinion), Minister Beck requested the Vice Minister for Foreign Affairs, [Mierosław] Arciszewski, to convey to the German Chargé d'Affaires [Johann von Wuhlisch] Poland's reply to the effect [that] Poland would regard any future intervention by the German Government to the detriment of Polish rights and interests in Danzig as an act of aggression.[3] Minister Beck dined with me that night, and informed [me] of the foregoing.

AUGUST 10

As near as I can recall, it was on this date, during the visit of Post Master General [James] Farley and his daughters, that Marshal Śmigły-Rydz, General [Kazimierz] Sosnkowski, General [Wacław] Stachiewicz, and officers of their respective staffs, dined at my house. In the course of after dinner conversation, Mr. Farley asked the Marshal how well prepared Poland was for war in [the] event of a Polish-German conflict. The

Marshal replied that in numbers of able and courageous troops, Poland was rich; however, Poland was in serious need of additional equipment both for the air and ground forces. In fact, Poland was more in need of equipment than money at the moment, for the potential outbreak of war would immediately result in cutting Poland's communications with the west, in the Baltic, thereby delaying if not to a large degree preventing Poland's receipt of raw materials and equipment.

The Marshal went on to say that he was well aware that Poland would have to bear the main brunt of the early stage of any war in the near future. Moreover, he realized that this brunt would take the form of an attack unprecedented in fury. He had full confidence in the courage of his troops and in their willingness to resist an attack, but he wanted to furnish them with every possible chance to defend themselves with adequate modern equipment against the form of attack he anticipated. The Marshal felt that for a period of between two and three weeks after the outbreak of war, the weight and swiftness of attack would undoubtedly tend to disrupt communications and cause a general state of confusion. In fact, Poland would probably be cut off from the outside world during that stage. In the meantime, the Polish armies would be endeavoring to adopt their tactics to the adversary's strategy. He estimated that the Polish forces would be able to readopt their tactics effectively in about two weeks after the commencement of hostilities. (The first signs of definite victory by Polish forces under the leadership of General Sosnkowski at Lwów on September 15, tended to bear out the Marshal's forecast on the above score, in that General Sosnkowski demonstrated a readoption of tactics during this battle against the German forces. For further details see my observations under date of September 16). The Marshal concluded by stating his belief that despite [the] anticipated unprecedented violence of attack, the individual courage and persistence of the Polish soldier would eventually enable a reconsolidation of the Polish forces to emerge from what might possibly appear at first to have been chaotic conditions.

AUGUST 11

In the course of the day I learned from our Consul in Danzig, Mr. Kuykendall, and from Polish official circles, that (a) League High Commissioner [Carl J.] Burckhardt conferred with Herr Hitler at Berchtesgaden, having flown there by plane from Danzig, and (b) concurrently, a meeting between [Italian Foreign Minister] Count [Galeazzo] Ciano and von Ribbentrop took place at Salzburg. Information subsequently indicated (a) that while there was reason to doubt that Herr Hitler was cognizant of the full text of the Polish response of August 10 (to Herr Hitler's aforementioned démarche of August 9) at the time of his meeting with Dr. Burckhardt on August 11, since it was transmitted to the Foreign Office in Berlin only that same day, (b) that there was but little doubt that Herr Hitler was fully aware of the text when he received Count Ciano shortly after his conference with Dr. Burckhardt.

In this connection, I was subsequently informed that reports from Berlin indicated that the contents of the final paragraph of the Polish response of August 10 had thrown Herr Hitler into a towering rage. This, together with other information I received at that time led me to feel that while all signs indicated Herr Hitler had already laid out his intended campaign against Poland, this reported fit of anger might possibly have served to hasten his decision to strike. By this I do not mean that had the Polish reply been conciliatory in tone Herr Hitler might have called off his intended campaign, but rather it might conceivably have served to the extent merely of postponing the German thrust for a matter of days or possibly weeks. (Later in the month reports reaching Warsaw indicated that having studied their meteorological reports which forecast a spell of clear weather in the first half of September, the German High Command were pressing for early action if a march on Poland was to be effected.)

At the time, I gained the impression that: (a) on the one hand, Minister Beck felt Herr Hitler would compromise at the last moment rather than risk coming to grips with Britain and France. Moreover, the Minister felt and earnestly hoped that through diplomatic tactics he might stall off as long as possible—at least until late autumn—what was then assuming the complexion of an inevitable Polish-German conflict; and (b) on the other hand, Herr Hitler was led by his close advisers to believe Britain and France would not intervene in Poland's behalf. If my impressions were correct, then subsequent events proved them both to have been mistaken.[4]

AUGUST 21

Reports reaching official circles in Warsaw indicated acceleration in the pace of concentration of German troops vis-à-vis Poland. Major Colbern, Military Attaché, and I had long regarded the degree of discernible troop movements, especially in the Breslau-Oppeln area, a barometer of Germany's possible military intentions vis-à-vis Poland. By August 21, moreover, our information led us to expect a potential German attack to take the form of a frontal drive from the Breslau-Oppeln area in the direction of Warsaw, under cover of a flanking attack from the southwest, driving towards Warsaw.

AUGUST 22

With the approval of the Department of State, I entered into a formal lease for the estate belonging to Mr. and Mrs. Vierzbicki, about 10 kilometers from the Brześć railway station which Mr. C. Burke Elbrick of my staff, Vice Consul E. Tomlin Bailey, and clerk of Consulate, Mr. Sadler had recommended as an appropriate evacuation center after a careful search of the countryside. I called a meeting of the members of our Mission and stated in effect (a) my apprehension of the imminence of war, and (b) my belief that we should take steps to notify American Citizens in Poland that they should make up their minds whether to evacuate or remain in Poland in face of possible hostilities. My associates all being in accord with these suggestions, we subsequently released by mail on August 22 the following message which had already been prepared before the aforementioned conference:

"1. In view of the recent developments in the unstable

situation of which you are undoubtedly acquainted through the press and otherwise, it is suggested that you give immediately serious consideration as to whether in case an emergency arises, you would remain in Poland or depart. In case you should have the intention to depart from Poland in such circumstances, it is further suggested that as transportation and other facilities might be interrupted or made difficult, arrangements for a planned departure should not be delayed too long.

"2. American citizens in Poland are expected at all times to comply fully with Polish law and regulations including the measures promulgated recently for the defense of the country, such as anti-air, gas defense, and similar measures.

"3. American citizens should study carefully all requirements of this nature with a view to being thoroughly familiar with them in case any emergency arises."

AUGUST 23

In Moscow, von Ribbentrop and Molotoff signed the German-Soviet Pact of Non-Aggression.[5] President Roosevelt made an appeal to King Victor Emanuel [of Italy] for intervention in the cause of peace. The King of Belgium broadcast a peace appeal in behalf of the Oslo States.[6] Reports reaching Warsaw indicated that the British Ambassador to Germany delivered to Herr Hitler a message from the British Government and a personal letter from the British Prime Minister. I subsequently learned that the main points in the Prime Minister's letter were: (a) reemphasizing Britain's resolution to fulfill its obligations to Poland; (b) affirming his willingness to discuss all Anglo-German problems provided a peaceful atmosphere could be created; (c) expressing earnest desire that a détente might be brought about permitting direct Polish-German discussions on reciprocal treatment of minorities. The main points in Herr Hitler's reply to the Prime Minister's letter were: (a) Britain's resolution to support Poland could not modify the policy outlined in the German Government's Note Verbale of August 9th to the Polish Government; (b) he was prepared to accept even a long war rather than sacrifice German honor and national interests; (c) if Britain persisted in its own mobilization measures, he would immediately order the total mobilization of German forces.[7]

President Roosevelt sent messages to the Polish President and Herr Hitler urging peaceful settlement of differences by direct negotiation, arbitration or conciliation at the hands of a disinterested power. Minister Beck imparted to me that Polish Ambassador Lipski had an interview with Field Marshal Goering during the course of the afternoon. According to Lipski's report, the interview had been most cordial. The Marshal expressed regret that his policy of friendly German-Polish relations had met with failure, and admitted his influence no longer counted in the matter; he added that he did not exclude the possibility of war with Poland. Goering stated that the main obstacle to any diminution of German-Polish tension was Poland's alliance with Britain.[8] Upon receipt of the foregoing report, Minister Beck, after consultation with President Mościcki and Marshal Śmigły-Rydz, determined that if Berlin made any further suggestions along this line, the answer would be decidedly in the negative. This, together with previous reports of like bearing, led Minister Beck to look for Berlin to resort vigorously to such methods, in hopes of detaching the Western Powers from Poland, and thus gaining a free hand in Eastern Europe. He emphasized to me his determination that Poland should not be drawn into intrigues of this character. With further reference to the Lipski-Goering conversation, Lipski reported that Goering asserted that Germany, faced with the two possibilities of going along with Britain or with Russia, was forced to go with Russia.

By decree of [the] Danzig Senate, dated August 23, Herr Forster was appointed Chief of State of the Free City of Danzig. Peace appeal broadcast by His Holiness the Pope.

I was informed by reliable Polish officials that British Ambassador Sir Nevile Henderson called on Herr Hitler at the latter's request at about 1:30 p.m. I subsequently learned that Hitler made proposals concerning two groups of questions: (a) necessity for an immediate settlement of Polish-German differences; (b) an offer of eventual friendship and alliance between Britain and Germany. Herr Hitler urged the Ambassador to fly by plane to deliver his proposals to the British Government.[9]

Minister Beck informed me that the President of Poland had that day replied to the peace appeal broadcast by the King of Belgium on August 23. Minister Beck pointed out that in his reply, President Mościcki expressed his admiration for the ideas expressed by His Majesty, and stated Poland had always defended the idea that peace, if it was to last, could not be based on the oppression of others. Similarly, Poland had always considered the best guaranty of peace to be the settlement of international disputes by the method of direct negotiations based on justice and respect for the rights and interests of those concerned.[10]

An official of the Foreign Office informed me that the Anglo-Polish Accord of Mutual Assistance was formally signed at about 4 o'clock that afternoon. (I later learned that a Polish official who had arrived in London that morning was urged by an official of the British Foreign Office to return immediately by plane to his country, in that London had received information indicating the stage was set for a German march on Poland on August 26).[11] A report which reached official circles in Warsaw indicated that that night, Hitler learned from his Ambassador in London of the signing of the Anglo-Polish Accord.

Reports from informed quarters in Berlin indicated (a) that, comforted by the strategic bearing of the German-Soviet Pact upon his own forward-looking schemes, Herr Hitler was inclined to waver after receiving the Prime Minister's personal letter on August 23, and (b) that while he was subsequently offended by the news of the formal signing of the Anglo-Polish Pact, tending to consider it in form of a response to his message to the British Government (imparted to the Ambassador at 1:30 p.m. the same day), he was still inclined to waver, and refrained from renewing marching orders which he had reportedly meanwhile countermanded. It is not inconceivable to my mind that Herr Hitler's hesitancy over the next five days was in part attributable to a combination of the report on the formal signing of the Anglo-Polish Pact, and the previously broadcasted announcement of Moscow's postponement of ratification of the German-Soviet Non-Aggression Agreement. Moreover, I gained the impression that during those days of hesitancy, Herr Hitler had hopes less for a compromise in Polish-German differences than for a detachment of Britain from Poland.

Reports reaching official circles in Warsaw disclosed that during the afternoon, Berlin's telephonic communications with London and Paris were suspended several hours. Other reports indicated [that] Signor Mussolini had been several times in telephonic contact with Herr Hitler throughout the day. Moreover, I learned from Kuykendall in Danzig, as well as from informed Polish officials, that the pace of military preparations in Danzig had markedly accelerated.* During the evening I was informed that at about 5 p.m., Herr Hitler asked the French Ambassador to transmit a message to Premier [Edouard] Daladier. In effect this message suggested that France, with whom Germany had no motive to quarrel, should abstain from continuing to support Poland, against whose attitude Herr Hitler complained vehemently.

Polish President Mościcki replied to President Roosevelt's appeal of August 24. In effect, Mościcki accepted President Roosevelt's proposal, stating: (a) Poland considered direct talks between Governments to be the most suitable method of resolving difficulties between states; (b) on [the] basis of these principles, Poland concluded non-aggression pacts with Germany and Russia; and (c) Poland considered also that the method of conciliation through the intermediary of a disinterested and impartial third party was a just method of restoring differences between nations. President Mościcki added that although he clearly wished to avoid even the appearance of desiring to profit by the occasion to raise points of litigation, he deemed it his duty, nevertheless, to make clear that in the present crisis, it was not Poland which was formulating demands and demanding concessions of another State. President Roosevelt made a second appeal to Herr Hitler for maintenance of peace, enclosing the reply from the Polish President.

German merchant ships reportedly [were] ordered by the German Government to remain in or return to German ports.

During the course of the evening, Minister Beck told me that despite an intensification of efforts of German provocateurs to inspire incidents along the frontier and in Danzig, he and his associates would continue not to permit their emotions to cloud their perspective.

AUGUST 26

I learned that the British Ambassador to Germany flew by plane to London, delivered Herr Hitler's message of August 26[12] to his Government, and sat in the Cabinet meeting which considered the question of a reply.[13] Herr Hitler cancelled [the Battle of] Tannenberg celebrations. Reports reaching Warsaw indicated a further exchange of messages took place between Herr Hitler and Signor Mussolini. Major Colbern and I were informed by Military and Governmental circles respectively that their reports revealed German troop concentrations vis-à-vis Poland were reaching a point indicating readiness for an attack.

AUGUST 27

Herr Hitler cancelled the Nazi Party "Congress of Peace" at Nuremberg. Reports reaching Polish governmental circles indicated [that] (a) all German airports [were] closed, and that except for the regular civilian lines, flights over German territory as a whole were forbidden. All German aviation services were suspended, and (b) rationing was introduced in Germany. The Polish-German frontier was closed to railway traffic. I was told by informed Polish officials (a) that the British Admiralty had assumed control of British shipping; (b) that reports indicated France had about 3,000,000 men under arms; (c) that Herr Hitler received Premier Daladier's response to his letter of August 25;[14] (d) that Herr Hitler had rejected Daladier's proposal [of August 26] that one more attempt be made at direct Polish-German negotiations; and (e) that at the conclusion of Herr Hitler's letter [of August 27] to Premier Daladier, he had made the demand that the Corridor as well as Danzig must become a part of the Reich.[15]

In my conversation with Minister Beck in the late afternoon, he stated [that] he earnestly believed Poland was demonstrating its sense of responsibility to its allies as well as to the cause of peace, through restraint which it had practiced in the face of accumulative incidents obviously inspired by Nazi agents in Danzig and at other points along the Polish-German frontier. Moreover, he emphasized his and his associates' determination to keep cool, and remarked that he had the impression that Herr Hitler had not yet made up his mind to go to war.

British Ambassador Sir Howard Kennard, in a later conversation, imparted to me that following inquiries in the matter of German allegations of mass ill-treatment of the German minority by the Polish authorities, he had found that these allegations were characterized by exaggerations, if not complete falsification. Moreover, he had already telegraphed his Government at length to this effect on August 24th, and was, previous to our talk, preparing a further cable in the same sense based upon additional investigation.[16]

In connection with the foregoing, I was aware that the German press alleged that one Mr. Karletan, who had been arrested in connection with the murder of a Polish policeman, was beaten to death and his wife and children cast out of the window. The *Manchester Guardian* correspondent who subsequently made it his business to check the allegation, told the British Ambassador and a member of my staff that upon visiting Mr. Karletan in prison, he found him well, that he had not been beaten, and that the allegations regarding his wife and children were erroneous.

I was, moreover, aware that in May 1939, a considerable exodus of members of the German minority of the Katowice and Łodz districts took place. Mid-August, according to usually reliable sources in Katowice and Łodz, marked the commencement of a further illegal exodus, under pressure from the German side of the frontier. When a number of them asked to return, the Poles evinced their disapproval, since they held they had reason to suspect the members of the German minority had, during their sojourn in Germany, been schooled in espionage propaganda activities and sabotage. In this connection, the Polish authorities uncovered a training center of this character in Katowice, conducted by the *Junge Deutsche Partei* and several centers of similar nature in Łodz.

I was aware that numerous Germans were discharged particularly from plants engaged in war industry. However, there were cases drawn to my attention in May as well as August, by plant managers of Łodz, wherein the attitude of individual German provocateurs amongst the combined Polish and German working forces became so obnoxious as to force the managers to discharge a number of the Germans in each case to avoid serious clashes between them and the Polish element. In such cases, moreover, according to my informants, the usually well behaved German element had unfortunately been forced into a false position by the provocateurs, and consequently suffered discharge along with the latter.

My sources of information in southwest Poland held, moreover, that many Germans left Poland in order to be on the German side of the frontier, should war break out. Of pertinent bearing, informed Polish officials maintain that the number of refugees from the German minority approximates nearer the figure of 16,000 to 17,000 than the exaggerated figure of 76,000 alleged by the German press.

AUGUST 28

Late on the night of August 28th, I was told by informed Polish officials that British Ambassador Sir Nevile Henderson had returned to Berlin. He was received by Herr Hitler about 10:30 p.m. that same evening, and handed the latter the British Government's reply dated August 28, to the German Government's communications of August 23 and 25.[17] I was aware that this reply, previous to delivery, had been communicated to the French and Polish Governments. Pursuant to the Polish Government's authorization, moreover, this reply informed the German Government that Poland was ready to enter immediately into direct discussions with the German Government. The aforementioned British reply of August 28th, to my mind, represented the key document of the British-German exchange of Notes, in that it announced Poland's declared willingness for direct negotiations, and thus served importantly to place on Germany, the responsibility for waging war. My aforementioned informant told me moreover, that Herr Hitler, after reading a translation of the text of the communication, stated he would study it, and would give the British Ambassador a written reply the next day. I learned the following day that during the course of the conversation which took place between the British Ambassador and Herr Hitler, when the former handed the latter the British Government's aforementioned reply, Herr Hitler expatiated on Poland's misdeeds, spoke of his generous March offer to Poland, and stated it could not be reiterated. He said, moreover, that nothing short of the return of Danzig and the whole of the Corridor, as well as a rectification in Silesia, would satisfy him. Moreover, Hitler held that Poland could never be reasonable, and he spoke of annihilating Poland.

AUGUST 29

On the night of August 29th, I was informed by Polish official circles that at about 7:30 p.m., Herr Hitler handed the British Ambassador his reply to the British Government's Note, at the same time offering verbal explanations.[18] The Ambassador thereupon cabled the message to his Government. Later, Minister Beck imparted to me the following: in brief, the message stated that, though skeptical as to prospects of a successful outcome, the German Government accepted the British Government's proposal of direct Polish-German negotiations, provided a Polish plenipotentiary with full powers arrived in Berlin during the course of the following day, Wednesday, August 30th. The communication concluded by stating that the German Government would at once draw up proposals for a solution acceptable to themselves, and, if possible, would apprise the British Government thereof before the arrival of a Polish negotiator. In response to the British Ambassador's observations that this condition smacked of an ultimatum, Herr Hitler and von Ribbentrop both assured him it was only intended to stress the urgency of the moment.

The Polish Government issued a protest against the German

occupation of Slovakia, stated to have been effected in order to protect Slovakia against the Poles.[19]

As a result of urgent requests by the British and French Ambassadors that the Polish Government postpone its call for general mobilization in order to avoid provoking Herr Hitler at this crucial hour, the Polish Government reluctantly accepted to postpone the order from 11 p.m., August 29, as was originally planned, to August 30, at 3 p.m. o'clock. On the morning of August 30, Minister Beck in imparting to me the reasons for postponement of general mobilization orders, stated in marked earnestness that while his Government had consented to comply with the requests of their allies, they had done so contrary to their own realistic views on events current and in-the-making. However, he had agreed with his associates that Poland, fully aware of her responsibilities to her allies as well as to herself, was capable of proving herself a worthy ally under all circumstances. (I am aware [that] this delay in mobilization proved costly to Poland, in that it served to prevent many reserve troops—estimated by Polish authorities at between 350,000 to 400,000 men—from reaching the western theater of operations before the German aerial attacks had bombed the rail junctions, thus crippling east to west transportation facilities).

AUGUST 30

I learned from Polish official sources (a) that the British Cabinet met to consider Herr Hitler's last communication of August 29, and sent a reply thereto; and (b) that in behalf of his Government, the British Ambassador in Berlin delivered an interim response to the German ministry of Foreign Affairs, between midnight of the 29th and 6 a.m. of the 30th, wherein it was pointed out, among other factors, that it was unreasonable to expect that the British Government could arrange for the appearance of a Polish representative with full powers in Berlin within the course of the following day and that the German Government should not count upon it.[20]

During the course of the day, the British Ambassador [in Berlin] received three messages to transmit to the German

Government. The first was a message from the British Prime Minister direct to Herr Hitler; it informed him of having made representations urging Warsaw to guard against frontier incidents, and asked the German Government to take similar precautions. The second informed the German Government that the British Government's counsel of restraint had met with the Polish Government's assurance that the Polish Government had no intention of provoking further incidents, and it asked for a like attitude on Germany's part. The third pointed out that the demand that a Polish Emissary with plenary powers come to Berlin to learn of German proposals was unreasonable. It suggested the German Government invite the Polish Ambassador to come and hand him the proposals for transmission to the Polish Government. This communication, moreover, recalled to the German Government that it had promised to communicate its proposals in detail to the British Government, which would undertake, if a reasonable basis were offered, to do its best in Warsaw to facilitate negotiations.[21]

At about midnight, (the hour set in the "ultimatum" embodied in Herr Hitler's Note of August 29, as the limit for the arrival of a Polish Emissary with Plenary powers), the British Ambassador called on von Ribbentrop and handed him the British Government's formal reply to the German Government's Note of August 29. In the final paragraphs of this reply, the British Government, in pointing out the necessity of an early commencement of discussions, insisted upon a military standstill on both sides, during the period of negotiations. It expressed, moreover, its confidence in acquiring a like engagement from the Polish Government, provided the German Government gave similar assurances. Finally, it suggested the establishment of a temporary *modus vivendi* in Danzig, of such nature as to avoid incidents which might render Polish-German relations still more difficult. Von Ribbentrop's attitude throughout this meeting was, according to reports, markedly hostile and excited, and according to Polish officialdom's subsequent reports, this hostile attitude exhibited by von Ribbentrop became increasingly violent as the British Ambassador conveyed in turn each communication received from his Government during that day.

After the Ambassador had finished making his communications, von Ribbentrop produced a lengthy document which he rapidly read aloud in German. The Ambassador thus found it possible to gain only the gist of about 7 of the 16 points contained in the document. When, at the close of von Ribbentrop's reading, the Ambassador asked for a copy of the text of those proposals in order to communicate the substance thereof to his Government, von Ribbentrop refused, stating the proposals were now out of date, in view of the failure of a Polish Emissary to come to Berlin by midnight. The Ambassador thereupon observed that in such case, the clause in Herr Hitler's Note of August 29 to which the Ambassador had drawn Herr Hitler's and von Ribbentrop's attention the preceeding night, actually constituted an ultimatum. Von Ribbentrop denied this was the case, and reiterated it was intended only to stress the urgency of the moment. The Ambassador asked why, then, could von Ribbentrop not adopt normal procedure; let him have a copy of the proposals; invite the Polish Ambassador to call on him, and hand him the proposals for transmission to the Polish Government. Von Ribbentrop replied in violent terms that he would never ask the Polish Ambassador to come to him. Von Ribbentrop hinted, however, that it might be different if the Polish Ambassador were to ask him for an interview.[22]

About 10:30 p.m. Minister Beck telephoned to ask me to come to his house. The Minister met me at the door and escorted me to his living room where we joined a group consisting of several members of his family and officers of his staff. The ensuing hours were devoted to an informal review of events of the day. Moreover, the Minister "filled me in" on details concerning what had recently transpired between the four capitals, Warsaw, London, Paris and Berlin. Touching on the German demand for the appearance of a Polish Emissary in Berlin by midnight, Minister Beck stated that neither he nor his associates intended that he should go to Berlin to be treated as another President Hácha.[23] I left Minister Beck shortly after midnight, the hour which marked the commencement of the heated conversation between Sir Nevile Henderson and von Ribbentrop in Berlin.

AUGUST 31

I subsequently learned that Henderson was informed during the early hours of the morning of the 31st that the German Government had decided to issue orders for a march on Poland by 1 p.m. o'clock, should a Polish Emissary with plenary powers not arrive before that hour.[24] It is conceivable, to my mind, that the Ambassador was correct in having attributed a further delay in the attack until dawn of September 1 to a final attempt on the part of the Italian Government to preserve European peace. In this connection, I later learned that during the course of August 31st, the *Duce* sounded out Paris and London as to their willingness to collaborate towards a peaceful settlement. While the replies from the French and British Governments were reportedly favorable in principle, lively interest being evinced by the French Government, the replies were not received by the Italian Government until September 1, after Germany and Poland had already come to grips.[25]

The following day, I learned from an informed officer of Minister Beck's staff that at about 2 o'clock that morning in Berlin, the British Ambassador disclosed to Lipski the substance of his midnight conversation with von Ribbentrop, and pointed out that the plebiscite in the Corridor and cession of Danzig were the two main points in Hitler's proposals. The British Ambassador moreover observed his doubts as to whether any negotiations might succeed if conducted with von Ribbentrop, and suggested that Lipski recommend that his Government propose immediately a meeting between Field Marshals Śmigły-Rydz and Goering. Following his talk with the British Ambassador, Lipski communicated the substance of the foregoing to Minister Beck.[26]

During the course of the same night, August 30–31, British Ambassador Kennard communicated to Minister Beck the British Government's (a) reply to Herr Hitler, and (b) comments contained in Lord Halifax's cable of August 30, to [the] effect 1/ that [the] British Government had proposed in Berlin a military standstill during discussions, to which it was hoped the Polish Government would have no objections, and 2/ that since the Polish Government had authorized the British Government to say Poland was prepared to enter direct discussions with the German Government, the British Government hoped that, provided a method and general arrangements for discussions could be satisfactorily agreed, the Polish Government would proceed without delay.[27]

Following Kennard's early morning telephone call, I called on him at about 8:40 a.m. whereupon he imparted to me a summary of the foregoing and asked me whether I thought any further peace efforts might be expected to be exerted by President Roosevelt. In response I pointed out that Herr Hitler had failed to reply to messages the President had already sent him, and that I had no indication that the President was contemplating further steps.

Subsequent to the above meeting, I learned from official sources that [at] about 9:30 Kennard called on Minister Beck. Minister Beck handed the Ambassador the Polish Government's reply to his aforementioned démarche which had taken place during the night of August 30–31. (Count Joseph Potocki attended this conference, in case the necessity arose to translate Poland's reply which was written in the Polish language). Minister Beck told the Ambassador that he would at once instruct Lipski in Berlin to seek an interview either with the Minister of Foreign Affairs or the State Secretary, with a view to stating Poland had accepted [the] British proposals. In response to the Ambassador's question as to what attitude the Polish Ambassador would adopt if von Ribbentrop handed him the German proposals, Minister Beck said that the Polish Ambassador would not be authorized to accept such a document as, in view of past experiences, it might be accompanied by some ultimatum. In this view, it was essential that contact be made in the first instance, and that then details should be discussed as to where, with whom, and on what basis negotiations should be commenced. Beck subsequently informed me that in the text of the Polish Government's formal reply, which the British Ambassador telegraphed to his Government, the Polish Government confirmed its readiness for a direct exchange of views with the German Government on the basis proposed by the British Government and communicated to the Polish Government by Lord Halifax's telegram of August 28, addressed to the British Ambassador to Poland. The Polish Government also expressed its readiness, on a reciprocal basis, to give formal guarantees that in [the] event of negotiations Polish troops would not violate German frontiers, provided a corresponding guarantee were given regarding nonviolation of Polish frontiers by German troops. The Polish Government moreover, stressed the necessity of securing a simple provisional *modus vivendi* in Danzig.[28] At noon, following his talk with Kennard, Minister Beck telephoned instructions to Lipski in Berlin to seek an interview at once, either with the Foreign Minister, or the State Secretary, and inform either or both that Poland would accept the British proposals of August 28 as a basis for direct negotiations. Accordingly, about 1 p.m. Lipski telephoned State Secretary [Ernst von] Weisäcker to request an early appointment with the Foreign Minister. About 3 p.m. the State Secretary telephoned Lipski to ask him whether he would appear as Ambassador or Emissary with plenary powers, to which question Lipski replied he would appear as Ambassador. At 6 p.m. o'clock, the State Secretary telephoned Lipski to say that the Foreign Minister would receive him at 6:30 p.m.

I was subsequently told by an officer of Minister Beck's staff that during the meeting which took place, Lipski stated he was appearing solely in capacity of Ambassador without plenary powers to discuss or negotiate, and handed von Ribbentrop a brief communication to effect that the Polish Government was weighing favorably the British proposal for direct discussion, and that a formal answer in this matter would be communicated to the German Government in the immediate future. Neither did Lipski ask for the German proposals, nor did von Ribbentrop offer to give them to him. Their meeting, which lasted but a few minutes, proved futile. Lipski subsequently described the meeting to me as "ceremonious".[29] Following this occasion, Lipski failed in his efforts to establish contact with Warsaw, due to the German Government's having closed all means of communication between Poland and Germany.

At about 9:30 p.m. the German radio broadcast their 16

FINAL STEPS OF THE CRISIS

point proposals, in spite of the vigorous efforts (which I later learned) Henderson had made to forestall the broadcast.[30] I also learned that previous to the broadcast, the Ambassador pointed out to Goering that this procedure would probably wreck the last prospect of peace. Moreover, when the Ambassador begged the Field Marshal to intervene in the matter, the latter said he could not, adding that the German Government felt obliged to broadcast their proposals to prove their "good faith".

This conversation, which according to the Ambassador's report was his last one with the Field Marshal, lasted about 2 hours. The Ambassador gained the impression from certain of Goering's remarks that it represented a last effort on his part to detach Britain from Poland. Moreover, the Ambassador augured the worst from the fact that Goering was in a position at such a moment to give him so much of his time. The Ambassador felt that since Goering had been made President of the New German Defense Council (war cabinet) a few days before, he could scarcely have afforded at such a moment to spare time in conversation if it did not mean that everything down to the last detail was then ready for action.

I later ascertained from authoritative sources that orders had that night been issued to march on Poland.

In Warsaw, Minister [Stanisław] Łepkowski, Counselor to President Mościcki, was at Minister Beck's house during the early part of the evening. While listening in to a German radio station about 9:30 p.m., Łepkowski heard the broadcast of Germany's 16 point proposals. He immediately imparted to Minister Beck the substance of what he had heard, and [the] Chief of [the] Foreign Office Press Bureau, [Wiktor] Skiwski, who had taken down a shorthand record of the broadcast, gave the Minister the details. (This radio broadcast marked the Polish Government's first receipt of the full text of Germany's 16 point proposals). Minister Beck immediately informed Marshal Śmigły-Rydz thereof by telephone. Later, in response to Łepkowski's question, Minister Beck stated there was no use in waking up the President and bothering him with a recital of these points.

In bidding good night to Count Joseph Potocki, Chief of the Anglo-Saxon Division of the Foreign Office,[31] who had dined with Minister Beck that night, the Minister stated in effect that he felt they could go to bed feeling that at least that night there would be no war. In discussing this with Count Potocki at a later date, he shared my impression that Minister Beck's remark might conceivably have been attributable to the following thoughts in the back of his mind: (a) that Herr Hitler, deeming Britain's acquiescence essential to the success of his aspirations, might at the last moment refrain from marching on Poland if he became convinced Britain would come to Poland's aid; (b) that in accepting Britain's proposals of August 28 as a basis of direct negotiations with Germany, Poland had given Herr Hitler a face-saving formula for at least a postponement of a conflict with Poland; and (c) that Minister Beck's proposal of a provisional *modus vivendi* might prove a potentially effective card.

I later was apprised shortly before dawn on September 1, that Kennard received from Lord Halifax a telegram in response to his own message of August 31 imparting Poland's acceptance of Britain's proposals of August 28 as basis for direct discussions, together with Minister Beck's appurtinent observations. Lord Halifax felt that while the British Government was glad to learn that the Polish Ambassador at Berlin was being instructed to establish contact with Germany and while the British Government fully agreed as to the necessity of discussing detailed arrangements for negotiations, and agreed as to the undesirability of Minister Beck's visit to Berlin, the British Government failed to see why Poland should find difficulty in authorizing the Polish Ambassador to accept a document from the German Government. Moreover, the British hoped that Poland might see its way clear to modify its instructions to him in this respect. Lord Halifax then went on to point out that there was no mention of ultimatum in the report on the German proposals which had been sent by Ambassador Henderson to the British Government, and the suggestion that the demand for the appearance of a Polish Emissary in Berlin on August 30 amounted to an ultimatum was vigorously repudiated by von Ribbentrop. If the document did contain an ultimatum, the Polish Government would naturally refuse to discuss it until the ultimatum was withdrawn. Lord Halifax went on to point out that he should have thought that the Polish Ambassador could be instructed to receive and transmit a document, and to say that (a) if it bore the complexion of an ultimatum, he anticipated the Polish Government would be unable to negotiate on such a basis, and (b) in any case, in the view of the Polish Government, questions as to the *venue* of the negotiations, the basis on which they should be held, and the persons to take part in them, had to be discussed and decided between the two Governments.[32]

In response to the foregoing communication from Lord Halifax, Kennard telegraphed that Lord Halifax's telegram had been decoded at 4 a.m. the morning of September 1, and that Lipski had already called on von Ribbentrop at 6:30 p.m. the previous day. The British Ambassador pointed out, moreover, that in view of this fact, which had been followed by the German invasion of Poland at dawn that day (September 1), it was clearly useless for him to take the action suggested.[33] Several points in connection with the foregoing exchange of diplomatic communications stand out clearly in my mind. Had Hitler honestly desired a peaceful settlement, he could have taken full advantage of the British Government's offer of good offices in the matter of direct negotiations between the German and Polish Governments. The Polish Government's practice of restraint under trying circumstances, and its further assurances of continued restraint to the British Ambassador in Warsaw, as late as August 30, in spite of an intensification of increasingly intolerable German provocation in Danzig and at other points along the frontier, revealed the Polish Government's willingness to contribute its share towards an improvement of the atmosphere. It seemed unlikely that Hitler believed it reasonable to expect a Polish Emissary with plenary powers to come within 24 hours to Berlin without even knowing in advance the basis of negotiations in which he would be required to engage. It also seemed that Herr Hitler and von Ribbentrop attached more importance to the appearance of a

Polish Emissary with plenary powers in Berlin than to the demands contained in the 16 point proposal.

In Warsaw, on the night of August 31, I turned on the radio about 9:30 p.m., and heard the announcement of Russia's ratification of the German-Russian Non-Aggression Pact. This engaged my suspicion, lest it serve as a signal to set the German military machine in motion against Poland. This suspicion, on top of my previous uneasiness about the situation, prompted me to put in a telephone call for Kuykendal, our Consul in Danzig. The operator said it would be difficult to complete the call, as lines were occupied to such extent that I would have to await my turn. I let the order stand, requesting her to call me regardless of what hour she could put me through. At about 11:30 I again called the operator, and was told there was trouble somewhere along the line; she thought however, this might be repaired in short order. This aroused my concern. I thereupon telephoned Mr. Jan Wrszelacki, officer of the night at the Foreign Office, and asked whether his night reports indicated that conditions along the frontier were more than hitherto disturbing in character. He replied in the affirmative, adding that all along the line, and especially down towards Katowice, border incidents had been rapidly increasing during the evening. Moreover, the atmosphere in Danzig was becoming disturbingly more tense.

Immediately following this conversation I sent a cable to the President and the Secretary [of State], stating in effect that while the Germans might conceivably still be bluffing, the situation was becoming more tense along the border and called for even closer watching than hitherto. As a matter of fact, I felt that matters had reached a point whereat anything could happen.

I then retired for what I instinctively felt would be a night of uncertain length.

1. For a good discussion of Danzig's domestic developments and international role during this period, see H. S. Levine, *Hitler's Free City: A History of the Nazi Party in Danzig, 1925–1939* (Chicago, 1973).

2. The text of the German note is in *DGFP*, D, 7:4–5.

3. Wühlisch's report on the Polish reply is in *DGFP*, D, 7:9–10.

4. Biddle's impressions as to what Beck and Hitler were thinking at this time were absolutely correct.

5. The text of the nonaggression treaty and the secret protocol attached to the treaty is in *DGFP*, D, 7:245–47.

6. The "Oslo Powers" to which Biddle refers included Belgium, the Netherlands, Luxembourg, Finland, and the three Scandinavian states.

7. The minutes of the meeting between Hitler and Henderson on August 23, along with the text of Chamberlain's letter to Hitler and the latter's reply, are in *DGFP*, D, 7:210–16. Henderson's account of his meeting with Hitler is in *DBFP*, Third Series, 7:161–63.

8. Lipski's account of the meeting with Göring is in his *Diplomat in Berlin*, pp. 590–92.

9. Hitler's statement to Henderson is in *DGFP*, D, 7:279–81. Henderson's description of the meeting is in *DBFP*, Third Series, 7:227–31.

10. The text of Mościcki's reply to Belgium is in *PWB*, no. 88.

11. The Polish official sent to London to negotiate this treaty offered a different version in his comments to the editors. W. W. Kulski, currently professor emeritus as James B. Duke Professor for Russian Affairs at Duke University and a noted expert on Soviet and East European affairs, was then serving as the chief of the legal division in the Polish Foreign Ministry. As the ministry's chief legal advisor, he was sent to Britain to work with the British Foreign Office Assistant Legal Adviser Gerald Fitzmaurice, later a judge at the International Court, in drafting the actual pact of mutual assistance. The treaty was completed on August 23, whereupon the British urged Kulski to return at once to Warsaw, for the reasons indicated by Biddle. Accordingly, Kulski left London by plane on the morning of the treaty's signing–August 25–and, in his words, "I found the situation normal upon my return in Poland."

*See supplementary note attached to section on military aspect. [Biddle's own footnote—Eds. The section on military aspects of the war is printed below as Chapter five of the report.]

12. Biddle undoubtedly meant August 25.

13. For a description of the cabinet meetings and the formulation of Britain's reply to Hitler, see Aster, *1939*, pp. 340–42.

14. Biddle was undoubtedly referring to Hitler's message to Daladier delivered to French Ambassador Robert Coulondre, noted in *DGFP*, D, 7:284. Daladier's reply to Hitler is in a letter dated August 26, ibid., pp. 330–31.

15. The text of Hitler's letter of August 27 to Daladier is in *DGFP*, D, 7:356–59.

16. Kennard's report on the alledged mistreatment of Germans in Poland is in *DBFP*, Third Series, 7:203–4.

17. The minutes of the Hitler-Henderson talk of August 28, and the text of Britain's reply to Germany are in *DGFP*, D, 7:381–84. See also *DBFP*, Third Series, 7:330–33, 351–55.

18. The text of Hitler's reply to Britain is in *DGFP*, D, 7:413–15. See also *DBFP*, Third Series, 7:388–90.

19. On March 14, 1939, the Slovak Republic was formed out of the ruins of Czechoslovakia as a theoretically sovereign, independent state, although German influence was obviously felt in every facet of the country's existence. However, by summer the Slovak leadership had grown increasingly restless under the strict controls imposed by Berlin; consequently, when Germany requested permission to mass its troops along the Polish-Slovakian frontier preparatory to the September invasion, the Slovak

leadership agreed only after long and surprisingly detailed negotiations between the two states had been concluded. It is therefore misleading to characterize the German military buildup as an "occupation"; Slovakia was not formally occupied by German forces until 1944, in reprisal for the abortive uprising in October. See the excellent study by Jörg Hoensch, *Die Slowakei und Hitlers Ostpolitik* (Köln/Gräz, 1965), and his brief article "The Slovak Republic, 1939-1945," in *A History of the Czechoslovak Republic, 1918-1948*, ed. Victor Mamatey and Radomir Luza (Princeton, 1973), pp. 271–95.

20. Hitler's message of August 29 is in *DBFP*, Third Series, 7:374–75, 388–90; Henderson's instructions for a reply and his report of the reply are in ibid., pp. 391, 400–401.

21. The texts of the three messages to Hitler are in *DBFP*, Third Series, 7:403, 405, 410.

22. Henderson's reports of his talks with Ribbentrop are in *DBFP*, Third Series, 7:429–30, 432.

23. Dr. Emil Hacha, the chief justice of the Czechoslovak Supreme Court, replaced Edouard Benes as president of the rump Czechoslovak state on October 5, 1938. An infirm, aging mild-mannered gentleman, Dr. Hacha found himself continually confronting increased German pressure on what remained of his country, until finally he was forced to appeal for an audience with Hitler. Hacha and the Czech foreign minister, Frantisek Chvalkovsky, arrived in Berlin the evening of March 14, 1939; early the following morning, after the well-known marathon session with Hitler during which the hapless Hacha fainted and was revived, the beleaguered Czechs yielded and signed a declaration formally requesting Germany to exercise complete control over their country. The secret German minutes of this meeting are in *DGFP*, D, 5:263–69, and the text of the joint communique announcing the agreement is in ibid., pp. 270–71. See also the account by Hitler's interpreter, Dr. Paul Schmidt, *Hitler's Interpreter* (New York, 1951), pp. 123–26.

24. Henderson to Halifax, August 31, 1939, *DBFP*, Third Series, 7:434–35.

25. On Mussolini's efforts to prevent war, see the documents in *DBFP*, Third Series, 7:434–39, 442–43; *DGFP*, D, 7:457–65; and Hugh Gibson, ed., *The Ciano Diaries 1939–1943* (Garden City, 1946), pp. 134–35.

26. Lipski, *Diplomat in Berlin*, pp. 606–8.

27. Halifax to Kennard, August 30, in *DBFP*, Third Series, 7:410–11, 434.

28. Kennard's report on the conversation with Beck, and the text of Beck's reply to Germany, are in *DBFP*, Third Series, 7:450–52.

29. Lipski, *Diplomat in Berlin*, pp. 609–10.

30. The full text of the German 16 points is in *DBFP*, Third Series, 7:459–62. The proposals included the surrender of Danzig to Germany, a plebiscite for the Corridor, Germany's right to build roads and railroad lines across the Corridor until the plebiscite, the granting of extraterritorial rights to Germany for the construction of an autobahn if the plebiscite went against Germany, the demilitarization of Danzig and Gdynia, the appointment of an international committee of inquiry to investigate the minority problem, the conclusion of a mutual guarantee regarding minority rights, and a demobilization of the German and Polish armed forces.

31. Biddle is in error here. Joseph (Józef) Potocki was the head of the western division of the Polish Foreign Ministry; there was no separate "Anglo-Saxon" department.

32. Halifax to Kennard, September 1, *DBFP*, Third Series, 7:469–70.

33. Kennard to Halifax, September 1, *DBFP*, Third Series, 7:481–82.

CHAPTER THREE

The Polish-German Conflict

and

The Embassy's Activities

SEPTEMBER 1

I awakened at 5:30 in the morning. At first I did not understand what had disturbed me. I went to the window and
peered over a tranquil city. All was quite—and yet I felt trouble
was in the air. (It was only later that I ascertained it had been
Warsaw's first air alarm that had disturbed my rest—I had evidently been subsconsciously aroused by the sirens, which had
ceased by the time I awoke. The plane which had caused the
sounding of the siren had bombed the race course at the edge
of town). When I put in a telephone call for Mr. Jan Wrszlacki
at the Foreign Office, the night operator (still on duty) informed me his line was busy. It remained busy so long that I
felt confident something was wrong. Finally I succeeded in
getting through to him, and in response to my question, he
said I was correct in my expressed suspicion that the Germans
had attacked. He had just been able to confirm preliminary
reports that German troops had been attacking at various
points along the frontier, including Danzig, since dawn. The
air fields at Katowice had already experienced air attacks.

Aware that I should lose much time in getting word to the
President and the Secretary of State by cable in that this
would entail coding at our end and decoding at their end of the
line, I requested my house telephone operator to try making

a call to Ambassador [William] Bullitt in Paris, who could relay the message to Washington. When the operator later told me that a call to Paris over lines through Berlin was impossible, I suggested he take a chance and try placing the call via Copenhagen. To my happy surprise, the idea worked— and with no undue delay, under the circumstances, I succeeded in reaching Bullitt. Realizing we might be cut at any second, we were brief—I told him war had started, and asked him to apprise the President accordingly by telephone. He assured me he would. Having long known the ambassador to be a man of clear thinking, energy, and action, I felt confident the President and the Secretary would learn the news in a matter of minutes. (I later learned to my profound sense of satisfaction that this turned out to be the case).

After my telephone talk with Mr. Wrszlacki, I awakened all members of my household, telephoned Consul General J. K. Davis and members of my staff, and notified them that war had commenced. In that I had been inclined to place considerable credence in the substance of the Turkish Ambassador's disclosure as to what his Military Attaché had some weeks before been able to learn of Germany's contemplated plan of attack, envisaging among other factors an aerial bombardment characterized by flights of about 100 planes at 20 minute intervals (which I subsequently reported to the Department, and which subsequent events proved approximately correct in many cases); and in that early morning aerial bombardments within the close proximity of several cities, including Warsaw, had already been officially reported to Mr. Wrszlacki at the Foreign Office, I decided to install, at the earliest moment, the clerks and all American women members of my staff in the house which preparatory to just such eventuality I had previously rented for them at Constanscin,[1] a resort in the midst of a pine forest about 18 kilometers from the heart of Warsaw which the Foreign Office had in February recommended as a reasonably safe haven from aerial bombardments in event of an attack. I felt they would be safer there, at least, until I might have been able to gain a clearer picture of what tactics the Germans intended employing via-à-vis Warsaw. Besides, I felt that even if, in the preliminary stage, the city itself did escape bombing, there might possibly be planes passing over and around Warsaw, causing air alarm sirens at various intervals during the night as well as day time. Hence, I believed my staff would be able to get a better night's sleep, (so important during tense times) in Constanscin than in Warsaw. Moreover, conditions permitting I planned to have them come into town to work at the Embassy during the day time. As I was warned by the police authorities that all roads leading out of Warsaw were already under guard and that passes would be required to go beyond the city limits, I personally escorted the women members of my staff to Constanscin. I thereupon returned to Warsaw for a prearranged conference with Minister Beck and his associates at the Foreign Office.

During the course of this conference, the Minister and several officers of his staff disclosed the substance of their reports of aerial bombardments which had taken place at various intervals over a wide area of Poland. Minister Beck stated his opinion that Herr Hitler pictured himself sovereign of a pan-German continent, and that Poland had decided to contribute her part towards halting Herr Hitler's drive towards that objective. Minister Beck told me confidentially that in a message from Lord Halifax, the latter indicated he now understood the Minister's policy vis-à-vis Rumania.[2] Later, during a conversation at the Embassy with officers of my staff, I urged that following further air raids in and around Warsaw, one and whenever possible two of us together should proceed to the scenes of bombardment for the purpose of making eye-witness reports on the circumstances and the damage incurred. From the very outset of the conflict, the importance of recording only eye-witness reports was clearly understood by all the members of our Mission.

Towards the close of the afternoon the first sizable flight of German planes took place over the city. From the courtyard of our Chancery we watched maneuvers between Polish pursuit planes and German bombers. Since the German planes were flying at an altitude of between 12 and 15,000 feet, the fire from the anti-aircraft batteries and heavy machine guns fell short of their marks. (We could see the tracer bullets shoot through space like balls of fire, headed for their objectives). There was a heavy machine gun battery on the roof of a house next door to our Chancery. However, the anti-aircraft fire appeared to prevent the planes from risking flying lower and diving. This raid entailed no bombardment of the heart of the city. I thereupon decided to have the women members of my staff whom I had that day left at Constanscin, come to work in town during the day and return to Constanscin to spend the night, pending a turn for the worse in the aerial attacks over Warsaw.

During the course of the day, (and again on September 2) the following message at our request was radio-broadcasted over the government-controlled broadcasting station:

> It is requested that American citizens who desire to leave the country and who may experience difficulty in doing so, report to the American consular officers at Brześć nad Bugiem where efforts will be made to arrange for their departures.

These measures contributed importantly towards the evacuation of between 300 and 400 American citizens before the railway communications to the north were cut after the commencement of hostilities.

During the course of the afternoon I was informed by an official of the Foreign Office (a) that at about six A.M. o'clock that morning Herr Hitler issued proclamation to effect he would meet force with force; (b) that the scrapping of Danzig's constitution and the annexation of Danzig was proclaimed; and (c) that subsequently Herr Hitler in [an] address to [the] Reichstag declared he would not call upon Italy for assistance. (It later came to light that in an exchange of views which took place between Count Ciano and Herr von Ribbentrop on May 6th and 7th in Milan they concurred, among other points, 1/ in the need of striving to preserve peace in Europe for a long period, in order to afford both Italy and Germany time to perfect their internal reconstruction and military preparations, and 2/ the duration of this period was to be

September 1st. Watching the first large-scale air raid over Warsaw from the courtyard of the Chancery.

fixed by Italy at three years; by Germany at four or five. These among other points formed the foundation of the Treaty of Alliance signed by Berlin on May 22nd.)

Motoring out to Constanscin that evening (it was still light) we were stopped by military guards at the outskirts of Warsaw. The guards pointed to an air raid which was taking place a short distance ahead of us, over what was reportedly an ammunition dump in close proximity of the Wilanów Palace. When the attack appeared to be over, we continued on our way. A few minutes later, however, we spotted a plane, evidently one of the same group of German planes which had engaged in the aforementioned attack. It was flying at about tree-top height, from the direction of the Vistula, and turned to cross the road ahead of us. To our discomfort, the pilot gave every sign of intending to swoop in behind us. Just as he started up the road after us, however, he apparently spotted a heavy machine gun nest in the field at his right—and as they opened fire, he sped off like a sky-rocket. It was not until later that night at our villa in Constanscin that I found that the day's bombardments had severed the telephone connections between Constanscin and Warsaw.

SEPTEMBER 2

I had already talked on August 29 with Mr. Brooks, managing director of the Giesha Mines of Katowice,[3] with whom I had previously been in frequent contact regarding serious developments. After ascertaining from him that the affairs of his company had been taken over by the Polish Government as a war emergency, I urged him to evacuate his American engineers and employees as soon as possible. He assured me he would act on this advice immediately. On that same day I discussed the serious trend of events with executives of the Gydinia-America Line, and ascertained that they were taking all possible precautions under the circumstances against the occurrence of an early emergency. Moreover, I discussed with Count Czapski, of the American Scantic Line, the seriousness of the current trend of developments, and ascertained that he and his associates were taking all pre-cautionary measures possible under the circumstances in con-nection with American business interests, direct or indirect. Mr. Sztoleman, of the Vacuum Oil Company informed me on September 2nd that he was removing the headquarters of the company's operations to Lwów.

In my early morning meeting with Minister Beck and several officers of his staff, the Minister told me that at about 2:00 A.M. the first secretary of the Polish Embassy in Berlin had telephoned Count Potulicki, Officer of the night at the Foreign Office, that in line with President Roosevelt's initia-tive, Herr Hitler wished to notify the Polish Government that he had given orders to limit aerial bombardments to military objectives.[4] Minister Beck pointed out that it was evident that the German Government had re-established telephone communications with Warsaw specifically to enable the sec-retary of the Polish Embassy in Berlin to transmit this message to the Polish Government. The Minister said that he would discuss this matter further with me later in the day. Air alarms became more than hitherto frequent throughout the day.

During luncheon in the garden restaurant of the Euro-pejski Hotel my family and I, as well as the other guests of the restaurant, watched an air raid overhead. No one evinced other than calm interest, and aside from an occasional glance upward to note the progress of the aerial action, the waiters served the various tables, as if the raid were a usual occur-rance.

In the course of my second call at the Foreign Office, about 4:00 P.M. o'clock, an air alarm sounded. The officials with whom I was talking received warning from the guards on duty at the Ministry that the raid was expected to be of serious character. They therefore invited me to continue our discussion in the air-raid cellar of the ministry. Once in the cellar I found it most efficiently fitted out for the emergency, in fact I have seen nothing since, anywhere so well equipped: a special air ventilation system connected with the roof, tele-phones, for inner-office and inter-ministry communication, operated on electric power system, independent of the regular city service. Moreover, there were several guards trained on the technique of gas defense and several trained nurses.

Minister Beck eventually came down and joined our conversation. He informed me that his Government was then replying through the Hague to the German Government's aforementioned proposal to limit aerial bombardments to military objectives. The Polish reply stated that the Polish Government had given "similar" orders, that it was maintaining them despite bombardments which had caused numerous casualties amongst the Polish civilian population, but that it reserved the right to retaliate should this happen again. Minister Beck went on to say that despite Herr Hitler's message, his reports indicated that at 8 o'clock that morning German planes had bombarded Ciechanów, a town close to the East Prussian border, killing 21 civilians and 4 soldiers, and wounding 36 civilians, 9 of whom were women, [and] 4 children; and Lublin, killing 30 inhabitants. Minister Beck added that his Government took a grave view of these acts and particularly in view of Herr Hitler's message transmitted both through the Hague and by telephone from Berlin to Warsaw; the Polish Government was considering what action to take.

Of pertinent bearing, I was aware that Polish Government circles attached considerable significance to the fact that Herr Hitler, transmitting his aforementioned message to Warsaw, had not only called upon The Hague to serve as intermediary, but had also re-established telephone communications with Warsaw for the purpose. These circles were inclined to ascribe this "double-barreled" action to Herr Hitler's anxiety lest, when Britain and France honored their respective alliances with Poland, they might bombard the industrial areas of Western Germany (after Britain's and France's intervention, Berlin was quick to discern the Western Powers' disinclination to engage in aerial bombardments of German industrial areas. At least during the course of the Polish-German conflict).

In connection with air raids, I anticipated that any delay in intervention by the Western Allies might make the Germans less apt to observe scrupulously the conditions embodied in their September 2nd agreement with the Poles, i.e., limiting aerial bombardments to military objectives. In fact, I considered that potential fear of reprisals in form of allied aerial attacks over the industrial areas of Western Germany about the only factor which might serve to restrain the Germans from broadening the scope of their aerial activities from strictly military objectives. Subsequent developments appeared to bear out my thought on this score. At 6 P.M. the Polish radio broadcasting station addressed a broadcast to the then-convened French Chamber of Deputies, refuting a report which Minister Beck had just learned was being circulated amongst the Deputies, and which Minister Beck was inclined to ascribe to Berlin's inspiration, to [the] effect that German troops had suspended all attack. During the broadcast a German air raid was taking place over the outskirts of Warsaw.

In the late afternoon Major Colbern, Military Attaché, and I met to review the course of military and aerial activities since the outbreak of war. The Major reported that, as in the case of the previous day, the German air force had continued on an extensive scale its attacks on objectives throughout Poland. As far as either of us could ascertain at that juncture, attacks were directed chiefly at military, industrial, and communications centers. We ascertained at the same time, however, that many casualties amongst civilians had resulted due in part to the fact that garrisons existed in all Polish cities. The effect of the bombs, in most cases reported, indicated light incendiary bombs. We concurred, moreover, in our observations that in the course of that day, German bombers had flown over Warsaw at two hour intervals at [an] estimated height of 12 to 15,000 feet; moreover, neither of us had observed any hits by Warsaw anti-aircraft batteries. The Major then stated that the Polish General Staff estimated 600 German planes had taken part in these raids, and that the direction indicated they were shuttling back and forth between East Prussia and former Austria.

Major Colbern furthermore reported the following resumé

of German ground attacks which had taken place up to noon that day (September 2); Danzig Division which had attacked in direction of Gdynia was driven back by Polish counter-action at Orlowo. East Prussian front: four German infantry divisions and one cavalry brigade attacking in direction of Neidenberg-Mława, reached Mława vicinity; Pomorze frontier: two German infantry divisions and one light armored division attacked on front Chojnice-Notec River, advancing 25 kilometers to Nakło vicinity; Poznan frontier: One Land-wehr division and mechanized units, elements of one fortress division attacked in direction Zbaszyn-Poznan, advancing about 15 kilometers; On front Wartenberg-Nanslau, one mechanized and two infantry divisions attacking in direction Wielun and Kepno reported making slow progress. Silesian front: one armored and four infantry divisions attacking on both sides of Katowice to Rybno and Czestachowa; Katowice uncaptured. Slovakian frontier; one armored and one infantry division attacking on either side of Zakopany advanced about 30 kilometers to Nowy-Targ. At no point had the Polish main defensive positions been reached or broken through. The Polish forces claimed to have captured or destroyed one Ger-man armored train and 100 tanks during fighting of Septem-ber 1.

Dined that night at Europejski Hotel and went afterwards to the Foreign Office to ascertain reports on latest develop-ments before motoring out to Constanscin for the night. We were awakened by the drone of German bombers, which at about 6:30 A.M. began passing over Constanscin and War-saw in flights of threes and fours at about three-quarters of an hour intervals. They seemed to be flying at about 15,000 feet. Suddenly a medium-sized bomber swooped down in a low power-drive, so low that it seemed as though the plane had scraped our roof, dropping eleven bombs in rapid suc-cession (6 of which fortunately proved duds). One bomb ex-ploded and another landed unexploded in our yard, about an acre in size, while a dud went through the roof of the adjacent villa (situated about 200 feet apart from our villa), landing unexploded in the cellar. The pilot started releasing his bombs close to and between a small brick factory (about 200 yards distant) and the villa adjacent to ours—and he continued releasing his bombs in rapid succession as he dove down towards our villa. As we heard the explosions coming nearer and nearer, and as our villa correspondingly shook with increased intensity, we stood crouched against the wall of the stair-well expecting each moment that the next bomb would crash in on us. It was therefore with a sense of relief that I saw the tail of the plane, signalling the end of the raid. I subsequently discovered how fortunate we were in having swiftly sought refuge in the stair-well, in that the concussion and flying fragments of the bombs had burst and scattered the glass of the windows of the rooms which we had previously evacuated.

I was later informed by the police authorities that in their investigation, shortly after the bombing they collected in various rooms of our villa, 20 pounds of fragments of exploded bombs. These fragments had come in through the windows. Moreover, I saved as a souvenir of the occasion, a piece of metal about half the size of my hand. It served as a sort of signal of attack as it whistled in its flight through space and with a dull clang, landed against the wall several feet from where I was standing on the second floor veranda, previous to entering the villa to take refuge in the stair-well.

Having experienced the worst, short of a casualty, both my family and I became more or less fatalistic; we gained a sense of being, so-to-speak, veterans of the more violent aspect in the "war of nerves". In fact, this experience served psychologically useful in dealing with what was to come.

One of the two following possibilities, as in effect I cabled the [State] Department after the incident, represent to my mind about the only conceivable explanation for the pilot's action: (a) he might conceivably have dived to bombard the nearby small brick factory, mistaking its comparatively broad wooden shingle roof line for a hanger (for it was close thereto that he started releasing his bombs), or (b) having dived to bomb what he may have mistaken for a hanger he might possibly have seen a Polish pursuit plane take off at the pilot's school some three and one-half kilometers distant, in which case he might have released his rack of bombs regardless in an effort to lighten his load preparatory to a quick get away. As regards the Foreign Office's recommendation in February as to the safety of Constanscin from the theater of aerial attacks over Warsaw, I am aware that my informants had in mind the following:

The nearest objectives of possible military bearing from our villa were 1/ a small aerodrome used as a school for civilian pilots a little over 3 kilometers distant, 2/ an electric power plant about 5 kilometers distant, and 3/ a wooden bridge across the Vistula river about 8 kilometers distant.

After the bombardment, I preceeded immediately to the nearby house wherein the women members and several of the clerks of my staff were quartered, to see whether they were all right. They had experienced several vibrations from the bomb explosions but suffered no injury or damage.

I then proceeded into Warsaw. Due to the damage to our villa, and the fact that the line-men had failed to restore telephonic service between Constanscin and Warsaw, I decided to take up quarters for my family and myself in the apartment on the second floor of the Chancery. During one of my two visits to the Foreign Office, in the course of the day, my conversation with several officers was again adjourned to the air raid cellar, where the discussion was continued in an atmosphere of calm. On this occasion my informants disclosed: (a) The British Government's final note presented in Berlin about 9 A.M. giving Herr Hitler until 11:00 A.M. to give an undertaking to withdraw his troops from Poland;[5] (b) at 11:15 A.M., Prime Minister Chamberlain radio-broadcasted to the nation that no such undertaking had been received and that consequently Great Britain was at war with Germany; (c) the ultimatum of the French Government was presented at 12:30 P.M. [and] expired at 5:00 P.M.[6]

When I dropped by the Foreign Office after dinner about 9:30 P.M., I received a message inviting me to Minister Beck's house adjacent to the Ministry. There I was greeted by the Minister and Mrs. Beck who were dining informally with a few officials of the Minister's staff and their wives. I joined them at the table until dinner was over. Subsequently over coffee, Minister Beck told me that he and his associates profoundly appreciated France's and Britain's honoring their respective alliances with Poland. He went on to say, moreover, (a) that in the course of September 2, twenty-seven Polish towns and cities had been objects of German aerial attacks; (b) that during the course of the day, September 3, Dęblin, Toruń, Poznań, Kraków, Płock, among other cities and villages had experienced attacks from the air. Moreover, bombs had been released in several cases amongst the peasants working in the fields; (c) about 1500 civilians had to date been either wounded or killed in Poland. The Minister then stated that Polish forces had since the outbreak of war brought down a total of 64 German planes. Poland meanwhile lost a total of 11 planes. In concluding our talk the Minister said that his Government was immediately transmitting a vigorous protest to the Hague, wherein would be listed violations of the Polish-German agreement of September 2, to limit aerial bombardments to military objectives.

On leaving the Foreign Office and in walking through the fore-court I discerned signs of packing up archives, an indication which at the moment I was to mark down as a precautionary measure. During the course of that day, September 3, the tempo of air raids over Warsaw was about the same as on the previous day. The suburbs and several localities close by experienced bombings.

I was aware that Minister Beck and his associates had been hoping that the Western allies would stage a diversion activity either in the air or on the ground or both. After the close of the conflict, I met [the] Polish Ambassador to London, Count [Edward] Raczyński, in Paris. In strictest confidence he imparted the following: He had engaged in numerous conversations with Mr. Winston Churchill just previous to and immediately following September 1, the date of the outbreak of Polish-German hostilities. During earlier conversations, Churchill had expressed his personal feelings that Britain as well as France should make some effective move in terms of a diversion activity in order to allow Poland to reconsolidate her armies. On the day that.Churchill was appointed first Lord of the Admiralty, Ambassador Raczyński had another conversation with him. At that time Raczyński pressed him for an explanation as to why neither Britain nor France had undertaken some form of effective aerial activities vis-à-vis Germany. In response, Churchill stated that his Government refrained from waging aerial bombardments over Germany for fear of antagonizing American public opinion. Raczyński was not satisfied with this explanation, feeling that it was being put out to camouflage the real motives for lack of aerial action. Hence, he continued daily to press Churchill until finally the latter told him the following in utmost confidence: He said that France was still weak in the air and depended upon British air strength to support her in the event of a German attack. Accordingly, if France were to engage in aerial activities at that time which might provoke retaliation measures, and if the British air fleet became engaged in the North Sea area, France might find herself a victim of the same type of aerial warfare which the Germans were then conducting against Poland and that France might fare no better than Poland. Britain at that moment had to look to the French army for ground resistance while the French had to look to the British air force as the main stay for her air resistance. Raczyński told me in strictest confidence that he realized that Churchill was telling him straight facts.[7]

SEPTEMBER 4

Awakened by early morning air raid. A number of raids occurred at regular intervals throughout the day. Other than when the broadcasting station warned that the raids might be of a serious character, however, the alarm, after the morning attacks, was not sounded. In the afternoon at about 4 o'clock, while I was at the Foreign Office, the alarm sounded shrilly, warning of a large-scale bombardment. Again the conversation in which I was engaged was adjourned to the cellar. A few minutes after our arrival there, Minister Beck, with whom I had had an appointment within a quarter of an hour of that time, came to join us. He had been on his balcony watching the machine gunners on the roof of the Ministry shoot down a comparatively low-flying German bomber directly overhead.

This air raid was longer than usual. The flight, consisting of about 60 or 80 planes, seemed to be trying to destroy the main bridges leading across the Vistula. The German pilots demonstrated a reckless daring in swooping down low over the city, and dropping bombs on their objectives. The Polish anti-aircraft guns were able to defend the bridges, and after a lengthy attack, the Germans abandoned their efforts in that regard. Before leaving, however, they dropped incendiary bombs in the outskirts, causing a circle of fire to be laid around the city. The Polish authorities were apprehensive lest this circle of fire had been effected deliberately in order to facilitate the bombing of the city on a return flight that night. Three German bombers were shot down that day. I left the Foreign Office just as the last one met its end. Damage resulting from the raid was considerable. On this, as on previous days, all members of our Mission at various times personally checked on all accessible scenes of bombings. Dined at the Europejski. An officer of G-2 joined us. He mentioned among other things his concern over the reported effectiveness of the drive of German columns in the direction of Modlin.

Upon entering the Foreign Office at 11:30 P.M., I immediately gained the distinct impression that the Ministry in general was uneasy over reports of the turn of military developments in the vicinity of Modlin, north of Warsaw. Mrs. Beck, who together with a number of the wives of officers of the Foreign Office, had been working like a trojan, was in charge of the information desk. On this occasion she was assisted by Countess Joseph Potocka, who took turns with Countess Michael Lubieńska and Countess Paul Starzyńska, wife of Minister Beck's secretary, in operating the telephone switch board while Mrs. Beck answered the questions of the numerous callers at the Ministry. I watched them while I was awaiting word to go upstairs. They worked fast and efficiently. I recognized in this scene another example of the admirable capacity and willingness of Polish womanhood to meet a crisis.

I went upstairs. It was dark save for the meager rays of a blue shaded lamp in the corner of the enormous gallery on to which open the offices of the officials. There were small groups of officers speaking together in whispers as they walked up and down the carpeted gallery. The atmosphere was charged with electricity; uneasiness. My conversation with several officers of Minister Beck's staff confirmed my previous impression: the turn in developments in the vicinity was causing grave concern. If anything arose which they thought I should know, they would telephone me. I departed, and as I walked through the Ministry courtyard, to get into my car, I perceived in the clear light of the moon that what had the night before looked like a packing up of the archives had now the earmarks of an evacuation move in the near future. I noted that along with the archives, army cots were being packed in several large motor trucks.

Chief of Protocol, Major [Aleksander] Łubieński imparted next day that Minister Beck had called him at midnight to inform him that reports from the direction of Modlin indicated an early heavy attack in a southerly direction, towards Warsaw. He then told Major Łubieński to come to him again at 5:00 A.M., adding that at that time he would either tell him to go back to bed or instruct him to notify the Diplomatic Corps to evacuate Warsaw by gradual stages throughout the day.

At about 2:00 A.M., night of September 4–5, I was awakened by sounds of motor lorries and tanks passing by the Chancery. I found it was a lengthy mechanized column consisting of troop-filled lorries, heavy guns, and medium-sized tanks which were rushing through the heart of the unlighted city toward Modlin. The column travelling at a speed of approximately 40 miles per hour took about two hours to pass our chancery. It was evident, in view of my talks earlier in the night, [that] these were reinforcements being rushed to check a threatened break-through at Modlin. It was a grim picture.

SEPTEMBER 5

At 5:00 A.M., Minister Beck conferred again with Major Łubieński, this time informing him of the Government's decision to evacuate Warsaw, and of his decision to evacuate the Diplomatic Corps gradually during the course of the day. Moreover, he instructed the Major to notify the various missions accordingly. Between 11:00 A.M. and noon (September 5) military developments north of Warsaw had taken so unfavorable a turn as to cause Minister Beck to call in Łubieński and instruct him to accelerate the pace of the diplomatic Corps's evacuation. On this occasion Minister Beck emphasized he wanted the entire corps out of Warsaw by the end of the day.

During the course of the preliminary phase of Poland's mobilization in March, I learned in strictest confidence from an official of President Mościcki's household as well as from an official of the Foreign Office that the Polish Government was considering, among other precautionary measures, the possible necessity of removing the seat of Government to another section of Poland in [the] event the capture of Warsaw was threatened during a potential Polish-German conflict. While the Government guarded with utmost secrecy this possibility as well as the designated evacuation point, I later became aware that confidential instructions had been issued to plant managers of the "industrial triangle" to start moving their machinery to the Lublin area, and that the President secretly sent a representation to the Lublin-Zamość area to make a census of billeting possibilities, to organize a communications center, et cetera. This and other information prompted [my] belief that the Government had decided upon the same area for its own possible evacuation.

It was still in March that my aforementioned informants divulged in strictest confidence the following broad outline of Poland's plan of defense: (a) to keep the Polish army intact, (b) to resist as long as possible an attempted capture of Warsaw and/or the "Industrial Triangle", (c) withdrawal of the main body of Polish forces under cover of delayed action, if and when pressure from a potential German attack made it necessary, to the main defensive position, on the line of the strategic Narew, Bug, Vistula, and San rivers, (d) to delay the adversary's advance 1/ until the advent of rainy and wintry weather and 2/ until assistance from Poland's Western allies might have diverted the full brunt of the German attack from off the Polish front. My informants went on to say that while this was the Polish defense plan in terms of the broad sweep, the Government and the General Staff had decided that, in [the] event the capture of Warsaw by the adversary became imminent, the Government and the General Staff would withdraw from Warsaw—the Government re-establishing its seat in Eastern Poland, the General Staff setting up its headquarters at some point between the newly established Government seat and the fighting front.

In other words, allowing for unforeseen turns in the course of a potential conflict, the Polish Government and High Command (a) regarded as their paramount aim: to hold the Polish fighting forces intact, awaiting the effects of wet and subsequently winter weather, and effective action of Poland's Western allies to alleviate pressure on the Polish front; and (b) had come to feel that they could less afford the loss of any sizable portion of their first line fighting strength, which would be difficult if not impossible to replace, than the loss in the preliminary stage of a conflict, of territory and even of their capital, the recapture of which changed conditions and counter attacks in a later stage might permit.

Still later I was informed confidentially by an official of the Foreign Office to the effect that, in event the Government decided to evacuate Warsaw, (a) it would want the Embassies and Legations to follow, (b) that the Government would supply each Embassy and Legation with a large motor truck, (c) that besides motor trucks a special train would be placed at the disposal of the diplomatic corps to transport the Chiefs of Mission and their respective staffs to whatever new capital might eventually be designated; and (d) that our respective automobiles might join the trucks in a military guarded "caravan" to their destination. While I appreciated the good intentions of

the Government, to extend us these conveniences, I anticipated that a potential German campaign would entail aerial as
well as ground attacks aimed at crippling at the outset
transportation and communications lines, which might tend to
cause confusion to such an extent as to render unlikely the
Government's ability to place transportation facilities at our
disposal. Hence, I purchased a large truck, with a view to providing against the possibility of our Embassy's being forced to
spend the winter in Eastern Poland (even possibly on the edge
of the Pinsk marshes). I loaded the truck with canned goods,
kerosene lanterns, candles, et cetera, for I felt that I should
provide our Embassy group at least with enough of the bare
necessities of life to tide them over a possible preliminary
shortage of food in event we suddenly found ourselves forced
to set up headquarters at some eastern point inaccessible to
supply centers.

In conversation with General Carton de Wiart, V.C. (Chief
of the British Military mission) at about 10:30 A.M., he expressed his apprehension lest Warsaw be surrounded and possibly come under the fire of German guns within several days.
(From these remarks I gained the distinct impression that
little, if anything, in the form of an effective diversion activity might be expected from the British and possibly the French
forces in the course of the next few days at least).

Pursuant to Chief of Protocol Łubieński's notification, at
about noon members of our Embassy staff evacuated Warsaw
by automobile at various hours throughout the day, arriving
towards the end of the afternoon at the newly designated
Foreign Office headquarters at Nałęczów, about 23 kilometers
west of Lublin [see map]. In accordance with cabled instructions from the State Department, the Consulate General
moved into the Chancery and the Embassy remained with the
Government.

As we crossed the bridge from Warsaw to Praga an air raid
took place and the police authorities stopped us, counseling us
to pull over to the side of the road to await the end of the
attack. When the authorities realized that the planes were
headed eastward, they let us continue our journey. As we

POLAND:
SEPTEMBER 1–17, 1939

Evacuation route
described by Biddle

DANZIG

INDUSTRIAL
TRIANGLE (C.O.P.)

LATVIA

LITHUANIA

GERMANY

EAST
PRUSSIA

RUSSIA

Gdynia

Poznań

Wilno
(Vilna)

Vistula R.

Narew R.

Bug R.

WARSAW

Brześć

Breslau

Lublin

Nałęczów

Chełm

Katowice

Włodzimierz

Luck

Sandomierz

Dubno

Kraków

Krzemieniec

Cieszyn (Teschen)

Sereto

Zaleszczycki

Tarnopol

CZECHOSLOVAKIA

Stanisławów

Kolomyja

Sniatyń

Kuty

Dniester R.

Cernauti

HUNGARY

ROMANIA

turned from the outskirts of Praga, into the road for Lublin, we ran into a second raid from the same flight of planes. Antiaircraft units along side of the road fired over our heads at the bombers. Further along the road, British Ambassador, Sir Howard Kennard accompanied by his Counselor, Mr. Clifford Norton and Mrs. Norton, having passed us in a fast moving car, stopped a little way ahead of us to ask if all was well with our group.

Before leaving Warsaw I decided to leave my motorcycle with attached sidecar, at the Chancery in case stranded American citizens who might wish to evacuate Warsaw, lacked means of transportation. Besides, I left two 200 liter barrels of gasoline. I also left a sack of flour and several boxes of canned provisions, at the Chancery in case food stock might run low.

Pursuant to Mr. Harrison's earnest request that he be allowed to delay his departure in order to attend to some outstanding personal matters, I requested him to accelerate completion of his business, and to join us as soon as possible at Nałęczów. (Pursuant to a conversation with the Under Secretary of State for Foreign Affairs, Count Szembek, the next morning (September 6) I telephoned Mr. Harrison and Major Colbern, who had postponed his departure in order to contact the General Staff, requesting them both to come to Nałęczów at the earliest moment. Accordingly, they assured me they would leave Warsaw that afternoon at about 4:30 P.M.)

Upon arrival in Nałęczów I made arrangements with Foreign Office officials and the Chief of Police to billet and board my family and the members of my staff. As I cabled the Department, Nałęczów is a small cure resort. We were billeted in several rooming houses. Part of the diplomatic corps was billeted in and around Nałęczów and part in Kazimierz about 7 kilometers distant. Together with a number of our colleagues we had dinner that evening in the dining hall of the newly established Foreign Office, formerly the cure house of the resort. French Ambassador [Leon] Noël joined our table and remarked to Mrs. Biddle that he did not think we would remain long in Nałęczów.

At that time, and under war circumstances, living conditions were comparatively primitive, gasoline for the automobiles scarce, and communications difficult. We soon found Nałęczów was in the direct path of a regular run of German bombers, shuttling back and forth between East Prussia and Slovakia. However, as I cabled on September 6, the nearest point thus far bombarded was the local railway station, three kilometers distant from the civilian community in which we were billeted. This bombardment, however, took place a few hours previous to our arrival on September 5. Subsequent investigation revealed that several German planes had, on a low power-dive, bombed two trains which had come to a stop alongside the little station; one was a troop train, the other filled with civilian passengers. The bombing had been concentrated, severe. Many civilian passengers, and to a lesser degree the troops, received serious injuries. (I was aware of the blunder both of the station master and of the conductors of both trains, in having permitted a train of civilians to stop alongside a troop train). Upon arrival at one of the rooming houses to which we had been assigned I found a number of the injured women and children receiving first aid treatment inside the house, and on the back porch, one woman who was due shortly to give birth to a child, had had her leg severed at the knee. Most of the others had suffered head wounds. There were no proper dressings for the wounded available. We thereupon contributed some gauze and bandages which I had fortunately secured for emergency purposes in a Red Cross kit, from Mrs. Beck, Minister Beck's wife, on the previous night in Warsaw. After these unfortunate people had been taken off to a hospital in Lublin, we moved into the house. Counselor of Embassy, Mr. North Winship and Third Secretary, Mr. C. Burke Elbrick joined us shortly thereafter.

SEPTEMBER 6

During my early morning conversation with Count Jan Szembek, Vice Minister for Foreign Affairs, he imparted that his reports indicated that the Polish forces, reinforced by the mechanized column which had rushed through Warsaw on the night of September 4–5, had succeeded in arresting the drive of the German mechanized columns, and were then holding position in the Zegrze-Modlin sector north of Warsaw. In the early part of the afternoon, the Breslau radio broadcasting station announced in the Polish language that our Embassy had arrived in Nałęczów. As the location of the new capital had until then been guarded confidentially by the Polish Government for protection of Government officials as well as the diplomatic corps, this announcement indicated, to my mind, [the] efficiency of German espionage activities.

During the course of the day, I cabled the State Department my observations on certain aspects of aerial bombardments. I pointed out that experience during aerial raids and subsequent investigations of outcome thereof, prompted my belief that the question of limiting bombardments from the air to objectives of military bearing bore serious consideration in light of circumstances which prevailed throughout the belligerent countries. In Poland, as in France, Britain, and Germany, during war time, mobilization involved the billeting of troops in civilian communities. As for Poland practically every village of, say, 500 inhabitants housed 50 to 100 troops. As regards industry, both the larger and the smaller manufacturing plants engaged in production both of armaments and articles for domestic consumption were usually surrounded by densely populated communities of employees. I felt therefore that the question concerning aerial bombardments called for consideration in the light of whether the bombardment of objectives of military interest was of sufficient value to the program of the adversary to warrant endangering the civilian population. (In view of the foregoing cabled observations, it was with more than ordinary interest that subsequently, on September 13, I learned of the German Government's announcement of that date that all Polish towns and villages harboring armed soldiers, snipers or marauding bands, would be regarded forthwith as military objectives.)

During a conference at about 7:00 P.M. between French Ambassador Noël, and myself, at the house where my family and I were billeted, Count Szembek telephoned me urgently requesting that both the Ambassador and I meet with him at the earliest moment at his headquarters. He added that British Ambassador Kennard was already on his way. Within a few minutes, we reached the Foreign Office. I recall that Szembeck, a charming character possessing the manners and general attitude of the 18th century Polish nobility, greeted us with characteristic cordiality. After friendly inquiries as to the state of our comfort in our new quarters, and after apologies for calling a conference on such short notice, he remarked with dignity and composure (as if he had just recalled the purpose of the conference) that the reason for calling us together was to inform us that a German mechanized column of considerable strength had unfortunately just broken through the Polish lines north-west of us, and was rapidly approaching Puławy, some 18 kilometers distant from Nałęczów. He went on to say that it was difficult at the moment, due to poor communications, to ascertain the exact strength of the German force. However, in the absence of full information in regard thereto, his Government, after consulting General Headquarters, had considered it advisable that the Foreign Office and the diplomatic corps move on to some point whereat they were less likely to be surrounded, cut off from General Headquarters, and possibly captured.

At the close of our conference, and as I was taking leave of Count Szembek in the garden outside the newly set-up Foreign Office, a Polish pursuit plane brought down a German light bomber directly overhead. The German pilot, wounded in the shoulder, landed by parachute at the other end of the garden, a comparatively short distance from where we were standing.

Count Szembek stated that the Ministry of Foreign Affairs and the Diplomatic Corps were to evacuate Nałęczów immediately and proceed directly to Krzemieniec, located about 480 kilometers from Nałęczów and about 30 kilometers from the Russian border. The Prime Minister would establish headquarters for himself and staff at Łuck, and the President would set up his headquarters at a point in the vicinity of Łuck. I thereupon earnestly requested Count Szembek's assurance that members of my staff driving automobiles be allowed enough gasoline to carry them at least to Łuck, where I understood there was a supply of gasoline sufficient to afford refueling. Count Szembek admitted that the scarcity of gasoline in Nałęczów was deplorable, but assured me he would do all possible to see that the gasoline requirements of my staff were met. Forseeing, however, the hectic rush for fuel, I urged Mr. Winship and Mr. Elbrick to drive their automobiles, at the earliest moment, to the gasoline pump and remain in their cars in order to avoid confusion.

I was anxious, moreover, to save the women members of my staff the confusion and discomfort of becoming envolved in what promised to be more or less of a "tussle" for gasoline around the pump of the service station. Fortunately, finding, therefore, that I could spare some gasoline, I turned over to Miss McQuatters, who throughout the entire trek from Warsaw to Krzemieniec at the wheel of my Ford station wagon, drove Miss Saunders, Miss Hillery, Miss Pinard, and Mr. Aneksztejn, assistant to the disbursing officer, a sufficient amount of gasoline in tin containers to carry the car through to the refuelling service station at Łuck. (Miss McQuatters, the only woman to drive a car during the trek, gained the respect and esteem both of Polish official and diplomatic circles, for having safely conducted her car and passengers through the lengthy and exhausting, as well as dangerous day and night runs which the trek entailed). Furthermore, I subsequently succeeded in obtaining a "best-efforts" promise from the Chief of Police (with whom I had previously established a friendly relationship) to furnish American citizens, who might come through during the course of the night or the next day, with sufficient gasoline to see them at least on their way to Łuck. Following these preliminaries, the members of our Embassy, commencing at about 11:00 P.M., departed from Nałęczów at various intervals throughout the night.

I endeavored to arrange the distribution of passengers amongst the automobiles of our caravan in such a way as to have (a) two drivers per car where possible, and (b) some one who spoke the Polish language in each car. In cases where this was not possible due to lack of space in any car, I urged that a car lacking someone familiar with the Polish language, accompany a car occupied by one.

Night travel under war conditions then prevailing, was, to say the least, a difficult, and dangerous task. Only the most meagre amount of illumination was permitted from our headlights which, according to regulation, were covered by a blue cloth hood. Moreover, upon approaching towns the military authorities stopped all cars and instructed the driver to extinguish all lights. This, coupled with the fact that "blackouts" in Polish towns were practiced in the literal sense of expression, made driving throughout the cities and towns a precarious matter. One had to slow down to a speed of about 3 or 4 miles an hour and frequently come to a stop, due to loss of bearings. I recall that the night we passed through Tarnopol enroute from Krzemieniec to Zaleszczyki I had to walk ahead of the car with one hand on the radiator, literally feeling my way and calling back to Mr. Charles Moszczyński (a member of my staff) who was then at the wheel.[8] We progressed thus for some 6 to 7 city blocks' distance, until we reached a part of the town where the buildings were sufficiently low to permit the glow of the moon to light the street.

On the other hand, night driving along the open road entailed other difficulties. Dry weather had made the roads exceedingly dusty—a white pulverized dust arose in the wake of each car like a thick fog, and frequently took from 3 to 4 minutes to settle sufficiently to permit visibility. Moreover, the military authorities chose the cover of night to effect their major movements of troops, supplies, and heavy guns. Hence, one frequently passed lengthy lines of troop-laden buses and lorries, and columns of mechanized equipment, including artillery of varying calibre. This, the lack of light, the narrowness of the average road, and the exasperating dust contributed towards making the automobile driver's position an uncomfortable one.

After the first few days of hostilities the German pilots discovered that, aside from anti-aircraft measures at Warsaw, several other important cities, armaments, communications, and other centers of vital military interest, there was little if any resistance to fear. Hence, these pilots soon became increasingly daring in their general operations, power-diving to surprisingly low altitudes, and frequently "hawking" traffic along the highways. The latter usually entailed machine-gunning. The drivers and passengers of automobiles were usually prevented by the hum of the automobiles' motors from detecting the approach of a plane. We finally developed a technique along the following lines: we left open the radio switch, for the approach of a plane usually registered a distinct clicking noise, and we constantly kept an eye on peasants working in the fields. If we noted their faces turned skyward, we instantly made for the nearest trees (if any were within a short distance)—and if they were not; we instantly stopped the car. We then shut off the motor, opened the doors of the car, and ran for the nearest cover. If woods were at hand, so much the better, if not, we sought the culverts at either side of the road, lying face up, to keep an eye on the plane. If the plane went on, we would immediately shift backwards or forwards from our positions in case the pilot returned with an idea of maching-gunning the spot whereat he had originally marked us (this proved to be the practice of the pilots).

Another measure, but more extreme in character, in event of emergency was the following: if one was suddenly found to be the objective of a plane close overhead, and in the absence of nearby cover, the best procedure in event of machine-gunning was to stop and stand absolutely straight; in event of a bombing, to drop instantly to the ground and lie flat. Careful study of maps and inquiries as to the terrain along the route preparatory to embarking on day trips, moreover, were essential. Bombardment flights usually occurred at dawn; again about 11:00 A.M., and again between 4 and 6 P.M. It was therefore only prudent for one to have in mind the probable necessity of seeking shelter (for one's automobile) just previous to or during these periods. Leaving Nałęczów we drove throughout the night. In passing through various towns along the route, I gave the *Starostas*[9] lists containing the names of those members of our Mission, who were driving automobiles, requesting that, should they run short on gasoline in those vicinities, the *Starostas* replenish their supply. At the same time, I urged the *Starostas* to assist any other Americans who might be in need of gasoline.

Several kilometers west of Włodzimierz, and just as we were approaching a railroad crossing, we noted ahead of us an automobile accident. It turned out to be a collision between a truck and a small sports model automobile belonging to the officer in charge of the French Embassy's codes. While he had escaped injury, his wife was seriously shaken up, and had received a deep cut on the head as well as a concussion. By good fortune, Mrs. Kulski, wife of the assistant counselor of the Polish Foreign Office (as Mr. and Mrs. Kulski lacked transportation, I had invited them to accompany us from Nałęczów), proved herself an expert at First Aid. By the side of the road, with ordinary needle and thread, she stitched the head wound. (I recently received a report that the young French woman finally reached Rumania in safety and was well on the road to recovery).

SEPTEMBER 7

After refueling in Łuck, each car of our Embassy Group in turn proceeded through Dubno to Krzemieniec. At the outskirts of Dubno the car I was driving was halted by military guards. We stopped under some trees during an aerial bombardment of the railway yards, not far distant. I arrived at Krzemieniec at about 10:30 A.M. (Thursday, September 7). Mr. Kulski (assistant Counselor of the Foreign Office, who together with his wife had accompanied us from Nałęczów in one of my two cars) took charge of preliminary arrangements towards setting up the Foreign Office and billeting the various Embassies and Legations.[10] I was informed by the Foreign Office that their reports indicated (a) the Polish forces were experiencing a major three-column attack; in the north one column was headed for Warsaw; in the central region another column was headed for Warsaw via Częstochowa; still another column was headed for Kraków from the direction of Slovakia; (b) Polish forces in Pomorze consisting of about 100,000 troops were threatened by a pincer movement consisting of columns from East Prussia and from the direction of Częstochowa; (c) that day was considered critical concerning success or failure of German flanking attacks vis-à-vis Warsaw.

Observation during our lengthy motor trek eastward had revealed that at the very outset of the conflict, the first day, the German bombers engaged in a series of effective attacks on all important railway junctions. Shuttling back and forth between Slovakia and East Prussia in three main broad bands of flight in the general direction, respectively, [of] Białystok-Lwów in the east, Mława-Jarosław in the central part, and Gdynia-Katowice in the west, these bombers had succeeded in putting most of the main railway junctions out of business in short order. To this perhaps to more than any other factor was attributable the disruption of the transportation of reserve forces, which in turn caused the failure to complete mobiliation.

By this time, I was aware of the effectiveness of the German mechanized thrusts under cover of the withering effect of efficiently coordinated aerial bomb and machine-gun barrages. The German mechanized columns were breaking through wherever possible and pressing forward in swift long-distance thrusts, frequently leaving the opposing divisions behind to fight it out. It was estimated by official circles at this point that the Germans were employing between 85 percent and 90 percent of their first line air force. It was found necessary by the Polish command to limit the main part of the Polish air force to collaboration with the troops in the line, thus leaving but few planes to combat effective efforts of the German bombers to disrupt communications, cripple industrial operations, and render general confusion.

After the close of the Polish-German conflict, the newly appointed Prime Minister of the Polish Government, General [Władysław] Sikorski, imparted to me in strictest confidence the following: on November 11, General Georges, Chief of Staff of the French Army, had told him that on the seventh day of the war, the French High Command urged the French

Government to permit the French army to march on Germany, pointing out that there were less than 20 German divisions vis-à-vis the Maginot line, whereas France at that time had about 46 divisions prepared for action. The High Command felt that an opportunity which would not again present itself was at hand. The French Government however refused this suggestion.[11] Assuming this disclosure to be exact, I should attribute the French Government's refusal to reasons confidentially cited by the First Lord of the British Admiralty in his aforecited conversation with Polish Ambassador to London, Count Raczyński, on September 3rd. In other words, I am inclined to believe that the hesitancy on the part both of the French and British Governments to permit their military forces to launch an attack against Germany was primarily due to their desire first to gain equality if not superiority in terms of air strength.[12]

During a subsequent visit at the Foreign Office I was informed (a) that the Prime Minister was establishing his headquarters at Łuck, (b) that President Mościcki was establishing his headquarters in three different locations within the district between Krzemieniec, the President's headquarters, and Łuck. While I found that proper communications from Krzemieniec had not yet been established, a spokesman of the Foreign Office expressed his hope of placing at our disposal in the near future short wave sending facilities. We were meanwhile experiencing difficulties in receiving and sending communications. Under the extraordinary circumstances prevailing, and as I was aware that the American Press correspondents lacked means of communications with the outside, I cabled our Minister in Bucharest, Mr. Gunther, asking him to notify the respective agencies that the following correspondents could be contacted if addressed care of our Embassy: Mr. Petersen, Associated Press, Mr. Walker, *New York Herald Tribune*, Mr. Neville, *Time Magazine*, Mr. Small, *Chicago Tribune*, and Mr. Shapiro, *New York Times*.

Having expected Mr. Harrison, Second Secretary of Embassy at Nałeczow, pursuant to my telephone instructions of September 6, to join us there that day, and having had no information as to his whereabouts since that telephone call, I became concerned regarding his welfare. Accordingly, I asked the *Starosta* of Krzemieniec to telephone other *Starostas* along the line for news of Mr. Harrison. The *Starosta* subsequently reported no information available. The first news I learned from him was from an American newspaper correspondent who arrived in Krzemieniec. He had seen Mr. Harrison leaving Warsaw in his car on September 6 with a Polish friend and much luggage. I was relieved when Mr. Harrison finally arrived in Krzemieniec on September 9. It seemed that his delay in arriving at Krzemieniec was due to his having conducted some Polish friends to their country place in the area northeast of Lublin.

SEPTEMBER 8

News reaching the Polish Foreign Office from G[eneral] H[ead] Q[uarters] during the course of September 8 continued to indicate an unfavorable turn for the Polish forces. It moreover became clear that the preliminary objective envisaged in the rapid eastward advance of the German troops in south Poland was the capture of Lwów. A German seizure of Lwów might conceivably have presaged a further German advance toward the Russian frontier, a possibility which might have spelled a severance of our connections with Rumania.

[I] cabled [the] Department to the following effect: Aerial bombardments by German air force includes railways (frequently endangering trains of refugees and wounded); factories engaged in war production (endangering surrounding communities) bridges (endangering public in transit and people living near bridge-heads) and all places resembling airports, troop centers, and barracks. I went on to point out that while they were ostensibly giving the appearance of adhering to the principle of limiting aerial bombings to objectives of military bearing, the German planes, in my opinion, were straining the point, and taking advantage of every opportunity irrespective of danger to the civilian population. It was, moreover, evident that the crews of the German bombers released their bombs even when in doubt as concerned the identity of the objectives.

By way of illustrating this point, I cited the following cases: 1/ bombardment of a sanatorium in the woods nearby Otwock; ten children living there were killed; 2/ bombardment of modern flats one kilometer from barracks on Warsaw outskirts; 3/ bombardment of hospital train (clearly marked with Red cross on roof) standing alongside of uncovered Warsaw East Station, and during the process of unloading wounded soldiers. This and the demolition of a girl guide hut (12 girls killed) resulted from the heavy bombardment of the East Station; 4/ bombardment of a refugee train bound eastward from Kutno.

SEPTEMBER 9

Shortly before 9:00 A.M. on the morning of September 9, I sent Miss McQuatters, Miss Saunders, Miss Hillery, Miss Pinard of my staff, in my Ford station wagon, and Mrs. Pedersen in the car driven by her husband, to Sniatyń, a Polish-Rumanian border town, where, thanks to the friendly assistance of one Mr. Agerton Sykes acting in behalf of the British Embassy in Poland, they were enabled to acquire sufficient gasoline to enable my car and that of Mr. Pedersen of my staff to return to Krzemieniec, as well as to procure transportation from the Rumanian border to Cernauti.

Shortly after my arrival in Paris, in late September, Polish Ambassador to France, [Juliusz] Łukasiewicz, imparted in effect the following: Either on September 9 or 10, (he was a little vague as to the exact date) he was taken a-back when General [Stanisław] Burckhardt-Bukacki (Polish General Staff Officer attached to the French General Staff) told him that [French Commander in Chief] General Gamelin had emphasized his opinion that the Polish armies should withdraw to a position in southeast Poland behind a contracted line somewhat described by a line drawn from the southwest corner of the Pinsk marshes, to the western junction of the Polish-Rumanian border. The Ambassador's immediate reaction to the foregoing was unfavorable. To him it indicated that Poland could count on little if any effective help from France. Moreover, he pictured that a move of this character might conceivably lead to a Russian advance through the Vilno area, and to a grim outcome for the Polish forces, under continued and probably redoubled ferocity of German aerial attacks, if the former were concentrated in a contracted area. The Ambassador thereupon wrote, in his own handwriting, a report on his aforecited reactions, requesting General Burckhardt-Bukacki to transmit it to General Gamelin. (This had taken place during the night of Paris' first alarm).[13]

As of connected bearing both on General Gamelin's aforementioned remarks and Ambassador Łukasiewicz's subsequent reactions thereto, the Ambassador told me that in reflecting on the full implications of General Gamelin's remarks, he called to mind the following: In the first half of August during a meeting between British and French representatives with Soviet Commissar for Foreign Affairs M. Molotoff, in Moscow, M. Molotoff had bluntly remarked that an agreement between the Western powers and Russia could be practical only if Britain and France could persuade Poland to permit Russian troops to enter Poland via the Vilno and east Galician areas at any time that the Russians deemed such action necessary.

The British and French representatives had replied that this was a matter which M. Molotoff should take up directly with Poland. In response, M. Molotoff said that Russia had only non-aggression and commercial agreements with Poland and that since Britain and France were Poland's allies, they were the proper parties to put the question to Poland.

French Minister for Foreign Affairs Bonnet had later sounded out Ambassador Łukasiewicz on the above score. In response the Ambassador had remarked to Minister Bonnet that the latter was unquestionably aware of the answer before putting the question. Moreover, the Ambassador had pointed out his opinion that M. Molotoff's remarks along the above lines represented merely a tactical play. Indeed, while on the one hand M. Molotoff was undoubtedly playing for time, on the other hand he had deliberately posed the one question which might cause tension between the Western powers and Poland. The Ambassador had added, moreover, that he would therefore prefer to consider that the question had not been broached by Minister Bonnet—and emphasized that if France pressed the question formally, it would be a mistake, for such action might lead to an "all round" serious misunderstanding.

The Ambassador went on to say to me that about the same time, Minister Beck had replied along similar lines to British Ambassador to Poland, Sir William Howard Kennard's soundings on the above score. Ambassador Łukasiewicz then told me that following these unfruitful soundings on the part of Minister Bonnet and Ambassador Kennard, he personally gained the impression that the British and French representatives in Moscow resorted to stalling the issue in their further conversations with the Soviet authorites. In concluding his remarks Ambassador Łukasiewicz told me that about the 19 or 20 of August, Minister Bonnet in conversation with him evinced considerable optimism over the prospect of coming to a deal with Moscow. The Ambassador had replied frankly that while the representative then negotiating in France's behalf was no doubt a military expert of high standing, nevertheless, the Ambassador felt it would be difficult for the French representative to gain a clear insight as to what was in the back of the Russians' mind, in that the French representative was not familiar with the Russian language, and had been in Moscow but a short time. At a later date, Minister Bonnet had admitted to Ambassador Łukasiewicz that he had been right as to his reaction on this score.

SEPTEMBER 10

I walked to the heighth of the mountain adjacent to and overlooking the town of Krzemieniec. From that point I peered down and studied the effect of the reflection of the sunlight both on the nickel trimmings and the shiny roofs of cars of our Embassy group. I had in mind that the parking of automobiles in a group served according to our experience to invite the attention of passing German pilots. I thereupon decided that, in the interest of protecting our motor vehicles, it was essential to construct a shed to shelter them from the sight of passing German pilots. Hence, I ordered the construction of a lean-to shed for our automobiles. Moreover, I requested as a further precautionary measure, that the nickel trimmings on all of our cars be painted a dull gray. (Besides, my chauffeur and I together did a quick, if not artistic job, in giving one coat of dark gray paint to my yellow cadillac. I subsequently threw several buckets of dust on the paint before it dried. The result proved an excellent form of camouflage.) Contrary to the counsel of a number of my colleagues and their chauffeurs, I painted the roof so as to leave a yellow U.S.A. They held it would only draw attention from the sky.

Lunched quietly in the back room of a small restaurant at the north end of the village, with Soviet Ambassador [Nikolai] Charanov,[14] Mrs. Charanov, their small son and daughter, their military attaché, and Estonian Minister Marcus. In the course of conversation the military attaché remarked that he had just talked by telephone to the Soviet Consul at Lwów, who said the bombardment, especially of the railway station and yards, was becoming steadily more intensive. Moreover, the German southern forces were advancing rapidly towards the City from the west. The Ambassador then mentioned the large scale mobilization which was currently taking place in Soviet Russia. In response to my question as to whether the mobilization was attributable to Moscow's anxiety lest, if the thrust of the German southern forces towards Lwów succeeded, the Germans might declare Lwów the Capital of an independent Ukrainia[n] state under German auspices, the Ambassador merely smiled, and shifted the trend of conversation. When Minister Marcus had departed, however, Ambassador Charanov referred to my question, stating that, "strictly off the record" and quite unofficially speaking, I had probably hit the nail on the head. However, he was lacking in sufficient information to be clear on the situation. Either his Government had not communicated with him or what communications they had sent had failed to reach him. He would therefore ask Minister Beck the next morning for permission to go to the town on the Russian side of the frontier, in order to telephone his Government. In response to my question as to whether he believed his country, in view of its own oil requirement for its agricultural structure based upon about 65% to 70% motorization, and now for this reported augmentation of mobilized forces, could afford to satisfy Germany's oil requirements, the Ambassador stated his belief that Germany would suffer a great disappointment. His own country's oil requirements would increase rapidly in proportion to the increase in mobilization. In concluding our conversation he informed me that many of my colleagues had requested him to grant them and their respective staffs visas for Soviet Russia in case the Government and Diplomatic Corps were cut off from Rumania. This was another matter regarding which he wanted to discuss with his Government by telephone.

Soon after my arrival in Paris in late September, Łukasiewicz told me the following: He had requested General Burckhardt-Bukacki (just arrived in France to consult with [the] French General Staff) to inform the French General Staff that if Britain and France did not at an early hour lend Poland some assistance in terms either of ground or aerial diversion activities vis-à-vis Germany, the Polish military situation might be expected to disintegrate rapidly. Moreover, Łukasiewicz asked Burckhardt-Bukacki to warn the French General Staff that if they did not quickly lend aid along the foregoing lines, they must beware of Russia's eventual entrance into the conflict. In this connection, Ambassador Łukasiewicz pointed out that Russia would be motivated (a) by a desire to relieve Germany of the apprehension and necessity of fighting on two effective fronts and thus give Germany a free hand to turn against the west, and (b) by a determination to prevent the possibility of Lwów's being captured by the Germans and declared the capital of a Ukrainian state under German auspices, and (c) by a desire to gain sufficient part of Poland for herself to improve strategically her then currently vulnerable western frontier.[15] Economic Counselor of the Foreign Office, Mr. Jan Wrszlacki, came by our embassy in a droshky accompanied by three other members of the Foreign Office. They were a pathetic sight. Their laps were piled with suitcases; their faces looked haggard and worn. They had just arrived from the railway station about five kilometers distant. Their arrival in Krzemieniec proved a welcome sight, for we were aware that the train of which Mr. Wrszlacki and Count Potulicki (associate counselor of the Foreign Office) had been in charge, had left Warsaw five days before with the wives and children of the officials and the staff, as well as a number of junior officers of the Foreign Office. We were aware, moreover, that while this journey would have taken no more than over night under normal conditions, it had taken more than four days under the current circumstances.

During the train's journey reports reached Krzemieniec from time to time indicating that it had frequently been forced to change its routing because of repeated bombardments from the air. This led to its being referred to as the "Phantom Train." Mr. Wrszlacki subsequently told me that the train, carrying about a thousand passengers, had suffered aerial bombardments seventy-two times. Enroute he and Count Potulicki had adopted and successfully developed a system of protecting the passengers from the air raids. The planes began by releasing bombs directly at the train, fortunately missing, though narrowly in each case. At a signal either from Mr. Wrszlacki or Count Potulicki, the locomotive engineer would stop the train. All passengers who could, instantly left the train, running for the nearest woods at the side of the tracks. Those who failed to reach the door of the cars before the return of the planes to machine-gun the passengers, fell flat on their faces on the floor of the steel cars. Moreover, before the planes returned following the bombing to carry out their machine-gunning, the locomotive engineer usually reversed the train some distance in order to prevent the pilots from marking the place at which the train refugees had sought cover in the woods. Mr. Wrszlacki had the highest praise for the engineer's intelligence as well as courage. He said that on almost all occasions when the engineer had thus shifted the train's position, the returning bombers had blindly machine-gunned the woods directly opposite the train's new position, thinking the passengers had sought shelter there. Despite seventy-two bombardments of this character, there were no casualties among the passengers—though there had been many "close shaves." The German air force's continuous knowledge as to the whereabouts of this train is an outstanding example of the efficiency of the German espionage activities in Poland.

SEPTEMBER 11

Beck arrived in the morning. He informed me that, accompanied by several experienced members of his staff, he had for the past four days been maintaining a mobile position, in order to coordinate operations of the Foreign Office with those of the other Ministries as well as the High Command. The Minister went on to say with emphasis that until September 9 the Germans had given at least a semblance of adherence to Germany's agreement of September 2 with Poland (to limit aerial bombardments to military objectives). Since then, however, the activities of the German airforce had in his and his associates' opinion been characterized by "methodical bombardment of open towns". The Minister by way of illustration then cited (a) bombardment both of the Transfiguration and Piłsudski hospitals, the summer theater and civilian dwellings in Sienna street, all in the center of Warsaw; (b) what had amounted to the demolition of Siedlec (a communication center), and (c) the destructive bombardment of Zamość, which he emphasized possessed no military interest whatsoever; (d) intensive bombing of Brsześć on September 9 when five heavy bombs evidently aimed at the railway station missed their mark, landing one kilometer distant in the center of the civilian community rendering. a number of casualties and considerable property damage. He and his associates had been eye-witnesses on this occasion and had narrowly escaped with their lives.

Just outside the Foreign Office I was hailed by Soviet Ambassador Charanov, who told me he had just talked with Minister Beck. The Minister had granted him permission to cross the frontier to telephone his Government. He bade me adieu and walked to his house. About an hour later the Brazilian Minister told me he had seen Ambassador and Mrs. Charanov, accompanied by their two children and military attaché, leaving Krzemieniec in their large automobile. The Minister added that he failed to see why the Ambassador's desire to telephone from a point only about 25 kilometers distant necessitated piling at least five bags on the roof and 4 or 5 others on the side of the car. Events proved my Brazilian colleague's skepticism, as to the Ambassador's intentions, to have been correct. This was the last we saw of Ambassador Charanov.

General Carton de Wiart, V.C., Chief of the British Military Mission, imparted his opinion based on recent observation that the Polish soldier, in action in direct contact with his German adversary, was worth four German soldiers.

Had picnic lunch at top of mountain overlooking Krzemieniec, with British and French Ambassadors. We reviewed events current and of recent past.

During the night of September 11-12, Count Michael Potulicki, officer on duty during the night at the Foreign Office, received an urgent telephone call from the P.A.T. Office (Polish Telegraph Agency) in Lwów, stating that two columns of tanks were headed from the direction of Sanbor; one towards Łuck, aiming to cut off the Government from the south, the others towards Tarnopol, and that both columns were skirting Łwów. Count Potulicki was also told that the P.A.T. agency had received orders to evacuate Łwów for Łuck, as had the staff of the Łwów Radio Broadcasting Station. Count Potulicki sent a message to Minister Beck apprising him of this conversation. As a result Minister Beck gave orders to mobilize all Government officials for a conference in the morning.

SEPTEMBER 12

On the morning of September 12, at about 10:50 A.M., Krzemieniec, a defenseless, open village, suffered a severe bombardment, immediately following which I cabled the Department a full report. The little restaurant where I lunched on September 10 with Soviet Ambassador Charanov was blown and burned to bits. In brief, a flight of four German bombers suddenly swooped down on our section of the village. They commenced to release their bombs at the edge of the town and at a short distance just opposite to the British and American Embassies located on the main street. As they swung into line with the main street they continued to release their bombs. Thence they followed the main street to the crowded market place which they swept with a spray of machine gun bullets. Three more planes flew low over the village from another direction releasing bombs within even closer proximity of the other foreign Embassies and Legations as well as the Foreign Office.

Upon verifying the casualties I found they included 16 civilians killed, 40 seriously injured, and many slightly injured. Besides considerable damage to business and residential property resulted. Moreover, the population was terrorized by the suddeness and viciousness of the raid. The aftermath was a pathetic scene: burning houses, local inhabitants rushing hither and thither in meaningless fashion; unfortunates bewailing the loss or injury of their dear ones, small groups silently and grimly carrying off several fatally shot women and children; many run-away horses dragging their rattling peasant carts after them, and upsetting everything before them—in general a scene of panic. Almost all merchants and restaurant-keepers rushed into the hills, locking their places of business behind them. This forced our Embassy group thenceforth to take our meals in the cellar of the University which housed the Foreign Office, and where a restaurant had been provided for the officials and staff of the Foreign Office. The fires caused by the incendiary bombs were difficult to extinguish, in that the water supply of the village depended upon a primitive system: filling barrels with water from the nearby river, hauling them up to one's house, and emptying the barrels into the house tank. Water thus delivered cost 80 groscher per barrel. Hence, in several parts of the village whole sections of houses went up in smoke.

Shortly after my arrival at Krzemieniec I looked around

for some place which might serve as an air raid shelter in case of an attack. I concluded that the best place for the members of my staff and my family was a narrow gulley, about 18 feet in depth, directly opposite and about 300 feet from our Embassy. At the outset of the raid which actually took place, and recognizing the familiar drone of the bombers, I called to members of my staff and family who were in and around the Embassy at the time to make for the aforementioned gulley. On the way across the main street, Mrs. Biddle suddenly experienced a presentiment, she said she instinctively felt the gulley was a dangerous place. As the explosions were rapidly coming nearer—not only could we hear the whistle of the bombs on their downward course then, from what seemed almost overhead, but also could we see the shell fragments and pieces of clay, kicked up by the explosions, passing overhead and around us—a quick decision was essential. We reversed our course, and stepped in behind the back wall of the British Embassy. As matters turned out Mrs. Biddle's presentiment proved a fortunate one, in that three bombs exploded in the gulley I had previously chosen as a shelter.

Shortly after the bombardment, one of my colleagues, came to see me. Though calm, he expressed his annoyance over the Government's failure to provide the Diplomatic Corps with some measures of air-raid protection and with adequate police protection from what he had been led to apprehend might possibly develop into an uprising against both the Diplomatic Corps and the Foreign Office on the part of some of the more restive elements amongst the civilian population. He concluded by stating [that] he felt confident that in view of prevailing circumstances his own Government would sympathetically regard a recommendation, should he make one, that he and his staff leave Poland at the earliest moment. In response, I said the pace of the conflict was unprecedented in tempo and that, given several days wherein to "dig in" in its new quarters and reconsolidate its position, the Government might possibly ameliorate conditions for the Foreign Missions. Meanwhile, I believed the best thing he could do was to keep his "chin up," and make the best of a situation which was no more pleasant for the Government than for the members of the accredited Foreign Missions. This, I added, was a time when only the primitive factors of life counted—everyone had to shift for one's self—and if one wished an air raid shelter, one ought to get out and dig one; moreover, as regards the restive elements among the local population, I too was aware of their mounting recalcitrance towards the presence of the Diplomatic Corps as well as the Foreign Office in their village, in that they, since the morning's bombardment, regarded the combined presence of the Foreign Office and the Foreign Missions as having brought on the bombardments. The best measures I could conceive at the moment of meeting difficulties with these elements, was to walk in the middle of the street, especially after dark, and preferably not alone. I concluded by stating that as far as our Embassy was concerned, we were going to "sit tight" and stick with the Government either in Krzemieniec, or any other place to which they might possibly have to go. When I next encountered my same colleague several hours later, he said he had thought it all over carefully, and was going to remain at the Government's side, no matter what the circumstances, and he did.

Moreover, three others of my colleagues came to me towards the close of the afternoon and stated that the neutral mission chiefs were considering requesting either the Italian Ambassador or myself to urge in their behalf that the Diplomatic Corps be sent immediately to some point either on the Polish or Rumanian side of the Polish-Rumanian frontier in order to be out of the theatre of aerial bombardments and threatened thrusts. In reply I stated that our Embassy would remain with the Government, but that I believed that already there had been some talk amongst Polish official circles as to the possibility of moving further south.

By this time I became worried over the condition of Mr. Burke Elbrick's (third secretary) health. During the lengthy dusty run from Nałęczów to Krzemieniec he had contracted a bad throat. Now it had developed into an abcess, and he was running a high temperature. As he insisted upon being on the job day and night I had a difficult time persuading him to remain in bed even for a part of one day. Despite the doctor's energetic efforts, the throat went from bad to worse. As a long motor ride to the Rumanian border might prove dangerous for him in his weakened condition I hesitated to send him to Bucharest for treatment. His untiring energy, moreover, and conscientious and dependable application to his work—he was always on the job in spite of his temperature and painful throat—gained my high respect and esteem.

About noon that same day, the Papal Nuncio emphasized his desire that I attend a conference of neutral mission chiefs which he intended calling at 4:00 P.M. He stated his purpose was to acquire the consent of the conference to address a collective protest to some leading world statesman, and asked me whether I would personally approve his suggestion that the protest be addressed to his Holiness the Pope. I expressed my approval, emphasizing that in joining in such a protest, I should want it understood that there was no political significance attached to the protest and that I would do so merely as an objective observer of what had taken place and on humanitarian grounds. He expressed his appreciation of my attitude. I then consented to his request that he announce to the meeting my personal approval of his proposal on the foregoing grounds. The Nuncio thereupon chose as our meeting place a small grandstand at one end of a sports field, close by the Foreign Office, and at the edge of a series of freshly dug but still uncomplete trenches. Twice during the conference we were driven into these trenches by two separate flights of German planes at exceptionally low altitudes over the town. On these occasions, however, the planes refrained from releasing bombs, and it was believed they had returned for purposes of reconnaissance.

When the Nuncio announced the purpose of the meeting, stating at the same time my approval on the basis aforedescribed, the Turkish Ambassador declared his support thereof. Thereupon in turn, the Italian Ambassador, the Spanish, the Swiss and Bulgarian Ministers arose, and in most emphatic terms, stated their refusal to become a part to such a protest.

They each pointed out that, in view of the delicate political situation prevailing in Central Europe, they did not wish to go on record as having taken action which might conceivably be subsequently interpreted as a criticism of German military tactics. The Nuncio, the Turkish Ambassador, and I thereupon re-emphasized the fact that the Nuncio's proposal was devoid of political significance and was based upon a purely humanitarian standpoint, and entailed merely our observations as individuals who had been the eye-witnesses of an aerial bombardment of an open town. Nevertheless, our aforementioned colleagues refused to waver from their respective stands. The Nuncio thereupon proposed, and it was unanimously agreed, that he make a record, merely of the fact that the conference had taken place; and that each neutral Mission Chief present had stated his intention to transmit his observations to his respective government. Thereupon, the conference ended.

The Nuncio subsequently made the aforementioned record, handing it to Cardinal Hlond (then just arrived in Krzemieniec) with the request that he transmit it personally to his Holiness the Pope. In later conversation with the Cardinal, he expressed to me his disgust with the brutality and ruthlessness of German aerial tactics throughout the interior of Poland. I consider Cardinal Hlond a man of outstanding courage and intelligence; he is fair and just in his opinions, and not given to exaggeration. Cardinal Hlond and Mr. Elbrick enroute to Krzemieniec had had to leave their cars and seek shelter from an air bombardment in the same woods.

About 10:00 o'clock that night Major Colbern, our Military attaché, arrived in Krzemieniec by automobile from Tarnopol where he had been observing military activities. Enroute from Tarnopol, he had taken a short cut which had led him through back country. He had observed evidences of recalcitrance on the part of the Ukrainian population along the way. As a matter of fact, he came to a stop at a cross-road in order to read the signs for it was after dark. Suddenly he became aware that he was surrounded by 7 or 8 Ukrainian peasants who appeared to be closing in on him. The spokesman for the group bluntly declared that they intended to have his automobile, and ordered him and his chauffeur out of the car. Realizing his predicament, he whipped out his revolver, warning them that he would shoot the first one to touch his car. He then bade his chauffeur to go on, leaving the group behind without further incident. The Major cited this incident as a warning to us and the members of my staff, should we be forced to take the same road in event we evacuated from Krzemieniec.

During this conference with Major Colbern we compared notes as to our respective observations and reports we had received regarding the theater of military operations. Immediately subsequent to the aerial bombardment I discerned that the local population turned bitterly against the diplomatic corps as well as the Foreign Office, in the belief that their presence in the town was a danger. As a matter of fact, several officials in the Foreign Office imparted to me their concern over the rapidly mounting recalcitrance of the local population. Moreover, the *Starosta*, commencing that day, declared a nightly curfew between 9:00 P.M. and 4 A.M. In order to police this curfew, the *Starosta* armed a number of the local youths with old fashioned rifles. Most of them I feel confident had never had a gun in their hands before. This action alarmed several of my colleagues to such an extent that they protested vigorously to the Foreign Office, but without avail. The only practical steps I could take to insure the safety of my staff was to obtain special cards of identity for them which might serve to pass them by the guards at night. Even at that, however, the situation was difficult, in that a number of these armed youths could not read. Moreover, when one turned on one's flashlight to show his card of identity, these youths usually forbade the light, (unless the bulb had previously been rubbed with carbon paper and thus dulled the light to such extent as to render it useless for reading).

SEPTEMBER 12-13

At midnight, M. Sequin, Counselor of the French Embassy, rushed into the officer of the night at the Foreign Office, and informed him that an officer of the French Military Mission had just reported that a mechanized column consisting of tanks and motorized infantry was rapidly advancing in the direction of Krzemieniec.

Shortly after my arrival in Paris, in late September, Polish Ambassador to France, Łukasiewicz, told me that pursuant to Minister Beck's instructions, he had imparted in effect the following to [French Foreign Office Undersecretary Alexis] Léger on September 12 at about 10:30 P.M. He said that Minister Beck had proposed any one of the following courses in order to permit the Polish army a sufficient breathing spell to reconsolidate; (a) a ground attack, or (b) at least a feint in terms of preparation for a ground attack of sufficient magnitude to divert Germany's attention, and (c) an air attack over military objectives in the interior of Germany, 1/ to impress the German population with the fact that Germany was at war with France and Britain (many German prisoners taken in Poland up to and including September 12 professed ignorance of this fact) and 2/ to divert the brunt of German aerial attention from Poland. Łukasiewicz went on to say that during this talk he reiterated the same warning regarding the possibility of Russia's entrance into the conflict as he had informed the French General Staff through General Burckhardt-Bukacki on September 10.

In response to the foregoing, Léger had seemed inclined to agree with the strategic bearing of Minister Beck's suggestions, thus transmitted. Later that same evening, through arrangements made by Léger, Łukasiewicz had repeated to Premier Daladier the foregoing message from Minister Beck, together with his own observations regarding Russia's possible intervention, in the event Russia gained the impression that France and Britain would do nothing to help Poland. The Ambassador told me that at the outset of his talk Daladier evinced a sympathetic attitude. At the end of the conversation, however, Daladier had remarked that while he understood the position, the British were opposed to aerial bombardment in the interior of Germany, for fear of offending American opinion. In response to Łukasiewicz's request, moreover, Daladier said he had no objection to the former's verifying Britain's stand in this matter. In subsequently verifying the foregoing, Łukasiewicz found that while such an idea might have existed in the minds of the British Government the idea had not been based on any statement by official American sources.[16] Ambassador Łukasiewicz thereupon sought another meeting with Premier Daladier, and after considerable delay gained the impression that the latter was deliberately avoiding him. However, he finally gained access to the Premier, and frankly stated his findings on the above score. He felt that Daladier wished to avoid further discussion of this aspect. The Premier thereupon called in General Denain of the French General Staff who produced a military map of Poland. Upon examining it, the General stated that according to his report the situation in Poland appeared to be in hand and that Łukasiewicz's apprehensions accordingly seemed to be unfounded, adding that the Polish forces were in the process of being reconsolidated behind the Vistula-San line. Perceiving there was little use of arguing the point further, since he gained the impression that Premier Daladier welcomed this means of avoiding the issue at stake, Ambassador Łukasiewicz retired.

Reports reached the Foreign Office indicating (a) that the German Government announced that all Polish towns and villages harbouring armed soldiers, snipers or marauding bands would be regarded forthwith as military objectives, and that the civil population would be bombarded, and (b) that Lord Halifax warned Hitler that the British Government in consequence held itself free to take reprisals.

SEPTEMBER 13

Minister Beck invited me to have a talk after luncheon in the cellar of the University which was then housing the Foreign Office.[17] Minister Beck thereupon stated his concern over the lack of communication facilities with the outside world, and urged me to try to establish communications with my Government, either directly or through relays by way of Bucharest and Paris. He added that it would also be a source of comfort to him and his associates to know that a neutral mission had established touch with the outside world. Besides this, he discussed other aspects of current developments.

In a further conversation with Minister Beck he disclosed in effect the following: 1/ the German air and ground forces had succeeded in destroying all lines of Polish armament industry, 2/ that while the situation was now exceedingly difficult, both the Polish Government and the High Command were determined to reconsolidate their forces and continue resistance, 3/ that among military and other official circles, the impression was rapidly gaining ground that France and Britain were staging more of a demonstration than a serious attack vis-à-vis Germany; his reports indicated that Paris and London official circles were informing the Polish Ambassadors in both capitals that they hesitated to permit their respective air forces to bombard German communications and war industrial plants, for fear of the potential unfavorable effect thereof on American public opinion. (During this conversation, a ranking officer of the Polish army who was present stated at this point that he did not see why the French and British did not send planes for Polish pilots to carry out the disagreeable task, if the French and British hesitated to engage in bombardments of this character themselves. The officer concluded by stating his opinion that for the Poles, it would be a case of justified retaliation). At the end of my talk with Minister Beck, he emphasized that this was a dramatic moment for Poland; perhaps a matter even of Poland's life or death. He intimated moreover that we might possibly soon be on our way towards the south. I was aware that Minister Beck and his associates in the Government as well as the High Command felt that if the French and British did not launch immediately a major shock attack, it might spell the end for Poland.

About 3:00 P.M. that same afternoon, it was officially decided and announced that the Foreign Office and the Diplomatic corps were to evacuate Krzemieniec immediately and proceed to Zaleszczyki, about 250 kilometers distant. Later in the afternoon, I had another talk with Minister Beck upon which occasion he informed me (a) that his military reports showed that whenever the Polish infantry had come into direct contact with the German infantry, the former had proved themselves superior, (b) that Polish troops had succeeded in checking the German advance on Lwów by the previous day's capture of about 7 tanks which had been part of a reconnoitering mechanized thrust at the city's outskirts, (c) in the theatre of military operations in Western Poland, 1/ the Polish army hitherto trying to withdraw eastward from a "pocket" formed by the German forces between Warsaw and Modlin, had suddenly wheeled into a southwestward counter attack, recapturing Łódź, 2/ the German southward drive was threatening to break through the Polish lines at Modlin, 3/ Polish forces were still holding Warsaw.

Minister Beck stated that he had personally already participated in two wars; the Great War, and the Polish war with the Bolsheviks. In this third war, he had had to stand aside. However, he still hoped to take active part in a fourth war, and perhaps to end his days on a battlefield as had his forefathers. Minister Beck then stated he had urged Marshal Śmigły-Rydz during the first days of the conflict to launch every bomber at his disposal in an attack on Berlin—at any cost. The demoralizing effect in Germany, the inspiring effect it would have in the West, would have justified the sacrifice. I gained the impression during my talk with him that the Minister was suffering from deep emotions and mixed feelings about the performance of Poland's military establishment. In fact, I felt he knew at that time that nothing could really pull the chestnuts out of the fire for Poland.

At about the same hour that I received from Mr. Kirk, Chargé d'Affaires of our Embassy in Berlin, a telegram via Stockholm and Bucharest to the effect that the German Government was urging Consul General John K. Davis' and his staff's departure from Warsaw, Minister Beck received from the Polish Minister in Riga a radio message to [the] effect that Minister John Riley of our Legation in Riga had requested the latter to ask Minister Beck to issue instructions to cover the evacuation of Consul General Davis and his staff. In discussing the substance of Mr. Kirk's message with

Minister Beck, he disclosed his receipt of the message from
Riga. He then told me that both communications had reached
Krzemieniec when it was no longer possible to communicate
with Warsaw, even over military lines.

Though orders had been issued to proceed immediately to
Zaleszczyki, I decided it would be safer, based upon previous
experience, to proceed after nightfall, especially in view of
the customary flights of German planes between 4:00 and
6:00 o'clock in the afternoon. Several of our group decided
to proceed by day light. I preferred to wait until after dark
before starting out with the cars containing my family and
Mrs. Kulski of the Polish Foreign Office (who still lacked other
means of transportation. The Government by that time had
provided a place for her husband, Counselor of the Foreign
Office, in one of the official cars). Again there was considerable
confusion and difficulty in acquiring sufficient gasoline to fuel
all cars bound for the south.

Before leaving Krzemieniec I went back to the University
where Mr. Alex Small (correspondent of the *Chicago Tribune*)
was billeted, to make sure that he was aprised of the evacuation, and that he would have transportation south from the
town. (I had seen to it that all other Americans in the town
were notified and provided for in terms of transportation).
Armed with a flashlight I passed through the immense halls
of the University and entered what I believed to be his
(Small's) room. It appeared to have been recently vacated.
I then went outside the building and shouted for him, whereupon I felt the muzzle of a rifle in my back, and turned only
to find, to my added discomfort, that the young lad who held
the gun had his finger on the trigger. I knew sufficient Polish
to understand that in a Ukrainian dialect he was ordering me
not only to cease shouting, but also to cease using my flashlight. Having finally persuaded him that my mission was a
friendly one and an effort to help get another foreigner out of
town, (an action which I felt confident would appeal to him),
he accompanied me through six or more rooms in the University. Having made a thorough search for Mr. Small, and
having later received a report that several Americans had left

by a train which had departed for the north that same day, I decided it was best to go on, leaving behind one car for several hours, in case Mr. Small might appear. I learned subsequently from the Paris office of the *Chicago Tribune* that Mr. Small had actually left Krzemieniec on the afore-mentioned train and after a harrowing experience succeeded in keeping ahead of the incoming Russian troops and reached German-occupied Poland through which he traveled on a refugee train to Berlin, whence he proceeded to Paris.

Having made sure that all the cars of our group would be able to acquire ample fuel for the trip, we proceeded by way of Tarnopol, which as I pointed out in an earlier part of this report was in utter darkness, having suffered a severe aerial bombardment during the late afternoon, and again just pre-vious to our entry. (The black out was so intense that I found it necessary to walk in front of the car, with one hand on the radiator cap, and feel my way along, calling back directions to Mr. Moszczyński at the wheel of my car. It took us well over an hour to traverse this comparatively small city).

We continued to our destination, Zaleszczyki. The only incident worth recording enroute was that on attempting to pass a slow moving truck on a mid-country road, I was forced to turn on the dimmers of my headlights for an instant (having driven thus far entirely without lights) since the road was narrow and the driver of the enormous truck in front either failed to hear my claxon or refused to pull over. Just at that moment the canvas flap in the back of the truck opened and a Polish soldier, obviously intoxicated, pointed his rifle (which was far from steady in his hands) at us shouting he was going to shoot, because I flashed on the lights. Realizing he was drunk and suspecting we might be in "for it," I felt there was nothing to do but leave the lights on and make a dash to pass the truck. Pressing the accelerator down to the floor, the car lept forward, and missing the ditch by inches, we fortunately got around to the side of the truck before the soldier, whose brain at that point was fortunately functioning slowly, decided to pull the trigger.

The remainder of the journey was uneventful other than

that we passed several cavalry units on reconnaissance, and noted a number of mechanized units moving up into position under the cloak of darkness.

SEPTEMBER 14

We drew into Zaleszczyki about 2:30 A.M. September 14, and went straight to the *Starosta*, of whom I requested information as to whether there were rooms available for our party. He politely indicated there was one bed available, and that if we wanted it, we had better claim it at the earliest possible moment—before someone else came along. I said we would prefer to park our cars under trees, and sleep in the cars the rest of the night. With an expression of considerable relief he offered to conduct us personally to a nearby park, which he would gladly put at our disposal. Having subsequently parked each car carefully under the shelter of a grove of trees, we all settled down the rest of the night.

In the course of the morning, the Breslau radio announced in Polish the arrival of the diplomatic corps at Zaleszczyki, another example of efficient German espionage. At 6:00 A.M. we were awakened by the hum of a plane directly overhead. Everyone was so exhausted, however, that no one evinced any interest. In view of the low altitude of the plane I particularly welcomed the sight of the Polish insignia. We thereupon cooked breakfast on our kerosene.stove, and upon looking around, found we were drawn up in the park of an old estate on the edge of the Dniester River, and about 200 yards from the Polish bridge head of the International Bridge, connecting Poland with Rumania, which two days later became the object of a fierce German aerial attack.

The first action I undertook was to contact the *Starosta* again in an effort to billet the members of my staff and my family. By that time an officer of the Polish Foreign Office had set up headquarters in the building of the *Starosta*, and he indicated to us certain quarters which would be available during the course of the day. Meanwhile, Mrs. Biddle went to the old Palace on the estate whereon we had parked our cars, and inquired as to whether rooms might be available for our use. The proprietor said he would be glad to accommodate us provided we could supply our own beds, as the house was completely unfurnished. I subsequently succeeded in acquiring the approval of this move on the part both of the Foreign Office official and the *Starosta*. I thereupon procured beds in the town and assigned rooms to the various members of my staff. In the early morning we set up an office on the front lawn, and I succeeded in acquiring the services of two policemen; one for the day, and the other for the night, to guard our automobiles and trucks, and to see that all automobiles on the estate were kept under shelter of trees (this precaution became an essential throughout our trek).

About noon Mr. Kulski, Assistant Counselor of the Foreign Office, arrived from Kuty, where Minister Beck and his associates in the Government had decided [to stop] en route south to headquarters, instead of Zaleszczyki. Kulski imparted confidentially that the President and his cabinet had changed their minds about Zaleszczyki for several reasons, the main one being that the General Staff had decided to set up its headquarters at Kołomyja, and the Government wanted to be at a point nearby. (I feel, moreover, that two other factors had contributed to the Government's decision, notably: (a) disturbing reports of a large concentration of mechanized units in southwest Russia indicated a possible Russian move into Poland, (b) Kuty was further distant than Zaleszczyki from the Russian border and (c) the vehicular bridge across the Dniester river at Zaleszczyki seemed a more prominent objective for aerial attacks than the long but low wooden bridge at Kuty). Kulski then gave me Minister Beck's private telephone number in Kuty, stating that the Minister wanted me to have it but cautioning me not to communicate it to anyone else. Moreover, Kulski said that Minister Beck would appreciate my coming to Kuty after I might have established a communications relay bureau in Cernauti.[18] Minister Beck did not wish any other members of my staff, however, to come to Kuty in view of the shortage of food and inadequacy of lodgings. I immediately interpreted this message from Minister Beck to mean that Zaleszczyki would no longer be regarded as an official center for the Diplomatic corps. My impression on this score was subsequently borne out by a message received by my colleagues advising them to proceed to Cernauti in Rumania, from whence they could maintain contact with the Government at Kuty by automobile.

During the afternoon of September 14, I cabled the Department that Minister Beck on the previous day had earnestly requested me to communicate his conviction, based upon tragic scenes at various points, to which he had been an eye-witness, that from the outset Poland had been the "victim of methodical aerial bombardment of open towns", which too frequently had been defenseless and of no military interest. In this cable I added my own observation that in view of what members of my staff and my family had experienced and witnessed I found it difficult to ascribe the frequently wanton aerial bombardment by German planes to anything short of a deliberate intention to terrorize the civilian population with a view to its creating a state of general confusion, to demoralizing repercussions on the Polish fighting forces, as well as to discrediting the Polish Government in the eyes of its people and the accredited foreign missions. [Moreover] Major Colbern and his companions had witnessed during their passage through Siedlce and Brześć three distinct instances wherein unjustified bombardment had taken place; and my further investigation of the outcome of the aerial bombardment of Krzemieniec revealed that the low flying planes had dropped in the vicinity of the Foreign Office diminutive parachutes to which were attached glass bulbs and other small containers, which being suspected of containing bacteria were then under examination by official laboratories.

It occurred to me by way of illustration that if the world were forced to accept Germany's interpretation of objectives of military interest in connection with aerial bombardments, as demonstrated by [the] German air force during the Polish-German conflict, then the civilian communities of today, should they wish to safeguard themselves against being considered in any way of military interest, would have to undertake a radical re-vamping in terms of physical layout. Moreover, the planners, architects and engineers of civil communities of tomorrow would have to conceive of an entirely different adoption from what we have come to accept as a normal city plan. Accordingly they would have to consider the necessity of isolating by a distance of at least 10 kilometers, the center of civilian habitations, not only from military barracks but also from railways, factories, public utilities, and even churches and hospitals. Moreover, in order to guard against possible air attacks, the water and gas supply lines and communications lines running between the utilities plants and the center of civilian habitations, would have to be sunk no less than 30 and preferably 40 feet below ground—for it should be borne in mind that a 1,000 pound bomb, according to experience in the Polish-German conflict, can cut through 27–29 feet of reinforced concrete like a knife through butter.

Moscow's official *Pravda* attacked Poland for its treatment of the Russian minority.[19]

SEPTEMBER 15

In the early morning, after consultation with Major Colbern, I cabled the State Department the following observations: If the Polish Army were to effect a reconsolidation, a breathing spell was essential. In this connection, about the only means of diverting the attention of the German air force from Poland would be some form of diversion[ary] activity in the west. As matters then stood the Polish forces were unable effectively to counter attack, to concentrate at any threatened point for any protracted defense, or to maintain effective communications between what then appeared to be three Polish armies operating separately.

I also cabled the department on the same day that Major Colbern's and my observations indicated 1/ German mechanized units threatened to surround Lwów, 2/ German columns hitherto advancing eastward in direction of Lwów had divided, one element going forward towards Przemyśl-Stryj, in center of Polish oil fields, one other element going forward in the general direction of Rawa-Ruska-Jaroslaw, 3/ German column at Radom attacking in north-easterly direction towards Garwolin was reported encountering difficulty in forcing crossing of river Vistula, 4/ east Prussian force attacking in general direction of Minsk-Mazowiecka-Wyszków had reportedly reached the Siedlce-Minsk road, 5/ report that a second column was approaching Brześć on River Bug was unverified, 6/ advanced elements of the German forces above indicated [that they] consisted mainly of mechanized units; infantry of main bodies had reportedly advanced to line: San-Vistula-Bug Rivers, 7/ Polish-Poznań army under command of Bortnowski in area Kutno-Warsaw-Łódź was reportedly attempting counter-offensive in direction of Rawa-Mazowiecka-Skierniewice. Until 10:00 on the morning of September 14, the Polish forces were reportedly holding Warsaw-Torun-Kutno-Poznań, 8/ terrain and weather favorable for operations of German motorized and air forces. It was doubtful whether the Polish plan envisaged reorganization behind the San-Vistula-Bug line would succeed unless heavy rainfall restricted action of the German forces, 9/ the British military mission had reportedly recommended the withdrawal of all organized Polish military units east of the Vistula River to general area south of the Pinsk marshes in an effort to maintain communications with Rumania; current disorganization of the Polish army would make such concentration difficult.

Information which reached official circles indicated that on this date the German Government had invited (a) Lithuania to occupy Vilno and (b) Hungary to occupy the Polish oil fields up to and including Stanisławow.

Vice-consul Morton, who had just arrived in town from our evacuation center at Brześć, accompanied by Mr. Dzieduszyski, went with Mrs. Biddle in the morning to the Chargé d'Affaires of the Rumanian Embassy to assist Mr. Morton in obtaining visas for Rumania. Mr. Morton volunteered to remain at Zaleszczyki as long as possible to assist any stray American citizens which might find their way to that point. I highly approved of his suggestion.

Having ascertained that gasoline in Kuty, or at any place enroute on the Polish side of the border, was more scarce than in Zaleszczyki, and having gotten down to our last few liters, as well as having in mind Minister Beck's expressed hope that I establish some kind of a communications center in Cernauti before joining him at Kuty, I left Zaleszczyki. Before leaving however, I asked Mr. Harrison to remain there until the following day, when I planned to reach Kuty.

I arrived at Cernauti, Rumania, late in the afternoon. I immediately telephoned our Minister, Mr. Franklin Mott Gunther, in Bucharest asking his approval of my setting up a provisional relay communications office in Cernauti, and his good offices in requesting permission of the Rumanian Government to permit my carrying out this plan. Moreover, I asked Minister Gunther whether he would be so kind as to permit his counselor, Mr. Fred Hibbard to come to Cernauti in order to facilitate me in organizing the mechanics in connection with my aforementioned plans. Through the helpful cooperation of Minister Gunther and Mr. Hibbard, I was able to set up a provisional office in Cernauti.

Miss McQuatters and Miss Saunders arrived early in the morning by train from Bucharest. Mr. Hibbard arrived the following day by train.

SEPTEMBER 16

Mrs. Biddle and I left Cernauti for Kuty during the morning. On arrival at Kuty we were assigned quarters in a small cottage in the center of town. The British Ambassador and his Counselor, Mr. Clifford Norton, (who was accompanied by his wife) were assigned quarters in a small house nearby. The French Ambassador and his Counselor were also billeted nearby upon their arrival later that day. I had numerous conversations with various officials of the Government as well as with Minister Beck.

In an informal conversation with a group of Polish officials at Stare Kuty, on September 16, they all expressed their concern over Russia's mobilization in general and over the concentration of Russian mobilized units vis-à-vis Tarnopol, and along the Polish-Russian border south of Tarnopol. This concentration indicated either a move against Poland or Bessarabia; they were apprehensive lest it be the former. Minister Beck's Chief of Cabinet, Count Michael Łubieński, remarked at this point that in his opinion Russia's paramount aims in terms of imperialism were the same today as during the reign of the Czars; (a) Control of the Baltic (b) Control of the Dardanelles, and (c) possession of India. All other moves were comparatively insignificant in terms of imperialistic ambitions.

Before my conversation with Polish Government officials terminated, one of them disclosed that between the 15th and 17th, the Germans had succeeded in piercing the Polish front lines by 6 motorized raids. These raids penetrated in most cases to the extent of about 200 kilometers behind the Polish armies.

Aside from combatting each raid in an effort to localize the effect thereof, Polish G[eneral] H[ead] Q[uarters] remained comparatively unperturbed thereby. (Nevertheless, I am aware that the sudden appearance of mechanized columns in areas formerly unentered by German troops created a demoralizing effect upon the civilian populations in each respective case). These motorized raids took place somewhat as follows:

1.   One column broke through from a point between Łomza and Ostroleka, eastward, reaching the outskirts of Białystok.

2.   Another column from somewhat the same point of origin penetrated in a southeasterly direction reaching the outskirts of Brześć.

3.   Another column penetrated from Wyszków southward, reaching the neighborhood of Warsaw from the east. After this column had retreated to Kaluszin, it was attacked and defeated by the First Division of Polish infantry.

4.   Another column originating at a point between Sobata and Kutno penetrated to the outskirts of Warsaw from the west. This column reached the outskirts of Warsaw and after an encounter with defense forces retreated to the neighborhood of Raszin. On September 14, this column was defeated by the army of General Kutrzeba which first fought its way out of the Kutno-Łódź line and later out of the Skiernevice-Lawicz line into Warsaw to form part of the city defenses.

5.   Another column succeeded in crossing the Vistula and

the Bug rivers at about Wlodawa, penetrating eastward to the outskirts of Wlodzimierz-Wołynski.

6. Another column originating at a point near Rzeszów penetrated eastward to the outskirts of Lwów, dividing at a point west thereof into two columns, one proceeding in a southeasterly direction, the other in a northeasterly direction, with a view to encircling the city. The main forces of this column were attacked by divisions under the orders of General Sosnkowski, at the time when he was leading them from the neighborhood of Przemyśl en route to Lwów.

In connection with columns mentioned in sub-sections 1,2,5, above, it was hoped by the High Command that they could also be successfully turned back by reserve divisions.

In the course of a conversation that evening with Minister Beck he said he (as in the case of other Government officials with whom I had previously talked) was apprehensive in connection with Russia's mobilization and concentration of troops vis-à-vis the Polish frontier. He recalled that Herr Hitler had spoken to Marshal Piłsudski in 1934 regarding Germany's possible association with Poland in a campaign vis-à-vis Russia. Goering had spoken in like terms to Marshal Śmigły-Rydz on one occasion in 1935 and on [one] occasion in 1937. Even during von Ribbentrop's January 1939 visit to Warsaw, he had significantly alluded to the possibility of joint Polish-German action vis-à-vis Russia.

He then recounted with marked enthusiasm the report of General Sosnkowski's victory of the previous day (September 15) against an attempt of the German forces to capture Lwów. He said that General Sosnkowski's troops had succeeded in defeating the German thrust and had captured 10,000 prisoners, besides having put out of business about 100 tanks. News of this victory had served to instill the Polish forces with renewed fighting spirit. Moreover, it indicated that General Sosnkowski had been able to adopt his tactics to the strategy of the German forces. (This statement recalled to my mind Marshal Śmigły-Rydz's forecast on August 10 to the effect that it would probably take the Polish forces between two and three weeks to readopt their tactics to German strategy.)

In response to my question as to whether the Polish forces had sufficient ammunition to continue an effective resistance behind the new defense line then being established, Minister Beck frankly admitted that Poland was then low in ammunition and he was aware that every possible effort had to be made to obtain fresh supplies. (At this moment I was of the opinion that even if the Poles succeeded in setting up a contracted line of defense, they could not be expected to hold out for perhaps more than three weeks at the most against continued concentrated German aerial bombardment and redoubled mechanized thrusts, unless the Western powers extended to Poland effective assistance in terms of guns and ammunition, and some form of military diversion activity in the west to draw off at least part of the German forces from the Polish front).

Minister Beck then told me that King Carol had been "very chic" in his attitude especially during the past several days. (The Minister did not develop this point further, however.)[20] At this point, Minister Beck turned to me and in marked earnestness, asked whether I could and would cable immediately to President Roosevelt, stating that he sincerely hoped that if the President found occasion again to mention the possibility of the United States' sending raw materials to France and Britain, that the President might see his way clear to include the mention of "Poland". (Minister Beck said he had learned that on a recent date, President Roosevelt had made a public statement to the effect that he did not believe that our neutrality law would prevent the United States from shipping raw materials to France and Britain). The Minister went on to say that he realized the difficulty if not the impossibility of sending raw materials from the United States to Poland; however, since Britain and France were belligerent countries as well as their ally, Poland, he felt that it would not be too much to ask that Poland be included in any subsequent statement of like character.

Minister Beck informed me at this time that President Mościcki had set up his headquarters at Załucze about four kilometers from Śniatyń. Moreover, general headquarters was being re-established at Kołomyja, a short distance from Kuty. The Polish army, at this time, was considered by the High Command to be almost intact, and the High Command was already commencing the re-establishment of a new Polish front line behind which it was intended that the Polish army would adopt a definitely defensive position. Minister Beck stated with convincing sincerity that for Poland it was now a matter of life or death, and every hour counted. Reconsolidation of Polish forces on a new line had to be effected and munitions had to be made immediately available.

At the conclusion of our conversation, Minister Beck urged me to start in motion at the earliest possible moment at least some measures which might form a basis of establishing the means of aiding the wives and children of Polish officers engaged in the war, and who then were rapidly accumulating as refugees in Rumania. He said that individually and collectively their case would shortly become a pathetic one in that the few *zlotys* that they did possess would soon be of little value. In response I told him I would go immediately to Cernauti and cable the President. I would at the same time take steps towards setting up some form of relief for the aforementioned Polish refugees. This would probably take me until about 11:00 or 11:30 o'clock the next morning, at which time I would return to Kuty. He thanked me warmly and asked me to come to see him upon my return.

While I was engaged in conversation with Minister Beck, Mrs. Beck told Mrs. Biddle that enroute from Brześć to Krzemieniec, the Minister told her that, not having slept for three nights and days, he must have a nap. They turned their car into a nearby wood, where in the shelter of the trees, he stretched himself out on the ground and slept for two hours. Up to that moment they had been driving rapidly but at a steady speed, and each town they encountered enroute was bombed severely just as they arrived. This unexpected break in their journey had evidently put the German bombers' schedule out of balance, for both Mrs. Beck and the Minister had noticed that on continuing their trip southward, each town they passed through had been bombed just about two hours previous to their entry. They believed that they had been spotted by spies who had communicated to the planes overhead at the outset of their journey. They felt very fortunate in having escaped what had appeared to be a plan to net their car in the bombardments of the villages.

Once in Cernauti I endeavored to communicate with Ambassador Bullitt with a view to discussing with him the means of informing relief organizations in the United States of the increasing plight of reportedly accumulating Polish refugees in Rumania, only to be informed by the operator that only an officer of the American Mission accredited to Rumania would be permitted to telephone out of the country. I was therefore forced to await the arrival of Mr. Fred Hibbard, before being able to contact Ambassador Bullitt by telephone.

SEPTEMBER 17

About noon Major Colbern, Military Attaché, came to my room, having arrived from Kuty. He confirmed reports which I had learned previously during the early part of the morning. (The Major had not awaited my return to Kuty, since he had been informed that the Government itself would leave Polish soil for Rumania that day, due to the fact that they had been cut off from their army by the entry into Poland of Russian mechanized columns which were rapidly closing in on Kuty and Kołomyja).

The Major went on to say that between 8 and 9 o'clock that morning he had talked with officers both of the British and French Military Missions, both of whom in response to his question said they had no news other than the massing of Russian troops at the Polish frontier. While he was subsequently out on a reconnoitering trip, in an eastwardly direction from Kuty, at 10:00 o'clock in the morning, he met coming towards him, a column of Polish infantry, marching side by side with a lengthy column of tanks. He stopped his car and the first tank in the column also stopped. As the door of the tank opened, he was surprised to see a young Russian officer step out, for at the outset, the Major believed these tanks must be either Polish or French, since they were going along side of and in the same direction of the Polish infantry. In response to his question in Polish as to where the tanks were going, the young officer stated in apparent sincerity that they were going to fight the Germans. About one half hour later, he encountered a group of Polish officers, who told him that the Russians had come to their aid against the Germans, and what was more they were willing at that point to accept help from the devil himself.

British Ambassador Kennard accompanied by Mr. and Mrs. Norton came to my rooms about noon and confirmed news of the Government's intended early departure from Kuty.

When I finally reached Ambassador Bullitt in the early part of the morning he informed me that he had just heard a radio broadcast announcing the entrance of Russian troops into Poland. Shortly after this telephone call I met several newspaper men in the lobby of the Hotel in which I was stopping who confirmed the report which Ambassador Bullitt had imparted. One of the correspondents stated that streams of Poles were already pouring into Rumania, in most cases blocking the roads at the bridge heads at Zaleszczyki and Kuty and that the Polish Government was expected to leave Poland at any minute, if they had not already done so. A little later while I was discussing with my chauffeur over a map as to the best way I might skirt around the blocked roads in order to get back to Kuty, several of my colleagues as well as the chauffeur of an official of the Polish Foreign Office came along the street. They informed me that there was no use in attempting to return to Kuty as the Government had decided to leave during the day and that the roads leading to Kuty were so jammed with traffic and refugee pedestrians that I could not hope to get near the bridge leading across the river to Kuty anyway. Besides, the bridge itself was jammed with refugees making their way into Rumania.

A few moments later as we were talking together we were informed by another colleague that we should remain in Cernauti [to wait] for Major Alexander Łubieński, Chief of Protocol, who would transmit a message to the diplomatic corps in behalf of Minister Beck. Shortly thereafter, Major Łubieński appeared and stated that Minister Beck wished to convene a meeting of the diplomatic corps upon his arrival in Cernauti and that the Major would keep us posted as to the hour of his arrival. As matters turned out events thenceforth moved rapidly and I subsequently learned that we were to meet with the Chief of Protocol at 4:00 o'clock that afternoon. Even before the hour appointed for this meeting I learned that it was uncertain whether Minister Beck would be permitted by the Rumanian authorities to meet with the Diplomatic Corps either individually or collectively. Accordingly, I came to the conclusion that if Minister Beck and his associates in the Polish Government were granted safe conduct through Rumania they would eventually foregather at the Polish Embassy in Bucharest. My thoughts on this score were later confirmed by Major Łubieński who said that if the Government were permitted transit through Rumania the most likely place for a meeting would be at the Polish Embassy in Bucharest.

I therefore telephoned our Minister, Mr. Franklin Mott Gunther, in Bucharest and asked his cooperation towards arranging for our railway transportation from Cernauti to Bucharest for the members of my staff and family. Before leaving, however, information which I received convinced me that a meeting between Minister Beck and myself in Cernauti would be prevented by the local Rumanian authorities. I had already learned that German pressure on the Rumanian government was already causing them to waver in their expressed intention to grant the Polish Government safe conduct through their country. Subsequent events proved this information to be correct.

As we boarded the train we counted 40 or more Polish planes flying into Cernauti. The Rumanian Government had permitted these planes to enter Rumania provided they maintained an altitude not exceeding 200 feet. These among other Polish planes which flew into Rumania composed the last stand behind the formerly envisaged contracted line of defense which had been in the process of forming when the entry of the Russian troops provided the "coup de Grace."

I later learned from President Mościcki's Counselor, Minister Łepkowski, that at 6:30 A.M. that morning (September 17) he had been telephoned at Załucze, the President's headquarters 4 kilometers from Śniatyń, by the Polish Prime Minister, then headquartering at Kosów, near Kuty, that Russian troops had already entered Poland at various points along the Polish frontier. The President, accompanied by his Counselor had subsequently proceeded to Kuty where he called a Council of Ministers meeting. Among other matters, it was decided at this meeting (a) that President Mościcki send a message to the Polish nation by means of radio, to be transmitted by means of Minister Beck's mobile radio station in Kuty, to Ambassador Łukasiewicz in Paris, with instructions that he rebroadcast it in the President's name. The message was to the effect that the Polish Government would continue its struggle for the Polish nation even if forced to evacuate into an allied country, (b) that since the Government had already been cut off from the army, the Government would evacuate into Rumania, but only when this move was found absolutely essential in order to avoid capture by the Russian troops.

Later in the afternoon, President Mościcki had, according to his rights under the Constitution, told Łepkowski that he felt it necessary in order to insure the Constitutional succession, that the latter prepare a decree voiding his decree of September 1, 1939 nominating Marshal Śmigły-Rydz as his successor. The President realized the urgency of this action and of dating the document from Polish soil, since he could not foresee the fate in Rumania of Marshal Śmigły-Rydz, should the latter as well as the Government be eventually forced into Rumania. He later signed the decree prepared according to his instructions in the presence of his associates at Kuty.[21]

Towards evening, when the Government learned that a Russian mechanized column had reached Śniatyń, 28 kilometers distant from Kuty, the Government decided to proceed to Rumania. Accompanied by members of his Government, the President started across the bridge between Kuty and Syznica on the Rumanian side. At the bridge Minister Łepkowski, the President's Counselor, and General Schalley, Chief of the President's Military Household, encountered Rumanian Ambassador to Poland [Gheorghe] Grigorcea and Secretary of the Rumanian Embassy Rosetti, who stated that the Rumanian Government proposed either one of the two following procedures: (a) safe transit through Rumania to a neutral country, or (b) residence for the Polish Government in Rumania provided it ceased to function politically. The Ambassador then stated he understood the President would prefer the former proposal. He then offered to lead the President and his group in automobiles to Cernauti.

During the course of the day of September 18, Polish Government circles learned that under threat of aggression Berlin had forbidden Bucharest to allow safe transit of the Polish Government through Rumania. During the latter part of September 18, Grigorcea transmitted to President Mościcki an invitation for him, his family and his official household, to occupy the shooting lodge of Prince Nicholas at Bicaz. Moreover, the Ambassador invited Beck, his staff and other Cabinet Ministers including the Prime Minister to proceed to Slanic where they would be afforded temporary quarters. At the same time Łepkowski learned that Marshal Śmigły-Rydz had been conducted to Craiova.

On September 21, President Mościcki received King Carol's Minister, Mr. Flonder, at Bicaz. Following this conversation, the President became convinced that there was no hope of safe conduct for him and his Government through Rumania. He consequently instructed his Counselor, Łepkowski, to proceed at once to Paris to see that his aforementioned decree [nominating Wieniawa-Długoszowski] was put into effect. Meanwhile, in Bucharest I found that it would be impossible for me to make contact either with Mościcki or with Beck or any of the officers of the Polish Government due to their strict internment by the Rumanian Government.

SEPTEMBER 19

In the lobby of the Hotel Palace Athenée I spotted Colonel Gestenberg, former German Military Attaché in Warsaw and

an officer whom Polish official circles came to regard as Goering's local "mouth piece", and then currently accredited to
Bucharest. I remarked to Dutch Minister to Poland, Mr. Rosenthal, with whom I then was talking, that since he had been
charged with the protection of German interests in Poland, I
thought it would not be inappropriate if he were to engage
Colonel Gestenberg in conversation with the view to ascertaining information regarding conditions in Warsaw. Rosenthal
accepted my suggestion in good spirit, promising to inform
me later as to the substance of his talk with the colonel.
Subsequently Minister Rosenthal told me the following: In
response to his question as to why the German air force had
released bombs close by the two villages at Constanscin,
Gestenberg said that since he lacked information on this incident he was unable to offer any explanation therefor. In referring, however, to the bombardment of Krzemieniec the
Colonel admitted that this had been a blunder on the part of
the German planes. Gestenberg then went on to say in response to the Minister's further questions that the German
High Command expected Warsaw to surrender shortly. Already the population was suffering from a shortage of food
supplies and he thought that this together with the growing
tendency to loot would cause early civil strife amongst the
inhabitants. This, in turn, would undoubtedly result in a call
for truce. He understood that in the meantime the air force
would refrain from releasing highly explosive bombs. This he
thought was no longer necessary. As a matter of fact the air
force had up its sleeve other methods even more effective at
this stage of the game (he later admitted under questioning
by Rosenthal that what the air force had up its sleeve was
the use of incendiary bombs containing thermite). The Colonel
concluded his remarks by saying that he understood that the
German High Command would shortly renew an offer to permit the evacuation of whatever staffs of foreign missions still
remained in Warsaw. This indicated to my mind that once
this evacuation had taken place, and in event Warsaw refused
to surrender, the German air force would concentrate upon
"firing" the city into submission. In my opinion, moreover,

the German High Command's desire to remove whatever mission staffs were left was motivated on the one hand by the desire to avoid harming the foreign representatives, and on the other hand to clear the city of all possible foreign witnesses to what the German air force had in store for the city.

Of pertinent bearing, it is interesting to note the following inconsistency in Germany's attitude in connection with her tactics vis-à-vis Poland: During and immediately subsequent to the Polish-German conflict, any public references to the barbaric character of German aerial tactics drew from the "propaganda factory" in Berlin, the most vigorous denials as well as most energetic efforts to discredit the sources of such references. By contrast, however, in late October, the Germans assumed actually a boastful attitude as regards the destruction rendered Poland in general and Warsaw in particular. They appeared to be attempting to exploit the extensive destruction wrought with a view to impressing and instilling fear in visiting neutral diplomats—perhaps even with a view to scaring them into the German camp. Indeed, German agencies in Budapest were openly advertising excursions to visit the scenes of destruction in Poland. Moreover, the Reichkomissar of Warsaw, when he delivered a "welcoming" address at the Warsaw station to the passengers (mostly diplomats) of an incoming train about October 28th, urged in effect that they look around carefully at the extensive destruction. He went on to say that while he deplored the outcome of the bombardment, nevertheless, the Poles had brought it on themselves. Moreover, he felt confident that close observation of the vast amount of damage would lead the visitors to recommend that their respective Governments intercede for peace. A former officer of my staff who was present on this occasion and reported the foregoing to me stated his opinion (a) that the expedition conducted by a Dr. Stracha, an officer of the Whilhelmstrasse Protocol Division, had been organized mainly in the interest of propaganda, and (b) the Reichkommissar's aforementioned address was obviously directed towards instilling fear in the foreign representatives, by drawing their attention to damage to Warsaw as an example of the capacity of the German air force and to a lesser extent the German 105 and 150 millimeter guns to render destruction.

After President Mościcki and the members of his Government had been interned at various points in Rumania, direct communication between them was prohibited. This served seriously to impede the mechanics of arranging for President Mościcki's Government's retirement with a view to setting up a new Government in Paris. I learned authoritatively that Minister Beck had at once recognized the necessity of a Governmental change, and that he and Mrs. Beck worked diligently to facilitate the matter. In fact, due to his being prevented from leaving his place of internment, Mrs. Beck served as liason between the President and his Ministers, thus conducting the necessary negotiations. I later talked with a close friend and associate of Minister Beck, who had just left him in Rumania. He said that the Minister had earnestly bade him to be loyal to the new Government. However bitterly opposed the latter might be towards him, he said he would not lift a finger to obstruct them. In fact, he recognized that support from all quarters behind the new Government was a matter of vital necessity.

1. The correct spelling is "Konstancin."

2. Throughout 1939, the French and Romanians eagerly pressed the Poles to expand the 1921 Polish-Romanian Pact of Mutual Assistance, which was specifically directed against Soviet aggression, to include Germany as well; in fact, Paris had attempted to have Britain make a Polish guarantee of armed aid to Romania in the event of a German attack a condition of the Anglo-Polish Pact. Beck refused persistently, however, on the grounds that such a move would not only arouse the Germans against the Poles, whom they could charge with not acting in the spirit of the German-Polish Non-Aggression Pact, but also would push Hungary completely over to the Nazi camp, since it would imply Polish acceptance of Romanian claims against Hungary. See Beck's views as expressed during his April, 1939, visit in London, in *DBFP*, Third Series, 5:2, 15.

3. The Giesche mine referred to by Biddle was formed in 1922 as a result of the American takeover of the old German firm Bergwerksgesellschaft Georg von Giesches Erben. Known formally as Giesche S.A., it was one of the W. A. Harriman financial holdings and specialized in zinc production. Because of its origins and operating procedures, it has been held up as an example of German capital active in Poland under the cover of another national firm. See Z. Landau and J. Tomaszewski, *Kapitały obce w Polsce 1918–1939* (Warsaw, 1964).

4. Here Beck was apparently confused. According to Dr. Kulski, *he* was the officer on duty that evening at the Foreign Office, and hence took incoming calls from the Polish Embassy in Berlin. He immediately contacted both military headquarters and Beck (waking the latter), who agreed that Kulski should officially accept the German message. Shortly thereafter, still in the middle of the night, the Dutch minister, acting as a liason between the Poles and Germans, repeated the message to Kulski, who informed him of the Polish answer.

5. The text of the British reply to Germany is in *DBFP*, Third Series, 7:535.

6. The text of the French note to Germany is in *DGFP*, D, 7:534.

7. The issue of British refusal to unleash a major air offensive against Germany in the opening days of the war became a point of bitter debate. In his diary Raczyński noted that Churchill conversed with him on September 4 about the problem of a joint Anglo-French offensive, and reported that London was exerting great pressure on Paris to launch a massive ground attack on the greatly weakened Siegfried line. Churchill then remarked that "unfortunately, the British had no divisions in the field themselves and were therefore not in a position to put strong pressure on the reluctant French. Britain would support a land offensive with the whole strength of the RAF; but the military were not in favour of a long-range air offensive independent of land action, since it could not achieve any strategic result and would mean heavy losses in men and planes." See Raczyński, *In Allied London*, p. 31. Throughout the first weeks of war, Churchill nonetheless continued to encourage the Poles to expect Allied action. In his own memoirs Churchill explained the situation in terms that corroborated his story to Raczyński, noting that "the French government requested us to abstain from air attacks on Germany, stating that it would provoke retaliation upon their war factories, which were unprotected. We contented ourselves with dropping pamphlets to rouse the Germans to a higher morality." Winston S. Churchill, *The Gathering Storm* (Boston, 1948), pp. 422–23. No mention is made of the secret conference of the British Chiefs of Staff in July, 1939, when British bombardment of Germany in the event of a Polish-German conflict was ruled out on the grounds that, as Biddle reported, the French would receive the brunt of German retaliation and would collapse beneath the strain. See J. R. M. Butler, *Grand Strategy* (London, 1956), vol. 2, *September 1939-June 1941*, p. 56.

8. Charles Moszczyński remained with the American Embassy to Poland which had later set up headquarters in Angers, France until, March, 1940. He then returned to his native United States, and that same year received his doctorate in history from the University of Wisconsin. Today, as Charles Morley, he is professor of Russian and Polish history and vice-chairman of the history department at Ohio State University. He has written the foreword to this volume.

9. The "starosta" was the chief political figure in the Polish county government system (*powiat*).

10. See Chapter 2, note 11 above. Biddle incorrectly described Kulski's position, which was head of the Polish Foreign Ministry's legal division.

11. A concerted French attack on the Siegfried line, manned only by a skeleton force of German regulars without armor support and a poorly trained and equipped home militia, was the main fear of the German high command; at the Nuremburg trials, both Field Marshal Keitel and General Jodl stated that only the complete inactivity of the British and French prevented a collapse of the German war machine during the Polish campaign. See Keitel's testimony in *Trial of the Major War Criminals Before the International Military Tribunal* (Nuremburg, 1947), 10:513–22; and Jodl's testimony in ibid. (Nuremburg, 1948), 15:350.

12. Although this was certainly a consideration of the Allies, it was not the decisive argument against immediate land and air operations on a massive scale. London and Paris viewed the German assault on Poland as merely the first phase of

what would be a long, drawn-out conflict, and had no intention of exposing their military establishments to what could have been a devastating attack. Accordingly, though German generals later expressed their belief that a concerted Anglo-French attack would have crumbled the German army in its tracks, the Allies were not prepared to gamble their national existence in the opening round of a mortal conflict; moreover, neither the British nor French were ready militarily or psychologically to move against Germany at that point. See Bethell, *The War Hitler Won*, chaps. 3–5.

13. This section agrees with the episode as related by Łukasiewicz in his memoirs, *Diplomat in Paris, 1936–1939: Papers and Memoirs of Juliusz Łukasiewicz, Ambassador of Poland*, ed. Wacław Jedrzejewicz (New York, 1970), pp. 297–301. The full text of Łukasiewicz's note to Gamelin is in the same source.

14. The name is correctly spelled "Sharanov."

15. Łukasiewicz, *Diplomat in Paris*, p. 298.

16. According to Łukasiewicz, ibid., pp. 303–5, immediately following this conversation with Daladier he telephoned his good friend Bullitt and requested him to obtain a precise and final opinion from Washington on the American view of British and French strategic bombing of Germany. Within several hours, Bullitt replied that no such American position against the bombing, as described by Daladier, existed. On September 13, the Polish ambassador to the United States, Jerzy Potocki, informed Raczyński that Hull had told him categorically that "the United States government had no talks with England aimed at restraining its air attacks on the territory of Germany," since Roosevelt's September 1 appeal had only called on the belligerents to refrain from bombing open cities and civilian populations. At the same time, however, Hull told Potocki that "in his opinion the Allies are fully carrying out their obligations toward Poland . . . and that the concentration of Russian troops is not offensive in character." Łukasiewicz, *Diplomat in Paris*, pp. 307–8, citing a document from the archives of the Sikorski Museum in London (file no. A.12.53/24).

17. There was no university in Krzemieniec; the school building in question was a lyceum, equivalent to a junior college.

18. The frontier town in Romania selected as the rallying point for the withdrawing Polish and foreign civilian and military establishments.

19. The Russian minority in Poland was quite small, consisting of about 137,700 people, though Poland did have about 4,440,000 Ukrainians. See *Concise Statistical Yearbook of Poland* (Warsaw, 1938), p. 22.

20. On September 17 the Romanian ambassador assured Beck in the name of King Carol that the officials of the Polish government would be accorded free passage through Romania. See Beck, *Final Report*, p. 228.

21. According to article 13, paragraph 2b, of the Polish constitution, the president could nominate his successor in time of war. Mościcki nominated Bolesław Wieniawa-Długoszewski to the post, but because of opposition from General Sikorski and from the French government, this was voided in favor of Władysław Raczkiewicz, whose appointment was confirmed on September 29. See Łukasiewicz, *Diplomat in Paris*, pp. 342–70.

CHAPTER FOUR

Factors Contributing

To Poland's Defeat

In the belief that it would enable the reader to gain a clearer perception of events covered in the subsequent chapters of this report, I take occasion at this point to cite below a summary of factors which to my mind contributed towards Poland's defeat:

1. Suddenness of the attack. Fighting commenced between 4 and 5 a.m., Friday, September 1, simultaneously at Danzig and at numerous points along Poland's western and southern fronts. Warsaw experienced its first air raid at about 5:15 a.m.

2. Failure of the British and French as well as the Polish military authorities to visualize the full capacity of the German air force to disrupt communications, to cripple industrial operations and to render general confusion by harassing civilian communities as well as the military forces in the field. As matters turned out, Germany employed between 85 and 90 percent of her total first line air strength, a ratio of 4 or 5 to 1, in relation to the Polish air force.[1]

3. At the commencement of the conflict, the German air force effectively bombed all Polish airplane, spare parts, and motors manufacturing plants, as well as pilot training schools. In fact, within four days after the commencement of hostilities there no longer existed the means of turning out more planes and pilots, and Poland could thenceforth count upon no planes

other than those in actual use—upon no pilots other than those already trained.

4.   Upon the outbreak of hostilities German bombers, continually shuttling back and forth in three broad bands between East Prussia and Slovakia, as well as former Austria, effectively bombed all important rail junctions in Poland. This crippling of the main east-west as well as north-south transportation lines was largely responsible for preventing (a) the completion of mobilization which had been postponed for 16 hours at the urgent request of the British and French Governments (according to Polish official circles, between 300,000 and 400,000 Polish reserves failed to reach their assigned positions), and (b) the prompt movement of supplies and ammunitions and reinforcements.

5.   Failure of Poland's system of communications to stand up under the destructive effects of aerial bombardments. It is safe to say that after the first few days of hostilities there was no Central Command. Too much reliance, in my opinion, was placed on mechanical methods such as tele-wiring which events proved impractical for operations in the field against the violent effects of the modern offensive. The inner communicating above ground wiring proved vulnerable to aerial attack and to cutting by parachute technicians who were frequently dropped from planes behind the Polish fighting lines. In brief, this tele-wiring system proved too dependent upon line maintenance to be practical. The field commands were, to my mind, inadequately provided with field short-wave radio apparati and there was a lack of sufficient motorcycle despatch riders and messengers.

6.   Failure of the Central Command, when at the outset it became clear that the Polish army was faced with about 75 percent of the entire German armed forces, to execute its original plan to withdraw the main bodies of troops under cover of delayed action to the main defense lines along the strategic rivers. (This plan had gained General Ironside's expressed approval, according to the British Embassy, during his visit to Warsaw). The Polish army allowed itself to become engaged in pitched battles instead of effecting a delayed action either to

cover an orderly withdrawal to the rivers or a maneuvering position.

7. Lack of an organized fortified main line of defense. On September 12, Minister Beck told me that while he had been aware of the desirability of constructing a fortified line of defense along the strategic rivers, Narew, Bug, Vistula and San, he and his associates had realized that the expense involved in such an undertaking was more than Poland could afford. Indeed, it was all Poland could do to raise through its recent internal loan, funds to purchase the bare necessities in terms of planes and anti-aircraft equipment, without permanently crippling Poland's economic structure. Even at that, however, these funds could not be expected to afford Poland adequate resistance against 85 to 90 percent of Germany's first line air strength. In other words, Poland had had to spread whatever moneys she had at her disposal to the maximum extent in terms of war preparation.

8. German air mastery permitted the reconnaissance and bombing planes to uncover and to a large extent prevent the secret concentration of Polish troops for counter attack.

9. After the first phase of the conflict, the continual German aerial bombardments served to terrorize the civilian communities, prevented the Government from functioning effectively, and harassed General Headquarters.

10. Long lines of civilian refugees frequently cut across the Polish troops on [the] march. This had a demoralizing effect upon the troops in that they thus ascertained that their homes were being detroyed, and their families injured and killed. In many cases, moreover, these lines of refugees requisitioned military rail transportation, and appropriated supplies destined for the army.

11. Failure of Poland's Western Allies to afford relief in terms of diversion activities particularly in the air (I am inclined to believe that this was largely attributable to the Western Allies' joint desire to gain equality if not superiority in terms of air strength).

12. The delay on the part of Poland's Western Allies in declaring war on Germany. While this delay is understandable

in each case for various reasons, nevertheless, the fact remains that the Poles were rushed off their feet. This delay, moreover, served undoubtedly to render Germany confident that she had no great cause to fear a major attack in the west.

13.   The Poles were given no time for revision of military leadership where required or to revise their tactics to meet the strategy of the adversary, or to give their troops a breathing spell. There were many Polish soldiers who never saw a German soldier—only tanks and planes. In most cases, however, when Polish infantry or cavalry came into direct contact with the Germans, the former proved themselves superior.

14.   The unusual dry weather, which prevailed throughout Poland previous to and at the time of the conflict, rendered the country as a whole a sort of dry hard plain which greatly facilitated the employment of tanks and other elements of mechanized divisions. Moreover, the excellent visibility permitted the German planes to operate anywhere at all times.

15.   The large minorities in the loosely knit Polish state had served as fertile ground for the skillful and effective subversion machinations of German agents previous to the conflict. In fact, elements thus organized in advance of the conflict proved valuable aids to the German totalitarian form of campaign in terms of internal sources of information as well as agents in fomenting internal unrest and division during the course of the conflict.

16.   The disadvantage of a mainly agricultural state fighting a highly industrialized state. Only an industrial country organized along totalitarian lines, and equally ruthless as the adversary, could have resisted the recent thoroughly equipped modern offensive which Germany launched unless the following factors existed: (a) climatic, geographic and geological conditions, (b) a previously constructed fortified defense line, supplemented by strong air defense elements, which might have enabled it to hold out long enough, and (c) a highly industrialized ally to "knock out" the adversary's factories, communications, and air bases.

In all these essential conditions Poland was lacking.

At the outset of the conflict the main bodies of the Polish

fighting forces were divided into three army groups covered by advanced attachments at about 7 different points: the north army group based on the Vistula river southeast of Torun. This group, according to the original defense plan, was to withdraw to a position ranging from the Narew-Bug-Vistula rivers' junction and up to cover Warsaw. The Central army group was based on an area southeast of Łódź. This group, according to the original defense plan, was to withdraw to a position on the Vistula, mid-way between Warsaw and the junction of the Vistula and the San rivers. The southern army group was based on the Nida river in an area northwest of Tarnów and northeast of Kraków. This group was to withdraw to a position along the San river. Moreover, the plan called for an extension of the line along the Narew river by moving up reserve divisions.

Reports indicated that the northern group, contrary to plan, allowed itself to be drawn into pitched battles with the adversary. This, in the face of overwhelming odds together with the swiftness of the German pincer-like thrusts (which developed from the converging major drives from the German army groups in the northwest, and in the southwest of Poland as well as from the "Condor Legion" frontal attack on the Polish defenses in front of Katowice) tended to cut off this group's retirement, and served to prevent its executing its withdrawal according to the original plan. This upset in the original plan caused the central army group to alter the scheduled direction of its withdrawal and instead to take up the position originally assigned to the northern army group in covering Warsaw. At the same time, the southern army had to withdraw likewise in a northeasterly [direction] instead of its scheduled direction north to maintain contact with the central army group. This left the San river line insufficiently defended to check a swift moving powerful German mechanized thrust aimed at Lwów.

Notwithstanding the aforecited among other difficulties and set-backs, there was still a possibility of the Polish forces reconsolidating behind a newly massed contracted line of defense, for the Polish forces had actually taken up position along part of their main defense river line. At this juncture, however, Russia delivered the "coup de grace" by suddenly marching in and occupying the very territory whereto the newly envisaged Polish position would have necessarily looked for supplies and reinforcements.

The following are a few examples of the important role which espionage played in the German campaign:

1/   The system of communication between the spies behind the Polish lines with the German forces both ground and aerial was conducted with marked efficiency. The spies had been organized in Poland to such an extent previous to the outbreak of war that in many cases they commanded key positions in the communications as well as in other fields. After the commencement of the war, numerous spies were dropped behind the Polish lines by parachute from German planes. These men engaged in cutting communications lines, spreading alarming rumors amongst Polish communities and in many cases, disguised in Polish officers' uniforms, intercepted and countermanded military orders.

2/   Shortly after the outbreak of war an official of the Foreign Office in Warsaw noticed from his office window, the continued presence of a man in the side street below, onto which gave the private entrance to Minister Beck's house. The Minister frequently used this entrance, and whenever statesmen and diplomats were received by him confidentially in his home, they likewise made use thereof. Suspecting the man was up to no good, the forementioned official of the Foreign Office ordered his arrest. Subsequent police investigation revealed that the man had been noting on a piece of paper the license numbers of Minister Beck's and visiting diplomats' automobiles. It was moreover disclosed that he intended to communicate these numbers to agents in the eastern part of Poland in order that they might be able to identify the cars in the case of their possible arrival in that region during further stages of the conflict. While this spy wore Polish clothes, he was identified by his German shoes.

3/   Again, an officer in command of troops near Krzemieniec sent orders for the delivery of a given amount of supplies for a certain time of the day. The supplies failed to arrive. Upon investigation, the officer commanding found that his orders had been countermanded. In subsequently tracing back to Krzemieniec, he found an individual in the uniform of a Polish officer walking along the roadside. Something about the man caused the officer commanding to stop and question him. He replied in broken Polish with a discernable German accent. He put the man under arrest and discovered under further examination that it was this spy in the uniform of a Polish officer who had countermanded his order.

4/ It was found by the Polish military intelligence that German aviators were receiving signals from German spies (dressed as Polish peasants) who stepped out numbers and other signs with their feet in plowed fields throughout the countryside.

5/ I personally became suspicious of telegraph operators in small towns along the line of our trek. My suspicions were supported by remarks of some of my colleagues who felt that while telegraph operators accepted their cables, they destroyed instead of dispatching them; in other cases, they deliberately juggled the message in such a way as to arrive at the other end of the line in a garbled state. I am convinced that this happened to some of my own cables.

1.   On every vital point—manpower under arms, the degree of mechanization in the army, and potential firepower available—the German war machine was vastly superior to the Polish by September, 1939. On September 1, the Polish army contained 840,000 troops, or 70 percent of the total called for in the mobilization plan; they were organized in 27 regular infantry divisions, 3 reserve infantry divisions, 8 cavalry brigades, 3 mountain brigades, 1 armored motorized brigade, and numerous special units and volunteer militia battalions. The Wehrmacht opposed this with about 1,400,000 troops—88 percent of the total called for in operational plans—organized into 37 regular and 9 improvised infantry divisions, 1 mountain division, and 14 mechanized divisions, of which 6 were regular armor, 4 light armor, and the remaining 4 mechanized infantry attack units. Tadeusz Rawski, Zdzisław Stapor, and Jan Zamoyski, eds., *Wojna wyzwoleńcza narodu polskiego w latach 1939-1945*, 2d ed. (Warsaw, 1966), pp. 128-37. The disparity in equipment between the two forces was even more revealing. The Germans had 2,700 tanks to the Poles' 887— of which 574 were reconnaisance vehicles; 6,000 cannon and mortars to 4,800 for the Poles; 4,500 antitank guns to 1,250 for the Poles; and 1,900 aircraft to the 388 at the disposal of the Poles. The figures are more striking when drawn from a comparison of the firepower available to the average regular infantry division in the German and Polish armies. The ratios, all in favor of the Germans, were: artillery, 2:1; mortars, 2.7:1; and machine guns and pistols, a crushing 10:1. Added to this were the problems

encountered by the Poles in transport. While the average German infantry division was fairly well mechanized, its Polish counterpart relied heavily on horse-drawn transport, with its many inherent shortcomings. Eugeniusz Kozłowski, *Wojsko Polskie 1936–1939* (Warsaw, 1964), pp. 90, 164. An exhaustive breakdown of the material strengths of each side on the eve of the war is contained in *Polskie Siły Zbrojne*, vol. 1, pt. 1, chaps. 4 and 5.

CHAPTER FIVE

Military Aspects of the Polish-German Conflict
And Lessons To Be Learned Therefrom

Reports previous to the outbreak of the conflict indicated, and campaign operations following the commencement of hostilities revealed, that the German plan vis-à-vis Poland envisaged the lightning destruction of the Polish armed forces before the development of an effective threat from the West. It was clear from the outset that Germany had pitted against the Polish forces an efficiently organized, modern, and powerful fighting machine. The outstandingly efficient co-ordination of air and ground force operations proved highly effective in the forward thrusts of Germany's swift moving campaign. That the conception and execution of the German plan of campaign were brilliant, was demonstrated by events—Germany had gained complete domination over Poland in less than a month's time. In brief, it may be said that against Poland the German High Command applied their entire "bag of tricks" in terms of Blitzkrieg tactics, formerly tried out and perfected in the military laboratory of the Spanish civil war.

In tracing the successful course of numerous swift, long-range thrusts of German mechanized columns (which in some cases left far behind them important bodies of German and Polish forces in the throes of combat), and in reviewing reports describing the effectiveness of these thrusts, it is well to bear in mind the following:

1. Weather conditions prevailing throughout Poland were highly favorable for this campaign of swift, long-range movement.

2. The comparatively flat terrain in Western Poland and the parts of Central and Southern Poland traversed, offered little if any effective check to the advance of these columns.

3. The exceptionally dry weather had so dried up the rivers that they were reduced in effectiveness as strategic barriers.

4. The Polish forces were inadequately equipped with anti-tank guns.

5. The Polish forces were quantitatively out-mastered in the air.

6. The possibility of German reconnaissance as well as bombing planes to shuttle back and forth from East Prussia to former Austria as well as to Slovakia. This permitted the discovery of any and all attempts of the Polish troops either to concentrate or maneuver their forces.

As of connected bearing on the military aspect, I take occasion to draw the reader's attention to the following angle. Professor Dr. Yakimowicz,[1] formerly professor in charge of the general clinic of Warsaw University, told me that previous to the outbreak of war he had received confidential reports through what he considered reliable channels in the international medical fraternity, that Germany in its totalitarian war program was prepared to engage in bacterial as well as other forms of warfare, not only against Poland, but also if subsequently deemed necessary against Poland's Western Allies. He had brought this to the attention of his Government, and while his Government were distinctly averse to the employment of any such type of warfare, they permitted him to proceed with research in connection therewith, with the view merely (a) to ascertaining the practical possibilities in this field, and (b) to keeping up their sleeve whatever formula the professor might conceive.

Accordingly, Dr. Yakimowicz had, after considerable research, worked out a formula which he called the "bacterial cocktail". This entailed the mixture of certain quantities of the germs of dissentery, typhus, and pneumonia, in bouillon in a container about the size of a small water glass. This according to the Professor, was sufficient to permeate fifty or more gallons of bouillon. This bacterial lotion could be spread in the adversary's territory by several methods: (a) it could be dispersed on a rainy or misty night by a type of spray gun over a given objective from an aeroplane, (b) it could be dropped from the plane over the villages or countryside selected, in small colored glass tubes attached to small parachutes (the tubes must be colored in order to keep out the light which renders the germs ineffective), or (c) a specialist in bacterial warfare might be let down from the plane by parachute— once landed he could empty the contents of the bacterial tubes into artesian wells, water supply tanks, and other vital places.

The Professor emphasized that while daylight tended to diminish the effectiveness of the bacteria, damp or wet weather at any time was the most favorable condition for spraying bacterial lotion from a plane. He then went on to say that because villages as a rule depended mainly upon artesian wells, and in general an open water system, this type of community would serve as the easiest victim of bacterial warfare such as above described. Fortunately, for both sides in the Polish-German conflict, this type of warfare was not resorted to.

After the close of the conflict, Dr. Yakimowicz informed me that he had imparted the results of his bacterial research to the head of the Pasteur Institute, pointing out to the latter that he had reason to believe that the Germans were prepared to resort to this, among other forms of totalitarian warfare. In response to the remark of the head of "Pasteur" to the effect that such a thing was too horrible to contemplate and that he refused to entertain such barbaric ideas, Dr. Yakimowicz pointed out that if and when the Germans did resort to this type of warfare, the French and British laboratories would be forced to conceive of some form of retaliation. Moreover, they would have to prepare large quantities of serums to fight the spread of disease thus introduced. Dr. Yakimowicz told me that he was surprised at the attitude of the Head of the Pasteur Institute, for he felt that it was indicative of Western Europe's lack of comprehension of the extent to which their adversary was prepared to go under pressure.

Observations and study of the course and effect of military tactics provided by the Polish-German conflict brought to light the following lessons, which in my opinion might be usefully applied in considering our own national defense problems.

1. That success in the modern offensive is largely dependent upon complete co-ordination of air and ground force operations.

2. That success in defensive action against modern offensive operations necessitates (a) a completely organized fortified position, (b) adequate equipment essential for standing off the adversary's air raids. This includes the integral essential, an air force at least equal to that of the adversary.

Superiority or at least equality in the air is essential to challenge effectively the adversary's planes (a) operating in coordination with the efforts of the troops and mechanized units in the theater of combat, and (b) bombing and otherwise harassing various points in the interior of the country. In Poland, during the first several days, the German air force made at least a pretense of limiting its intense aerial bombardments to objectives of military interest. The German pilots soon abandoned all pretense, however, and resorted to indiscriminate and large-scale use of incendiary bombs over cities, towns, and villages.

This new phase raised the question of the necessity of adequate fire prevention and fighting apparatus and organization, as an essential defensive factor. Most cities, towns, and villages other than Warsaw, many of them composing industrial, rail and other communications centers, were short of and in many cases totally lacking in anti-aircraft cannon. Poland, with her meagre supply of this essential equipment, was only able to distribute it sparsely throughout the country.

After witnessing a number of air raids, I came to the conclusion that in centers where machine gun batteries composed the only element of defense against air attacks, the machine gunners would frequently have proved themselves more effective, had they held their fire until the planes risked flying in low and power diving. Instead, as in a number of cases I recall the machine gunners started firing ineffectually at the planes when they were still out of range, thus exposing their positions to subsequent attack from the planes.

Experience through the conflict taught us that from the standpoint of comparative safety for the civilian, large cities, provided they were afforded the maximum requisite in air defense measures, afforded more security than the smaller towns and villages throughout the comparatively sparsely defended countryside. In the latter centers, air defense as well as bombproof shelters were practically non-existent.

From the reports of Major Colbern, Military Attaché, as well as from observations of Polish official circles, I gained the impression that in sectors along the battle front where the character of fighting permitted patrolling operations, patrol units would have derived considerable advantage from the use of sub-machine guns (the kind frequently employed in the past by "gangsters" in the United States). The lightness and mobility as well as intense volume of fire of this gun would render the patrol the maximum capacity to cope with surprise attacks of opposing patrols without diminishing his essential mobility.

I furthermore noted with interest that in General Sosnkowski's defense of Lwów against the eventually overpowering forces of his adversary, General Sosnkowski brought into use a number of 7.92 mm anti-tank rifles, secretly developed by the Polish armament industry previous to the conflict. The General later told me that this weapon, fired from the shoulder, proved effective especially against the comparatively thinly-armored German tanks. (The latter, he said, were inferior to the tanks formerly manufactured in Czechoslovakia).

Major Colbern observed that during the recent conflict, the Germans replaced their old 77's with 105 mm guns. These 105's, not much heavier than the old 77's, have about the same mobility and fire a heavier projectile with a range of some 2,000 to 3,000 meters greater than the 77's. In fact, reports indicated that the 105's had an effective range of about 10,000 meters.

Moreover, in their artillery bombardment of Warsaw, the Germans brought into play, in addition to their 105, their 150's which, with a range of from some 12,000 to 15,000 meters, proved effective for counter battery work and in cases where destructive power was required. However, according to the judgment of Major Colbern (who visited Warsaw about October 29) he believed that notwithstanding the intense artillery fire, Warsaw suffered less therefrom than from aerial bombardment.

Further lessons derived from the Blitzkrieg campaign against Poland, as well as from reports on German aerial tactics vis-à-vis British and French naval and commercial tonnage, raise the following additional factors for consideration in connection with our own national defense problems.

1. A two-power air force of *no less* than 10,000 first line planes, including strategically placed air bases with under-ground hangers.

2. Sufficient naval aircraft carriers.

3. A two-coast swift, long-range light navy, equipped with guns of the maximum caliber possible.

4. A two-coast fleet of submarines, mine layers, and mine sweepers, equipped with the most modern devices.

5. A great quantity of mines stored and ready for immediate use on both coasts.

6. Sufficient tank and mechanized divisions.

7. Rapid-fire rifles for the infantry, cavalry and motorized troops, and sub-machine guns for patrol units.

8. Sufficient quantity of anti-tank guns and anti-tank rifles.

9. Motor transport sufficient to enable at least the military forces to be independent of railways.

10. Anti-aircraft elements: longest possible range anti-aircraft cannon and heavy machine guns—being governed as to requisite quantity by realistic appraisal of Germany's and Russia's recently manifested interpretation of military objectives, as an example of what to provide against in modern totalitarian warfare.

We as citizens of the United States should come to regard this necessity in the light of a national insurance policy and accept the necessary annual military and naval appropriations as a constant over that period. In arriving at this opinion I have taken into consideration the following factors: If an early cessation of current European hostilities materializes before a definite victory by either side, then such a cessation, in my opinion, would prove more in the light of a truce providing a breathing spell for recuperation and realignment of forces, than a prelude to durable peace.

Even if however, a definite victory were attained by either side in current hostilities, I can foresee little better than a post-war period of say, 10 years or more, marked by economic and social unrest, growing out of shutdowns in war industry and leading perhaps even to revolutions and counter-revolutions, particularly on the Continent. Besides, another factor which I do not overlook and which may conceivably have an important bearing on future trends, is that current-day youth both in Germany and Russia are born and raised in an exclusive spartan atmosphere, all trace of the athenian having been elbowed out by totalitarian leadership. Conquest in one form or another is the keynote of their upbringing—they know little else. Hence, with the mentality of the oncoming generations of two major powers of the world attuned to warlike thought, we, even as geographically remote as we feel ourselves today, must take into account the possible developments from this condition over the next fifteen to twenty years.

1.   The correct spelling is "Jachimowicz."

CHAPTER SIX

The Russian Aspect

As a matter of interesting background in regard to the Russo-German Non-Aggression Agreement and its implications, I recall Minister Beck's having said that there were two times when Russia became dangerous: (a) when the Russian Government derived a measure of self-confidence from prosperity throughout the country, in which case, the Government felt it had a free hand to engage in world revolutionary tactics abroad, and (b) when the Government was on the defensive in relation to the peoples of Russia due to the country's experiencing hard times—in which case there was a danger of the Government's deciding that foreign conquest was necessary to divert the attention of the masses from their internal difficulties.

Minister Beck's expert on Russian affairs imparted to me that according to Lenin's works and in the records of the 6th [Congress of the] International, Moscow had envisaged a Russo-German Block eventually under Russian domination—that the Russians did not plan to attack Germany, but rather to let the Western powers weaken her, then at the psychological moment jump in and liberate the German people, decompose Germany, then Bolshevise her.

As far back as March 1937, I reported from Oslo that informed circles there had confidentially disclosed to me that through usually reliable channels they had received a report that during a conference in London between Foreign Minister Eden and German Ambassador von Ribbentrop (shortly before the latter's departure for Berlin to sign the Anti-Comintern Pact) Mr. Eden stated he had information that conversations had been taking place between certain Generals of the German and Russian armies and that their discussions envisaged a military alliance. While Eden admitted receipt of the foregoing report, he omitted reference to the fact that his information also indicated that von Ribbentrop was aware of these conversations and their purpose. In response to Eden's question as to whether his information was correct, von Ribbentrop reminded Eden that he had undoubtedly been long aware of the close relationship between the military circles of Germany and Russia. Mr. Eden said yes, but that was before Nuremberg, where Herr Hitler had taken occasion to attack Bolshevism. In response von Ribbentrop lamely offered to try to ascertain further light on Eden's report. Eden then concluded by stating that the British Government would regard with grave concern any such negotiations. While I was unable to confirm the substance of this report and in that I regarded this talk (if true) and its implications one of the potential pivots of history in the making, I considered it of sufficient interest to pass it on to the State Department for its information and verification.[1]

Previous to my arrival in Poland, I had been informed by a Polish diplomat whom I consider not only extremely well-informed on his own country's affairs, but also one of the most able diplomats in Europe, that Poland due to her geo-political position had to practice a policy of "balance-diplomacy" between Germany and Russia. It was not long after my arrival in Poland that I found my informant's appraisal of Polish policy to be exact. Moreover, it was clear to me that in Poland's interest Polish foreign policy was directed towards the maintenance of correct relations with each of her neighbors and towards preventing collaboration between the two—a prospect which would prove fatal to Poland.

In connection with this policy of "balance-diplomacy", I was interested in Minister Beck's remarks that as far back as 1935, Goering had proposed to Marshal Śmigły-Rydz Polish-German collaboration vis-à-vis Russia.[2] Moreover, I was informed by a leading official of the Polish Foreign Offiice, that the period 1935–37 was marked by several further German overtures on this score. Indeed, he recalled that on several visits to Berlin during that period German people from the bootblack to the intellectual, greeted him with some direct or indirect reference to eventual Polish-German collaboration vis-à-vis Russia. In other words, it had become common talk. Moreover, Minister of Finance Kwiatkowski told me that as late as January 23–25, 1939, von Ribbentrop during his visit to Warsaw significantly alluded on several occasions to a possible collaboration between Poland and Germany against Russia.[3]

Appraising Polish-Russian relations, I felt that in spite of the existence of a non-aggression and a commercial agreement,[4] there was a deep sense of distrust and hatred between these two Slav nations. Moreover, I had my doubts whether if Russia had a chance to make a turn to her own advantage she would stand steadfastly by the sanctity of these agreements. As for Poland, she represented to my mind the last western window looking east and in such light could be depended upon to adhere strictly to her obligations. To be sure, while Poland manifested no affection for Russia, Poland did her best to maintain correct relations. Outside the non-agression agreement, Poland was determined to confine her relations exclusively to the commercial aspects in line with her commercial agreement. She wanted no political "trucking" with the Soviets.

Of related interest, Polish Ambassador to France Łukasiewicz informed me after my arrival in Paris following the Polish-German conflict, that in the first half of August, during a meeting between British and French representatives with Soviet Commissar for Foreign Affairs Molotoff in Moscow, Molotoff had bluntly remarked that an agreement between the Western powers and Russia could be practical only if Britain and France could persuade Poland to permit Russian troops to enter Poland via the Vilno and East Galician areas at any time that the Russians deemed such action necessary. The British and French representatives had replied that this was a matter which Molotoff should take up directly with Poland. In response, Molotoff said that Russia had only non-aggression and commercial agreements with Poland and that since Britain and France were Poland's allies, they were the proper parties to put the question to Poland.[5]

French Minister for Foreign Affairs, Bonnet, had later sounded out Ambassador Łukasiewicz on the above score. In response the Ambassador had remarked to Minister Bonnet that the latter was unquestionably aware of the answer before putting the question. Moreover, the Ambassador had pointed out his opinion that Molotoff's remarks along the above lines represented merely a tactical play. Indeed, while on the one hand Molotoff was undoubtedly playing for time, on the other hand he had deliberately posed the one question which might cause tension between the Western powers and Poland. The Ambassador had added, moreover, that he would therefore prefer to consider that the question had not been broached by Bonnet— and emphasized that if France pressed the question formally, it would be a mistake, for such action might lead to an "all round" serious misunderstanding.

The Ambassador went on to say to me that about the same time, Minister Beck had replied along similar lines to British Ambassador Kennard's soundings on the above score. Ambassador Łukasiewicz then told me that following these unfruitful soundings on the part of Minister Bonnet and Ambassador Kennard, he personally gained the impression that the British and French representatives in Moscow resorted to stalling the issue in their further conversations with the Soviet authorities. In concluding his remarks Ambassador Łukasiewicz told me that about the 19 or 20 of August, Bonnet in conversation with him evinced considerable optimism over the prospect of coming to a deal with Moscow. The Ambassador had replied frankly that while the representative then negotiating in France's behalf [General Doumenc] was no doubt a military expert of high standing, nevertheless, the Ambassador felt it would be difficult for the French representative to gain a clear insight as to what was in the back of the Russians' mind, in that the French representative was not familiar with the Russian language and had been in Moscow but a short time. At a later date, Bonnet had admitted to Ambassador Łukasiewicz that he had been right as to his reaction on this score.

I recall having felt that after Poland had decided to cut its bridges with Germany, she was inclined to pay insufficient attention to her relations with Russia. Moreover, I was inclined to feel that at about that time the Polish Intelligence Service in Russia was not functioning up to standard—had failed to keep Warsaw fully apprised of developments in the making.

While I fully understood Poland's reluctance to permit the Red Army to step one foot onto Polish territory, I questioned in my mind, whether in the event of a German invasion, Poland might not be inclined to accept help from the Devil himself. The thought therefore occurred to me that if Poland and Russia could work out a formula whereby Poland could attach Russian forces to the Polish war machine, and whereby the Polish Government were the sole judge as to the character, extent and timing of Russian assistance, Poland might have held this up her sleeves as an effective weapon vis-à-vis Germany.

In the early part of August, [Deputy] Commissar for Foreign Affairs [Vladimir] Potemkin came to Warsaw and conferred with Minister Beck. The Minister subsequently imparted to me his opinion that Potemkin throughout his conversation had shown full comprehension of Poland's position. Moreover, Potemkin had remarked that Poland's attitude towards Russia was not as bad as had been widely suspected, for it was clear that Poland was not playing ball with Germany. He added that enlightenment on this score had led towards greatly facilitating a clearer Polish-Russian understanding.[6] (I was aware that at this time, Poland felt that all she needed from Russia were raw materials and that she entertained hopes of obtaining further requirements whenever needed, within the framework of the commercial agreement).

After the signing of the Anglo-Polish Accord, I looked for Russia to relax in that the accord removed the possibility of a Russian-dreaded Polish-German collaboration vis-à-vis Russia. In this light, the Accord offered Russia a strategic advantage in a political sense and thus allowed her to sit back and take her time before making her next move.

Following March 31, whereon British Prime Minister Chamberlain announced Britain's and France's support of Polish independence, and the British and Polish Government's "covering note" of April 6, Herr Hitler reportedly reacted violently in that the completion of the agreement envisaged in this covering note implied a potential two-front conflict should Herr Hitler embark on further adventures—a prospect to which Germany was historically opposed. Both Germany and Britain shortly thereafter bid vigorously for Stalin's hand. Thus Stalin was afforded the opportunity to choose with which side he would throw in his lot, both of which powers Stalin, in my opinion, considered imperialistic.

A leading official of the Polish Foreign Office informed me that in February his Government had received secret reports from Berlin indicating that the German Government had reached a conclusion that unless its efforts to detach the Western powers from Poland succeeded, war was inevitable. It was at this point that, according to my informant, Berlin seriously started laying the ground work for a German-Russian rapprochment. Again, Polish official circles received reports in early April which indicated that after March 31, Germany initiated in earnest the conversations which were signed on August 23 and ratified in Moscow on August 31, 1939.

There was no logical reason for Stalin to back Great Britain which he considered as the personification of capitalistic imperialism and regarded rightly as not yet ripe for Communist propaganda. (Indeed, Trade Unionism in England is too healthy and too politically strong to admit Bolshevist theories). As regards Germany, there was from Stalin's point of view, every reason to back it.

1. The obvious gains to be achieved in Poland.

2. Both systems are based on totalitarianism and near-Communist ideals.

3. Similarity of ultimate aims. Germany or Hitlerism aims at world domination by conquest; Stalinism or Communism at world domination by world revolution.

4. Only one barrier existed to prevent an understanding—Herr Hitler, a professed anti-Communist, was after all just one mortal man.

5. Germany, as a reaction to Nazi rule, was becoming internally ripe for Communist propaganda and social unrest.

Cooperation with Germany in conquest or occupation of Central and Eastern Europe would bring the Russian ideology closer to Germany and sap theirs, speed up internal trouble, liquidate Nazism and natural evolution towards something closer to Stalinism and less dangerous for Moscow. In both Germany and Russia, statesmanship had given way to novel experiments in general, based upon the glorification of the state as a super deity in itself, upon the suppression of the individual, upon the worship of one man who regards himself as the exclusive master of the fate and souls of his people, upon the doctrine of one given race over all others, and of its consequent right to bid for world domination—in cases of Germany and Russia, the objective was the same, though the approach to that end differed at the outset.

Moreover, National Socialist totalitarianism is in my opinion a general adaptation of Bolshevism, [which,] as Communist totalitarianism, entails a policy of world domination through conquest primarily in the name of militarized National Socialism. In assessing the real strength of the National Socialist doctrine it is well to bear in mind that while declaring a ruthless crusade against Communism to destroy the Communist Party in Germany, Herr Hitler borrowed some of the most characteristic axioms of Communism for his State Totalitarian and Social program. The explanation of this phenomenon rests in the fact that in Germany, dictatorship was instituted as the direct result of growing social unrest.

Shortly after Hitler came to power in Germany there was a break in cordial relations between Moscow and Berlin. This was brought about by the necessity of ideological shadowboxing: Berlin's so-called anti-Bolshevist crusade, and Moscow's so-called anti-Fascist line-up. When, however, ideological tactics were no longer useful there was a natural tendency on the part both of "National Bolshevism" of Germany and "Bolshevist Nationalism" of Soviet Russia, to come closer together—both are opposed to the so-called capitalist democracies.

Russia's participation in the European conflict substantially augmented the complexities of the scope of the war. The implication of German-Russian collaboration are far-reaching.

1. In the current state—for Europe.

2. In a later stage—for Asia and possibly for the world at large unless broken up before it gained momentum. Herr Hitler and Stalin might be expected to collaborate against the rest of society which upholds the principles of human freedom and the rule of right over might, so long as it suited the interest of one or the other. At the same time, however, like two gangsters, they might attempt to "do each other in" at every turn and perhaps even work subversively towards each other's downfall.

With ideologies now so to speak "out of the window" and with the lid off "power politics," western civilization finds itself faced with an unlimited menace in the combination of imponderable sinister imperialistic forces.

Seen from the Warsaw angle the following observations stand out as important bearing on what eventually developed into a Russo-German Pact of Non-Aggression. I recall that during the formative period of the anti-aggression front, all signs indicated that Moscow was deliberately giving encouragement to Britain, France, Turkey, Poland, Rumania and other links in the anti-aggression chain. During the course of Moscow's encouragement to these powers, I gained the impression that Moscow discerned signs of concern in Berlin over growing resistance abroad, which Hitler chose to label "encirclement". At about this juncture, my interest was engaged by what I considered the significant implications of remarks on the part of Russian Ambassador to Poland, Charanov. He inferred that Russia was not going to permit itself to become an instrument of British policy, whereby so frequently in the past Britain had looked to others to fight her battles for her. These remarks indicated to me that Moscow was still making up its mind as to which side to choose.

Later, Moscow offered Berlin a Non-Aggression Agreement. At the time, I interpreted this as a move aimed among other factors at boosting Berlin's confidence in the face of increasing resistance from abroad. Moreover, aside from whatever subtle designs in behalf of Soviet imperialism Stalin might have envisaged, he undoubtedly had in mind laying the groundwork for world revolution. Hence, I felt that while Moscow had on the one hand lent its encouragement towards building up resistance against Germany, on the other hand Moscow had deliberately taken steps to relieve Berlin of the worry of a Russian attack in the East by agreeing to conclude a Non-Aggression Agreement. As observed in my previous writings, Moscow's machinations smacked of a deliberate attempt to foment a European conflict. In line with this thought, Moscow ratified the Non-Aggression Agreement on the night of August 31, and Germany attacked Poland between 4 and 5 o'clock the following morning, September 1, indicating to my mind, that ratification had served as the final factor which released the German forces against Poland.

Reports just subsequent to the entry of Russian forces into Poland indicate (a) that German military observers had accompanied the former and (b) that the German observers upon their return to Berlin pointed out that judging by organization and performance of the Russians on this occasion, Germany could crush the Russian military establishment at any time it decided to do so. These reports might possibly lead Herr Hitler to believe he could afford to permit Russian forces to engage in a westward thrust, feeling he could arrest the thrust whenever he chose. Once Herr Hitler gained such an impression, he might let the Russians lunge westward with a view to "bringing home" the Bolshevik menace in the minds of western Europe, feeling at the same time that if he thus succeeded in sufficiently frightening the Western powers, he might either enlist their active assistance towards checking the Russians, or at least count on their neutrality while he turned against Russia.

If he failed, however, in his efforts to frighten the Western powers with the Bolshevik "bogey," and/or with the implications of a German-Russian Pact, either into a compromise peace or into giving him a free hand in the East, he might conceivably embark upon a set plan for joint action with Russia, to break up the British and perhaps even the French Empires. By that time, Russia might request, and Hitler might be glad to accord her, technical assistance towards reorganizing Russia's military and economic forces. This process might involve a period of as much as two years, during which time Herr Hitler might attempt to freeze the Western front while he whipped the Russian army into shape.

As for possible joint action between Germany and Russia, it might in a preliminary stage involve in terms of Russian aspirations a diversionary thrust against Britain via Scandinavia, with a view to gaining submarine and aviation bases from which to hold the major portion of the British fleet in the North Sea and Home waters to cover a Russian move—vis-à-vis possibly India, Turkey, and perhaps Iran. In this connection, I was aware that between 65 and 70 percent of Russian agriculture is on a motorized basis, and that an air or naval attack from the Black Sea or effective air attacks from Iran vis-à-vis Batum or Baku, might paralyse Russia's economic as well as military structure. Accordingly it is not inconceivable that with a view to protecting her oil bases, a campaign against Iran may later figure in Russia's military plans.

I feel that when Herr Hitler authorized von Ribbentrop to sign the German-Russian Pact on August 23, he was willing to pay a high price for Russia's neutrality, and an even higher price for Russia's support should he subsequently require it. Herr Hitler's plans previous to the outbreak of the Polish-German conflict, according to all indications, had envisaged a swift "blitzkrieg" victory over Poland, with subsequent vigorous efforts towards bringing about a peace with the Western powers. Towards this end, he had probably hoped (a) to neutralize Russia during his "blitzkrieg" vis-à-vis Poland, and (b) subsequently intimidate the Western powers by the implications of a German-Russian Pact. In other words, he hoped to make the Bolshevik "bogey" and its implied joint action with Nazism serve as a pressuring instrument vis-à-vis Britain and France, in an effort to make them more responsive to peace proposals in the western theater.

Failing in these efforts, Herr Hitler might conceivably enter into a joint program with Stalin, envisaging the redrawing of the map of Europe. During the period of Herr Hitler's efforts to free himself of a conflict in the West, I should look for him to put the wheels of his "propaganda machinery" in motion towards subtly building up the Bolshevik "bogey" and picturing it as the "world's menace No. 1". In this connection, Herr Hitler would probably work on the neutrals. Moreover, he might possibly encourage Italy, (the sole member of the Axis free to express openly its consistent dread of the Bolshevik doctrine) to launch a propaganda campaign aimed at playing up Bolshevism as Europe's paramount danger. Indeed, were Signor Mussolini to perceive anywhere along the line that the Western powers were gaining superiority over Germany, it is not inconceivable that Signor Mussolini, fearing Herr Hitler's fall might spell his own undoing, and therefore hoping to keep the Nazi regime intact, might spare no effort in staging a propaganda "play-up" along the above lines.

The foregoing observations are all based upon the assumption that Britain and France do not contemplate initiating offensive action, due mainly to the desire first to acquire equality if not superiority in the air. If action by Germany and/or Russia should in the meantime prompt the Western powers to take the initiative, this of course might change the whole picture. It is, moreover, not inconceivable that the Polish-German conflict represented only one of several episodes in the current war. Should the scare methods of Herr Hitler and the political pressures of the "peace-at-any-price" elements in Western Europe fail towards giving Herr Hitler a free hand in the East, by say March, I should be inclined to look for present hostilities to endure for a minimum of two years.

1. Although there is no published record of this conversation, Eden's concern over a possible Russian-German alliance was such that in 1937 he sent a memorandum to the British Chiefs of Staff warning about the possibility. See *The Memoirs of Anthony Eden* (Boston, 1962), vol. 2, *Facing the Dictators*, p. 590.

2. In January, 1935, Göring visited Poland ostensibly on a hunting expedition but with far-ranging political objectives as targets. He delivered an expansive speech before several high-ranking Polish diplomats and military officials; although

no available source mentions Rydz by name as having been present at this meeting, since he belonged to the latter group in Poland he could well have been there. On this occasion, Göring stressed the common bond of Western civilization that had traditionally joined Poland and Germany together as a "bulwark" against the "Tatar barbarism" of the East, of which Soviet Russia was the latest version, and then proposed that Berlin and Warsaw join forces in an attack on the Soviet Union. In dividing the spoils, Göring assured his listeners that Germany would be content with the northwestern portion of Russia, while Poland could have the entire Ukraine. He subsequently repeated this proposal to Piłsudski himself; in each case, the Polish reaction was openly cold and discouraging. Undoubtedly Beck had this incident in mind in his remark to Biddle. See Szembek, *Diariusz*, 1:230–31. The first clear mention of a Göring-Rydz conversation concerns a meeting in Poland in early 1938, when Rydz had become a major political figure. During Göring's visit to Warsaw on February 23–26, he held a lengthy conversation with Rydz, during which the Nazi leader repeatedly stressed the common threat of the Soviet Union to both Poland and Germany but stopped short of renewing his earlier proposal. See Szembek, *Diariusz*, 4:41–42.

3. Ribbentrop's conversation with Beck is in *DGFP*, D, 5:167–68. The Polish version is in *PWB*, nos. 50–56.

4. The text of the Polish-Soviet Non-Aggression Pact of 1932 is in *PWB*, no. 151. A number of commercial agreements covering a variety of topics were concluded between the two countries in the period following the signing of the non-aggression treaty. Texts of all such trade pacts are in *Dokumenty i materiały do historii stosunków polsko-radzieckich* (Warsaw, 1967), vol. 6.

5. This report is not entirely accurate. During the initial stage of the Moscow talks, the British and French agreed to obtain Poland's approval for the passage of Soviet troops through her territory in the event of war, and they even speculated that mounting German pressure would force the Poles to agree. See *DBFP*, Third Series, 7:2–5. The talks with Russia came to a standstill, however, and Molotov then made this demand as described by Biddle. *DBFP*, Third Series, 7:155. That Beck was unaware of the earlier Anglo-French stance is clear from his *Final Report*, pp. 192–94.

6. The Potemkin-Beck meeting took place on May 10, not in August. Beck, *Final Report*, pp. 191–92.

PART THREE

Diplomatic Documents

As noted in the introductory essay, Ambassador Biddle was particularly skilled at amassing information from widely diverse sources, evaluating and digesting it, and then presenting his conclusions to Washington in a manner that was comprehensible and remarkably prescient. He was a prolific producer of dispatches, situation reports, and analytical memoranda, all distinguished by insight and clarity. Moreover, because of his close personal relationship with President Roosevelt, Biddle frequently corresponded directly with the White House. Irrespective of form, however, all of his reports reveal the impressive breadth of interest and wealth of personal contacts that Biddle employed in his work. In addition to such obvious topics as Poland's relations with Germany, the Soviet Union, Britain, France, and the United States, he was also concerned with domestic political developments, especially the problem of the national minorities. Biddle's sources ranged from Foreign Minister Beck and other high-ranking Polish officials to American labor leaders, Nazi Party propaganda officials, and fellow diplomats in Warsaw. Thanks to his diligent research and reporting, Washington obtained a complete and, as it transpired, extremely accurate picture of the Polish as well as the international political and economic scene.

In selecting the documents presented below, the editors

were guided by a desire to demonstrate the skills in observation and deduction that Biddle manifested consistently. Particular care was taken to choose materials that would complement those few dispatches already published in the series *Foreign Relations of the United States*. Two items have been published elsewhere, in part or in their entirety, and this fact has been duly noted. Nonetheless, they are included herein either because of their direct pertinence to the events that Biddle was describing, or as excellent examples of his superb analytical and reportorial abilities. With these exceptions, however, all documents appear for the first time in print in this collection.[1]

In preparing the documents for publication, the editors have proceeded as they did in editing the lengthy report. As a convenience to the reader, the involved formal introductions and closings of dispatches and letters have been omitted. Furthermore, all of the code ciphers and diplomatic transmittal formulae have been removed from the papers; unless the document in question is identified specifically as a "memorandum" or "telegram," or is obviously a personal letter to Roosevelt, it is a routine diplomatic dispatch. The editors assigned the number that heads each entry, and only materials not originating from Warsaw have the point of origin noted. Otherwise, the material is presented exactly as it left Biddle's office. All parenthetical expressions, indications of emphasis, and colloquial phrases are his; moreover, footnote material added by Biddle himself is carefully acknowledged as such. The listing of the documents in chronological order reveals not only the unfolding panorama of European politics on the eve of World War II but also the evolution in perspective and interpretation of Biddle and the Polish government.

---

1. All of the documents published below are deposited in the Franklin D. Roosevelt Library, Hyde Park, New York.

July 26, 1937

My dear Mr. President:

With the passing of each day both Margaret and I are feeling more at home in Poland. We were fortunate to have arrived at the height of the short "spring season" during which the President and other Government officials were in Warsaw. This served to accelerate arrangements for the presentation of my credentials.

The occasion of my presentation was indeed a magnificent, picturesque, and efficiently conducted ceremony. I sensed a distinct effort on the part of the President, his Cabinet, and of officials all along the line to make this ceremony an especially impressive one, as a particularly friendly gesture to yourself and to our Nation. My impression has since been confirmed on numerous occasions by confidential remarks by leading officials here to the effect that they hoped I was pleased with the details of the ceremony, for they had been happy to carry out instructions calling for more effort in connection therewith than with any like ceremony in the past. In this connection, they pointed out that for the first time on record General Wieniawa-Długoszowski,[1] formerly a close friend and aide-de-camp to the late Marshal Piłsudski, had especially requested to be allowed to receive me on the occasion of my laying a wreath at the Tomb of the Unknown Soldier (this occasion immediately followed the main ceremony). In brief, it was gratifying for me to learn, by this gesture on the part of the Government, the high esteem in which you and our Nation are held in Poland.

Moreover, because of my profound affection for, and genuine pride in you I was in no small measure touched by the personal remarks which President Mościcki, in the presence of Colonel Beck, Minister for Foreign Affairs, made to me during my private audience. Colonel Beck, moreover, joined wholeheartedly in support of the President's remarks. In effect, the President stated that you had engaged his sincere interest from the very moment that you took over the reins of our Government. He had recognized the widespread difficulties with which you had been confronted on the very day you took office and had followed with the keenest interest your subsequent moves, the substance of your program, and the methods whereby you had so courageously and intelligently succeeded in arresting the vertical decline of prices and the panic tendency. Not only had it been a remarkable feat to arrest the momentum of a depression of such magnitude, but also an outstanding accomplishment to have set the wheels of industry again in motion, and to have restored confidence, and to have given the Nation— so to speak—a fresh start. Indeed, this had represented a great achievement—brought about by your own courageous intelligence, and withal your constant sympathetic regard for and understanding of humanity. What you had accomplished had engaged the interest and study on the part of the whole world. Your prestige and influence had advanced so tremendously that your constructive moves in the direction of world peace were being followed with utmost interest everywhere. President Mościcki hoped that, in view of all the many and important tasks with which you were daily faced, you could find time to rest, at least occasionally. Indeed, he stated with emphasis that it should be the duty of everyone close to you to see that you took excellent care of your health towards maintaining that extraordinary vitality and energy which was contributing so importantly to your courageous and able direction of the Nation's renewed forward movement.

At this point, Colonel Beck, with genuine sincerity, stated he heartily subscribed to all the President had said.

I then had the pleasure of describing to them both my last visit with you at the White House. It was on the morning of your departure for Charleston, where you boarded the boat to sail for the Buenos Aires Conference.[2] It was soon after the elections which had been preceded by a lengthy campaign in which you yourself had so energetically participated. I had never seen you in better health and spirits, despite your arduous campaigning activities. Indeed, I was at that moment more impressed than ever with your extraordinary combination of vitality, dynamic energy, and calmness.

The President was delighted to learn this and requested me to convey to you his every good wish for continued happiness, health, and success.

Another occasion which has afforded me a sense of real pleasure was that of my meeting with the Nuncio, Monsignor Philippe Cortesi.[3] He had just arrived from Buenos Aires, where he had served as Nuncio for some time. He is a man who, from all accounts, justly gained an enviable reputation during his period of service there, and even during the short time he has been here he has come to be regarded generally with affection and esteem. He told me with great sincerity that his meeting with you and your son in Buenos Aires had been a source of genuine pleasure for him. He had had a talk with you and had observed the unparalleled welcome accorded you in Buenos Aires. The spirit with which this welcome was given by the people on the streets, as well as by the officials, the expressions on the peoples' faces as they greeted you, all had made an indelible impression on the Nuncio's mind. Then, during his subsequent conversation with you, he felt that he had acquired a real insight into your inner self. He was profoundly impressed with your humanitarian outlook, your spiritual sense, your courageous intelligence, and innate kindness to all with whom you came in contact. Indeed, you inspired the best in everyone. Besides, the Nuncio was thankful that there was such a truly beneficial influence in the world of today. He entertained the hope of going to the United States in the not far distant future, at which time he sincerely hoped that he might have the honor of an audience with you. . . .

1. Brigadier General Bolesław Wieniawa-Długoszowski, a physician by training, was one of Piłsudski's most intimate collaborators. He had served the Marshal closely during World War I, the Russo-Polish conflict (1919–20), and the brief period when Piłsudski held supreme political power legally; he also played a major role in organizing segments of the Polish military establishment in support of the 1926 coup d'etat. He then served briefly in the diplomatic service as a military attaché in Paris and Bucharest, and later returned to the army as a ranking officer in the General Inspectorate of the Armed Forces and the commander of the Warsaw garrison. A strong backer of Beck, he was appointed ambassador to Italy in 1938, and served for a brief period in September, 1939, as the successor to President Mościcki. For an account of his Rome embassy, see Marian Romeyko, *Wspomnienia o Wieniawie i o Rzymskich Czasach* (London, 1969).

2. The Buenos Aires Conference took place in November, 1936.

3. Cortesi was the Papal Nuncio in Poland during Biddle's tenure, 1937–39.

July 10, 1937

Memorandum

Matthew Woll,[1] in my conversation with him during his visit here, stated in effect [that] the reason Warsaw had been chosen as the meeting place for the Congress of International Federation of Trade Unions was the following:

The British and French labor organizations, working in many respects along the same international political lines as their respective Governments, had engineered the meeting here in order to appeal to the laboring classes of Poland and other small neighboring states to bring pressure on their respective Governments to remain independent of the influences of the larger neighboring states. Both British and French delegates were careful not to mention the latter by name but their identities were obviously Germany and Italy. Britain realized she could no longer definitely count on her colonies as in the past and required some time yet before attaining her proposed peak in armament. The Dominions Conference[2] had resulted in a demand for a fresh examination of Britain's position *vis-à vis* Germany. The British Air Force and Navy would be up to standard in eighteen months, but a continued decline in enlistments would prevent the Army's being up to proposed strength by that time. Conscription would undoubtedly call for a general election. Hence, Britain's present attitude in respect to Spain as well as her currently adopted means of cir-

cumventing Germany's attempts to gain control, in one capacity or another, of smaller states in this part of Europe.
Including Sir Walter Citrine, President of the International
Federation of Labor Unions, the various delegates to the Congress had deliberately given Woll the following impression: if
Franco won in Spain they believed Poland would become the
scene for the next test between the two ideologies. Though
Citrine, at the meeting on July 2nd, had already publicly
stated he believed it would be Czechoslovakia, he subsequently confidentially told Woll he *really* believed it would be Poland. Citrine, moreover, had told Woll that, in his opinion,
the two ideologies, Fascism and Communism, had different
aims but applied similar methods towards obtaining their respective objectives.

Woll's discussions with various delegates had given him
the impression that labor circles looked for a military dictatorship to replace Stalin, such a dictatorship to be followed by a
gradual breaking up of the Soviet Union into autonomous
states. Moreover, Germany was exerting no little influence
towards this end.

Regarding the Comintern, Woll said that when Trotsky and
Lenin came to power, they were faced with a lack of ade-
quately armed and equipped, as well as coordinated, defense.
Hence, among other aims, the establishment of the Comintern envisaged holding at bay other nations which might wish
to intervene in Soviet affairs during the formative stages of
organizing the Communist State. The Comintern directed its
efforts along the lines of an "inside job", towards internally
weakening, if not crippling, and thus holding off the opposition. They, Lenin and Trotsky, so to speak, augmented their own
defensive forces by subversively enlisting the support of as
large a portion as possible of the other nations' manpower.
Woll had gained the impression that the Comintern's efforts
were not currently proving as effective on the Continent as in
the past, since they had provoked a forceful resistance. Hence
the Comintern had turned to the United States. In continuing
to apply like methods today, the Comintern aimed to gain
control of the merchant marine on a worldwide basis. In

this connection, Woll said the Comintern's efforts were now directed towards gaining a strong foothold in the unions engaged in our own shipping industry. He added that thus the Comintern aimed to control ocean transportation facilities eventually throughout the world with the objective of bringing about a paralysis of shipments of goods, food, and ammunition in the event of war.

Regarding the internal structure of the International Federation of Labor Unions, France and Belgium actually dominated the organization as a whole. French and Belgian delegates played up to the labor of the Latin countries, the British played ball with the French up to a certain point but avoided becoming involved in France's Communistic tie-up. Léon Jouhaux, President of *Confédération Générale du Travail*, the French delegate, though not formerly Communist-minded, now had to play ball with the Communists for he was accompanied here by a Communist Committee from his own labor organization. Besides, Jouhaux's long-time personal antipathy for Mussolini led him, consciously or unconsciously, to support the cause, opposed to Mussolini's doctrine. The British were none too sure of France's position due to these Communist leanings; hence there was an increasing desire on the British delegates' part to gain the cooperation of American labor organizations. The British admittedly would feel more secure were American labor represented at the Congress. Woll's own impression was that the Jews in the International Federation of Labor Unions were strenuously endeavoring to gain a foothold in the organization's control. This was becoming more obvious every day.

Various delegates, the British and French in particular, had, for Woll's benefit, deliberately painted a black picture of economic and labor conditions here. Moreover, they had obviously determined to discredit by inference the present Polish Government.

At the same time, Woll had been told that the underlying situation in Poland was a volcanic condition due to following facts:

(a) Poland had made a grave mistake in not having adopted

land reform such as the Baltic States had done. One of the contributing reasons for [the] peasants' difficulties here was that the landed nobility were allowed to retain their vast estates. These properties should have been split up into farms and made available to the surplus peasant population.[3]

(b)   Peasants' sons were raised on extremely meager living standard until reaching military age. They were thereupon taken into the army where they were fed well and generally well cared for. At the termination of the military training period they were released to go back to the farms and to return to their meager standard of living. The Government should establish and organize means for engaging these men after their training period in order to prevent discontent consequent to the drastic contrast between their welfare in the army and their subsequent return to poor living conditions. It was of utmost importance for the Government to create such means in order to secure these men as pillars of the State. Otherwise, they would become prey to the influences of radical organizers.

(c)   The Jews felt themselves steadily becoming the objects of intolerance. They were resentful, fearful, and bewildered.

(d)   In this connection, the Jews are apprehensive lest a continued lack of rainfall would mean a poor harvest and consequent bad times this winter. They felt that this would mean greater pressure against their race.

(In relation to the Jewish problem here, Woll believed the problem was fundamentally an economic one. However, it was an economic problem associated with and emphasized by the racial characteristics of the Jews.)[4]

(e)   It was generally believed here that the Fascist element in Government circles was behind the present drive against the Jews. In this connection, the labor delegates pointed out that three-quarters of the Government was Fascist-minded and only one-quarter liberal. So far the one-quarter had succeeded in tempering the otherwise more drastic actions of the majority. It was further felt by these delegates that the Hitler régime is playing for control of this Government.[5] . . .

1. Matthew Woll, a leading figure in the Photoengravers Union, was one of the chief representatives of the conservative wing in the American labor movement. First as head of the National Civic Federation and later as a spokesman for the American Federation of Labor, Woll emerged as a symbol of old-guard opposition to the industrial unionism exemplified by the Congress of Industrial Organizations, and led the "Red-baiting" campaign against that organization. Woll's views on European labor and Polish domestic conditions are quite well-founded; more important, they typify those opinions about Poland held by many Americans. Finally, this document is of interest as an example of the broad, diverse contacts employed by Biddle in shaping his own interpretations of the contemporary Polish scene.

2. The Dominions Conference of Prime Ministers took place in May, 1937, in London.

3. The state of Polish agriculture's structure was not as depressing as Woll presents it, although there were some serious problems. Despite well-organized opposition from church and landowning circles, land reform made substantial progress before the war: in the period 1919–38, a total of 2,654,800 hectares of arable land were distributed among Polish small and medium farmers or used to set up model experimental farms (1 hectare equals about 2.47 acres). In addition, over 5,000,000 hectares of scattered holdings were consolidated into efficient agricultural units, and another 558,700 hectares were reclaimed for agricultural use. Despite these gains, however, Polish agriculture was still structurally top-heavy: although large estates accounted for less than 1 percent of the total number of farms, they embraced 43 percent of arable cropland, whereas 65 percent of all farmers owned only 15 percent of the land. See the statistical studies, *Mały Rocznik Statystyczny 1939*, pp. 68–72, tables 1–6, and *Poland in Facts and Figures, 1944–1964* (Warsaw, 1964), pp. 31–32, 51–52. See also Ferdynand Zweig, *Poland between Two Wars* (London, 1944), pp. 130–34. However, given such serious internal problems as a steadily expanding population (due to a rising birthrate and a decline in emigration to the United States) coupled with the slow pace of industrial development caused by the shortage of investment capital, it is doubtful whether a more aggressive and effective land reform would have produced any immediate improvement.

4. Although the more than 3,000,000 Jews constituted only about 10 percent of the country's total population, they dominated much of the lower middle-class occupational levels (business, artisans) and professional groups, and were concentrated in the larger cities; hence, an expanding Polish population in search of industrial, commerical, or professional employment tended to view the Jews as competitors for a limited prize. Moreover, the Hasidic beliefs of many Polish Jews set them apart from the Christian population in terms of dress, customs, and language. Of the substantial literature of this topic, see especially Szymon Bronsztejn, *Ludność żydowska w Polsce w okresie międzywojennej. Studium statystyczne* (Wrocław, 1963), and Simon Segal, *The New Poland and the Jews* (New York, 1950).

5. While there is no evidence that Hitler actually or directly meddled in Polish domestic politics, there is no doubt that Polish crypto-Fascists had a powerful voice in government circles during this period; moreover, close ties existed between this element and the Italian Fascists. For details, see Edward D. Wynot, Jr., *Polish Politics in Transition: The Camp of National Unity and the Struggle for Power, 1935–1939* (Athens, Ga., 1974). For a discussion of the regime's Jewish policy during this period, see the same author's " 'A Necessary Cruelty': The Emergence of Official Anti-Semitism in Poland, 1936-1939," *American Historical Review* 76, 4 (October, 1971):1035-58.

August 28, 1937

My dear Mr. President:

I greatly appreciate your thoughtful letter of August 16 which came in yesterday's diplomatic pouch. I am especially gratified to learn that the State Department has told you that my despatches have been proving of interest, for I love my work, and have been doing my utmost towards acquiring a clear picture of Poland in terms both of domestic and foreign policy. I am happy to say, that the attitude on the part of Colonel Jozef Beck, Polish Minister for Foreign Affairs, towards me has been frank and most friendly. Indeed, this cordial relationship has proven extremely helpful to me since my arrival here. From my own observation, Colonel Beck is steadily becoming the leading force in the Polish Government, due mainly to his initiative, his willingness to make decisions, and to shoulder responsibility. I find in him a man of courage and intelligence.

He has frequently emphasized to me, that his determined objective is the maintenance of independence and peace for Poland. In line with this, he feels that if he succeeds in his aims, he will be contributing his part towards the maintenance of peace in this section of Europe. In this connection, I have noted during our frequent conversations, his increasing emphasis on the importance of what he calls "voisinage"—or the good neighbor policy. In this connection, it is clear to me that he has taken a leaf from your own book.

As regards his direction of his country's foreign affairs, he admits his "tight-rope walking" role is a difficult one. He enjoys it, however, and has so far proven himself capable of dealing with the various complicated phases entailed in Eastern European affairs. He was profoundly touched by the substance of a message which you transmitted to him through Ambassador George [Jerzy] Potocki,[1] who recently arrived here from Washington. The Colonel told me, in effect that it afforded him the sense of utmost gratification, thus to learn, that his own efforts to preserve peace in this part of the world had come to your notice. Indeed, he was frankly profoundly touched.

In closing, may I not express to you my most profound felicitations upon your grand address at Roanoke Island on August 18.[2] Both Margaret and I derived a real thrill from this forceful declaration. It was simply splendid! . . .

1. Ambassador to the United States from May, 1936, to December, 1940. Previously, he had served as Polish ambassador to Italy and Turkey.

2. The text of the Roanoke Island address is in Franklin D. Roosevelt, *The Public Papers and Addresses*, 6:326–33.

[June 19, 1938]

Streamline observations on various aspects of [the] complex effect of Hitler's expansion program—in terms of (a) Poland's short and long-term objective and (b) its general bearing on Eastern and Central Europe (from the Polish viewpoint)

In examining the forces which have influenced, and in many cases determined, the course of events leading to the present tense situation in Europe, I have herein endeavored to fit together some of the pieces of the international mosaic which have come under my observation here. My purpose envisages an attempt, from Poland's viewpoint, to peer over the hill of European political confusion, to gain a glimpse of what events are leading to.

From the Eastern and Central European, and particularly the Polish point of view, the potential outcome of events both current and the recent past, may best be evaluated by taking into consideration the implications and possible effect of the following aspects:

(a) Hitler's reportedly envisaged synchronization of an eastward expansion policy with his four-year economy plan.

(b) Mussolini's and Hitler's apparent attempts respectively to shake loose France and Czechoslovakia from their alliances with the Soviet. (According to the Polish viewpoint, Hitler sees in a severance of these ties a clearer pathway for his envisaged ultimate infiltration of the Ukraine, and Mussolini conceivably wishes to clear the path for Hitler's envisaged drive as a means of diverting his course from the Adriatic to the Ukraine).

(c)   Potential effect of Austria's annexation upon economic-political outlook of Central and Eastern Europe and of Poland in particular.

(d)   Poland's position in respect to Hitler's plans.

In the course of discrete inquiry as to Polish observations on a rumor going the rounds in diplomatic circles to the effect that Hitler envisaged a policy of German infiltration of certain states including the Ukraine, by stages, in synchronization with his four-year economy plan, a high ranking informed Polish official imparted to me in *strictest confidence* there had taken place informal discussions between certain Polish and German officials, wherein the Germans had in vague terms actually mentioned the *Ukraine* in the light of a German long-range objective. In these conversations, which were only of the most *informal* character, the *Germans had done all the talking.* The Poles had *listened only*! Indeed, my informant emphasized this point, and added that a policy envisaging a future aggression vis-à-vis the Soviet in collaboration with Germany was a dangerous one in terms of Poland's long-range interests. On the other hand, by listening, the Poles had at least to a certain extent gained confirmation of their suspicions as to Germany's long-range aims.

As to the likelihood of Minister Beck's (or his associates') agreeing to collaborate with the Germans in a Ukraine-wards move, Beck, in my opinion would not lend himself beyond the point of *listening* to any such proposal. For, on the one hand, he is not in the habit of committing himself so far in advance, while on the other hand, he could not fail to recognize that such a long-range project would spell eventual vassaldom for Poland (even his close associate, whose observations I have above recited, bore out in effect my opinion in this regard).

It is, moreover, well to bear in mind that notable among Beck's characteristics are his alertness and elasticity of mind; moreover, due perhaps to his military training, [considerations of] strategy discernably marks all phases of his direction of Poland's foreign policy. Hence for each move forward, he generally leaves himself two ways for retreat (see my despatch No. 194 of October 7, 1937).[2]

Beck's tendency to color the direction of his foreign policy with the effects of his former military training was also in part illustrated by his remark to me to the effect that according to Article III of the Polish cavalry and artillery regulations, once the command to "gallop" had been given, the direction of the "charge" could not be changed. Hence, it was necessary for the commanding officer to study every possible angle in advance, in an effort, not only to appraise his opponents' position, but also to make sure that the "charge" under consideration was properly conceived, timed, and directed. Minister Beck added significantly that this principle formed one of the cardinal considerations which guided his direction of Poland's foreign policy. Indeed, he realized that before embarking on any positive line of policy in one direction or another, it was essential to devote undivided study to the effect and implications, in terms both of short and long-range outlook; for once his country had actually embarked upon a given positive course, there was no veering as to direction, nor turning back.

It is safe to say that, if between now and the next four years, any feasible measure presents itself whereby Beck can avoid Poland's vassalage to Germany, he would take advantage of it. Moreover, to my mind, Beck aims to confine the German frontier to the minimum vis-à-vis Poland; consequently, at this point, I would not look for him to involve himself as a party to any envisaged extension of the Polish-German frontier. As to whether Poland might in the future become a party to such a scheme under certain circumstances, it is, in my opinion conceivable, *but only* if at the time the economic-political-military circumstances were such as to offer Beck no alternative. In other words, in such a case, he might conceivably be driven to collaboration in the German Ukraine drive.

In conclusion, it is well to bear in mind that one of Beck's guiding policies is to keep Poland in such a position as to jump at a moment's notice in the direction which Beck feels will serve Poland's interests to the best advantage.

Strict adherence to this policy would preclude his agreement to such a long-range German-envisaged Ukraine project which in the end would only accrue to Poland's disadvantage in terms of peace, independence and international prestige.

Poland's playing into the hands of Germany would be, I believe, in conflict with Beck's policy of counter-balancing German eastward expansion. Moreover, I do not believe that the acquisition of additional lands would hold any temptation for Poland. My observations lead me to feel that the acquisition of any part of the Russian Ukraine would fail to compensate Poland for having Germany on her East and South as well as her West. As a matter of fact, Poland is having none too comfortable a time as it is, with Germany at her West. Indeed, there is an undisclosed but deep-lying apprehension here over the potential threat of Germany vis-à-vis Upper Silesia, the Corridor, and Danzig. In the eyes of Polish officialdom, each fresh evidence of Germany's territorial appetite makes those three points loom more grimly as potential objects of German aspirations.

Poland has gained the impression that for the moment Germany welcomes a strong Poland to serve as a buffer between herself and the Soviet during Germany's consolidation of her position in Central Europe. Informed veteran observers in Polish inner Government circles, however, regard this merely as temporary comfort, for they have not forgotten their former Master's (Piłsudski's) warning to the effect that Poland must in all possible ways make friends with Germany during peace time, in order to allow Poland time to strengthen herself sufficiently to meet an inevitable eventual German challenge.

Of connected bearing, I take occasion to recite the following paraphrased excerpts from my cable No. 88 of May 23:[3] Further light might be thrown on the motives underlying the present Polish course of action respecting Czechoslovakia by the following:

1. Poland, in my opinion, may be expected more and more to recognize that a conflict of German and Polish interests is being led to by events in the making.

2. Briefly, I am cognizant that the deep-seated desire of Polish officialdom, although undisclosed, is to keep Czechoslovakia from becoming a German arrow pointing too far east and running along the southern border of Poland, as a direct and dreaded contact between Germany and the Polish Ukraine minority would thereby be allowed. [This] contact,

Polish official circles feel, Germany would employ as a way of indirectly contacting the Russian Ukraine, to the end of the ultimate infiltration with German politico-economic hegemony of the Ukraine, and as an instrument of pressure against Poland. Official circles in Warsaw in this connection see a possible German encirclement of Poland in the potential expansion of German hegemony along the eastern borders of Poland, which would be a threat to Poland's peace and independence.

3. The more positive, moreover, does the character of the politico-economic drive of Germany become, the more in my opinion, will the interests of Germany and Poland clash, for it is my belief that Germany's push at present has caused the rise of Polish hopes that a close tie-up with a Slovak minority, favorable both to Hungary and Poland, might strengthen Hungary's hand and serve to block Germany's infiltration of the whole of Czechoslovakia.[4] It would appear that this is in conflict with the suspected encouragement by Germany of Hungary's appetite in the direction of Transylvania.

4. German-Polish interests clash again in Rumania, for Poland is not pleased at the prospect of German infiltration into her ally's territory.[5]

Of further important bearing, in the course of conversation just previous to his departure for Stockholm, Beck imparted in strictest confidence what I consider to be a most enlightening disclosure of his foreign policy in terms of the long-range outlook. In effect he said he felt that some day, in the event that Germany might find an envisaged acquisition of the Ukraine impossible through Nazi-styled "peaceful penetration", Poland might have to fight to prevent passage of German troops over her territory, which from the German military viewpoint would represent the most direct route to the Ukraine. In such event, Germany would attack Poland, not as the *objective*, but as the *means* of reaching Germany's envisaged Ukrainian objective.

Poland would resist such an attack with every force at her command in order not only to eject the Germans from Poland's soil, but also to prevent them from seizing the Ukraine, for German occupation of the Ukraine would constitute a menace to Poland's peace and independence. In such efforts, Poland might face potential defeat, but she would delay and "bleed" Germany to such an extent that eventually through Poland's resistance, together with the force of an almost inevitable subsequent Anglo-French-German clash on Germany's Western front, Germany would be prevented from obtaining her objective.

In conclusion, Beck said he would, in effect, discreetly and strictly confidentially impart his aforementioned views to certain representatives of Scandinavian and Baltic states with whom he intended to confer in Stockholm, pointing out to them that particularly the Baltic states, due to their geo-political position, would inevitably suffer as potentially dangerous an outlook as Poland, in the event of a German seizure of the Ukraine. Moreover, he would make clear his opinion that the Baltics occupied a geo-political position similar to that of Poland's in respect both to Germany and the Soviet.

Even before his departure for Stockholm, he confidentially imparted the above line of thought to the Estonian Minister here, who had played so important a mediatory role during the Polish-Lithuanian dispute.[6] At the same time, Beck arranged with the latter a forward date for a formal visit to Tallinn, whereby Beck would be enabled both to express his profound sense of gratitude to the Estonian Government for their important mediatory contribution during the heated stages of the aforementioned quarrel, and to emphasize discreetly his aforecited views on the Baltics' sharing Poland's geo-political position.

Since Beck's return from his Stockholm and Tallinn visits, I have derived an impression in my numerous conversations with him that he was satisfied with the results of both trips. In brief, from my own observations, I feel that both voyages might be characterized, on the one hand, by Beck's soundings as to Scandinavian and Baltic capacity and willingness to resist ideological forces through the maintenance of a firm "active" neutrality policy, while on the other, "diplomatic shopping" on Poland's behalf. As to the effect thereof on Poland's position in the international political arena, my observations lead me to believe Beck made a good turn for his country in the light both of drawing closer to "Downing Street" through the medium of London-inclined Sandler,[7] and of strengthening Poland-Baltic ties.

In response to my further inquiry, an informed high ranking Polish official, and close associate of Beck's, frankly stated that to extend Germany's frontier vis-à-vis Poland along the south and east, would work a serious disadvantage for Poland. Indeed, the only conceivable way Poland might off-set the disadvantage of Germany's occupation of the Ukraine, would be a Polish tactical move to occupy White Russia.[8] Thus, Poland might gain a strategic position whereby she might hope to prevent Germany's eventually covering Poland's entire eastern frontier. Moreover, Poland might thus be in a position to counter any possible German attempt to attack Polish territory elsewhere. In other words, such a move on Poland's part would be mainly tactical to block possible German encirclement of Poland which would inevitably spell Poland's vassaldom to Germany.

In line with this explanation, my informant referred me to a book written in the Polish language by Mr. Bocheński, a Pole; the name of the book (translated into English) is, "Between Russia and Germany".[9] My informant recommended it as in many respects one of the most illuminating discussions of Polish policy vis-à-vis both Germany and Russia that he had ever read. While emphasizing that the substance of the book could be taken in no sense as illustrative of official policy, still it represented, to his mind, political observations which were full of possibilities. In brief, the book had pointed out that in the event of a German seizure of the Ukraine by troops transported via territory south of Poland and by air, Poland's only alternative would be to seize the territory immediately north of the Ukraine. In at least this respect, the book corresponded with my informant's ideas as to what Poland's course might necessarily be in event of German action vis-à-vis the Soviet.

In further discussing Germany's Ukrainian objective, my competent informant stated [that] his intelligence reports indicated that German officialdom expected a continued period of weakness in the Soviet's internal structure to lead to an eventual break-down, whereby resistance to aggression would be reduced to a minimum.[10] Indeed, the Germans felt that if present conditions lead to a military revolution, "skill-fully" supported in advance from the outside, matters might even develop so that German military "specialists" would be called in to assist both in the restoration of order and in the reorganization of the military structure. My informant then pointed out that German policy, vis-à-vis the Soviet has for long been one envisaging a long-range "inside job", entail-ing the secret enrollment of executives and officials occupying key positions in *coup-aimed* organizations, and a subsequent subversive propagandizing of the masses.

Of related bearing, the Japanese Ambassador to Poland, [Shuichi] Sakoh, came into possession of a confidential report covering a meeting as of December 24, [1937,] of the Soviet Government Council at the Kremlin (see my cable No. 33 March 25, 3 p.m.)[11] wherein among other points, it was con-cluded that of the two threats to Soviet security, Japan cur-rently comprised the more immediate danger as compared with Germany. Moreover, it was concluded that the Soviet was in no position to fight on two fronts, etc. I understand that the substance of this report is known both to the Govern-ment in Warsaw, and to that in Berlin. In addition to this, highest military circles here disclose their reports to the effect that the majority of Brigadier Generals presently being ap-pointed by the Soviet are officers who were made captains as recently as 1936. This, among other confidential information dealing with the weakened condition of the Soviet military establishment, are known to the Governments of Warsaw, Ankara, and Berlin.

In connection with the foregoing it is significant to me that during his recent participation in the examination at the Polish-Soviet border of prisoners returning home from Soviet prison camps, a responsible individual informed me that during the past several months he found these returning prisoners averaged ten to fifteen per day, all Germans. My informant felt that the preponderance of German prisoners in these various camps indicated Soviet distrust and a concentrated campaign against the German group in the Soviet by the authorities thereof. Moreover, in turn, he felt that this might indicate a concentrated German subversive effort against the Soviet Government.

In other words, this reported[ly] subversive German policy entailed reaching over and getting a firm grip on certain personalities in key positions for the purpose of using them in their scheme when the time was "ripe". Then, when there were sufficient signs of decomposition setting in, these agents throughout the [Soviet] political and military structure would operate, not only towards giving the situation the needed "shove" to bring on a revolution, but also to steer their respective departments in the direction of calling for German assistance.

In commenting upon Hitler's suspected envisaged methods of accomplishing his Ukrainian objective by means of an "inside job", an informed high military authority stated that the German General Staff were fully aware of the difficulties to be encountered in guarding the extensive northern line of [the] Ukraine against a possible eventual attack by Soviet forces. As a matter of fact, few people realized how enormous was the Ukraine, and amongst those who were familiar with that territory there was a division of opinion as to whether the Ukraine extended to the Don or even to the Caucasus. Besides the difficulty of guarding such a huge territory against the invasion, Hitler was aware of the risks entailed in a military seizure. In other words, why run a military risk, when there existed the possiblity of his machinations bringing about the Ukraine's falling into his lap.

It would seem from all reports that Mussolini has reverted to his policy of 1933: to endeavor to steer Germany into Russia as a means of leaving Mussolini's interest in the Balkans alone. In connection with this, informed veteran observers in official circles here discern through the fog of international political confusion, characterized by maneuvers and counter maneuvers, the earmarks of at least one development in the making: namely, an attempt both on the part of Rome and Berlin, but for respectively different reasons, to shake France and Czechoslovakia loose from their respective alliances with the Soviet. In this connection my informants' reports lead them to feel Mussolini is aware of Hitler's long-range aim to infiltrate the Ukraine with Nazi economic and political hegemony, in connection with which objective Mussolini perceives an "out" for his own prospective intra-axis difficulties—in other words, a means of getting Hitler "off his neck" in those states which Mussolini had hitherto regarded as lying within the sphere of Italy's economic-political influence and wherein Mussolini fears Hitler might eventually "muscle in" at the expense of Italian interest.

An informed Polish official confidentially remarked that despite a potential conflict of Italo-German interests in several domains, the Axis, in his opinion, would probably remain intact—if not as hitherto active—for after all, it had so far cost little to maintain and had proven a source of profit for both axis points. Indeed, so far, disadvantages were limited to intra-Axis differences—and in this connection just how long Mussolini would continue to accept the short end of the profits, remained the outstanding question.

Hitler, on the other hand, according to my informants' observations, seeing the Ukraine a potentially valuable consumers' market, as well as a source of commodities supply, aimed to gain economic-political domination there—not, however, by resort to arms, but by means of a typical Hitlerian "inside job" styled by Hitler and his Nazi associates as "peaceful penetration". Hitler's successes in carrying forward these methods of power-politics had given him added encouragement to believe he could perform a similar operation on the Soviet. Indeed, his cunning and insidious machinations had already been in operation throughout the Soviet political military structure for some time, "boring in" and preparing for the day when all that might be necessary to bring on a military revolution would be the essential shove at vital points at the psychological moment. In event that such a day dawned, a pre-conceived Berlin-inspired "invitation" might conceivably issue to Berlin, from a "newly-formed military Government" under influence of Berlin-planted agents in Moscow, inviting Berlin to send in "specialists" and "technicians" to assist in a program of reconstruction and reorganization. According to the observations of my competent informants, this was the scheme envisaged by Hitler, whereby he hoped eventually to gain political and economic dominance over the Ukraine. Moreover, such were the purposes respectively motivating the activities of Mussolini and Hitler as regards Hitler's envisaged control over the Ukraine.

I have gained the impression that as the picture now presents itself, Polish official circles perceive the following courses in the making:

(a) Germany's envisaged political-economic drive to the Black Sea, to Istanbul and beyond.

(b) Britain's vigorous role as an honest peace-broker in her efforts to liquidate the Spanish and Czechoslovak problems. (Regarded here as the first stage potentially leading to an Anglo-German settlement in a subsequent stage of Britain's envisaged ambitious program for European appeasement and pacification.)

Polish officialdom feels in this connection that Britain's concern lest France might become involved in a continental war and drag in Britain has led Chamberlain to press into force all possible measures towards preventing a continental eruption. Moreover, they feel that the British have been trying to get the French to soft-pedal their ire in respect to the Czechoslovak issue, and have been giving France encouragement to "put to sleep" her alliance with the Soviet, for they feel that Britain has come to suspect that Moscow's continued practice of her policy of irritation might conceivably lead to a European "jam" of major proportions.

(c) Polish officialdom foresees also the possibility of an alternative course on Britain's part. Should Britain fail in an attempt to bring Germany into line, Britain together with

France might conceivably resort to a counter-policy vis-à-vis Germany's envisaged expansion program—hoping that even though Italy might refuse to support such a counter-policy, she might at least remain neutral.

Of pertinent bearing, official circles here feel that Chamberlain is fully cognizant of the complexities entailed in an envisaged Anglo-German settlement. Indeed, my informants here are inclined to regard the prospects of such negotiations with considerable pessimism. This view is attributable in part to my informants' feeling that Chamberlain does not yet enjoy the full support of British public opinion, an important part of which is still opposed to any conciliatory deal with the dictators. However, my informants look for Chamberlain to continue in his persistent efforts to bring Hitler into a round-table discussion looking to a settlement of grievances. Should such a settlement fall short of success, Chamberlain would be in a position at least to draw not only the world's attention, but more importantly so, his dominions' attention, to the fact that Britain had left no stone unturned in her efforts towards bettering her relations with Germany. (My informants have not forgotten that at the Dominions' Conference a little over a year ago, the question was put to Chamberlain as to whether he was sure that his Government had left no stone unturned towards ameliorating Anglo-German relations. This question was put, according to subsequent reports, on the heels of Chamberlain's urge that the Dominions join Britain in rearming on an Empire scale).

Polish officialdom sees in the possible development of a counter-policy a potential opportunity for Poland to play a key-role, possibly in the formation of Poland's long-cherished hope of a neutral Baltic-Black Sea or even Baltic-Aegean Axis, aimed at cutting across Germany's envisaged eastward drive. Poland would want, however, to be assured of ample support from Britain, France, and possibly even Italy, for Poland would expect at least Britain and France to share in any burden of responsibility which the states of Eastern and Central Europe might incur in provoking German ire and suspicion.

On the one hand, Polish officialdom interpreted Chamberlain's conception of the recently concluded Anglo-French military-naval-air understanding as, among others, a strategic move to strengthen his hand for possible eventual conversations with Germany. In this connection, Chamberlain, recognizing Britain had not attained her desired measure of rearmament, considered the French army might fill the gap, Britain supplying other requisites. At the same time, Chamberlain felt that through such an understanding he could more readily exert a restraining influence over the uncertain political forces within France, whose machinations, he considered, might conceivably lead to a continental explosion. By thus gathering his forces behind him, Chamberlain felt he could face Hitler around the table with a "full hand".

With this interpretation in mind, Polish officialdom is aware of French irritation over the French-Polish alliance, whereof the French are apt to emphasize the political aspect, while the Poles emphasize the military. The Polish Government are not unduly concerned over the fact that the French might consider a withdrawal therefrom—for Polish officialdom feels on the one hand that the French would not move without the British, while on the other hand, (though not yet the British Foreign Office), at least realistic "Downing Street" is gradually coming to recognize more and more the merits of Poland's policy of drastic realism. In further connection therewith, officialdom here looks for Chamberlain to continue not only to direct Britain's foreign policy, but also importantly to influence that of France. As one informed official remarked, "France will continue to take her orders from 10 Downing Street and like it!"

Of pertinent bearing, I continue to discern that under Beck's rather confusing "mugwump" policy,[12] he keeps a close eye on British policy. *To my mind, Beck though mute on the subject, harbors a distinct hope that a potential eventual linking of forceful Polish action with that of Britain and France in countering Germany's expansion ambitions might prove Poland's best "out" from the grim prospect of becoming either a potential victim of German expansion, or the potential pathway for a German aggression against the Ukraine*, should Germany fail to acquire the latter through the alternative of "peaceful infiltration". In other words, I should look for Poland to be fighting on the side of Britain and France in the event they came to blows with Germany. Moreover, since in terms of long-term military-economic considerations, the combination of France and Britain might conceivably be expected to gain the upper hand, [for] in the long run, Poland's fighting on the Anglo-French side would be consistent with the Polish policy requisite, of "picking the winning horse."

Of connected bearing, Beck sees time playing in favor of Britain and France in terms of military preparations, and favoring Germany in terms of economic-political expansion and consolidation of her position in newly acquired areas. From the standpoint of Poland's objective policy, this expansion may be expected to come steadily more in conflict with Polish interests. Even a German-infiltrated Czechoslovakia would be for Poland, like one's trying to sleep peacefully with a strand of barbed-wire at the foot of one's bed. It is therefore well to bear the foregoing in mind when appraising Polish realistic foreign policy in terms of potential circumstances, over the long pull.

Beck, moreover, is aware that the combined armies of Poland, her ally Rumania, possibly Yugoslavia and Hungary, and even Czechoslovakia, would potentially present an effective resistance to a German eastward military action, provided the British and French forces simultaneously engaged the Germans on the German Western front. Though Poland and Czechoslovakia, fighting side by side might form incongruous military bedmates, their geo-political positions are at least vis-à-vis Germany similar, and an actual German aggression might conceivably throw them on the same side, particularly if Poland were assured of synchronous forceful action on the part of Britain and France in the West. Besides, in such event, Poland would march *not for Czechoslovakia, but against Germany*.

In evaluating Beck's policy, I wish to emphasize the im-

portance of bearing in mind not only Poland's potentially
black outlook in the event either of continued German military or peaceful infiltration eastwards, but also the already
reported disclosure that Beck, according to the Belgian Minister here, was bitterly disappointed over France's refusal to
march, subsequent to Hitler's march into the Rhineland. In
fact, Beck later told me personally that France had made a
great tactical error. To his mind, failure to march at that time
would prove costly in terms of the long-run, not only for
France, but also for Poland and Britain. In other words, they
had "missed the boat", for Germany, their common potential
menace, had at that time been less prepared to resist the
combined forces of France, Britain and Poland, in a lengthy
engagement, than she would be in another year or more.

*   *   *   *   *   *   *   *   *   *   *   *

MINISTER BECK'S VIEWS AS OF JUNE 19, 1938,
ON [THE] CZECHOSLOVAK SITUATION

Beck feels that prudence and caution should guide the
course of European statesmen just as rigidly during periods of
"breathing spells" conducive of optimism (such as the present one), as during volcanic periods conducive of pessimism.

In Beck's opinion the Czechoslovak situation continues to
be:

(a) A vital one, at the mercy of incidents and unpredictable developments.

(b) One calling for cautious observations: What might
for the moment appear to be a "breathing spell" should not
be translated into undue optimism.

Moreover, the situation held three especially potential
dangers:

(a) An attempt by either side to prolong unduly the
Hodža-Henlein negotiations.[13]

(b) The possibility of the Czech Government's answering
conceivable Sudeten resistance to the Government's terms,
(characterized by self-administration) by means provocative
of internal strife, conducive of outside intervention.

(c) Stalin's pursuance of a diplomatic policy aimed at wrecking attempts of appeasement and pacification west of the Russian frontier and the Comintern's reported efforts to keep open the Czechoslovak wound in the heart of Europe.

In connection with the sub-division (a) in the preceeding paragraph, the following observation may be of interest: Beck, whose personal feeling towards Beneš is far from cordial, and whose judgement of Beneš should therefore be considered in such light, feels Beneš' natural inclination is to stall for time, a dangerous course in the light of its conceivably abusing the other side's patience.[14] On the other hand, Beck is concerned lest Beneš, in the event of wanting company in his "misery", might conceivably "strike out" in an attempt to provoke real trouble while the cards are stacked in his favor, namely, among other factors, the support of Britain and France. Moreover, Beck is inclined to question whether, although the French General Staff was reportedly ready to move, and the British were prepared to come along subsequently, either might be so sanguine later, if Beneš overplayed his hand in an undue prolongation of negotiations. Of connected bearing, Beck is aware of France's rather embarrassing position in relation to bringing pressure on her ally, Czechoslovakia, to revise her national policy after twenty years of apparent approval thereof. Under such circumstances it was not easy for French diplomacy to point out to Beneš that he was now facing the necessity of adjusting the balance of political mistakes which his Government had made during the last twenty years. Hence, it was only natural that the Quai d'Orsay was unloading as much of this burden as possible on British shoulders.

* * * * * * * * * * *

MY OBSERVATIONS ON VARIOUS ASPECTS OF
CURRENT TREND OF GERMAN EASTWARD EXPANSION

Chafe at her fetters as she might, it was becoming steadily more apparent that unless "pulled out" by Britain and France, Italy might be expected to remain for some [time] to come an economic-political prisoner of the Berlin-Rome Axis. Whereas the Axis had so far served as an instrument of profit with little or no cost to the shareholders of the incorporated interests, in terms of the Axis' activities a-field the question of comparative intra-Axis profits was steadily becoming a matter of grave consideration for Italian interests. The startling fact was that Italy was not only reaping the short end of the profits, but also faced the struggle to sustain her economic and political position in the Balkans against a German effort to elbow Italian interests out of that area. Indeed, statistics each month show that the position of Italian interests in that sphere is becoming steadily less tenable.

The German export surplus in trade with Italy may be expected to increase as a result of the recently concluded Italo-German trade agreement. Economists here are inclined to feel that recent speeches by prominent Italian statesmen proclaiming confidence that the already demonstrated Rome-Berlin solidarity would be operative in the Balkans, was simply another way of "whistling in the dark". Not only were the Balkans becoming more dependent upon Germany in terms of trade, but, according to statistics, even Italy herself was becoming more so.

Statistics as of 1937, moreover, show that about 24 percent of Italy's total imports come from Germany and Austria combined, and that about 23 percent of Italy's total exports go to Germany and Austria combined, which means that almost 25 percent of Italy's total foreign trade is with Greater Germany.

The fact that a cardinal point in Italy's foreign policy was the maintenance of Italian interests in the Balkans indicated a growing clash of Rome-Berlin interests within that area. For example, a review of 1937 statistics disclosed that Italy's exports to Yugoslavia dwindled from 23 percent of Yugoslavia's total trade to 9 percent thereof. Moreover, imports from Yugoslavia to Italy dwindled from 13 percent to 8 percent.

On the other hand, glancing at the Axis picture from the Berlin end, statistics show that exports from Yugoslavia to

Germany had increased to 35 percent, and German exports to Yugoslavia had increased to 45 percent. In comparing Germany's and Italy's respective shares in Hungarian trade, available figures show that of Hungary's total exports, 53 percent went to Greater Germany against 15 percent to Italy. According to my informant, Hungarian economists held that a 50 percent rise in the cost of living within Hungary was mainly attributable to the straight-jacketing effect of German trade.[15]

About twenty percent of Greater Germany's total foreign trade is now tied up with southeastern and central Europe. Statistics indicate that Greater Germany's economic infiltration of southeastern and central Europe has taken on the form of a drive for a self-sufficient southeastern and central area under Greater Germany's political and economic domination. Moreover, statistics indicate that Italy is about five times more dependent economically upon Greater Germany than the latter is dependent upon Italy.

Nazi designs on gaining control of the Danubian trade, and Nazi hopes of turning the Danube into part of a Nazi-fied water route from the North to the Black Sea, have not escaped the long-range concern of far-seeing statesmen and economists in this part of Europe. Indeed, they are aware that through Germany's annexation of Austria, Germany had gained control over more than 50 percent of the Danube's trade. According to these economists, Germany placed great importance upon this river's aiding German infiltration in the regions throughout which it flowed. Cheap water freight rates, in addition to the "clearings" and other restrictive factors of the German "closed" economic trading system, comprised a combination which was expected to serve Germany as an effective aid to her eastward drive.

Germany's restricted economic system has penetrated into Central and Southeastern Europe with almost unbelievable speed, during the past three or four years, economically subjugating a number of countries in these areas—a condition wherefrom they are increasingly finding it difficult to shake themselves loose. Moreover, Germany's system is tending to elbow-out trade with these powers which practice a liberal trade policy. It is only a question of time, therefore, until Germany's competition in those areas may be expected to reflect itself unfavorably in the economic and industrial structure of such countries as Britain, Holland, France, Switzerland, and Scandinavia.

A review of trade returns brings to light the fact that a sizable increase in the German share of the imports of Yugoslavia, Rumania, Greece, Bulgaria, and Turkey has taken place over the past four years. In fact, Germany's and Austria's combined share in the imports of these countries shows a more rapid increase than their share in her exports—due in the main—to these countries' inability to liquidate their "frozen" accounts in Germany.

Country	Exports to Germany, percentage of total exports	Imports from Germany, percentage of total imports
Hungary	41	44.2
Rumania	26.9	38
Yugoslavia	35.2	42.7
Bulgaria	47.1	58.2
Greece	29.6	32.2

As for Poland, Germany's relative position remained somewhat similar in the period 1934–36 in terms of Germany's percentage of total imports.[16] For the year 1937, statistics show Germany as the foremost supplier to these [Balkan] countries and that Germany's share in the exports of these countries is greater than any other nation.

It is interesting to note the decline of trade between Czechoslovakia and Greater Germany. Between the years 1929–37, Germany's share in Czechoslovakia's foreign trade was about halved. Trade returns show that although the shares of Britain, France, and the United States in Czechoslovakia's foreign trade increased, their increase did not balance the losses which Czechoslovakia suffered in her trade with Greater Germany.

Having in mind that Gdynia's share of Czech export traffic this year amounted to about 2,000,000 tons, or an increase over last year of about 75 percent, I enquired of my informant whether he thought Poland might conceivably see her way clear to grant further traffic concessions on increased volume, to the ultimate mutual benefit of Poland and Czechoslovakia. In response, he stated that Poland would naturally welcome an increase in the flow of Czech traffic Gdynia-wards, and added that Poland would be willing to go far in terms of concessions to meet competition over the German rails and waterways. However, until the Czechs became fully conscious of a German attempt not to gain a strangle-hold over, but even to stifle Czech exports through increased tariffs, Poland could not take the surveys of Czech tariff delegations more seriously than as a gesture, on the one hand characterized by pressure on Germany for liberal tariff treatment, and on the other, an effort to ameliorate Polish-Czech relations by "caressing the Polish pocket nerve". Poland, indeed, was aware of the motives behind Czechoslovakia's recent gesture on this score, and before becoming excited over such a tempting prospect, Poland would await concrete evidence of Czech intentions.[17]

I am aware that Poland has been able to meet the competition of German tariffs to the extent of 2,000,000 tons of Czech export business over the past year. However, in the event that Poland showed signs of trying to swing much more Czech traffic from the German routing to Gdynia, I believe Germany's recognition thereof would give rise to another aspect; that is to say, the question would cease to be one between Germany and Czechoslovakia, and would inevitably become a conflict of interest between Germany and Poland. In this light, I should be inclined to look for German pressure against Poland all along the line.

1. The following three documents are situation analyses written by Biddle on June 19, 1938. They deal separately with German policy aims and their implications for Poland and East Central Europe; Polish-Czech relations; and Biddle's own assessment

of the general situation. They all provide a very penetrating and highly accurate analysis of Polish foreign policy, and the thinking behind it.

2. This dispatch is not reproduced in this volume but is deposited in the Department of State Files of the National Archives, Washington, D.C.

3. See note 2 above.

4. Hungarian uneasiness at the prospect of total German domination, or even annexation, of all of Czechoslovakia is underscored by a letter from the Hungarian regent, Admiral Miklos Horthy, to Hitler in September, 1938. Horthy pointedly warned Hitler that the Hungarian government would never accept a "solution of the Czechoslovak question" that was not "final," i.e., which left ethnic Hungarians outside the borders of Hungary, and concluded with the statement that the Hungarians were certain their opinion on this matter "is in full harmony with that of the German Government, viz., that peace in Central Europe cannot be assured unless the Czechoslovak problem has been resolved definitely and radically." *The Confidential Papers of Admiral Horthy*, ed. M. Szinai and L. Szücs (Budapest, 1965), p. 102. Hungary had already served notice of her determination not to be swept up in the German whirlwind by somewhat hypocritically signing the "Bled Agreement" of August 23, 1938, with members of the Little Entente: all parties renounced the use of force against each other, in return for which Czechoslovakia, Romania, and Yugoslavia recognized Hungary's right to rearm. For good, concise discussions of Hungarian foreign policy during this period, see the articles by Betty Jo Winchester, "Hungary and the Third Europe in 1938," *Slavic Review* 32, 4(December, 1973): 741–56, and Thomas L. Sakmyster, "Hungary and the Munich Crisis: The Revisionist Dilemma," ibid., pp. 725–40.

5. The defensive mutual assistance pact signed between Poland and Romania in March, 1921, was aimed specifically at the Soviet Union, with which Romania had a bitter and unresolved controversy over Bessarabia. It was mutually beneficial, giving both countries a degree of security along their long eastern frontiers, while for Poland it provided a safe and friendly relationship with the largest and potentially most prosperous nation of southeast Europe. Text of agreement in Arnold J. Toynbee, *Survey of International Affairs, 1920–1923* (London, 1927), pp. 504–5.

6. The Estonian minister to Poland was Hans Marcus. The Polish-Lithuanian dispute referred to involved a long-standing diplomatic confrontation, which had smouldered at varying degrees between the two neighbors since 1920, and had flared into a near war over a frontier incident in early 1938. For the diplomatic background, see Alfred Senn, *The Great Powers, Lithuania, and the Vilna Question, 1920–1928* (Leiden, 1966). See also Leonas Sabaliunas, *Lithuania in Crisis: Nationalism to Communism, 1939–1940* (Bloomington, Ind., 1972).

7. Biddle here refers to Rickard Sandler, the Swedish foreign minister (1932–39).

8. Biddle here means the area of Belorussia, located west of Russia proper.

9. A. Bocheński, *Między Niemcami a Rosją* (Warsaw, 1937).

10. Reference here is to the Great Purges, which racked the Soviet Union from 1936–38.

11. This document is not reproduced in this volume but is deposited in the Department of State Files of the National Archives, Washington, D.C.

12. The term "mugwump" is derived from a group of Republican party dissidents who broke with their party and refused to support the GOP ticket in the 1884 elections. The term is used to denote a group or individual given to pursuing maverick or independent actions or policies, without caring for the pressures brought on him to conform to an orthodox line.

13. Biddle here refers to the talks between Czech Premier Milan Hodža and the leader of the pro-Nazi *Sudetendeutsche Partei* among the German minority in Czechoslovakia, Konrad Henlein, over demands made by the latter for complete polit-

ical and administrative autonomy for the Czech Germans and their treatment as a separate, distinct legal entity within the Czechoslovak state. In keeping with Hitler's plans to use the minority issue as a provocation of sovereign East European states, these German demands were consistently escalated whenever the Czechs revealed a willingness to meet them. See Elizabeth Wiskemann, *Czechs and Germans*, 2d ed. (New York. 1967). pp. 197–283.

14. Eduard Beneš, one of the principal architects of the Czechoslovak state before and during World War I, was a key figure in that nation's politics, first as foreign minister and then, from 1935 on, as Tomas G. Masaryk's successor to the presidency.

15. The eminent historian C. A. Macartney, whose two-volume study *October Fifteenth: A History of Hungary, 1929-1945* (New York, 1956) is generally regarded as the definitive work on the topic, offers a somewhat different version of the German-Hungarian relationship. In 1937, Hungarian purchases from Germany accounted for 26.2 percent of her total imports, whereas she sent 24.1 percent of all her exports to Germany; these official statistics do not include expenditures on armaments, which were highly classified. Moreover, until 1938 the Magyars eagerly sought expanded trade with the Germans, who offered a ready market for their agricultural produce and bauxite while providing Hungary with finished industrial products (especially machinery, machine tools, and spare parts) and such raw materials as coke, coal, and petrochemicals. The primary motivation for this Hungarian zeal was a desire to industrialize and modernize their land as quickly as possible. However, this desire blinded them to the dangers that ultimately become reality: the two economies became interlocked in such a manner that virtually the entire Hungarian economy would have ground to a halt had Germany suddenly suspended trade relations. Macartney, *October Fifteenth*, 1:140–42. See also Antonin Basch, *The Danube Basin and the German Economic Sphere* (London, 1944).

16. According to official Polish statistics, the Polish trade balance with Germany had revealed a healthy surplus of exports over imports until 1937, when the advantage shifted to Germany. Nonetheless, total Polish-German trade continued to play a minor role in the overall foreign commerce of each country: in 1938, Germany obtained only 2.1 percent of all its imports from Poland, to which it sent 2.2 percent of its exports. *Mały Rocznik Statystyczny 1939*, pp. 166–68, tables 4–8. The German-Polish economic relationship is considered in more detail in Document 5 below.

17. In late April, 1938, Dr. Juraj Slávik, Czech minister to Poland, visited the deputy premier and minister of finance, Eugeniusz Kwiatkowski, who was known for his differences of opinion with Beck on foreign policy. Kwiatkowski was openly interested in developing closer relations with Czechoslovakia, and envisioned an expansion of trade between the two countries as the best start to this end. Slávik proposed that commercial relations between Poland and Czechoslovakia be broadened at once, and also offered to redirect the Czech export trade from Hamburg to Gdynia, and to conclude an air-agreement with the Poles. In concluding, the Czech minister proposed that a Czech trade delegation be sent to Poland at once. Polish diplomats were miffed that the Czechs elected to approach a member of the government directly on these issues, instead of proceeding through the normal diplomatic avenues set up to handle foreign trade questions. Szembek, *Diariusz i teki*, 4:139–40.

[*June–July, 1938*][1]

Observations of economic advisor to Foreign Office and those of a veteran observer of affairs in this part of Europe on the economic block resulting from Germany's annexation of Austria

Of almost inescapable connection with the political aspect, and with reference to the Department's Instruction No. 20, I take occasion herein to transmit the following results of my examination of the potential effect of Germany's annexation of Austria upon the economic outlook for this part of Europe and for Poland in particular.

Accordingly, I believe that the substance of observations disclosed in my several discussions with Mr. Jan Wszelaki, Economic Advisor of the Foreign Office, might prove illuminating. He possesses a liberal attitude towards trade in general and his intelligence and sound views are coming more and more to the fore in terms of influence on inner Government circles. His influence upon Poland's trade policy is consequently becoming steadily more effective.

In substance, he said that in 1935 there had arisen a vigorous argument in Government circles as to what extent Poland should be permitted to trade with Germany without eventually endangering, through potential German economic pressure, Poland's independence. In fact, the heated controversy which grew out of the issue as to whether Poland should be permitted to trade with Germany to the extent of 15 or 16 percent of her total trade had almost led to a cabinet crisis. (At this point he explained that 17 percent represented, so-to-speak, the "classical maximum" which Polish trade authorities set on the extent of Poland's trade with Germany). Finally, however, the majority, who, despite their desire to go even further, (since it had seemed to them a real sacrifice to limit their trade with Germany) compromised on 16 percent. Indeed, in their opinion, Poland might have temporarily at least, been economically benefited. However, according to my informant, by its decision to limit Polish-German trade, the Polish Government as a whole had manifested its foresight as to the possibilities of German domination through economic strategy, such as had since proved to be the case in Bulgaria, Hungary, Rumania, and Yugoslavia, and to a lesser degree, Czechoslovakia.

About that same time, [German Minister of Finance] Dr. Hjalmar Schacht had made a tour of the Eastern and Central European areas, offering German markets for a large portion of the trade thereof. The prices he had offered for the various products under discussion were tempting to all the countries except Poland and Turkey, who had foreseen the potential outcome in the form of a German economic-political domination, and they had eagerly accepted Dr. Schacht's terms.

These countries had been accustomed to dealing with9 France and Britain and other liberal trading countries on a basis of cash payments, and they did not realize until too late that Germany had no intention of paying cash—in fact was completely incapable of doing so. Later Dr. Schacht announced his regret to learn of these countries' disappointment over Germany's inability to pay cash, and thereupon explained the restricted formula of Germany's "closed" economic system, which has governed their trade relations with Germany ever since.

In my informant's opinion, the economic outlook for these countries was now far from rosy, in view of their having fallen victims of Germany's economic "straight-jacketing" system. Poland so far had fortunately avoided this pitfall by restricting her trade with Germany, and intended to continue this policy. In fact, my informant believed this was the only way to prevent Poland's falling prey to German economic and, in consequence, potential political domination.

He was, moreover, aware of an overhanging cloud of German potential penetration of the whole of Eastern and Central Europe. In such case, lacking Western aid, even Poland might conceivably be forced to accommodate her economic-political scheme to the German line of policy. In such eventuality, and from Poland's standpoint, it would be a case of trying to compromise with danger in an effort to hold on to her independence. Moreover, potential collaboration between Poland and Germany would prove a serious danger for the rest of the world.

On the other hand, Poland was at the moment endeavoring to find means of effecting an increase in her trade with those countries which were now being economically pressed by Germany, as Poland's contribution (infinitesimal though it might be) towards keeping this part of the world in almost a vain hope from falling completely into German economic clutches. Accordingly, Poland and Hungary were at the moment endeavoring to find some way whereby they might increase their trade with each other; unfortunately, however, their respective representatives had found it a difficult task, due mainly to the similarity of their respective exports.[2]

Moreover, my informant added that he felt I was aware that in addition to Hungary, Poland would like to be in a position to contribute towards keeping Rumania, Yugoslavia, and Bulgaria out of Germany's envisaged political-economic strangle-hold. Beck's policy (as I have previously pointed out in former dispatches) had already favored closer bilateral relations, both politically and economically, between Poland and each of the aforementioned states. In fact, Beck was now proceeding with renewed vigor in an effort to bring about an amelioration of Rumanian-Hungarian relations, and to bring Bulgaria into closer relations with Rumania. Moreover, Beck had considerable respect for the Yugoslav people—their courage and their ideals; and he felt that they had sufficient courage of their convictions to resist an attempt on Germany's part to draw them completely politically into the Nazi orbit. Besides, he felt that the Yugoslavs were strong enough to hold the Bulgarians in line in a crisis. Personally, from my own observations, I should be more inclined to feel that the Yugoslav people—aside from that uncertain political quantity, Stoydinowicz[3]—would be at this juncture a more reliable element to count on than the Bulgarians, whose forward-looking policy appears to have been based to a large extent upon the political success of Nazi policy. Nevertheless, my informants in Polish official circles are inclined to believe that with real evidence of an active Anglo-French counter-policy, and with pressure from Yugoslavia, Bulgaria might be expected to be brought into line against German expansion.

My informant had frequently been asked the question as to whether it would not be cheaper in the long run for Britain and France to devote at least some of the moneys now going to armaments into the channels of trade, by purchasing, for example, commodities and products of the Danubian area, in an effort to prevent Germany's becoming the economic and political master of Eastern and Central Europe—and potentially the economic dictator of that region. The answer, to his mind, was that Britain was prevented from taking such steps by her Dominions' situation, and that France, beyond possibly a gesture, could not be expected to take any positive or effective action on this score. Moreover, my informant doubted that France, under present-day circumstances, could take any steps without Britain's cooperation.

In response to my question as to whether he thought the peoples of the Danubian countries were at heart pro-German, he said that at the moment he did not think so, for Germany's annexation of Austria and subsequent happenings there had opened their eyes, and each country now feared that it might become the next victim of Germany's machinations. As concerns the peoples of the various German minorities in states contiguous to Germany, recent events in Austria had served as a two-sided lesson: (a) the individual's fear that he might not get aboard the "band wagon" in time to ride with the potential wave of Nazi penetration, and (b) the aftermath of disillusionment among the native Nazis, resulting from their experiencing the cold reality of Berlin's clamping down its iron claw.

The critical situation, however, was that so long as Germany had the preponderance of trade she would dictate to these countries in that, if these countries made an effort to throw off the yoke of German economic bondage, they might experience such acute sufferings, unemployment, etc. that the result might conceivably be revolutions in economic countries where such attempts were made. The only solution he saw for a happy outcome for the economic dilemma in this part of Europe would be the replacement by those countries now dominated by Germany of part of their German trade, by trade with liberal trade-minded and peace-loving nations.

There was one potential danger which he feared a great deal and that was something which he believed Germany was contemplating and might be expected to put into effect eventually, namely: that she would attempt to force the Central European countries to use only German railways and ports for exports of their goods abroad. From the Polish standpoint, this prospect presented an unhappy outlook, for such action would bring great hardship to ports like Gdynia.

He summed up his views of the situation by stating that through her economic victories Germany was steadily gaining political sway, and, although other countries were spending colossal sums for rearmament, they were doing little to combat the aforementioned economic victories. He was afraid that these other countries would be ready to take important steps in this line only when it would be too late to bring about effective action peaceably.

In evaluating a possible turn in future events, my informant remarked that the British Government's persistent desire for an agreement with Germany might conceivably serve as a force in the cause of peace, for he was aware that the British Government, in return for its willingness to consider concessions to Germany in the colonial domain, would necessarily exact certain conditions. The British Government would have to gain something tangible to satisfy its public opinion. Hence, in addition to Britain's known desire for aerial disarmament, particularly in terms of *bombers*, Britain might reasonably be expected to impose a condition entailing Germany's participation in an economic conference consisting of all European countries at least. In such event, efforts would be made to shake Germany loose from her walled-in economic system which she was now employing so effectively as an instrument of penetration abroad. To his mind, success in such efforts would undoubtedly prove the quickest and most effective means of curbing Germany's economic-political penetration eastwards, and to release those countries now in the path of German envisaged expansion from the iron shackles of the German political-economic orbit. Whereas he was not unduly optimistic over the prospects of getting Germany to sit in an economic conference envisaging Germany's dislodgment from her present system, Britain's conception and envisaged effort along these lines was constructive and admirable, and if and when put into motion, would justify the support of all countries practicing a liberal trade policy. After all, perhaps in terms of the long-pull, this might prove a more effective first stage approach towards reducing the Danubian States' dependence upon Germany than a temporary measure proposed and discussed during the recent Anglo-French conversations in London, i.e. an emergency scheme entailing the purchase of Danubian products and commodities.

In scanning the objectives on both sides of the gap separating Germany's "closed" economic system and the liberal trade policy of the Western world, I feel that the following forms, in effect, the basis of resistance which Berlin may be expected to offer in the event of a British invitation to sit around the European economic conference table. Accordingly, as I see it, Germany is fighting for a policy which to date she cannot support by reason of the lack of adequate raw material and food sources. Germany is therefore faced with the following two alternatives:

(a) To make a deal with Britain and France which would entail shaking the Nazi Government loose from its "closed" economic system. The liquidation of this system would in turn spell the loosening of the Nazi Government's grip on the people, not only within the Reich, but also in those countries which the Nazi Government has already succeeded in bringing under the clutches of her economic penetration, or,

(b)   To gain control of the raw material and food sources of Eastern and Central Europe in order to strengthen Germany's hand towards meeting Britain and France on a more equal footing.

Of connected bearing, in my recent coversations with a veteran observer of affairs in this part of Europe (whom I have usually found to be objective in his point of view) he made in effect the following observation.

Regarding the Central European situation he remarked that neither he nor anyone else in this part of Europe who was willing to judge the reality of events had any serious belief in the scheme which the Quai d'Orsay had reportedly suggested for the opening up of new markets for the Danubian powers in Western Europe, in order to lessen the latter's economic dependence upon Germany. For such markets as could be perhaps artificially established for the benefit of those powers—except in regard to a few essential commodities such as oil—could not compete whether in volume or in matters of long-term credits, or again in the domain of barter, with the facilities that Germany was offering and would continue to offer them. My informant described this "rehash" of old-time projects as a "pill for an earthquake". Not even Italy could compete with Germany in that field. The doubtful prospect of any genuine competitor with Germany down the Danubian Valley would go a long way to persuade the Germans how mistaken would be a policy which might incur ultimate war risks for the sake of an objective envisaging economic penetration and political hegemony, when that penetration could be realized by economic and diplomatic means without such risks. My informants' information through various channels was to the effect that Italian diplomacy was not setting to mobilize, against German penetration, every element of resistance in the various Danubian states, notably in Hungary, Rumania, and Yugoslavia, and Albania. But according to my informant, Italian diplomacy was doomed to failure in this respect, because it could not offer to the countries in question the advantages which Germany could offer. As a matter of fact, my informant took the view that not only would all these Italian activities fail to make any deep and lasting impression, but that, wriggle as he might, Mussolini remained the prisoner of the Rome-Berlin Axis. He fancied, therefore, a second Axis to play with; hence, the Anglo-Italo Agreement.[4]

My informant then went on to say that he had serious doubts as to the permanent effectiveness of any attempt on the part of either Britain or France, or both, to step into the economic breach in Central Europe, and more particularly the Balkans; in the first place, Germany was historically the chief market for the products of that region. Germany took commodities and goods from the States of that Region which were not required by Britain and France, for in many cases the latter had other markets to which for economic-political reasons they had to reserve their purchasing power; for example, Britain had her dominions markets and France her colonies. In addition they both had their regular-line outlets which they had in effect to compensate with purchases. In other words, the flow of commodities and manufactured goods between Germany, and especially the Balkans, was a natural and historical movement.

I suggested that the reopening of international trade channels which were profitable to all parties would seem the only practical and fundamentally sound means whereby the international community could stiffen its front against the extraordinary social-economic conditions now confronting it. In this direction, I felt that my country had gone a long way toward blazing the trail, and leading the way along the path of sound treatment of the world-wide problem. Accordingly, the world would do well to devote a serious and objective study to the principles underlying our trade liberation policy, which represented in my opinion a constructive contribution toward the alleviation of the world's social-economic-political tension.

He agreed that this policy represented the one ray of hope, emerging from the present state of politico-economic confusion. He only hoped that our trade agreements program might be pressed forward with renewed vigor.

1. There is no date on this document. However, judging from its position among Biddle's other dispatches and from the information contained therein, it was probably written in early summer (June–July) 1938. It contains an excellent analysis of the economic factors underlying Polish policy toward Germany.

2. Official Polish statistics support this observation. In the years following the Depression, Poland's trade balance with Hungary was exactly in equilibrium, with imports matching exports, until 1937, when Poland imported goods worth 1,000,000 *złoty* more than she exported to Hungary. In 1938, as a result of the increased attention of both countries to mutual commercial interaction, the balance swung to Poland's favor by over 500,000 *złoty*. Yet this trade claimed an insignificant portion of each country's total foreign trade program: in 1938 Polish goods accounted for only 1.5 percent of all Hungarian imports, while Hungary sold only 1 percent of her goods to Poland. In that year Poland purchased fruits and vegetables, certain cereals, machinery and electrical equipment, and wine from Hungary, to whom she sold raw and finished wood products, zinc, unfinished hides, and flax. *Mały Rocznik Statystyczny 1939*, pp. 166–82, tables 7–19.

3. Biddle here refers to Milan Stoyadinovič, the flamboyant Serbian radical politician who became premier of Yugoslavia in June, 1935, and kept Central Europe in constant suspense with his unpredictable political moves.

4. The Anglo-Italian agreement, signed April 16, 1938, in Rome, cleared up a number of nagging problems that had been disturbing relations between the two states. From the Italian point of view, it was particularly important as a vehicle for obtaining British recognition of Italian conquests and colonial predominance in Ethiopia. For the Italian viewpoint of the agreement's importance for them, see the memoirs of Italian Foreign Minister Galeazzo Ciano, *L'Europa verso la catastrofe* (Verona, 1947), pp. 280–300. Although the text had not been printed at this writing, the agreement is summarized and analyzed from the British perspective in *DBFP*, Third Series, vol. 3, Doc. 326.

July 28, 1938

MEMORANDUM

Memorandum of substance of my recent conversation with a high ranking Polish official wherein (a) he disclosed Polish and other European statesmen's interest in the question as to whether the United States might be expected to supply Germany with war supplies in event of a European conflict, and (b) he questioned me as to American public opinion's reported increasing antipathy for Nazi policy

The following is the substance of my informal and confidential conversation with a high ranking Polish official. In connection with my response to his question, he assured me upon my request that he would treat the information informally, unofficially, and in strictest confidence. Needless to say, I was guarded in my statement but owing to our close and frank relations, and to the fact that he has steadily proven an exceedingly helpful source of interesting information for me, I concluded to comply with his request in general terms.

In response to his remark that a vital question currently engaging the interest of European statesmen, in considering the possibility of a European conflict, was whether the United States might be expected to supply Germany either directly or indirectly with war materials and supplies, I drew his attention to the substance of our neutrality law, and recalled to him my previous remarks (imparted upon my return from the United States in March) to the effect that I had observed (a) that American public opinion in general was characterized by opposition to any entangling alliances, and (b) a rigid insistence on the part of public opinion that the United States guard its rights to independent and uncommitted judgment on all aspects of each and every foreign crisis as it developed; in other words, an unwillingness to make advance commitments. I added that, in effect, the foregoing reactions reflected the principles which had long formed an integral part of our foreign policy.

I emphasized that the majority of my countrymen manifested a strong will to "steer clear" of war, believing at the same time that war was not inevitable. However, it would, to my mind, be dangerous for opinion abroad to interpret this as an unwillingness to fight under any circumstances, aside from invasion. At the same time, it would be equally misleading for opinion abroad to assume that the United States might be unable to retain its neutral status in the event of a major European conflict. As a matter of fact, there was no barometric device whereby we might gauge what position our country might assume under unforeseen circumstances.

In response to the Polish official's further inquiry as to the correctness of reports he had recently received regarding American public opinion's growing antipathy for Nazidom's policies, I stated that in further examining American public opinion in general, I had personally discerned a growing antipathy for the principles and practice of Nazidom's policies; they were for the most part in direct conflict with the principles underlying democracy.

In clarification of this point I remarked that in appraising the full value of this antipathy, it was well to bear in mind (a) my Government's profound respect of the rule of law in international affairs, (b) Berlin's alleged implications in the recently-detected "spy-ring",[1] (c) the clash of our principles of tolerance and equal opportunity for all, regardless of race, creed or color, with Nazidom's neo-pagan policy of extreme anti-Semitism. Indeed, the effect of barbaric measures entailed therein upon the sensibilities of my liberal-minded countrymen was unfavorable, to say the least.

He then remarked that my observations as to my countrymen's continued belief that war was not inevitable, had especially engaged his interest. I thereupon offered my personal opinion that present European tension might be expected to be liquidated within the next year and a half, either through war or through statesmanship and diplomacy. Moreover, I personally believed that this current war-conducive tension could be liquidated by means of the latter provided there was sufficient will towards that end on part of Governments directly interested.

Throughout our conversation, I discerned his undisguised and lively interest in my remarks. In fact, he observed in conclusion that he was particularly interested, in that in substance nearly all phases of my observations had corresponded in effect with verbal reports on the part of recently returned Ambassador Count Potocki. Moreover, my remarks as to my countrymen's attitude in relation to the persecution of Jews in Germany had corresponded with observations recently and confidentially imparted to him by an important German diplomat to the effect that his Government had become seriously concerned over [German] Ambassador Dieckhoff's alarming reports of a frenzied wave of anti-German feeling throughout the United States due (a) to the "spy scare", (b) to repudiation of liability for the Austrian external loans, and (c) to Jewish persecution.

1. Biddle here refers to the FBI action taken against German spies in spring 1938, which resulted in the arrest and conviction of six Nazi agents in New York and other East Coast points. The episode, which received wide publicity in various newspapers, focused the attention of the American public upon this danger, and led to increased internal vigilance and an outburst of popular anti-German sentiment. See A. B. Magil and Henry Stevens, *The Perils of Fascism: The Crisis of American Democracy* (New York, 1938), pp. 228–29.

August 12, 1938

Subject: Further observations on secret, "flooding system" aimed at serving as a defense line from Pinsk Marshes to Dniester River; Further observations on roads and terrain in southeastern frontier

I have the honor to supplement my despatch No. 194[1] of October 7, 1937, regarding construction of a flooding system in Southeastern Poland aimed at serving as a line of defense into Polish territory and to report that my recent tour of inspection in that particular area brought to light the following information.

Along the two rivers, Styrpa and Seret, which run parallel southward to, and emptying into the Dniester River, have been constructed a series of dams which, when and if opened, would be capable of flooding an intervening area averaging about 20 kilometers in width for a distance of about 200 kilometers, within a period of several hours. This obstruction, combined with the quality of pasty clay-like soil which lies between the two rivers would seriously impede, if not completely hinder the passage of any motorized equipment.

In traversing this southeastern area I was careful to observe the roads and the terrain in the light of their bearing on potential military operations. The road which brought me to the border runs due east from Lwów, and is constructed and maintained as a main military artery. Hence, up to a point within about 20 kilometers from the border, it is broad enough for two lines of heavy motorized equipment, and the surface up to the aforementioned point is macadamized. East of the aforementioned point, however, as in the case of all roads running eastward to the frontier, the highway became very narrow and ceased to have a macadamized surface. At this point (which as I pointed out is about 20 kilometers from the frontier) there is a very broad belt of forest running north to south, maintained as a shield for tactical purposes.

In surveying the rolling plains which characterize southeastern Poland, and continue for several hundred miles into the Russian Ukraine, I gained the impression that the terrain is far better suited to cavalry rather than to motorized operations. Indeed, the undulating nature of this part of the country would lend itself admirably to the movement or deployment of cavalry or infantry. As to its lending itself to the operations of tanks and other motorized equipment, the black silt which characterizes the land over this area, reaches depth on the Polish side of about 18 inches, and in the wet season is practically impassable except on foot or horseback. Having reached these conclusions, I can now more readily understand why the Polish military authorities have maintained an exceptionally large cavalry establishment, and so much horse-drawn artillery.[2]

Examination of the map moreover, discloses that such an obstruction on Polish territory would throw the main burden of responsibility on Rumanian shoulders for the passage of Russian troops into Czechoslovakia.

As near as I could estimate upon careful examination, the main part of the work on this project has already been completed. In fact, I believe that outside of the present work, which is mainly devoted to the digging of sluices to connect up one river bed with the other in order to expedite the inundation, the system as a whole could be made to function effectively even now in an emergency.

During my tour of this district I was interested to find that the community inhabiting the area adjacent to a large estate belonging to Count Siemienski (whereon one of the large dams of the Styrpa river had been constructed) had become greatly excited over some incident which had just occurred. Upon inquiry, I was confidentially informed that on the day previous the Soviet military attaché had appeared near by in civilian clothes, motoring in a small car and was stopped by the military authorities and discretely informed that this particular area was under military control and advised to conduct his tour elsewhere. He had departed in the opposite direction without remonstration. Later I found that his departure from Warsaw had been marked by the secret police and though his trail had been lost during one night, he was picked up again the next day by the local police near Słoczów. I cite this to show how careful the military authorities are to guard the "flooding area" from inquisitive eyes—especially those of officials of the Soviet.

I was interested, moreover, in observing conditions in various frontier posts along the Polish-Russian border, from Podwołoczyska southward. At this particular point, I noted an exception in that there was the absence of the usual three strands of barbed-wire entanglements. Here there is a small river dividing the two center posts. Instead of the wires being visible as in the case of most frontier points, the wire is submerged in the stream. The Russian village opposite Podwołczyska has undergone a major change in terms of population during the past year. All inhabitants except the Jewish population evacuated the town and were replaced by immigrants from the interior of Russia.

Southward along the frontier I found that at all bridges and points of military concentration on either side, there were two Soviet soldiers on guard vis-à-vis one Pole. Inquiry on my part revealed that in Polish military opinion the reason for these two guards at each Soviet post was for the purpose of having one watch the other. An interesting sidelight on Polish frontier etiquette was that the Polish soldier on guard never takes his eyes off his opposite number on the other side. Thus when the officer whom I accompanied approached his guard, the latter backed to join us, advanced along side, and saluted the captain and myself without ever looking at us. The captain explained that this is a cardinal principle strictly adhered to by the Polish frontier troops on guard.

Having at the same time the flooding system in mind, I noted that the terrain southward to the Dniester offered itself advantageously for the operation of that defense scheme.

1. This dispatch is not reproduced in this volume but is deposited in the Department of State Files of the National Archives, Washington, D.C.

2. Although Biddle's perception of Polish domestic as well as international policies was, on the whole, surprisingly astute, he shared the misconception of foreign and Polish military strategists alike that the eastern regions of Poland were suited to cavalry use alone, and not mechanized warfare. This feeling was especially strong among British military observers, even such as Edmund Ironside; see Bethell, *The War Hitler Won*, pp. 98–99. It should be pointed out, however, that most of the Polish cavalry was designed to be used as a mobile fighting force, whose troops rode by horseback to their assigned positions, but then dismounted and fought on foot; each cavalry brigade was equipped with light artillery and machine guns. See Leszek Moczulski's controversial study, *Wojna Polska 1939* (Warsaw, 1972).

November 5, 1938

My dear Mr. President:

Many signs point to the Munich Conference and its immediate sequel's having already had far reaching repercussions throughout the whole extent of the European continent. As in effect pointed out in my previous letter, in view of the apparent check suffered by the western powers, the smaller countries, such as those of the Oslo group, which had already decided upon neutrality and upon repudiation of the compulsory sanctions clauses of the League Covenant, are already congratulating themselves on their foresight and wisdom. Belgium, Holland, Switzerland, and the Scandinavians are more than ever determined not to be drawn into any conflict between the major powers.

States east and southeast of Berlin, though rapidly falling in line with Berlin's orientation in an economic sense, are in many cases, still groping for some "out" (a) from eventual German political hegemony, and (b) from becoming the potential victims of "peaceful settlements" between the major powers. Poland is in this category.

The Chanceries of eastern and central Europe are now apparently practicing a "balancing policy", characterized by a search for the orientation whereby they may be the safest (at least temporarily so) and wherefrom they may acquire the most benefits.

Having interpreted recent events to mean Britain's and France's "evacuation" of eastern and central Europe, certain states, such as Poland, Yugoslavia and Hungary, have recently been evidencing an inclination to look to Rome in their pursuance of a post-Munich course of "balance diplomacy" between Berlin and Rome. Due to Italy's politico-economic position in central Europe, these smaller states looked for Italy to adopt measures towards preventing German penetration and domination in a region which Italy had hitherto regarded as her natural and legitimate sphere of interest. Moreover, the smaller states felt Italy might be tempted by the prospect of acquiring for herself in these parts the leadership which France had apparently abandoned.

For the second time however, since the Anschluss, and, in this instance, at the recent Italo-German arbitration conference in Vienna, Mussolini succumbed to Hitler, and this blasted the hopes of statesmen of the smaller countries to Berlin's east for Italian support.[1]

Though Italy may desire to resist the German drive down the Danube valley by diplomatic and economic means, and by domestic intrigues, she would not at this date, in my opinion, dare to challenge Germany by force of arms. Indeed, I find it difficult to believe either in the will or ability of Italy (unbacked by the western powers) to stand up to Germany. I find it equally difficult at this writing to foresee any development which in final resort will not imply a variable degree of German hegemony over the various individual states east and southeast of Berlin—a hegemony which certain economic and political arrangements between these states may mitigate, but not prevent. Moreover, as Germany's trade offensive effectively advances, the states in its path can hardly afford to quarrel with their best customer, from a trade standpoint.

As regards Germany's post-Munich position, it is interesting to note that as Germany emerges from the "have not" to the "have" category, Nazi inner circles are manifesting concern over the renewed vigor with which the western powers are arming.

Signs at the moment point to Germany's planning, on the one hand, a period of territorial reconsolidation and digestion, and continuance of her eastward trade offensive, on the other. Funks recent southeastern tour brought to light Germany's new form of approach to the various trade goals envisaged in Berlin's program. In brief, these bilateral negotiations may be characterized as an approach to meet the special circumstances prevailing in each country with which Berlin aims to do business. In cases where states are under-industrialized and thus unable to participate in the exchange of items of the character suitable to German requirements, Germany proposes to take in hand the organizing of an industrial structure within such states, providing them with technicians and materials—receiving in return food commodities and other products.

In connection with this eastward drive, Berlin's present mood was characterized in effect, by the following statement recently imparted to me by an experienced observer who enjoys close contact with inner Nazi circles: Germany was not building a ramshackle road, such as that which Napoleon built. The road which present-day Germany was constructing would not tumble. While Napoleon was a great General, he had lacked the opportunity to learn many things present-day Germany had learned, and which only the modern world understood—such as, economics and the regularized expansion of population. I interpret this to mean that an almost "power drunk" and super-confident Germany intends to have no unsympathetic or undigested portions along the way towards its eastward goal.

My informant furthermore stated that inner Nazi circles were now looking to Mr. Chamberlain to see what he would propose. Accordingly, they expect great efforts to bring about European appeasement and understandings to characterize the next three to six months. Moreover, these circles did not anticipate at the moment a Four-Power Pact, rather they looked for conferences of several or more powers directly interested in any particular settlement.

As for Poland's current position in light of Germany's eastward politico-economic ascendency, I am aware that while Poland has already given evidence of "playing ball" with Germany economically, as a temporary expedient, she realizes it is a risky game at the best, and is seriously apprehensive in terms of the long-range political outlook. Indeed, Warsaw deeply regrets increasing evidences of Britain's and France's eastern and central European evacuation—for, although Warsaw has for long ceased to expect British and French military intervention in affairs of this section of Europe, nevertheless, Warsaw regarded evidences of their active interest in the light of a healthy balance.

As regards near future policies of the present British and French Governments, current signs indicate that France, like Britain, will exert efforts towards making peace with the dictators, and that France will try to secure from Hitler a statement of peaceful intentions somewhat along the line of that which he made to Mr. Chamberlain.

Just how far the demands of Hitler and his Nazi "colony-mongers" will impede understandings of durable character between Germany, Britain and France respectively, remains to be seen.

1. The hopes that Biddle mentions were embodied in Beck's project for the creation of a "Third Europe," stretching from the Black to Baltic seas as a bloc of neutral states to form a barrier to either German or Russian expansion into East Central Europe. An integral part of the plan was the establishment of a common Polish-Hungarian frontier through cession of territory by Slovakia to both countries in the Carpathian-Tatra region. Hence, when the Vienna Award of November 1, 1938, denied most Hungarian claims against Slovakia and totally ignored all the Polish demands, thereby preventing the establishment of this border, the plan seemed doomed. The best discussion of this topic is in Cienciala, *Poland and the Western Powers*, pp. 149–76, and the two articles by Winchester and Sakmyster cited above in Document 4, note 4.

November 10, 1938

My dear Mr. President:

The plight of the Jewish populations as a whole in Europe is steadily becoming so untenable, and their hopes for some way out from their present and increasing dilemma becoming so dim with the passage of time, that I take the liberty of sending you this confidential outline of my recent observations.

First of all, it is steadily becoming clearer that you personally are the one to whom they all look more and more to take the lead in finding a solution for their unhappy situation. My impression on this score is daily corroborated by requests on the part of various Jewish factions here that I ask you to receive their representatives, should they proceed to Washington in the near future. Chief amongst those who have pressed me along these lines is one V. [Vladimir] Jabotinski,[1] leader of the Zionist Revisionists. He is now in the course of attempting to organize a Congress of Jews of this part of Europe, the total amount whereof he puts at about 7,000,000. In fact, he looks upon the Jews of this section of Europe as constituting the object of concern on the part of the Jews in the rest of the world—particularly in the United States.

You may recall that from time to time I have written and cabled regarding my conversations with Jabotinski. He has a brilliant mind, and an engaging personality, and has at his disposal a "grapevine" system for the gathering of information—hence, he is extremely well-informed. Moreover, he is diametrically opposed to the policies of Mr. Weisemann[2] and at heart extremely anti-British.

He correctly predicted (a) the British Government's scrapping the idea of partition in Palestine, and (b) a general disapproval amongst the Jews of the world to the idea of the Jews of Palestine assuming a minority position within the framework of an Arab State. He now informs me that as regards Palestine he felt the blackest of the menacing clouds of a month ago had been removed; it seemed now that the Jews were no longer faced with the prospect of a drastic and radical liquidation of the Balfour pledge. He felt that this intention had been frustrated and averted owing to your intervention. He believed that what is now likely to follow is a return to the status quo ante—meaning "ante the Peel reports"[3]—only perhaps veiled by a display of "a few well chosen words" intended to save everybody's face. According to his opinion, most people in Britain would feel thankful in that event and would "rest"—and the moment for the big move would be lost; while the only thing that *would not rest* would be the "disease". Hence, he took another occasion to state his fears that there was only one factor left, one man who could prevent this half-way stagnation, and this was President Roosevelt.

Naturally, in reply to his repeated question whether there was any chance that you might be willing to receive him, I stated that you had never lost sight of the problem, and that you and your associates were constantly engaged in a search for a solution. I did not think this was the time to request an audience with you—in fact, the committee which you had appointed to study the problem was in London and diligently at work.

I am aware that Mr. Jabotinski, like many of his confrères, is concentrating his thoughts and energies in an effort (a) to engage your good offices in calling another world conference to consider territorial outlets for Jewish immigration and (b) to enlist your influence and pressure upon a "Britain, desirous of American cooperation", towards making a generous settlement in Palestine.

Of importantly pertinent interest, usually well-informed circles here impart to me that their reports from London indicate that Chamberlain, or perhaps a member of his Cabinet, might possibly accompany the King and Queen to the United States for, among other purposes, discussing the Palestine question along the following lines: To retain Palestine as a Jewish homeland would be impossible, if immigration were increased. Hence, the British Government might be willing to consider favorably offering territory at one or more points in their colonies for the purpose of setting up a Jewish State— and, *provided* the *United States joined Britain in the guarantee of such a state*. This proposal, according to my informants, might be expected to be a part of an envisaged plan for a colonial settlement within the framework of a general European settlement.

At the present moment the following are highlights on developments in connection with the current European Jewish problem: (a) violent repercussions against the Jews throughout Germany as a result of the Jewish boy, Herschel Grünspan, murdering [Ernst] vom Rath, Secretary of the German Embassy in Paris;[4] (b) signs of an approaching storm over the community of Jews in Rumania;[5] and (c) difficulties encountered by the Polish official representatives in their negotiations in Berlin regarding the individual rights and properties of the Polish Jews recently ordered out of Germany to Poland (15,000 Jews recently crossed into Poland under 24 hours' notice from the German Government. From all accounts, German treatment of these unfortunate people was nothing short of brutal. On the other hand, the Polish Government went to great lengths in an effort to extend humane treatment under trying circumstances).[6] . . .

1. A Polish Jew, Jabotinski gained an international reputation with his eloquent pleas for the creation of a Palestinian Jewish state having the "historic borders" of the ancient Israeli kingdom.

2. Biddle probably meant Dr. Chaim Weizmann, like Jabotinski originally a Jew from Poland. However, he settled in England, where he headed the British Zionist movement. He had considerably more moderate views regarding the territorial outlines of the Jewish state than did Jabotinski.

3. The reports of the "Peel Commission," the Royal Commission set up to study the Middle East situation and the impact the establishment of a Jewish state would have on the area, took note of the deep, emotional hostility among Arab leaders to the award of the entire Palestinian area to Israel. In order to counter this animosity, and head off what would be certain conflict and bloodshed, the Peel Commission recommended that Palestine be divided into two separate states—an Arab and Jewish—and that the key cities, such as Jerusalem, be placed under British control in the form of a mandate. Needless to say, this recommendation pleased no one, and the report was ignored by both Arab and Jewish parties. An excerpt of the report is in Walter Laqueur, ed., *The Israel-Arab Reader*, 6th ed. (New York, 1970), pp. 56–58.

4. Hershel Grynszpan, a young Polish Jew living in Paris, assassinated vom Rath on November 7 as retribution for the deportation of his parents from Germany. His action touched off the most vicious Nazi anti-Semitic pogrom yet— the infamous *Kristallnacht*, or "Night of the Broken Glass."

5. Biddle doubtless refers to the sudden arrest, and subsequent murder, of Romanian Fascist chief Corneliu Codreanu by the Romanian authorities in November, 1938. Given the mood of Romania's radical Right, there was ample reason for expecting that mass outrage at this deed could easily take the form of another *Kristallnacht*, this one directed against Romanian Jews.

6. This is a somewhat simplified and incomplete presentation of the problem. The Polish government announced that, starting on October 29, within a two-week period all passports held by Polish citizens living abroad would have to be verified by Polish diplomatic outposts; penalty for failure to have a passport validated was the loss of Polish citizenship. For the numerous Jews living in Germany as resident aliens on Polish passports this could mean loss of the right to return to Poland freely, and the consequent necessity of remaining in Germany permanently—a situation obviously distasteful to Berlin. Hence, the German Foreign Office protested strongly to Warsaw; when it received no satisfaction at once, Berlin announced that it would begin expelling all Polish Jews immediately. By October 29, 17,000 Jews of Polish citizenship had been forced to leave Germany for Poland; in most cases, they were prohibited from taking any but their most essential possessions. When the Polish government threatened to retaliate with a wholesale expulsion of German citizens in Poland, the two countries commenced negotiations on November 2 that culminated in a January 24, 1939, agreement allowing those Jews expelled in the previous October to return to Germany for a stay sufficiently long to settle their financial affairs. Details of the controversy are in *DGFP*, D, Vol. 5, docs. 84, 88, 89, 91, 92, 95, 107, and 127.

December 7, 1938

Subject: Minister Beck's confidentially imparted observations (a) on his "balance diplomacy"; (b) Poland's and France's respective relations with Soviet; (c) French-German declaration of December 6 and 1/ its estimated effect upon Poland's pacts with France and Germany, and 2/ value of France's and Britain's declarations with Germany as a long-range basis for foreign policy; (d) Polish-French relations, and Beck's discernible desire for improved understanding and closer relations; Beck's clarification of Poland's pre-Munich and post-Munich position

In conversation with Minister Beck on various aspects of Polish foreign policy, he emphasized that, from Poland's angle, maintenance of the delicate balance between Moscow and Berlin was more difficult and even more important than maintenance of the balance between Berlin and Paris. Equilibrium in Polish policy between her two major neighbors was particularly difficult, mainly due to Berlin's inherent misunderstanding and mistrust of Moscow. On the other hand, however, Poland found it measurably easier to balance her relations between Berlin and Paris, in that the passage of time had served to mitigate Paris' first flush of resentment over the Polish-German Non-Aggression Agreement; in fact, in recent years Warsaw had found that fundamentally the Polish-German Non-Aggression Agreement had ceased to have an unfavorable bearing upon the Polish-French Alliance. On the other hand, Berlin had accepted the Polish-French Alliance as representing no hindrance to the Polish-German Non-Aggression Agreement.

Turning to Poland's and France's respective relations with the Soviets, and more particularly their comparative appraisals of the Soviets' potential military strength, Minister Beck remarked that in 1922, when he, as Military Attaché at the Polish Embassy in Paris, had remarked to General Foch that the Soviet Army (then in the course of reorganizing) would bear watching in terms of potential strength and European balance, Foch had manifested distinct annoyance with Beck's remark, adding that such an idea was illusory and preposterous. At that time, and subsequently, Poland, always in a better position than France to watch closely and appraise realistically Soviet internal developments, was aware of the Soviet's mounting military strength. Minister Beck then remarked that it had been with a combined sense of amusement and interest that years later General Gamelin had loudly acclaimed the Soviet Army as an outstanding force and as a potential balance in the European politico-military arena. The Minister then stated his opinion that, while Poland had kept abreast of military developments in the Soviet [Union] during past years, hence realizing its mounting strength, Poland had taken full account of the immediate and long-range bearing of certain weaknesses in the structure resultant from a series of "purges" over past years. Therefore, Beck felt Poland was apt to evaluate the Soviet Army's potential strength more realistically than France, which was apparently inclined to over-rate the Soviet's strength.

Turning then to the subject of the French-German declaration signed December 6, Minister Beck remarked with a sense of satisfaction that M. Bonnet had advised Polish Ambassador [Juliusz] Łukasiewicz well in advance of France's undertaking and had kept him abreast of negotiations. At the same time Bonnet had pointed out that his Government considered the French-German declaration would work no hindrance either to the Polish-German Alliance or the Polish-German Non-Aggression Agreement.

About the same time, Chancellor Hitler had advised Polish Ambassador [Józef] Lipski that Germany intended to join in a declaration with France and that he likewise considered that this declaration would have no unfavorable bearing upon the Polish-French Alliance and the Polish-German Non-Aggression Agreement. It was significant to me that Hitler failed to mention the possible effect of the then forthcoming French-German declaration upon the French-Soviet Alliance. In fact, I interpret this to mean that Hitler deliberately eliminated mention of the latter pact as a means of evidencing his non-acceptance thereof.

In response to Bonnet's aforementioned message to Beck through the Polish Ambassador in Paris, Beck had replied he was in accord with M. Bonnet's opinion that the French-German declaration would not affect the Polish-French Alliance nor Poland's Non-Aggression Agreement with Germany. In fact, he added his belief that France's action now removed any existent differences of views between Poland and France. In other words, the German-French declaration in effect had placed Poland's and France's respective relations vis-à-vis Germany on the same level.

Though Beck has not expressed it in so many words, I gain the impression he is not inclined to look for either France or Britain, in terms of the long-range outlook to base with any degree of permanency their respective foreign policies on the declarations with Germany. Minister Beck imparted his high esteem both for M. Daladier and M. Bonnet. He felt that of the two M. Bonnet had a clearer grasp of the fundamentals governing Polish policy. On the other hand, he felt that M. Daladier's political activities had been so confined to the internal affairs of France that he had had little time to keep abreast of problems confronting Polish policy. Beck had learned with sincere regret that, due to a combination of rapid post-Munich events, M. Daladier was inclined to be annoyed with Poland—especially in connection with Poland's action vis-à-vis Prague.[2] Beck particularly regretted this in view of his belief that M. Daladier had perhaps failed to grasp the whole picture from Poland's own objective standpoint.

By way of further clarification of Poland's position, the Minister pointed out that at no time during the past year had he or his close collaborators believed that either France or England would march for Czechoslovakia or that Czechoslovakia would fight Germany single-handed. (My conversations with Minister Beck, Marshal Śmigły-Rydz, and Chief of Staff General [Wacław] Stachiewicz over the past year bear out Beck on this point). Beck continued that meanwhile both London and Paris had vigorously pressed Warsaw to commit Poland to a line-up with France and Britain vis-à-vis Germany.

During the period leading up to the Munich Conference, and in response to London's request that Warsaw suppress its violent press attack on Prague, Beck had stated that he would rather be criticized for acting tactlessly at that moment than to be accused three months hence of having "let down" Czechoslovakia.

Here Beck emphasized that, with the conviction in the back of his mind that Paris and London would seek to negotiate rather than fight over Czechoslovakia, he had interpreted London's pressure for his commitment in the light of an attempt to use Poland's desired declaration of alignment in the nature of a "big stick" vis-à-vis Berlin. In other words, he foresaw that:

(a) London's immediate objective envisaged possibly trying to bring Berlin to terms by pointing out that, with Poland and Czechoslovakia in the East and Britain and France in the West, Germany faced a conflict on two fronts;

(b) London's possible longer-range objective envisaged, in event of bringing Germany to terms, calling a four-power conference to the exclusion of Poland. Moreover, Beck had foreseen that a four-power conference entailed potential dangers for the smaller powers; in other words, that the latter might possibly become the victims of "peaceful settlements" between the major powers. Moreover, he reiterated with emphasis his former statements to effect that Poland, whose claims for the Teschen district had pre-dated and were more justifiable than Germany's claims for the Sudetenland, had from the very outset consistently voiced her insistence upon equal and non-discriminatory treatment of Polish claims—and had so notified the capitals of the four major powers. Hence the London-Paris agreement to advance the scope of treatment of Germany's claims for the Sudeten territory from autonomy to cession, in which deliberation Poland had had no part, had placed Poland in a position whereat there was no alternative other than to settle her claims in her own way. (I am aware that Beck and his collaborators were faced not only with a question of prestige in the light of their internal political arena but also with what they considered the necessity of *"showing"* Germany they were willing to *fight* for what they considered their rightful objectives.)[3]

(c) the recent French-German declaration would undoubtedly have the effect of "putting to sleep" the French-Soviet Alliance. Moreover, Beck felt this declaration placed Poland's and France's respective relations with Germany on the same level. Hence, there should be little if any difference of views now between France and Poland.

From the foregoing and other conversations with Minister Beck, I gain the distinct impression that he has a sincere desire of clarifying Poland's position with Messrs. Daladier and Bonnet towards a better understanding and amelioration in relations between Poland and France.

---

1. This document has been published in the series *Foreign Relations of the United States 1938* (Washington, 1953), 1:108–11. It is included herein to preserve the continuity of Biddle's running narrative and analysis of Polish diplomacy, as well as to illustrate the evolution of his perception of both the Polish and general European diplomatic scenes. In addition, this document is an excellent presentation of Beck's thinking on the entire Munich question.

2. Reference here is to the Polish ultimatum to Prague on Teschen and the subsequent territorial changes involving that area.

3. Reference here is to the Polish-German dispute over the strategically important town of Bohumin (Bogumin) in Teschen; see Document no. 16 below.

December 22, 1938

Subject: Opinion of Turkish Ambassador[1] and discussions with passing Nazi agents bearing on schemes envisaged by the war lords and political dreamers of the Nazi extremist element; Observations on various aspects of Poland's position

Judging from my discussions with passing Nazi propaganda bureau agents, the Turkish Ambassador, and other informed individuals here, it is steadily becoming clearer that Hitler's ultimate objective entails Germany's eventually becoming the dominating power on this side of the Atlantic, and that the course envisaged, at least by the Nazi extremists now in the "saddle", toward that end is somewhat along the following lines: While the establishment of an independent Ukrainian state, or a "Greater Ukraine", as the project is now labeled by the revolutionary organization now operating under Berlin influence in Prague,[2] figures as Berlin's major objective, I do not look for Hitler to risk measuring his military strength with that of the Soviet until he might have accomplished the following envisaged program:

(a) Complete ascendency over the area between Germany's eastern and the Soviet's western frontier. In this connection, I understand he envisages the creation of a chain of small subjugated states to serve as a "buffer" between Germany and the Soviet until such time as Hitler is prepared for a thrust at the Soviet. (My informants added that when the time came to "go after" the Soviet Hitler would have organized an army of White Russians to go forward as the advance guard, and that Hitler would approach his object not only from the south, but also through a friendly Finland and an envisagedly amenable Estonia. They added that Estonia had already shifted her arms purchases from Britain to Finland, which was acting as agent for sales of German equipment.)

In line with this scheme he plans to divide Poland into several parts through (1) annexation of the Corridor, Danzig, and Upper Silesia to the Reich, (2) incitement of a rebellion in the Ukrainian minority with an aim to joining it up with Ruthenia, and (3) promise of delivery of Vilno to Lithuania as part compensation for Lithuania's envisaged adherence to a Berlin policy. (In this connection I understand that Berlin, well aware of the Slavs' historic recalcitrance and resistance vis-à-vis Germany and former Austria in their respective forward-looking programs, plans materially to disarm the Polish forces after Poland's envisaged dismemberment.)

I am aware that until recently Hitler has "soft-pedalled" the Danzig Nazis in their desire to "break out" beyond the limits set by Hitler into a bolder than hitherto offensive attitude. I believe, however, that the hour is fast approaching when Hitler might give them instructions to go on the "attack". Moreover, my afore-cited conversations prompt me to feel this may be timed with an even more vigorous agitation among the Ukrainian and German minorities.

Meanwhile the picture taking form on the northern and southern frontiers of Poland may be described by stating that what were previously two detached arms of the Soviet, namely Lithuania and Czechoslovakia, are rapidly becoming the attached arms of Germany.

In Prague, falling in line with Berlin policy with surprising rapidity, we find already a going organization of revolutionary character boldly supporting the Polish Ukrainian minority's bid for autonomy, and playing a leading role in a vigorous campaign envisaging the setting up of a "Greater Ukraine." I understand, moreover, that the efforts of this organization are coordinated with the propaganda broadcasts of Vienna and Leipzig, as well as a secret broadcasting station on Czech soil close to the Czech-Polish border in Trans-Olzan Silesia, disseminating anti-Polish propaganda. Furthermore, Ruthenia is rapidly being rigged up, under Berlin's direction, as a center for anti-Polish, anti-Rumania, and anti-Soviet activities.

I understand through usually reliable channels that in Kaunas there is evidence of a growing tendency to "play ball" with Berlin. Already large student bodies have demonstrated for the return of Valdemaras, for the adoption not only of a pro-German but an anti-Polish policy as well.[3] These demonstrations, I understand, are attributable to Berlin influence.

According to the Turkish Ambassador and the aforementioned Nazi agents who passed through here, Hitler's attention to Memel represents mainly a "play" to bring Lithuania into line—and eventually he aims either to buy off Smetona or support Valdemaras in a *coup d'état* with a view to setting up a Government in Kaunas which might definitively bring Lithuania into Berlin's orbit.

As regards Hitler's identification with machinations vis-à-vis the Ukraine, it is well to bear in mind that at the time Piłsudski and Hitler accomplished the Polish-German Non-Aggression Agreement, it was secretly agreed that Hitler should leave the Polish Ukrainian minority alone.[4] Until recently, mention of the Ukraine project was notably absent in the Nazi press. It is significant, however, that on December 14 the *Schlesiche Zeitung* of Breslau, a paper with conservative and military tradition dating from 1742, carried an article clearly disclosing Germany's interest in the establishment of an independent Ukrainian state, mainly at the expense of Poland and the Soviet. Besides, the article concluded by stating it was advisable that Europe follow events in this area, if it did not wish one day to be surprised. One thing was certain: "The Ukrainian race will live." This then marks a significant departure from Hitler's hitherto apparent desire to withhold Berlin's identification with a Ukrainian project, and a deliberate breach of his secret agreement with Piłsudski. As a matter of fact, Warsaw has on several occasions in the recent past discreetly complained to Berlin about the aforementioned Viennese and Leipzig broadcasts.

In other words, I discern increasing signs that Hitler is fast closing in on Poland, and I believe he means to press with intensified effort on all points, both internally and externally, to bring Warsaw to terms. It now appears he is deliberately "sicking" Czechoslovakia on Poland (such as he is now reportedly "sicking" Hungary on the Transylvanian area of Rumania). In fact it is even conceivable he might carry this to the point of provoking an open conflict with view to taking advantage of any pretext (such as protection of the German minority from possible harm in a disturbed area, etc.) to intervene actively.

Meanwhile, unless the Polish Government comes to terms, or succeeds in stalling for time through diplomatic tactics, I look for Hitler to stir up in every way possible internal restiveness in Poland, especially amongst the German minority, even perhaps with view eventually to creating a pretext for an open row. For I believe Hitler and his "extremist" associates, provided they felt sufficiently confident France had been neutralized by the recent Paris-Berlin declaration and that neither France nor the Soviet were in the mood nor of the capacity to come to Poland's aid, would welcome an opportunity "to try out" their Army in an envisagedly victorious war of short duration, in order to build up confidence amongst their armed forces and to offset what Hitler reportedly interprets as a lingering spirit of defeatism and pacifism amongst the German masses. Moreover, according to my aforementioned informants, the Turkish Ambassador and the Nazi agents, Hitler would like to accomplish this provided he thought he could "localize" it before France and Great Britain might have attained any further appreciable improvement in their respective armaments.

As regards the other links in Hitler's envisaged chain of smaller units between the German and Soviet areas, my aforementioned informants were of the opinion (a) Hitler counts upon Yugoslavia and Bulgaria as "friends" and counts upon their "sitting tight"; moreover, that Hungary will completely "board the band wagon" at an early date; (b) as regards Rumania, Hitler is already setting the scene for the amputation: Bukovina to line up with Ruthenia, and possibly even part or all of Bessarabia (The "extremist" element in Berlin figures on there being three million Ukrainians in Rumania. This, they hold, includes Bessarabia.); (c) Hitler aims that Bucharest should henceforth have its hands full with Berlin-inspired Hungarian pressure vis-à-vis Transylvania.

In discussing King Carol, the Turkish Ambassador unhesitatingly and bluntly labeled him a *voleur*, adding that if anything in the form of financial benefits were to come Bucharest's way Carol was always sure to get his usually important share of the "soap." The reason he had "bumped off" Codreanu and "Iron Guard" associates was not only to fortify his own political position, but also to clear the Rumanian arena of forces which might insist upon sharing the spoils with him. Carol had always had a price, took it from where he could get it, and the Berlin of today knew it. Carol, like his compatriots, suffered from sensitivity of the "pocket nerve" and would not be difficult to line up eventually when Berlin was prepared to assure itself of the Rumanian Government's alignment with Berlin policy.

Ascendency over the area between Germany and the Soviet in general, and over Poland in particular, is of paramount importance in terms of the immediate aspect of Hitler's program. In connection therewith, Hitler feels he must eliminate Poland as a force of potential resistance from the picture as speedily as possible, in order to make a thrust at France before she will have effectively prepared to meet a combined German and Italian attack. Hitler, according to the Turkish Ambassador, does not dare risk coming to grips with France until Poland may have been put down, for Hitler is convinced that Poland would jump on his back the instant the French, and perhaps the British, forces might have engaged the German forces in the field.[5] His plan envisages a joint German and Italian campaign vis-à-vis France, entailing the immediate closing of the Mediterranean and the Suez Canal to all British and French shipping. The attack would be one of lightning and destructive character. Ribbentrop, who is today in the "saddle", in terms of direction of foreign policy, continues to maintain that Britain is still in such a state of unpreparedness that she will have her hands full merely taking care of "home defense" and protection of her merchant fleet; that Germany may, in collaboration with Italy, consequently proceed against France without much worry of effective resistance from Britain. Of pertinent bearing, I am reliably informed that Ribbentrop (still Britain's "Public Enemy No. 1") is now frequently referred to by Hitler in his informal conversation as "my man Ribbentrop".

In fact, reports reaching the British Ambassador here from Berlin concur with the substance of my recent conversation with an agent of the Press Bureau of the Nazi Party (who recently passed through Warsaw) to the effect that Hitler had remarked, in the presence of several of his Ministers, that if he had only listened to "his man Ribbentrop" (instead of Goering and Neurath) he could have launched a victorious attack of short duration against Prague without effective interference from abroad. In this connection, the Turkish Ambassador stated that, through an envisaged victory over France, Hitler plans his "pay-off" to Mussolini by leaving him North Africa, retaining the right to exercise full sway over the European continent. The Ambassador, moreover, emphasized that upper Nazi circles are anxious to bring about their envisaged attack on France as soon as possible in order to strike before France and Britain will have become better prepared.

Of pertinent bearing, my inquiries during discussions with my aforementioned informants disclose that the fundamental explanation for Rome's outburst regarding Tunis, Corsica and Nice during Ribbentrop's visit in Paris was a tactical move previously agreed upon by Berlin and Rome. Ribbentrop was anxious to neutralize France during Berlin's period of "consolidation" in Eastern and Central Europe. Hence he had felt it would be tactically helpful, from a psychological standpoint, if Rome, the other axis partner, shouted for French possessions while Ribbentrop would be talking to Bonnet. Ribbentrop had felt that during the conversation Bonnet's mind might thus be divided between Ribbentrop's offer to sign a declaration along limited lines and the disturbing outburst of the other axis partner. Threatened by one end of the axis, and seeing the outstretched hand of the other end, Bonnet might thus the more readily be brought to grasp the outstretched hand, and to be content with Berlin's refusal to extend the scope of the declaration beyond the frontiers common to Germany and France. In other words, it might have been a preconceived "ploy", aimed primarily at bringing Bonnet to terms on Berlin's conditions, and secondarily as an opportunity for Rome to acquire whatever profits might eventually accrue to Italy as a result.

Now it seems that Ribbentrop is satisfied that he obtained Paris' signature and Rome is gratified over the prospect of (a) France's raising the status of the Italian population in Tunis (possibly to the point of extending agricultural loans to the Italian as well as to the French inhabitants), (b) coming to terms on the Djibouti railway, and (c) both France's and Britain's coming to terms on the Suez Canal. These disclosures, in response to my inquiries, are to the following extent borne out by the fact that the Polish Ambassador to Rome was told several days ago by [Italian] Foreign Minister Ciano that the latter did not expect the Tunis claims to give rise to serious consequences; the issue involved more a social than a territorial aspect and Ciano believed that in that light the matter would be settled satisfactorily. Moreover, Ciano expected France eventually to meet Rome's Djibouti claims satisfactorily and France and Britain to adjust the Suez issue.

In evaluating the substance of (a) the above-cited opinion of the Turkish Ambassador upon certain phases of Berlin's forward-looking program; and (b) the above-cited information imparted to me by Nazi secret agents who have recently passed through here in various guises, I do not lose sight of the fact that the Turkish Ambassador is an Italophobe almost to the point of fanaticism, and that though generally exceptionally well informed, "a professional pessimist". Besides, I do not fail to take into consideration that if and when Germany might have gained complete ascendency over whatever states still represent resistance points, such as Poland and Rumania, it might spell the approach of an early show-down between the Axis and Turkey. In line with this, I do not exclude the possibility that his expressed opinion might have been motivated by the tactical conception that by planting the thought that the "silencing" of Poland might presage a subsequent attack on France, he might serve to stir up more vigorous French interest in the Polish-French Alliance. After all Turkey, like all other countries in Eastern, Central, and Southeastern Europe, is seeking to divert Berlin's drive from all their own necks.

In evaluating the information imparted to me by the aforementioned Nazi agents, while I am inclined to mark it down partly (a) to the scare- and confusion-inspiring technique of Nazidom's formula of gangster diplomacy, and (b) to the speculative dreams of the "extremist" element of Nazi inner circles, I am aware that at the moment the "extremist" element is in the saddle. Moreover, it is well to bear in mind that previous to the Anschluss, and again in the period leading up to the Sudeten, the Propaganda Bureau in Berlin characteristically made an "open secret" of Hitler's intentions vis-à-vis both projects; as these rumored intentions gained widespread attention, they were generally received as the fantastic machinations of the war lords and radical political dreamers of Berlin. Therefore, in view of these recollections, the aforementioned opinion of the Turkish Ambassador and the Nazi agents' information, a large portion of which I am inclined to attribute to Nazi Propaganda Bureau inspiration, might conceivably serve in the light, at least from time to time, of watching the course of Berlin's diplomacy and other political maneuvers during the next few months.

Insofar as Poland is concerned, Beck is well aware (a) of Berlin's intensified pressure at all points above described, and (b) of the destructive designs of the Nazi "extremists". He is, moreover, alive to the necessity of coming to a decision at an early date as to what course to pursue henceforth vis-à-vis Berlin, and as he faces the problem I believe the two answers he awaits are: (a) Bonnet's reply to Polish Ambassador Lukasiewicz's soundings as to how far Poland might count on France in the event of a conflict with Germany (I am aware that until today, December 22, Paris has, to the disappointment of Warsaw, not made itself clear.);[6] and (b) Polish Ambassador to Moscow [Wacław] Grzybowski's impression as to Moscow's mood and capacity to support Poland's continued resistance to German pressure. In my opinion, the answers to these questions may be expected to prove the determining factors in Beck's forward-looking program.

At this point it is pertinent to recall that some time ago I discovered there was a school of thought in official circles here which had long envisaged Poland's collaboration with Germany in an envisaged establishment of an independent Ukrainian state, wherein this group pictures Poland's receiving her proportionate rewards for "services rendered" and territory contributed.[7] I am aware, however, that this school of thought received a shock when Hitler refused to permit the establishment of Poland's envisaged common frontier with Hungary. Indeed, their rude awakening to the realization that Berlin's "political engineers" were setting up Ruthenia as a "propaganda fortress", turned against Poland as well as the Soviet, dampened their enthusiasm for collaboration with Germany in connection with the Ukraine. Moreover, their pride was deeply offended—and for a Pole this is an almost unforgivable sin.

Moreover, my own observations of Nazi mentality convince me the aforementioned group's hope of Germany's willingness to collaborate with Poland in and after the establishment of any potentially fruitful scheme is nothing short of a "pipe dream". Indeed, to my mind, Berlin's idea of collaboration with a smaller state is decidedly foreign to the ideas of collaboration entertained by the aforementioned Polish group. Poland would do all the collaborating, and Germany all the profit-taking. Poland would be like a vehicle used by a person to reach some place on an important mission—after reaching his destination he would strip the car of all detachable parts and cast the rest on the "dump heap".

In that I realize Beck possesses a keen insight into the German mentality, I feel he entertains no illusions as to Poland's potential benefits from collaboration with Germany. Hence it would seem that his best "out" is the possibility of a French- and/or Soviet-supported Polish resistance to German pressure—or perhaps even a lightning thrust at Czechoslovakia (a) in a hope of "silencing" Ruthenia, a thorn of increasing discomfort in Poland's side, without intervention of a third power, and (b) in a hope that Germany's potential intervention might bring other powers to Poland's side.

As regards the likelihood of Paris' committing itself to forceful action in connection with the Polish-French Alliance, see Memorandum A attached hereto. As regards Moscow's potential capacity and mood to support Warsaw's continued resistance to Berlin pressure, see Memorandum B attached hereto. As regards the possibility of Poland's striking out suddenly against Czechoslovakia, see Memorandum C attached hereto.

In endeavoring to estimate Beck's future attitude vis-à-vis Berlin, it is pertinent to mention that at the conclusion of a conference of the inner Government circle with the President on December 14 at the *Zamek*,[8] Beck was requested to press Berlin for a clarification of its intentions in Eastern Europe in general and vis-à-vis Poland in particular. Beck later conferred with German Ambassador [Hans Adolf] von Moltke. In connection therewith, Under Secretary of State Count [Jan] Szembek imparted that Beck had been forceful in his conversation, emphasizing that Poland, "one of the Great Powers", insisted upon Berlin's explanation of its recent actions vis-à-vis Poland and insisted upon a clarification as to what Berlin intended to do vis-à-vis Memel, where Poland had interests, and vis-à-vis the Soviet. Moltke had replied that Berlin intended no annexation of Memel and was merely interested in seeing that it enjoyed full rights under the Statute. As regards the Soviet, Moltke would leave the explanation of Berlin's interest for some official of the German Government to clarify.

Moltke subsequently arranged for Ribbentrop to come here "on the Polish Government's invitation" about mid-January. Moltke yesterday imparted to the Rumanian Ambassador[9] that he hoped Warsaw would alter its recently adopted recalcitrant attitude towards Berlin before Ribbentrop arrived, adding that Berlin was seriously annoyed over Beck's declaration with Moscow. Moltke considered Beck had made a great mistake.

Beck departed from Warsaw December 21 for Monaco. Before his departure he sent me a confidential message, requesting me to guard it with secrecy, that he intended to go to Monaco for about ten days in order to have time to think out his various problems and to gain a clear perspective before making certain important decisions. He facetiously added he had chosen Monaco, since it was the only country to which he might go without being suspected of negotiating for an alliance.

It is pertinent to state that the Rumanian Ambassador, characterizing the opinion of several representatives of other nearby Central European states, has the impression that Poland would be willing to collaborate with Germany against the Soviet, provided she could be assured of generous compensation. He bases this impression (a) upon his belief that any positive action vis-à-vis Russia is of major interest to Poland—in fact, could not be carried out without Poland's collaboration, unless Germany were willing to fight both Poland and the Soviet; (b) upon the fact that the Ambassador's own Government circles cannot picture Poland's marching with the Soviet against Germany—rather it might be the other way round. The Ambassador concurs in my opinion, however, that if Berlin at the outset refused to talk terms satisfactory to Warsaw, such as withdrawal of objections to a "common frontier" with Hungary, Berlin might force Poland over to the side of the Soviet.

In this connection, I do not exclude the possibility that if Berlin strikes recognizable resistance during the forthcoming Beck-Ribbentrop talks, which Berlin felt might lead to widespread complications, Berlin might adopt the role of the "spider and the web"—or empty promises.

In considering the Rumanian Ambassador's impression, I am inclined to feel that his attitude borders on confusion and defeatism in view not only of the foregoing, but also because of his statement that he felt there was nothing for his country and Poland eventually to do but to collaborate with Germany in her Ukraine objective—in fact, he said that he and his Government circles felt London and Paris would welcome Germany's turning against the Soviet, that Germany could count upon their standing aside. Moreover, I recall having pointed out in a previous despatch that, while Beck might conceivably and eventually agree to collaborate with Germany in a venture vis-à-vis the Soviet, both his insight to the German mentality and his foresight might prompt him to regard such a venture as spelling a grim prospect for Poland in terms of the long-range outlook and, as such, to treat it in the light of a last alternative. Besides, in my opinion, Beck would not likely lose sight of the improbability of Hitler's attempting a military venture vis-à-vis the Soviet until he would have either sufficiently assured himself of Britain's and France's neutrality during such a campaign, or would have attempted to "silence" France through a potential campaign at the side of Italy. In connection with the latter, if Beck suspected that Hitler intended to strike at France, I am of the opinion that Beck would not commit himself to collaborate with Germany.

Hence I believe that Beck, during his visit to Monaco, will study all angles of events in the making in order to gain a clear perspective of the general trend and its potential bearing on Poland's position. He will, moreover, undoubtedly watch for signs indicating the possible outcome of Chamberlain's forthcoming meeting with Mussolini, for the outcome thereof will undoubtedly have an important bearing on Poland's forward-looking policy. I look for him meanwhile to continue a "wait-and-see" policy.

MEMORANDUM A

As to the likelihood of Paris' committing itself positively to forceful action in connection with the Polish-French alliance, it is interesting to note that according to information through usually reliable channels, Berlin's "political engineers" estimate that about 60% of leading political circles in Paris would oppose any definite commitment at this time to military action in connection with Eastern and Central Europe, and that this element favors "putting to sleep"—if not altogether cutting loose from, France's alliances with Poland and the Soviet. This estimate corresponds with that of political experts of the Angora [Ankara] Government.

Moreover, I am aware that Poland's press in France hit a

"new low" for all time in the early stage of the post-Munich period. In fact, there has been little if any improvement in French feeling towards Poland since the Warsaw-Prague "settlement" over the Teschen district. Besides, the Government here has adopted an antagonizing attitude toward France's economic interests in this city. As a matter of fact, French investors in the Warsaw Electric Company are now in the process of defending their interests against an attempt to sequester the property. Furthermore, for Poland's part, Warsaw has done little to improve relations with Paris by apparently going out of its way to lend moral support to Rome's recent outburst regarding Tunis, etcetera. Moreover, to make sure that Paris did not miss these articles, the Warsaw Government-controlled press agency, PAT, deliberately distributed the substance thereof to their Paris subscribers. In view of Beck's earnest desire to gain a sympathetic ear in Paris, adoption of such an inconsistent attitude in the Polish press is inexplicable, unless it might be put down to a complete lack of coordination between Beck and his Press Bureau, and/or both acute pique over France's declaration with Germany and subsequent rumors published in the foreign press that Ribbentrop and Bonnet have discussed the Polish-French alliance and implications that France had "cooled off" on this alliance. In other words, with France's not having yet attained her desired standard of military preparedness and with an already recalcitrant French public opinion *vis-à-vis* Poland (which certainly could not have been ameliorated by the moral support recently given Rome's outburst by the Warsaw Government-controlled press), it seems hardly likely that Paris would either be in the mood or of the capacity to greet with outstretched arms Beck's emissary when the latter seeks a definite commitment entailing French military action in the event Poland came to grips with Germany.

* * * * * * * * * * *

MEMORANDUM B

As regards Moscow's potential mood and capacity to lend support to Warsaw's continued resistance to Berlin pressure, the only indications I have so far had on this score, are the following:

The Rumanian Ambassador informed me confidentially that his Government had received a report that Litvinov, in recent conversation with a foreign diplomat accredited to Moscow, had given the latter the impression that until he might have had more time to judge Warsaw's actions, he was not inclined to take too seriously Warsaw's sudden turn towards Moscow. However, the Rumanian Government's source of information had interpreted Litvinov's attitude as a willingness to "play ball' with Warsaw in the hope that improved relations might possibly serve Moscow profitably in the end.

Of pertinent bearing, Minister Beck's Chief of Cabinet, Count Łubieński, in discussing current negotiations between Warsaw and Moscow looking to a trade pact, stated that while TAS[S][10] had recently reported that Moscow was prepared to offer a deal on a basis whereby Moscow would purchase goods here in 1939 amounting to 80 million *złotys*, he was disinclined to be hopeful that Moscow's purchases would exceed much more than about 20 to 25 million *złotys*. Naturally he hoped for considerably more but due to past experiences in commerce with the Soviet, figures cited in negotiations usually dwindled considerably in practice. On the other hand, experience had shown that in many cases Moscow directed its purchases along political tactical lines.

In this connection, Łubieński mentioned that Moscow had already evinced considerable interest in the possible purchase of Polish coal. Łubieński interpreted this more in the light of a political gesture than a commercial requirement.

He then stated signs now pointed to Moscow's continuance of steel orders formerly issued to the Trzyniec foundries, formerly in Czecho-Slovakia, now in Poland.

* * * * * * * * * * * *

MEMORANDUM C

As regards the possibility of a Polish-Czecho-Slovak conflict, it is well to bear in mind the following:

On December 14th, the inner Government conferred with the President at the *Zamek*. At the conclusion of the conference it was decided that Beck should press Berlin for a clarification of its intentions in Eastern Europe in general, and *vis-à-vis* Poland in particular.

Marshal Śmigły-Rydz moreover, reportedly inferred that army circles had been disappointed by their impression that a "silencing" of Ruthenia as a center of anti-Polish activities was no longer a question. Moreover, military circles continued to feel that the only solution was a lightening thrust at Ruthenia, which they felt would not encounter resistance from Rumania, Hungary, or Yugoslavia. They felt that even in the case of Germany, they would not encounter German intervention, provided the job was accomplished speedily.

I am, moreover, aware that high military circles here have been pressing for action *vis-à-vis* Ruthenia until several days ago, when there was a noticeable quieting of anti-Polish activities arising in Ruthenia, on the heels of Warsaw's vigorous note to Prague. I now learn, however, that due to a recent incident wherein a group of Czechs reportedly caused disorder in the Teschen district by hurling bombs, grenades, etc., Warsaw is planning to send a fresh protest to Prague. What effect this will have on the military hotheads is too early to forecast. It is safe to say, however, that their knowledge of this recent incident will not improve their mounting recalcitrance towards Czecho-Slovakia.

1. M. Ferid Tek.

2. Reference is to the Organization of Ukrainian Nationalists (OUN), which openly flaunted its connections with Germany and advocated the use of terrorist tactics to oppose Polish rule of the Ukraine. For details, see Ryszard Torzecki, *Kwestia ukrainska w polityce III Rzeszy 1933-1945* (Warsaw, 1972), pp. 121 ff.

3. Biddle here refers to domestic political developments in hostile neighboring Lithuania. In 1926, Augustine Voldemaras headed a Pilsudski-style coup and established himself as a "dictator of the Right"; but after he introduced a new constitution greatly expanding the power of the presidency, the incumbent president, Antanas Smetona, ousted Voldemaras in favor of his own brother-in-law, who retained the authoritarian character of the regime. Voldemaras especially hated Pilsudski and all that he represented in Poland; hence, the Polish worries transmitted by Biddle.

4. There is no evidence that such an agreement existed, not even in the form of a tacit understanding.

5. This observation is typical of the brilliant insight that Biddle had into the complexities of Hitler's diplomatic thinking, for it agrees completely with the latter's views as outlined in the famous "Hossbach Memorandum" of November 5, 1937—a highly secret document not revealed until after the war. *DGFP*, D, 1, Doc. 19.

6. See the extremely pessimistic reports sent to Beck by Łukasiewicz from Paris in mid-December 1938; Łukasiewicz, *Diplomat in Paris*, pp. 155–60.

7. There is no evidence that anyone in the Polish government counted on their country's cooperation with Germany in return for territorial compensation as a reward. Of course, there were individuals outside of official circles who advocated this kind of relationship—headed by Władysław Studnicki—but they don't appear to have exerted much influence over Beck or other responsible Polish leaders.

8. The *Zamek*, or Royal Castle, was the official residence of the president of Poland, and hence the scene of particularly important ceremonial functions.

9. Constantin Visoianu.

10. The official Soviet News Agency.

December 22, 1938

Subject: Polish Government's rejection of
Ukrainian Minority's demand for autonomy on
grounds of unconstitutionality; observations

I have the honor (a) to supplement my despatch No. 844 of
December 10, 1938,[1] page 1, wherein I reported that the
Ukrainian Deputies of the Sejm [Diet] presented on the part
of the Ukrainian minority in Poland a demand for autonomy;
(b) to refer to my despatch No. 848 of December 15, 1938;[2]
and (c) to report the following developments in connection
with the Ukrainian minority demands.

As anticipated, the Polish Government dealt with the legal
aspect of the Ukrainian demands, and in such light turned them
down as being unconstitutional.[3] Accordingly, at yesterday's
(December 21st) session of the Sejm, Speaker of the House
[Wacław] Makowski replied to the spokesman of the Ukrainian Deputies in the form of a private letter which in substance
read: That in view of regulations governing Sejm debates the
Ukrainian motion could not become the object of discussion.
According to these regulations, the Speaker classified the
motion as a proposal to amend the Constitution. Such proposal had to bear the signatures of at least one quarter of
the House, or 52 signatures.

Since conditions prevailing in the House preclude the
Ukrainian Deputies' hope of attaining no less than 52 signatures, the Speaker's action marks the death knell to the Ukrainian demands from a parliamentary standpoint. I now learn
from one of the Ukrainian leaders that the Ukrainian Deputies

of the Sejm plan to meet in Lwów on December 28, when they will discuss various aspects of the outcome of their parliamentary demands and will consider forward-looking action.

During yesterday's session there were current "Lobby rumors" to the effect that, as the result of the recent help of the Papal Nuncio, the Ukrainians had become more conciliatory and might be willing to "play ball" with the Government on terms more satisfactory to the Government standpoint. In conversation with one of the Ukrainian leaders, however, he denied that there was any truth in these rumors, contending that his and his associates' demands represented more of an effort to find a common footing for cooperation with the Poles than a move of anti-Polish character. The Government's answer to their efforts had been decidedly in the negative and he felt altogether that if Polish-Ukrainian relations were worse than they used to be, the fault was on the Polish side. He therefore felt that the first move should now come from the Poles.

While it is too early to forecast future developments, it is safe to assume that the Government will lose no time in taking conciliatory steps "behind the scenes"—and in these efforts, I look for the Vatican to take a hand through its intelligent and courageous and able Papal Nuncio here.

1. This dispatch is not reproduced in this volume but is deposited in the Department of State Files of the National Archives, Washington, D.C.

2. See note 1 above.

3. The Ukrainian National-Democratic Union (UNDO), the leading Ukrainian moderate organization which worked for the advancement of Ukrainian interests within the established framework of the Polish political system, had become increasingly upset with Polish attempts to Polonize forcibly the Ukrainian population. Accordingly, on May 7, 1938, it adopted a resolution demanding the "immediate recognition of the Ukrainian nation in Poland as a separate national entity," together with territorial autonomy for all those lands inhabited by Ukrainians which formed "one compact economic and geopolitical whole." The demands are printed in the contemporary Polish publication *Sprawy Narodowościowe* 12(1938):285–88, and an English translation is in Stefan Horak, *Poland and Her National Minorities, 1919–1939* (New York, 1961), p. 169. Since the UNDO had several deputies in the Polish parliament, it sought to reopen the question there when the government, as expected, rejected outright the demands. For a discussion of the Ukrainian question in Poland during this period, see Edward D. Wynot, Jr., "The Ukrainians and the Polish Regime, 1937–1939," *The Ukrainian Historian* 7(1970): 44–60.

December 22, 1938

Subject: Observations on current developments concerning the so-called Jewish problem in Poland

I have the honor to supplement my despatch No. 801 of November 15, 1938,[1] wherein (a) I described various developments, both current and in the making, as regards the Jewish problem; (b) to refer to my previous writings on this subject wherein I have taken frequent occasion to point out that events then in the making bore the earmarks of a more drastic wave of anti-Semitism here; and to report the following observations upon the current turn of events in connection with the Jewish problem here.

As forecast in previous writings, the position of the Jewish community in Poland is rapidly taking a turn for the worse. Preceded by a series of articles and editorials in the Polish press treating with the problem, and in most cases emphasizing the necessity for international treatment of the Jewish problem in a *global* rather than a *limited* sense, looking to a solution in terms of large-scale emigration, the following events took place during the past 24 hours. General [Stanisław] Skwarczyński, Chief of OZON and spokesman for what he numbered as 116 OZON Deputies, yesterday afternoon (December 21st) made an interpellation regarding the subject of Jewish emigration to the following effect:

On behalf of his group he took occasion to repeat with emphasis that OZON condemned any acts of peril and persecution, but contended vigorously that the number of Jews was excessive. The economic and cultural development of Poland called for large-scale Jewish emigration. Hence, they addressed the Government to ascertain what the Government intended to do in the matter. Aware of the Government's arduous study of the problem, they now wanted to have an account of what work had actually been done. More precisely, they wanted to ascertain the Government's plan (a) for emigration; (b) what territorial outlets were being considered; and (c) what financial plan was being worked out.

During that same evening, Colonel [Zygmunt] Wenda, Chief of Staff in the direction of OZON affairs, followed up the General's aforementioned interpellation by a radio broadcast to the following effect: Wenda referred to the aforementioned interpellation as having marked an occasion of great consequence in that it had been the first time that the Jewish problem had been taken up officially by Parliament. In contending that this move would cause the Government to seek arrangements for mass emigration of the Jews, Wenda emphasized that this could not be done at the cost of the racial Poles. He concluded by emphasizing that it must be done, however, in order that the Polish towns, villages, industry and trade might be properly Polonized.

Another significant event which took place on the heels of the parliamentary interpellation was the sticking of large posters on the walls in various quarters of Warsaw. These posters contain in effect what might be characterized as an "invitation" for the racial Poles to omit the Jewish shops in their lists of Christmas shopping. As reason therefore the posters point out that every *złoty* spent in Jewish shops is a crime against the nation and the country. This part of the "invitation" concludes by emphasizing that the money of the Polish people should go to the Polish merchants. In the second part of the poster it is pointed out that there are 4 million Jews in Poland (this, of course, is in excess of the actual number). Then follows a list of statistics showing the predominance of the Jews in the trades, industry, professions, etc., and calling for resistance to the dominant economic position of the Jews in Poland.

Another sign of the current trend is illustrated by the efforts of Sejm Deputy [Franciszek] Stoch, (non-partisan),[2] to obtain the necessary 14 signatures to enable him to present a bill aimed at the establishment of an anti-Semitic law along the following lines: (a) to classify Jews on a religious and not a racial basis; (b) all persons confessing to the Jewish Creed, or who were Jews until 1916, to be considered "temporary" citizens and to be deprived of all public rights. Exception in connection therewith to be granted in the case of those who have been recognized by the State for special merit; they and their families to be exempt. In further connection therewith, a limit of 50,000 families to be set as the maximum for those families who may be exempted from discrimination.

In connection with this projected bill, Deputy Stoch energetically endeavored for about 10 days to secure the number of signatures necessary to qualify his bill for presentation. Until yesterday afternoon he had succeeded in acquiring all but one. I understand that Deputies of the OZON Party are disinclined to support Stoch's proposal. Since OZON claims 159 out of the total of 208 seats in the Sejm, I look for OZON to wish to take a lead in the matter and to work out its own bills on the Jewish question.

In this connection I am inclined at the moment to look for the more liberal element in Government quarters, as well as the Church, to bring influence to bear on OZON circles to moderate the tone and substance of whatever bills OZON might eventually propose. In my various conversations I have gained the impression that the tendency is to model such bills after the Hungarian laws.[3] In other words, at least the present move of Government circles presages an attempt to mollify any and all legislative measures. While the Government may possibly support OZON to the extent of aiding OZON towards the enlistment of the nationalistic and anti-Semitic elements, the Government may be expected to exert vigorous efforts to avoid provoking scorn to the same degree as did Germany.

A factor which may possibly work in favor of the Jewish community is the prominence of the Socialist vote in the recent municipal elections, which should somewhat strengthen the hand of the liberal element in Government circles. On the other hand, however, the National Democrats (or ENDEK Party) likewise figured prominently in the results, a fact which might in some districts conceivably offset the Socialist gains. It is too early, however, to judge the full effect of these elections for the official figures will not be published until December 28th.[4]

Meanwhile we may expect an intensification of pressure against the Jews. Moreover, as I anticipated a number of months ago, and so reported, I now discern that the present surge of anti-Semitism is motivated in most cases, except in the case of the inherently anti-Semitic ENDEK Party, more by a desire to force the Jewish problem here into the arena of international consideration than by an acute sense of religious hatred.

On the other hand, I am aware that while Government circles frankly ascribe the so-called Jewish problem to an overcrowded "economic room", there is a certain element in these circles who are inclined to play up the Jewish question for reasons of internal political tactics—namely to enlist the support of the anti-Semitic nationalistic element. I continue to be of the opinion that (a) repercussions of recent anti-Semitic outrages in Germany and (b) the earnest desire of leading political circles here to have the so-called Jewish problem treated *globaly* rather than *limitedly* by inter-governmental conferences seeking a solution, may be expected to work increasing hardships on the Jewish community of Poland.

1. This dispatch is not reproduced in this volume but is deposited in the Department of State Files of the National Archives, Washington, D.C.

2. Although Stoch was officially listed as a "nonpartisan" member of the 1938 Sejm, he represented the extreme nationalist and anti-Semitic movement that sought constantly to push the existing government to the Right. His introduction of this particular bill typified the tactics of the nationalists: to strive to embarrass and force the hand of the government in delicate areas of widespread emotional appeal, especially anti-Jewish campaigns.

3. There were three anti-Jewish laws enacted in interwar Hungary, of which only one was in force at the time of this dispatch; the second had just been introduced to the Hungarian Parliament in December, 1938. The "First Jewish Law," passed under the sponsorship of Premier Kálmán Daranyi in April, 1938, limited the

number of persons defined religiously as Jews that could be admitted to professional positions in the press, theatre, film industry, law, medicine, engineering, and all financial, commercial, or industrial enterprises of a substantial size. Disabled Jewish veterans were exempted from these restrictions, and no attempt was made to break up Jewish capital operations. The "Second Jewish Law," introduced by the government of Béla Imredy and passed into law the following spring (1939) under the direction of Premier Pál Teleki, was more far-reaching in both its definition of what constituted a "religious Jew" and its restrictions on the rights and functions of the Jewish population. This time, severe limitations were placed on Jewish civil, legal, and political rights, and formulas were provided to insure that Jews would be progressively impoverished and driven out of the agrarian as well as commercial and industrial sectors of Hungary's economy. For an analysis of these laws and the circumstances surrounding their passage, see Macartney, *October Fifteenth*, 1: 218-19, 324-25. Biddle obviously had in mind only the first Jewish law when he made the above reference in his dispatch.

4. According to official figures, the government-front OZON on its own ticket won only 21.9 per cent of the total seats at stake in the city councils across Poland, with merely 29 per cent of the popular vote; however, it picked up additional seats by posing as a united nonpartisan bloc in some areas, giving it a grand total of 33.8 percent of all seats. The Socialists actually outpolled the OZON, with 27.3 percent of total council seats; of the rest, the National Democrats (ENDEKS) gained 17 percent, and the Jewish labor party, the BUND, accounted for 9.6 percent. The government's best showing came in Warsaw, where it won 40 of the 100 council slots, with the Socialists and ENDEKS getting 27 and 11, respectively; nowhere did the OZON win a clear majority. Complete figures and analysis of the municipal elections are in W. Jakubowski, "Bilans polityczny wyborów samorządowych," *Światło*, no. 6/7(1939).

December 23, 1938

Subject: British Ambassador's conversations with Minister Beck seeking (a) Polish Government's attitude in event of League High Commissioner's withdrawal from Danzig, and (b) Polish Government's attitude in event of Danzig question's coming to issue between Warsaw and Berlin; Current Warsaw-Berlin negotiations on Danzig

Britain's signature as one of the Big Four who approved the 1924 Statute giving Memel autonomous status under Lithuanian sovereignty is discernibly proving a source of headache for London in view of recent events in Memel.[1] In light of the potential bearing of these events, moreover, upon the situation in Danzig, Britain's membership on the Committee of Three is perceptibly becoming an increasing source of worry for London.

Accordingly, in anticipation of the possiblity of Hitler's releasing the pent-up energy of Nazi Danzigers in the near future, energy which he has hitherto confined to certain limits. London instructed its Ambassador here to sound out Minister Beck as to his Government's attitude in event the Danzig question came to issue in the near future.

In accordance with his instructions, the Ambassador took up the question with Minister Beck on December 21. In reply to the Ambassador's question as to whether the Polish Government might object to the withdrawal of League High Commissioner [Carl] Burckhardt from Danzig, Minister Beck bore out my belief that the Government here would be loath to have the High Commissioner retire in face of anticipated intensification of Berlin pressure concerning the Danzig question by his reply to the effect that his Government would be inclined to oppose the High Commissioner's withdrawal if the question were to come to issue at the League Council meeting in Geneva on January 15. In this connection, I am aware that while the Government here regards the position of the High Commissioner in the light of a "ghost" of the League, they feel that his presence "eases" the increasingly difficult relations between Warsaw and Berlin in connection with the Free City.

In response to Minister Beck's foregoing reply, the British Ambassador made it clear that his Government considered the High Commissioner's continued presence in Danzig ineffective, in fact little short of futile. The British Ambassador then put the direct question as to whether the Polish Government might be willing to make a deal with Berlin on the Danzig issue, adding that if such a deal were made along lines satisfactory to both Warsaw and Berlin, London would regard the matter only with the friendliest interest—as a matter of fact, London had come to consider the problem as one mainly between Warsaw and Berlin. Minister Beck replied that negotiations of a sort had recently begun.[2] However, at this early stage it was difficult to foresee the outcome. With holidays approaching, it would be almost impossible to accelerate the pace of these negotiations. However, by mid-January he should have gained a fairly accurate estimate as to where they were leading. Certainly, by early February he would be in a position to know whether the Polish Government could agree to a potential settlement which then might conceivably be in sight.

The British Ambassador then stated it would be difficult for his Government to postpone its decision in the matter much longer. Naturally London did not wish to do anything to embarrass Minister Beck during his negotiations, but after all both London and Geneva had to look to their own interests. Besides, neither London nor Geneva would welcome the prospect of having an arrangement accomplished without having been apprised thereof before the arrangement might have become public knowledge. Indeed, London might be glad to grant its approval to whatever arrangement might be in sight, but it would insist upon being consulted before the matter became a *fait accompli*.[3] The Ambassador added that it might be possible under the circumstances to make some arrangement whereby Commissioner Burckhardt might still serve to a certain extent as High Commissioner and yet reside in Geneva. Life was daily becoming more miserable for him in Danzig and his position was undoubtedly becoming increasingly the object of ridicule, at least in Nazi circles. The Ambassador was frank enough to point out that both the League and London would prefer to withdraw him before he were obliged to leave under even less favorable circumstances.

Minister Beck thereupon assured the Ambassador that his Government would keep the British Government informed as to the progress in Warsaw-Berlin negotiations. In conclusion, the Ambassador informed Minister Beck that he would inform his Government as to the Polish Government's attitude and hoped that some formula might be worked out whereby not only the faces of all parties interested might be saved but also Beck's position during his negotiations might not be embarrassed.

The Ambassador informed me subsequently that he realized Beck was in an extremely delicate position *vis-à-vis* Berlin as regards the Danzig issue in view, among other factors, of the trend in the recent [Polish] municipal elections which resulted in the predominance of the two parties most opposed to Germany, namely the Socialists and the National Democrats (ENDEK) for this decided trend would undoubtedly serve to limit the latitude of Beck's policy *vis-à-vis* Berlin.

I am aware that of two face-saving formulae the one of paramount desire in the views of London envisages Burckhardt's immediate retirement—before the Danzig Nazis, as London apprehends, might force him out. The alternative formula, a second choice from London's standpoint, envisages the setting up of the Free City along Hanseatic lines, entailing: (a) a customs union with Poland; and (b) Poland's release of the right to represent Danzig in foreign affairs.[4]

Before leaving yesterday for a trip, Beck sent me word through a confidential source, cautioning me to guard his secret, that he intended to be out of the country for about ten days as he wanted a complete rest and wanted to gain a clear perspective before coming to certain important decisions. He facetiously added in his message that he had chosen to spend the greater part of the time in Monaco with his good friend the Polish honorary Consul General there, for that was the only country wherein he dared relax without being accused of negotiations for an alliance.

1. Biddle probably meant recent "developments" rather than "events" in the key Lithuanian port town of Memel. Since Munich, the local German population there had been organizing and agitating for a return to German control in a manner reminiscent of the Austrian and Czechoslovak episodes. The Poles were especially uneasy over this situation, which they felt was a companion plan for the major German offensive against Danzig along similar lines. Their fears were justified in March, 1939, when Memel was actually occupied by German troops after the Lithuanian government "invited" Berlin to assume responsibility for the city. See Sabaliunas, *Lithuanian in Crisis*, pp. 113 ff.

2. There were no actual negotiations in progress between Poland and Germany on the Danzig question at this time. Beck here refers to the conversations held between Lipski and Ribbentrop prior to the latter's visit to Poland in January, 1939. See Jedrzejewicz, *Diplomat in Berlin*, pp. 465–81.

3. On December 15, 1938, the British government issued an official declaration stating that it would take no action on Danzig without first consulting with Poland. *DBFP*, Third Series, vol. 3, Doc. 504, enclosure I.

4. There already was a customs union between Poland and Danzig; hence, the change would have involved Poland's surrender of its right to represent Danzig in foreign affairs.

December 28, 1938

Subject: Increasing strain in Warsaw-Prague relations; reports from Prague; Polish officialdom's and other observations thereon

I have the honor to refer to my despatch of December 22, 1938 (Memorandum C), wherein I pointed out that Warsaw-Prague relations were rapidly going from bad to worse and that Warsaw, on December 19 through its Minister in Prague, had protested against the existence of "certain" organizations engaged in anti-Polish activities on Czechoslovak soil, and to report that on the heels of this protest, in fact at six o'clock in the afternoon of December 22, a squad of Czech terrorists found its way into Dziećmorowice, Frysztat, and threw two grenades at two policemen leaving police headquarters, wounding one in the stomach, the other in the skull.

Moreover, at midnight on December 22 another squad of Czech terrorists arrived in the town of Łaży, throwing two grenades through the window of the house of a resident of the community, locally known as a pronounced Polish patriot. While the explosion caused damage to the house, no persons were injured. About the same time the house of a Polish peasant, known throughout the neighborhood for his Polish patriotic feelings, caught fire. It was suspected by the Polish community that this fire was started by Czech terrorists. The following day, December 23, Polish Minister to Prague [Kazimierz] Papée made a vigorous démarche to [Czech] Foreign Minister [Frantisek] Chvalkovski regarding the general situation existent on the Polish-Czech frontier in the Teschen area.

These incidents and publication of the two Polish official protests have contributed towards a rapid rise of anti-Czech feeling throughout Poland and are adding to the already heavy strain on Polish-Czech relations. Subsequent to the second protest *Gazeta Polska*, the Government mouthpiece, played up the Teschen incidents prominently in a rather lengthy article, which in effect concluded with a statement to the effect that "We shall have to put an end to that."

Again on December 27 the Polish Minister in Prague made a vigorous protest as result of an incident which occurred in Morawska Ostrava during the Christmas holiday. It seems that a band of Czech terrorists had removed the Polish eagle, an emblem which adorned the entrance to the Polish Consulate in that town.

Meanwhile, however, the local police have run down the culprits and punished them, found the eagle and replaced it, thus rendering sufficient satisfaction in Polish officialdom's eyes to prompt their soft-pedaling P.A.T.'s (Government news agency) playing up the incident. As a matter of fact *Illustrowany Kurjer Codzienny* was the only Polish paper to carry the story—and this was due to their having had their own correspondent in Morawska Ostrava.

I now find that, in retaliation, the Polish authorities had issued orders that each incident would involve the expulsion of one hundred Czechs from Polish territory. Thus Czech raids have already cost several hundred expulsions. It is worthy of note, moreover, that during the ten-day period previous to the Christmas holiday *Kurjer Poranny*, which frequently represents the trend of feeling in high Army circles, daily played up reported disorders in sub-Carpathian Ruthenia. Today, December 28, I note a recrudescence of this play-up—this time in *Gazeta Polska* (the Government mouthpiece).

In connection therewith and in reply to my direct question, Minister Beck's Chief of Cabinet, Count Lubieński, in the absence of the Minister, admitted his Government considered that the Ruthenian question was not yet closed. Of pertinent bearing, Mr. Burke Elbrick of this Embassy, who has been temporarily assigned to Prague, and who came to Warsaw for Christmas, informed me of the following: En route to

Warsaw he was accompanied by a well informed Czech, formerly of the Czech diplomatic corps, widely conversant with Czech affairs, and enjoying intimate contacts with various categories of official circles in Prague. This individual, who is married to a Pole, does not entirely share the bitterness generally felt by his compatriots towards Poland. He informed Mr. Elbrick, in confidence, that one of his friends on the Czech General Staff had imparted that Berlin had instructed the Czech General Staff to be prepared to call upon the Czech Army to fight the Poles, perhaps in March. The General Staff officer had said such a campaign would necessitate a mobilization of about one million men.

On the one hand this information would seem to bear out my previously reported impression that Berlin was "sicking" Czechoslovakia onto Poland, perhaps even to the point of an open conflict. On the other hand, in an effort to evaluate fully this information, it is well to bear in mind the Polish Government's point of view. In this connection, I am aware that the latter is cognizant that the Czech General Staff had received word along the foregoing lines from Berlin. Moreover, my informants in official circles here, in appraising the possibilities of the Czechs' adoption of an offensive military role, are inclined to regard the situation along the following lines: They considered Prague was now in a process of complete upheaval, economically, politically and spiritually. As a result, the Army has had to be demobilized, and the chances were that it would not only have to be considerably diminished, but also must experience somewhat of an overhauling. The Czech state, as presently set up, would naturally call for alterations in the military structure—and current circumstances presaged Prague's adoption of more of a neutral than an offensive policy. Meanwhile, however, Berlin was trying in every way possible to weaken Poland preparatory to Warsaw-Berlin negotiations along various lines—primarily on the Danzig issue. Hence, part of Berlin's weakening technique was to stir up the Czechs to the prospect of a combat with the Poles, probably baiting them with the recovery of Teschen, among other factors. It was therefore pertinent to take into consideration that Berlin's propaganda along the above lines might naturally find fertile ground amongst the Czech officers, who were now apprehensive lest they might soon be out of a job through a potential diminution of their military establishment. Hence, in view of their resultant concern they might readily seize upon a potential Polish danger to the Czech state as a pretext to keep the Czech Army intact.

I am aware that, while my informants are inclined at the moment to regard the situation in the above light, they do not shut their eyes to the possibility that Berlin might conceivably employ the Czech Army in the end as a tool against Poland.

Of connected bearing, my interest was engaged by my informant's remark that his current reports indicated that while Government circles in Rumania and even Hungary were dealing with the Nazi Government with apparent grace, there was a mounting apprehension and resentment at heart amongst these same circles. My informant thought even the Czechs might eventually experience a like change of heart. If such a turn took place, and Berlin ordered a Czech Army to make war on Poland, it was not inconceivable that either a rebellion amongst the Czech troops might take place or that an important section of the Czech Army might prefer to join the Poles in a potential conflict with the Germans.[1]

---

1. A "Czechoslovak Legion" was actually formed in Kraków and fought alongside the Poles against the Germans in September, 1939.

January 5, 1939

Subject: Substance of conversations with League
High Commissioner Burckhardt during his New Year's
visit to Warsaw; observations on various
aspects of Polish-German relations

High Commissioner Burckhardt, who admittedly dislikes
the suspicion, in German as well as Polish quarters, which
usually attends his visits to Warsaw, resorted to our New
Year's reception as a pretext to spend several days here. The
reception afforded him an excellent opportunity to confer
with the British and French Ambassadors, the Swedish
Chargé d'Affaires, an officer of the German Embassy, and
officials of the Polish Government without arousing undue
suspicion or publicity.

The following day Burckhardt and I had a lengthy conversation covering not only his impressions gained in his
discussions with the aforementioned officials here, but also
various aspects of Polish-German general relations.

At the outset of our conversation, Burckhardt recalled our
former talks in Danzig wherein he had pointed out that he
expected to confer with Ribbentrop and associates in Berlin
with a view to persuading the former to "soft-pedal" Nazi
boisterousness in Danzig (though at that time he had even
entertained the hope of persuading Ribbentrop to withdraw
Foerster, he failed in attaining that end). He was gratified
that his recent visit to Berlin had resulted in Danzig Senate
President [Arthur] Greiser's and Gauleiter [Albert] Foerster's
respectively promising to forward a letter to the "Committee

of Three", acknowledging the unconstitutionality of the four recent decrees.[1] They had promised, moreover, to state in this letter their intention to withhold putting these decrees into force until they could be acted upon properly by a new Volkstag to be elected in April. While admitting this letter represented little more than a gesture in view of the damage already done by the declaration of the four decrees, Burckhardt felt that such a letter might conceivably serve in the nature of a face-saver for the Committee of Three in any event.

In such light, I am inclined to interpret this gesture as a reflection of Berlin's present desire to retain Burckhardt in Danzig until the April elections at least. Moreover, I am inclined to concur with Burckhardt's expressed reaction to the effect that it reflected a hitherto state of uncertainty in Nazi high circles as to what definite line of action to adopt vis-à-vis Poland on the Danzig question.

Commenting upon Berlin's attitude vis-à-vis Warsaw, Burckhardt said that during his last Berlin visit he had gained the distinct impression that there were two schools of thought in upper Nazi circles as to what line of policy to pursue relative to Poland. There were the "extremists" who advocated weakening Poland through ruthless pressure; they aimed thus to bring her to Berlin's terms, envisaging no doubt Poland's collaboration in Berlin's forward-looking expansion program. To the extent that the "extremists" advocated weakening Poland, they now enjoyed the support of the "old-line" Prussian diplomats and politicians—for the latter envisaged the weakening of Poland as a preliminary step towards an eventual *rapprochement* with Moscow, in pursuance of the Prussian policy of former days. This was a new feature and had to be taken into consideration when gauging Berlin's potential near future attitude.

On the other hand, the so-called "moderates", headed by Goering, advocated "going easy" with Poland, perhaps with a view to coaxing Poland, through stages, into Berlin's orbit with a view to Poland's proving a potentially helpful factor in Berlin's eastward-looking expansion program.

Of pertinent bearing, *Gestapo* Chief [Heinrich] Himmler's message to Burckhardt—to the effect that Himmler expected early important political changes in high Nazi circles—during his previous visit to Germany, had evidently left a deep impression in Burckhardt's mind. Indeed, Burckhardt, in referring again to this message, said that during his recent visit to Berlin he himself had gained the impression that important changes were in the offing. He wondered what form of government might take the place of the present régime, in the event it failed as a result of internal "dog eat dog" conflicts. (My reports through other reliable channels indicate that while tension exists among upper Nazi circles, there is no likelihood of an *early* fall of the Nazi régime.) In response to his conjecture that Communism might seep in and take the place of Nazi-ism, I observed that, in terms of their relationship to the capitalist system and doctrine of democracy, there was fundamentally little difference, in my private opinion, between the two "isms"—they were both of the same litter only differently striped, but headed in the same direction. He could hardly gainsay this and concurred with my feeling that a military dictatorship would probably "take over" in event of a fall of the present régime in Berlin. This might hold out until some other form of dictatorial government were conceived. Indeed, I thought there was little hope the doctrines of democracy might be applied with any degree of effectiveness to present-day German mentality. The older generations had apparently already submitted and attuned themselves to the Nazi politico-economic formula: the "man-hours-based" economic aspect, so inseparably interlocked with that of the political. There were undoubtedly great numbers who preferred a more normal form of life under a more liberal form of government. There were undoubtedly many who distrusted its capacity to endure the test of time and who at heart were opposed to it. However, even these had shown a lack of capacity to resist the Nazi revolution at the outset, and had fallen in line with others, who had manifested a willingness to submit to the strong-arm dictum of the Nazi minority. On the other hand, Nazi youth had been raised on a Spartan formula to the exclusion of scarcely a trace of Athenian culture. In other words, German mass-mentality of today, as in the case of that in former days, showed signs of being more attuned to forceful direction than capable of understanding and enjoying the full benefits of democracy. The difference between the German-American population of the United States and the Germans in the Reich was largely attributable to the former's having lived under a liberal form of Government in an atmosphere of liberalism and having gradually acquired enlightenment as to its advantages. To bring today's German mass-mentality up to a point of understanding and enjoying the full value of democracy would require time, patience, and education.[2]

Burckhardt was inclined to concur with the substance of my observations; he remarked that as far as Hitler was concerned, the latter was regarded by the masses as a "Jehovah", and in such light his position was reasonably safe; it was merely his associates who were at sword's points with each other, an erruptive condition which might easily come to the exploding point. I remarked at this point that how much was conflict within certain limits, and how much was taken advantage of by Hitler for tactical purposes, remained to be seen. Burckhardt then stated Hitler kept abreast of internal and external affairs through daily reports presented to him by his closest associates. As regards foreign affairs, the first thing each morning he read the German-Swiss newspapers, subsequently receiving reports from other sections of the foreign press. He searched the democratic press abroad for political weaknesses which frequently gave rise to fresh ideas in carrying forward his "pin-pricking" technique.

In this connection, Burckhardt's discussion with a competent officer of the German Embassy here disclosed that the latter was apprehensive lest German Ambassador von Moltke, now in Berlin, might soon return with instructions of disturbing character. He had been led to believe, confidentially, that Ribbentrop had given von Moltke orders which might prove conducive to added tension between Warsaw and Berlin. Burckhardt expressed surprise at this disclosure for during his last visit to Berlin he had gained the distinct impression that Goering's policy was gaining ground and reflecting itself favorably in the Berlin Foreign Office's attitude vis-à-vis Warsaw. In response, the officer of the German Embassy had pointed out that at the time of Burckhardt's last Berlin visit Goebbels, Goering's *bête noire*, had been taken ill. This probably accounted for the temporary ascendency of Goering's less drastic policy. Goebbels' recent recovery, however, might conceivably account for any potential change in the Foreign Office's attitude. He then added his own impression that Berlin at this time was suffering from increasing strife within upper Nazi circles. Berlin was consequently not pursuing a set line of policy—rather, acting from day to day on impulse which found its roots either in the "pet aversions" or "fancies" of the individuals who at a given moment happened to be "in the saddle". Burckhardt admitted that his aforementioned informant had given a clear picture of conditions presently prevailing in Berlin high circles. Burckhardt hoped, however, that Goering's influence would rule, at least in the matter of Danzig.

As regards Polish-German relations in general, Burckhardt said Hitler was seriously annoyed with Poland, among other reasons, over Poland's having "swiped" Bogumin from under Hitler's nose, Poland's efforts to gain Italy's support towards accomplishing a common frontier with Hungary, and Poland's recent declaration with the Soviet.[3]

Burckhardt went on to say that in Geneva, moreover, there was no lost love for Poland, nor could the *Quai d'Orsay* be expected to feel any degree of deep sympathy for Beck in his pending difficulties—Paris had usually manifested an unfortunate lack of objectivity in its regard for and dealings with the affairs of its Eastern and Central European allies. Characteristic of this cramped point of view, [French] Ambassador to Poland [Leon] Noël, in his recent conversation with Burckhardt, had failed to conceal an obvious secret sense of pleasure when he observed that Beck faced troubled waters both internally and externally. Burckhardt had both esteem and liking for Noël, but felt he typified French mentality on affairs beyond the frontiers of France.

While admitting that Beck's suppleness in the direction of Poland's foreign policy was exasperating in many cases for foreign observers, including at times himself, he felt Beck had proven himself masterful, at least up to this point, in his "balance-diplomacy" against great odds, inherent to Poland's delicate geo-political position. It was a tough job at best, and was eventually bound to let Beck in for "digs" from all sides.

Were Beck replaced today, however, it might be either by someone less adept at "balance-diplomacy" and who might consequently fumble the ball in trying to carry on the delicate game, or by someone who might pursue a radically anti-German policy. With this observation I concurred, and asked Burckhardt whether (a) Berlin was aware that the recent municipal elections in Poland had resulted in an important showing by the anti-German parties: ENDEK, the Socialists, and the Jews, and (b) whether Berlin perceived that this might tend to cramp Beck's latitude in his dealings with Berlin. Unless Berlin was looking for trouble, it might discern the advisibility of "going easy"—otherwise, it might conceivably "torpedo" Beck's efforts to maintain friendly relations between Berlin and Warsaw. Burckhardt replied that due to confusion in upper Nazi circles and the fact that Ribbentrop was in the "saddle" he did not look for Berlin to appraise these aspects with any degree of astuteness. Ribbentrop was a "fool", drunk with power, [who] not only wanted but felt home conditions required Germany to "go places" at top speed. Anyway Ribbentrop did not believe the Poles would offer any more resistance than the Czechs in the event of a show-down. Upon Ribbentrop's questioning him as to the mood and capacity of the Poles to fight, Burckhardt had told Ribbentrop that one could not compare the Poles with the Czechs on this score. The Poles were romantic, inflammable, proud, and entertained fighting proclivities. Moreover, they had less to lose and more to gain economically speaking than had the Czechs before their early October amputation. The Czechs were more docile and through their former comparatively comfortable economic status had over a period of years become more economic- than fight-minded;

they preferred to trade out a situation than to fight it out, hoping to hold on to whatever they could. Moreover, one had to take into consideration that Poland had served as a battle-field at frequent intervals not only during her period of partition, but even as recently as 1920. The men who had fought then were still comparatively young, fit, and better trained and equipped. It would be dangerous to push them too far.

Reverting to the Danzig question, Burckhardt was aware that while Britain and France preferred his withdrawal they did not want to weaken or embarrass Poland's trading position during continued negotiations with Berlin and were, therefore, inclined to grant Beck a reasonable amount of latitude in terms of time, provided he kept them informed as to progress. On the other hand, Burckhardt was aware that Berlin, Warsaw, and now Danzig Senator-President Greiser and even Gauleiter Foerster (perhaps for different reasons— Greiser because he feared his position might be liquidated in event of Danzig's annexation to Reich, and Foerster perhaps reflecting Goering's "soft-pedalling" influence) favored Burckhardt's retention in Danzig at least until April. Moreover, Swedish Foreign Minister Sandler, a member of the "Committee of Three", might be inclined to favor particularly Berlin's desire in that he would like to find a means of relieving the strain recently placed on Stockholm's relations with Berlin.

I am aware that, while Burckhardt believes his role in Danzig, though cramped by recent events, in terms of potential effectiveness, serves the interests of peace, he has also his personal interests at stake. He gave up a professorship to take on the Danzig job, and the fact he is devoting part-time to writing a book, in addition to the fact that his salary is a matter not to be overlooked, may reasonably be expected to figure in his considerations. I should not be surprised, therefore, if for the above combination of reasons he welcomed the possibility of Sandler's support of Warsaw's and Berlin's desire to retain him in Danzig at least until April.

As regards Warsaw-Berlin negotiations on Danzig, what

in the early stage might have been considered merely conversations suffered a lapse due to Polish objections to the size of Berlin's appetite and were subsequently renewed on the basis of negotiations. With reference thereto Burckhardt said that while Warsaw had hinted it might possibly consider a somewhat independent status for Danzig, Berlin had evinced an inclination to oppose any arrangement bearing the semblance of a definite and final settlement. Indeed, Berlin appeared to want an arrangement of more or less temporary character—to leave the question open for further treatment later. The negotiations rested thus for the time being.

Burckhardt added that Ribbentrop was now tentatively planning coming to Warsaw to confer with Beck. Though the date was still unsettled, some rumors indicated he would arrive here in mid-January. Both Berlin and Danzig Nazi circles, however, looked for Ribbentrop to come to Warsaw at the termination of the Danzig negotiations in time to sign a potential agreement—probably about April.

At this point I recalled to Burckhardt's mind our former conversation in Danzig wherein our expressed impressions had concurred to effect Beck would prefer to talk directly to Hitler. I still thought so and believed that if he felt it essential to talk to anyone in Berlin, he would manage to see Hitler despite likely attempts of Ribbentrop to prevent it—probably he [Beck] would arrange it through the offices of Ciano. (I am aware circles here close to Beck are anxious that he talk directly with Hitler, contending that such a conference would stand better chances of a favorable outcome for Poland than a conference with Ribbentrop, whom they dislike and distrust. Moreover, while in the event Beck found his way to Berchtesgaden his move would undoubtedly be widely interpreted as spelling Poland's alignment with the Axis, I should be inclined to put it down, preliminarily at least, to more of a game than an intention to tie-in to the Axis—after all, Beck would prefer putting a number of essential questions directly to Hitler than to his Foreign Minister, Ribbentrop, whom I am aware Beck neither likes nor trusts, and whom he suspects

of desiring to present Hitler with a series of ruthlessly conceived schemes at frequent intervals for his own aggrandise-
ment. Accordingly, Beck would want to sound out Hitler as to
the potential limits whereto he might be willing to trade on
Danzig. Moreover, Beck would want to put the following questions: (a) does he intend to leave Poland in peace; (b) what
are his intentions 1/ vis-à-vis the Ukraine question, 2/ vis-
à-vis Soviet, 3/ vis-à-vis Eastern Europe in general. In brief,
a talk with Hitler would not necessarily require an immediate
reply and might enlighten Poland as to what to expect.

On the one hand, a meeting between Beck and Hitler
would serve Beck as a means of making soundings as to what
Poland faced in terms of continued pressure from Berlin, and
it would serve Hitler as an opportunity to appraise Poland's
mood and capacity to resist Germany, and thereby tend to
guide him in his immediate course vis-à-vis Poland: whether
to increase pressure to a ruthless degree, or whether to adopt
tactics of cajolery and bribery to win over Poland's collaboration through stages. It should be borne in mind, however,
that with a steadily mounting anti-German sentiment among
the masses here, Beck would not be in a position to come to
terms with Hitler on the spot. The best he could do would be
to put his questions, to listen, and subsequently consult his
associates of government circles here.) I was therefore interested to hear Burckhardt's remark that Hitler had a certain
liking and esteem for Beck, and might give Poland a better
break in direct conversations with Beck than Ribbentrop
would be likely to give.

Burckhardt is now going on a shooting trip in northern
Poland, returning to Danzig for the New Year diplomatic
ceremonies on January 8. Shortly thereafter he intends to
leave for Switzerland, where he will remain at his home
nearby Geneva pending the forthcoming meeting of the
Council and of the "Committee of Three". He believes that
shortly thereafter the "Committee of Three" will meet for
further discussions either in London or Paris. In this connection I am aware that a meeting in London would particularly
suit Minister Beck's book, for he would thus be afforded a
much-desired pretext for conferring with British statesmen.

1. Biddle here undoubtedly refers to the series of four decrees promulgated in November, 1938, that introduced Nazi Germany's "Nuremburg Laws" into Danzig, over the objections of Britain and to the discomfort of the Poles, who felt forced to insist on the protection of Polish citizens in Danzig who were Jews. For a concise discussion of the problem, see Herbert S. Levine, *Hitler's Free City: A History of the Nazi Party in Danzig, 1925–1939* (Chicago, 1973), pp. 126–47.

2. Biddle's impression of Nazism and its reception by the German people, offered on the eve of war, offers an interesting contrast with those of his predecessor in Warsaw, John Cudahy, who in December, 1933, characterized Nazism as a harmless form of social-fraternal activity that appealed to the German love of things military—an impression doubtless shared by many American and European observers at that time. See Cudahy to Roosevelt, December 27, 1933, FDRL-PSL, 50, "Poland."

3. Bogumin (Bohumin, Odeberg) was a town in the Czech portion of Teschen Silesia that possessed considerable economic, strategic, and demographic significance as a major railway junction. Despite Polish claims to it well before the Munich agreement, the Germans had tried to include it in their zone of control out of fear that the Poles would use Bogumin as a launching pad for a push into the vital industrial center of Moravska Ostrava. But the firmness of Beck in the face of Nazi threats and bluster, not to mention the methodical military occupation of the town by Polish military forces while Berlin raged, resulted in Poland's acquisition of Bogumin, although at the expense of worsened relations with Germany. The entire incident appears to have been the work of Göring and his cohorts in the German Foreign Ministry, for an October 5 declaration by Hitler stated that he was not at all interested in the issue and would not quarrel with Poland over one relatively minor town; *DGFP*, D, 5, Doc. 62. For Polish documents on the problem, see Józef Chudek, "Sprawa Bogumina w dokumentach polskich," *Sprawy Międzynarodowe* (Warsaw), no. 5(1960), pp. 108–14. This incident moved Beck to push his plan for a "Third Europe," and he pressured Italy to support the Polish efforts; Mussolini, however, yielded to German policy on the disputed area of East Central Europe, and ignored Polish exhortations for assistance.

January 13, 1939

Subject: Substance of my several conversations with Minister Beck upon his return from conversations with Hitler in Berchtesgaden and Ribbentrop in Munich

I have the honor to supplement my cables Nos. 2 and 4 of January 10 and 11, 1939,[1] respectively, and to report in greater detail the following substance of my several conversations (therein referred to) with Minister Beck upon his return from Berchtesgaden.

At 9:30 p.m. Saturday, January 7, shortly after Beck and his Chief of Cabinet, Count Łubieński, had reached their office from the train they together telephoned me. Beck stated he had been profoundly impressed by the contents of President Roosevelt's address.[2] Moreover, he could assure me that it caused mental and moral "jitters" both in Berlin and Berchtesgaden. In fact, he was aware that Hitler was not only furious but also extremely worried. He then stated he wanted to see me at the earliest possible moment. While en route from Munich to Warsaw he had remarked to Łubieński that there were a number of things he wanted to talk to me about. I saw Beck at the New Year's diplomatic reception at the *Zamek* when he made a point of repeating he wanted to see me at the first moment he found himself free.

The following morning Beck was in a great rush when I saw him during a short encounter. It was during my conversation with his Chief of Cabinet, Count Łubieński. He knew I was there and came in between his conferences with Government officials. He explained he had wanted to see me at length that morning but had been up to his neck in conferences with his own Government associates. He then hurriedly outlined his talk with Hitler, substance whereof I transmitted to the Department in my cable No. 2 of January 10, 5 p.m.[3] At the conclusion of this conversation, Minister Beck invited me to join him informally for dinner at his house on Tuesday evening, adding we could talk more at length at that time. Subsequently at dinner, attended by the Minister and family, Count Józef Potocki, head of the Anglo-Saxon Division of the Foreign Office,[4] and later joined by the Chief of Staff [Stachiewicz] the Minister and I had ample time to discuss various aspects of his conversations in Germany. The following morning I again had a brief talk with the Minister by way of clarifying certain points discussed during the preceding evening.

The following is a digest of my aforementioned three talks with Minister Beck:

In view of all circumstances, of which I was aware, he had deemed it advisable to talk directly to Hitler. Indeed, as he had previously told me, he had wanted to talk to Hitler before Ribbentrop. In general the conversations with both had proven fairly satisfactory in that Hitler had given him the definite impression that Poland might expect no "surprises"—that all matters bearing on Polish-German relations were negotiable —and that Poland might take these negotiations in her stride. I am aware that in his own evaluation of the foregoing Beck regards the potential course of such negotiations with cautious optimism. By nature not credulous, he is ever on guard, particularly as concerns Germany. He will accordingly no doubt endeavor to insure against eventualities.

Beck had for some time gone on [the] hypothesis that the recent Ukrainian "play-up" was not so much the work of Hitler —it had not borne the traces of Hitler's hand—rather it had smacked more of the machinations of his "extremist" subordinates—all the more reason for his desire to talk with Hitler directly, not with Ribbentrop first. Without his (Beck's) having broached the subject, Hitler brought up the Ukraine and Sub-Carpathian Ruthenia and bore out Beck's hypothesis by disclaiming an immediate interest to any measurable degree in the Ukrainian question. Moreover, he gave Beck an impression that whatever interest he did have in the Ukrainian situation was mainly a question of distant consideration and involved the Soviet in general. Indeed, Hitler made it clear he was distinctly anti-Russian, not merely anti-Soviet and anti-Communist, and that the Ukraine figured merely as a part of Hitler's envisaged future treatment of Russia as a whole. Moreover, his interest in the Ukraine was more economic than political. Beck told me he now believed, as he had felt before his talk with Hitler, that while the latter had a long-range interest in the Ukraine, it had thus far been greatly exaggerated. Even von Moltke and Ribbentrop had been obviously taken aback when Hitler disclaimed categorically an immediate interest in the Ukraine in general and in Sub-Carpathian Ruthenia in particular.

In response to my inquiry as to how Hitler could reconcile his denial with the fact that his representative, Ribbentrop, at the Vienna Conference had gone so far as to prevent Hungary's annexing Ruthenia, Beck amusedly stated that Hitler had gone to considerable lengths to allay Beck's suspicions and misgivings on this score. Hitler had accordingly pointed out that when Budapest had demanded the right of a plebiscite in Ruthenia, Hitler and his associates had assumed the position that the entire matter should be settled along ethnographical lines. Subsequently, when he had learned Budapest planned attacking Czecho-Slovakia about November 21 he had sent word he did not want an open conflict to further complicate the situation in Central Europe. At this point Beck had to admit to me he was aware that the Nazis had evinced more than common interest in "rigging up" the mechanics in Ruthenia, reiterating that Hitler went to considerable pains to allay Beck's suspicions that Hitler's immediate plans envisaged Sub-Carpathian Ruthenia as a strategic base of activities. Moreover, Beck had been led to look for Hitler henceforth to "lay off" Poland's Ukrainian minority in the course of his forward-aimed program.

Beck added [that] Hitler had obviously been down at his

mountain haunt alone for some time, with a few exceptions uninterrupted by his "group", resting after the fatigue of his Austrian and Czechoslovak *coups*—and examining the trend in an effort to gain a perspective as to the future turn of events. Of this Beck had gained a distinct impression. When Hitler had greeted him, he was philosophical and pensive in demeanor—and only during his oration wherein he reviewed his accomplishments over the past year did he evince a spirit of boastfulness.

At this point Beck reiterated his impression that as far as Hitler was concerned—and he was the deciding factor—Sub-Carpathian Ruthenia did not figure in his immediate considerations. In fact, Beck believed Hitler's interest in the Ukraine up to this point had been exaggerated. Though the "stories" regarding it were not devoid of foundation, they had been exaggerated. Beck then added with emphasis that if that region continued to prove a menace for Poland, Poland would liquidate the situation in short order.

Of pertinent bearing, Beck stated that in recent representations to Prague Beck had asked whether Prague had complete control over Ruthenia or not; or whether Ruthenia had become a disorderly center subject to the influence of a third party with designs opposed to Poland's interest. In response, Prague, through its Minister Slavik here and even the Prime Minister of Ruthenia, had gone to great lengths to apologize and assure Beck that no third-party influence prevailed in that region.

Beck would wait and see. Moreover, Poland was prepared to deal in Poland's own way with the situation, should it require action. As I have previously pointed out in connection with Ruthenia, both high military and Government circles here have not considered the projected common frontier with Hungary a closed question. However, Hungary's having backed off when she had a pretext to come to grips with the Czechs at Munkacs recently has given rise to considerable discernible but not generally expressed skepticism here as to the mood and capacity of the Hungarians to come through. Hence I feel the Poles are in [such] a mood that, in the event potential anti-Polish activities in Ruthenia reached an acute stage, the Poles might conceivably move in and clean up the disorder without waiting on the Hungarians.

Whether the Germans, in the final analysis, would tolerate this is still doubtful in my mind. Besides, insufficient time has passed for me to judge as to how far to ascribe Beck's statement on this score to talk for "home consumption" or full intention to act forcefully in event of further disorders. At the moment I am inclined to believe he means to act. Moreover, the Rumanian Ambassador imparted his surprise, if not concern, over his impression gained in conversation with Beck, who had spoken to him along lines similar to those he adopted with me regarding Ruthenia. The Ambassador remarked that the more he saw of the Poles, the more he realized they were a "determined lot".

In summing up his impression of Hitler's attitude both as to the Danzig and the Ukrainian issues, Beck stated Hitler was more conciliatory than aggressive. It was apparent that he desired Poland's friendship. As to the negotiations now going forward regarding Danzig, while Hitler had discussed the subject, his remarks had been more general than specific. Moreover, the negotiations were still in a formative stage. Beck was vague and guarded with me in discussing them, stating that Hitler had not clearly defined his position with respect thereto.[5] The British Ambassador subsequently imparted that during his conversation with Beck the latter had adopted a similar line regarding Danzig. In response to the Ambassador's reminder that Beck had promised to keep him advised as to progress and that he was under instructions from his Government to keep them posted, Beck said he was fully aware thereof and would not fail to let the Ambassador know as soon as the negotiations assumed sufficiently definite character to permit a clearer than hitherto appraisal as to their outcome. I discern that the Ambassador is nettled over a lack of more information to transmit at this point to the "Committee of Three" shortly scheduled to meet.

Pending more definite clarification of Danzig negotiations, I am still disinclined to exclude the possibility of the Germans' pressing for the inclusion of a right of way across the Corridor as part of a Danzig settlement—the right of way to assume somewhat the following form: combined rail and motor way within a mutually recognized neutral zone; elimination of customs and passport control.

Reverting to my conversation with Beck, while he felt that Hitler's quick successes over Austria and Czechoslovakia complicated matters for Europe, Beck believed that these successes had not diminished Hitler's respect for Poland; Beck was of the opinion that this was extremely important.

The two questions which were now engaging Hitler's immediate attention were the Jews and colonies. On every topic other than the Jews, Hitler had evinced a calm attitude, but when he spoke of the Jews he manifested rage, pounded the table and breathed hard. He shouted that he was absolutely determined to rid Germany of every single Jew within the current year. Beck said the subject was positively an obsession with Hitler, adding his own opinion that Hitler, realizing that internally all matters were not running smoothly and that a conflict of personalities within his regime was in course, undoubtedly made the Jews bear the brunt, laying the fault for everything at their door. As for colonies, Beck looked for this question to become Hitler's paramount interest in near future.

Regarding the axis, Hitler was obvious in his efforts to give the impression that the axis was more secure than ever and that he and Mussolini were pals. In response to my question as to what effect on this "paldom" Hitler's potential insistence upon assuming Austria's rights in Trieste might eventually have, Beck admitted that if proved an eventuality, it probably would not sit so well with the Italian public.

As regards Italo-French friction, Rome was using Tunis (more of a social than a territorial issue) and Corsica and Nice as a "smoke screen" for the serious questions of Djibouti and Suez. Whether the Italo-French controversy would break into an open conflict was not yet clear. Ciano had told the Polish Ambassador in Rome about a month ago he did not expect the dispute to come to an open conflict—as reported in a previous dispatch. However, Ciano, realizing Poland was

France's ally, might conceivably have made this remark for tactical reasons. Hitler, during the talk, had spoken rather sympathetically of France.

The waiters in the hotels at Menton, all Italian, were boasting that it would not be long now before their brethren took the place over. Beck admitted in response to my conjecture that it was perhaps mainly for the Italians' part a confusion- and fear-inspiring campaign. Nevertheless, the French in that region were convinced that they were in for a fight. Moreover, the French people along the Riveria were convinced there would be a war between France and Italy, were accordingly living in their valises prepared to evacuate the area, and were fully confident of a victorious conflict of short duration. How far, in final analysis, the French politicians might go was another matter and had not yet crystallized. The only nation to profit by an Italo-French conflict would be Germany, who would undoubtedly swoop down on the Danube area, taking advantage of Italy's being tied up at the front. Poland would continue to devote efforts as a peace broker between the French and the Italians, for such a conflict would do neither any good.

Hitler would like to have given the impression that he was prepared to go "all out" in support of the Italians. When I ventured the conjecture that the Germans might avoid going beyond the point of diplomatic support, Beck said that it was so difficult to gauge that point and so easy to ride beyond it into an explosion that it would be a delicate game at best, and was pregnant with danger in a jittery Continent—a diplomatic offensive of severity was risky business nowadays. Moreover, it was well to bear in mind that the axis was still in vigor. However, I do not think Beck believes Germany would deliberately risk war with the West and thus weaken herself in advance of an eastern venture, her major strategic objective.

Beck then emphasized there must be a meeting between France and Poland. They must face the realities and understand them. Their respective positions vis-à-vis Germany today, more than ever before, were similar in character. Appraising their respective positions, it would seem today that Poland enjoyed friendship of closer character than France with Germany, while on the other hand France being involved with Italy offered little chance of France's offering effective assistance to Poland. Yes, they must sit down at an early date and clarify their positions vis-à-vis one another and vis-à-vis Germany.

At the outset of Italo-French friction, Polish official circles' reports from London had indicated the British Government were assuming the attitude that the course of European events depended mainly on Chamberlain and Hitler; that while Hitler had the bark of a wolf, Mussolini had the bark of a fox; and that at most current Italo-French friction might be put down to a diversion to keep France busy. Subsequently, French Ambassador Noël remarked to me the other night that France had no worry as to whether she might enjoy Britain's active support if she required it in the event of a conflict over Tunis, for the fact that the Tunis issue brought Bizerta into the picture made it more of a British than a French problem. Evidently Noël had made a similar remark to Beck, for the latter gave me the impression that the French entertained ideas along somewhat similar lines.

Personally I am of the opinion that if France and Italy came to grips, and if Paris and London felt Britain's potential neutrality might mean Germany's neutrality, both Paris and particularly London might favor this course—provided, of course, France felt capable of handling Italy alone, and provided France could be reasonably sure Germany would not suddenly jump in against her.

Beck went on to say that up to the point of a potential ultimatum London might conceivably continue to influence French foreign policy—*but a decision for a war could be made only in Paris today.* Britain was augmenting her air and naval strengths but not her army to any effective degree. This meant she could not take a lead in determining the issues of the Continent. While France had hitherto appeared to be turning more towards her colonial domain then maintaining her interest in the Continent, this move had served the politicians more than it represented the characteristic interest of the Frenchman. Beck now felt that the Frenchman's natural interest in the Continent would re-express itself.

Commenting upon Chamberlain's and Halifax's approaching visit to Rome, Beck did not look for the British statesmen to accomplish much. The latter, due to public opinion both at home and in France, would be limited in terms of potential "hand-outs", and would have to "tread easy" during the talks. Mussolini, who had already assumed a position of positive character vis-à-vis particularly belligerent rights in Spain, Djibouti and the Suez, might not be expected, in view of his own public opinion, to give much ground. Moreover, Beck doubted whether the Rome meeting would go far towards immediately bringing about new four-power talks—anyway, the latter would only prove costly to other powers in terms of "peaceful settlements".

Up until about three or four days after the New Year discussions on the European political arena could have covered little beyond a review of past events, events which could be left to the historians. Only shortly after the turn of the year did there appear any indications of what might be in the offing. After all, since the Czechoslovak event, statesmen and diplomatists had been suffering from shock—dismay. Then came the Christmas holidays, affording much needed relaxation, then New Year's, then fresh thought and now we begin to discern signs of what we may expect.

Beck added in conclusion that Ribbentrop would come here January 26, and that Hitler had remarked during the conversation that he regretted that his progress on his architectural projects had been retarded by the necessity of sending so many men to the Siegfried Line. However, in case he were not able to finish it during his own lifetime, Goering was well versed in his objectives and could carry on readily. Beck added this had been the first time Hitler had ever frankly intimated he expected Goering eventually to succeed him.

My impression of the Beck-Hitler conversation was that Hitler made a *tour d'horizon* of about three hours, thinking out loud in a conciliatory rather than aggressive tone. Beck seemed fairly well satisfied and under no apparent tension as a result of Hitler and Ribbentrop conversations. Beck has so far avoided receiving the British and French Ambassadors, who evidently under instructions from their Governments, are making constant efforts to see him.

1. These dispatches are not reproduced in this volume but are deposited in the Department of State Files of the National Archives, Washington, D.C.

2. Biddle here refers to Roosevelt's speech of January 4 to the Congress, in which he asserted that he would do everything short of war to halt German aggression. See the *Public Papers and Addresses of Franklin D. Roosevelt, 1939* (New York, 1941), pp. 1–2.

3. This dispatch is not reproduced in this volume but is deposited in the Department of State Files of the National Archives, Washington, D.C.

4. Potocki headed the "Western Division" of the Polish Foreign Ministry; there was no "Anglo-Saxon" department.

5. Hitler had actually proposed the return of Danzig to Germany but assured Beck there would be no faits accomplis; Beck responded that he could see no "equivalent" that Poland could accept in return for Danzig. Beck was correct in so far that Hitler did not press the point, having raised it apparently only to sound Beck's reaction. See Lipski, *Diplomat in Berlin*, pp. 482–85, and *DGFP*, D, 5, nos. 119, 120, 121.

February 15, 1939

Subject: Beck's further disclosures regarding
Ribbentrop's Warsaw visit; observations

I have the honor to supplement despatch No. 950 dated February 3, 1939[1] regarding the aftermath of Herr Ribbentrop's visit to Warsaw, and to report the following additional observations.

Beck informed me that he was satisfied with the outcome of Ribbentrop's conversations during the latter's visit here.[2] In effect, these talks had "boiled down" to a "re-hash" of Beck's former conversations with Hitler at Berchtesgaden.

He was pleased to have had Ribbentrop confirm his [Beck's] impression previously gained during his talk with Hitler to the effect that Ruthenia did not figure in Hitler's immediate forward-looking program. Moreover, he had gained the impression from Ribbentrop that if Ruthenia continued to represent a center of activities threatening the security of the Polish state, Hitler would not be opposed to Poland's adopting military measures to restore order in that quarter. Hence, the Polish Government continued to regard Ruthenia as an "open" question. (In important connection with this statement, I shall report later on an interesting disclosure made by the Rumanian Ambassador to Poland.) Beck then stated in effect that his recent reports indicated that German direct interest in Sub-Carpathian Ruthenia was already on the wane and that a number of German agents hitherto

assigned to activities in Ruthenia had already been withdrawn. Recently, moreover, conditions had taken a turn for the
better in Ruthenia. Prague was taking a stronger hand in
terms of efforts to restore order in that quarter and had
adopted forceful measures against the influx of Ukrainians
across Ruthenian frontiers.[3] Beck hoped this would continue
to prove the case.

Beck had moreover gained an impression from his discussions with Ribbentrop that in the eyes of Berlin the position of
Czechoslovakia was still far from settled, the boundaries not
definitely determined, the status of internal policy not yet
clearly and satisfactorily defined from the standpoint of Nazi
policy.

Beck then stated that, as regards the general outlook from
Germany's angle, the impression he had gained in his talk
with Hitler had been subsequently confirmed in his talk with
Ribbentrop to the following effect: (a) January and February
were the months wherein Hitler would come to a decision as
to a definite line of action; (b) Hitler would turn his main
attention from the pursuance of his reportedly major objectives in the East to the West; (c) Hitler would concentrate
in the West upon his colonial claims. In connection with these
claims, and in response to my inquiry, Beck said in effect the
following: he looked for Hitler's campaign in the West to
develop into a *major play* for colonies, and Beck had the
distinct impression there was a decided disinclination on
part of Hitler's close associates, as well as Hitler himself,
either to bargain or to consider the imposition of conditions,
such as arms limitation or treatment of the claims within
framework of a general agreement, in connection with Hitler's
colonial claims. In fact, Beck's impression was that Hitler
would flatly refuse to consider any such condition as *disarmament*. Moreover, Hitler felt that the colonial aspect
represented the last important unrectified injustice of the
Versailles Treaty, and in such light Hitler would undoubtedly
assume that the return of colonies constituted Germany's
right. Moreover, his extremist associates were urging him to
adopt this line of policy. In other words, Hitler might be

expected to shy off from any attempt either to impose conditions to potential colonial concessions or to treat the question within the framework of a general European agreement.
(Of further interesting and pertinent bearing on this question
were (a) the remarks of an unofficial but prominent figure in
Central European affairs, Prince Max Hohenlohe, and (b)
substance of Beck's reports regarding Berlin's views of
colonies as recently conveyed to London, which I shall re-
count in separate supplementary dispatches.)

Beck told me he had the impression that Hitler still did
not want war. He stated that so far reports he had received
since his talk with Hitler at Berchtesgaden had borne out his
impression that Hitler would not deliberately wage war this
year, as Beck felt that Germany, from the standpoint of
military training, adequate fuel supplies, and raw material
reserves, was not yet up to a major conflict of lengthy duration. He added, however, that if the present grave state of
affairs between France and Italy went from bad to worse,
there was always a possibility that Mussolini might strike
out against France in a conflict wherein Hitler might conceivably become involved. Indeed, a conflict between Italy and
France would be most unfortunate—the differences at stake
should be liquidated bilaterally through statesmanship and
diplomacy rather than war; it was only Germany which might
conceivably profit by such a conflict.

As regards Danzig, Beck said that, while Hitler had in
broad terms discussed the question of Danzig and the transit
of German rail and motorized traffic across the Corridor to
East Prussia and Danzig, and while Ribbentrop had subsequently, during his visit here, touched upon these questions,
Ribbentrop had confirmed Hitler's previously expressed willingness to agree that these issues should be negotiated quietly
in a neighborly spirit, and not be allowed to disrupt good
Polish-German relations. Beck added in strictest confidence,
however, that in the Warsaw-Berlin negotiations regarding
Danzig, the position assumed by the German negotiators was
still unsatisfactory to the Polish Government. From the
Polish standpoint, the Germans were still seeking too much.

In other words, the terms Germany had thus far pressed went beyond the capacity of Polish public opinion to stomach them. The matter was therefore still in the course of negotiations and, if continued at the present rate, would probably consume some little time yet before coming to a head. As regards the "Committee of Three", it continued in its course of consideration of the Danzig question, and the status of the League High Commissioner in connection therewith, in the light of the confidential Warsaw-Berlin negotiations. Thus far the Committee had shown a disposition to grant Warsaw and Berlin latitude in terms of time.

Beck was aware that both the Foreign Office in London and the Quai d'Orsay were concerned lest the already enfeebled status of the League might be further burdened by a *fait accompli* in terms of an agreement between Warsaw and Berlin over Danzig. However, Beck had given his assurances to the British Ambassador to keep him posted as to the progress of these negotiations.

In concluding our conversation, Beck reminded me of his prediction before my departure for "leave" from Warsaw on January 18 to the effect that Ribbentrop's visit here would amount to little more than the creation of "atmosphere" and stated that such, in effect, proved to be the case.

As a result of my inquiries in various conversations with Beck, his closest associates, and other competent individuals here, I have gained the impression that during Ribbentrop's conversations with Beck, the former had on several occasions actually touched on issues outstanding between Warsaw and Berlin; in only the most delicate manner he had tested out Beck, and the instant he had detected Beck's stiffening, he had dropped the question in point. This, according to my impression, occurred in connection with the question of a right of way over the Corridor, as well as other questions of potential dispute between the two countries. In thus having retreated from a preliminary delicate approach on these touchy points, he at least learned Beck's reaction, and I believe he was accordingly carrying out Hitler's willingness to let these issues "ride" as a means toward the main objective, namely, the creation of an atmosphere of friendly German-Polish relations, with an aim of giving the western powers the impression that Germany might possibly enjoy Poland's friendly neutrality during Hitler's course of action vis-à-vis the West.

1. This dispatch is not reproduced in this volume but is deposited in the Department of State Files of the National Archives, Washington, D.C.

2. January 25–27, 1939.

3. These were Ukrainians coming from eastern Poland.

February 17, 1939

Subject: Minister Beck's observations on current French mass and official attitude; his comments on Bonnet's recent declaration regarding the French-Polish alliance

I have the honor to report that in recent conversation with Beck, he stated that his reports tallied with my expressed impression that France was consolidated to a greater degree than it had been for some time, and that Daladier's forceful declaration of recent date enjoyed the support of the country at large.[1]

Commenting then upon the attitude of the French Government as a whole, Beck intimated his doubts as to whether Daladier and Bonnet saw eye to eye on all issues at stake. Beck considered Bonnet likeable, but felt he lacked a comprehensive grasp of his present job. He then repeated what he had stated to me on a previous occasion—that Bonnet was given to an unfortunate weakness of occasionally divulging indiscretions which some times proved embarrassing to capitals whose affairs were entailed in his disclosures. Beck still believed, however, that such indiscretions were due to a weakness in terms of desire to please the press during comparatively dull periods, rather than to a deliberate intention to embarrass anyone.

Commenting then upon Bonnet's recent declaration before the Chamber of Deputies regarding the Polish-French Alliance, Beck stated that, while on the face of it the declaration appeared to be satisfactory, still a careful examination of the text of Bonnet's reference to Poland had led official circles here to greet it with less enthusiasm than if it had been otherwise worded. Instead of having treated the French Alliances with Poland and the Soviet separately, Bonnet had covered them both in the same statement. Warsaw could hardly be expected to evince any great degree of satisfaction over Paris' having put the French-Polish and French-Soviet Alliances in the same "casserole", since the Polish Government was well aware that Paris placed little, if any, confidence in the Soviet Alliance. In other words, this treatment had not proven very convincing for the Poles.

In response to my suggestion that perhaps Bonnet had not deliberately meant to give that impression, and that his having so coupled the two Alliances in the same statement might have been an oversight, Beck said he believed my observation was correct on this score, but that such an oversight was all the more lamentable, for it showed a distinct lack of grasp of the situation on either Bonnet's or Quai d'Orsay's part, or both.

---

1. French Foreign Minister Georges Bonnet on January 25 denied to the Chamber of Deputies that French policy signaled the virtual abandonment of alliances with Poland and the Soviet Union, and Premier Edouard Daladier followed this up with a declaration stressing that all existing agreements would be maintained. Apparently, however, the French government had made these affimations of faith under considerable domestic political pressure; Bonnet later told the German ambassador to France that they had both spoken "for internal consumption." *DGFP*, D, 4:497.

February 17, 1939

Subject: Minister Beck's observations on Ciano's forthcoming visit; Polish Chief of Staff's observations on military capacity of Axis in event it came to grips with the London-Paris axis; Polish Government's recent reports from Rome; observations

I have the honor to report that in recent conversation with Minister Beck he expressed his sense of real satisfaction over a letter which he had just received from Italian Foreign Minister Ciano regarding the latter's forthcoming visit to Warsaw, scheduled for February 25. Beck was pleased to note from Ciano's personal communication that the latter would bring his wife with him, marking the first time that he would have done so on an official visit. Moreover, Ciano would be accompanied by a formidable group of Italian journalists, headed by Signor Gayda.[1]

In view of what Beck considered the gravity of the situation in connection with strained Italo-French relations, Beck would welcome the opportunity to discuss with Ciano all aspects of the dispute. Indeed, Beck would do what he could in a conciliatory role. Though he did not know how much his own efforts might count on this score, still he was willing to have a go at it.

Of significance and at least indirect bearing in light of its potential effect on Polish Government's attitude is today's strictly confidential disclosure by Polish Chief of Staff, General [Wacław] Stachiewicz, to effect that the Polish General Staff estimated that in event the two axes came to grips, the French and British would for the first two months find "rough going"—thereafter, however, the tide would undoubtedly turn in their favor. Moreover, the Staff excluded the possibility of a victory of the Rome-Berlin Axis in a lengthy conflict. Furthermore, in a conflict between Italy and France, Italy would be defeated. The General went on to say Mussolini was said to have changed the Italians' soul—maybe to a certain extent, but not sufficiently to meet the crisis now staring them in the face—it would take more than the past fifteen years, at least fifty, and probably twice that.

Moreover, the officer corps of the Italian Army was not up to that of the French. Neither, in terms of quantity, was the German. Besides, in terms of trained reserves, the Germans trailed the French to a marked degree. Moreover, Germany was definitely not yet prepared in terms of raw materials or fuel reserves. Besides, Britain and France had both effectively stepped up their plane production—and the availability of American planes was an enormous factor, and should be taken into important consideration. The Chief of Staff, with whom the Marshal is in accord, had so informed the Government here during the past twenty-four hours. It is moreover pertinent to add that today's reports from the Polish Embassy in Rome, to effect that political circles there were discernibly increasingly nervous lest Mussolini make some unexpected bold move, have made a marked impression in official circles here.

In consideration of the foregoing, I feel the Government now looks forward to Ciano's visit with mixed feelings. On the one hand, Poland, since its regeneration, has developed a natural sympathy for Italy which, due to a lack of conflict in Italo-Polish interest, Poland can afford—and Ciano's visit will mark an occasion permitting Poland an opportunity to express its friendly feelings. On the other hand, in view of mounting tension between Italy and France, the Polish Government does not welcome an occasion at the moment which might afford Ciano an opportunity to put questions—the Government here will want to steer clear of commitments; besides, it is reasonable to suppose that Beck will wish to avoid offending France at this time.

1. Virginio Gayda, editor of the influentical newspaper *Il Giornale d'Italia* (Rome) from 1926 to 1943, was considered the semiofficial spokesman for Italian Fascism in matters of foreign policy. His editorials were closely read by diplomats, and his presence in Ciano's party was therefore justifiably interpreted by the Poles as an indication of the importance Mussolini attached to the visit. Ciano was returning Beck's visit to Rome in March, 1938. Ciano's impressions of the visit to Warsaw between February 24 and March 2 are in *The Ciano Diaries*, pp. 33–35. For a discussion of Italian-Polish relations see Philip V. Cannistraro and Edward D. Wynot, Jr., "Polish Foreign Policy in 1934: An Unpublished Document from the Italian Archives," *East Central Europe* 1 (1974): 71–81.

March 4, 1939

My dear Mr. President:

Permit me to assure you, in all sincerity, that I am pro-foundly impressed by your realistic appraisal of the current developments in Europe and their potential bearing upon events apparently in the making, as well as your combined foresight and courageous intelligence, which prompted your sound and far-reaching policy, aimed at averting war in Europe.

Your firmness of attitude, your armament program, and your decision to afford the French and British opportunity to purchase planes from us, have been greeted by official circles here with a genuine sense of satisfaction. While leading Government and military authorities in Poland are frank in expressing this to me, they are careful to treat the matter confidentially, for, due to Poland's delicate geo-political situation during this period of mounting tension, they are careful not to say or do anything which might provoke Germany's suspicion and ire.

Moreover, my numerous conversations with diplomatic and Government circles here, reveal in effect, the following:

The firm attitude you have manifested, and the effective steps you have taken, have served (a) as a "stop, look and listen" sign to the dictators; they have driven them to cover, and forced them to reexamine their respective and joint positions vis-à-vis the West; (b) to stiffen Paris and London; (c) as an important contribution towards consolidating the British dominions behind a firmer attitude in London; (d) to "ginger up" the French, whose leading political circles had previously been given somewhat to a spirit of defeatism; (e) to curb the tendency of the Italian press to minimize Chamberlain's statements in reference to the binding character of Britain's alliance with France; Rome is reportedly no longer indifferent to Chamberlain's assurances on this point; (f) to dampen Rome's war-mongering boisterousness, at least up to this point; Polish official circles· confidentially inform me, that during Ciano's visit here, his close associates imparted that the attitude of the United States had now become a consideration of major importance in the minds of the ruling circles of Rome.

It is, moreover, interesting to note that competent observers here hold that, mainly attributable to your reported attitude, [there] are traces of a desire in Berlin for a four-power conference, traces first brought to light in a leading article in the *Frankfurter Zeitung* of February 5. The gist of the article may be characterized as a ballon d'essai for a four-power conference. Competent observers here interpreted this as an attempt on the part of Berlin to keep the United States out of the European picture, and to circumvent the potential influences of our attitude upon the Western European capitals, as regards the demands of "gangster diplomacy". . . .

March 11, 1939

MEMORANDUM

Minister Beck's views on general European situation, in terms of near-range outlook; substance and potential bearing of Polish Government reports from abroad; observations

In discussing with Beck various aspects of the current European political trend and their potential bearing on the period immediately ahead of us, he stated his opinion: (a) that Spain still constituted a potential source of worry; it was still too early to forecast the outcome of the current play of forces in connection therewith; in other words, Spain still bore watching in terms of a potential breeder of international complications; (b) as long as Czecho-Slovakia remained an unsettled question—and it was still far from settled—the consequent uncertainty thus created, and the potential confusion which might arise from disturbing developments in that country, might be expected to work an unsettling effect on Central Europe; (c) otherwise, although diplomatic circles, still suffering from the shock of last autumn's events, were tense, the chances of war in the near future were less than last fall, when the situation growing out of mobilizations in various quarters and attendant acute tension had failed to lead to war.

Moreover, and of pertinent bearing, in the opinion of official circles here, their persistent reports of "behind-[the-] scenes" conversations between the capitals of Western Europe and those of the Axis afford grounds for a greater than hitherto degree of composure in estimating events of the immediate future. In this connection, it may be recalled that I formerly drew attention to the persistence of reports reaching here to the effect that, on the one hand, Monsieur Bonnet was inclined to attempt to avert a show-down with Rome by soundings on the possibilities for a potential compromise settlement, while on the other hand, Mr. Chamberlain was preparing for a "second major peace effort."

While my informants' reports are not sufficiently definite in character to gain a specific grasp of the aforementioned "behind-[the-]scenes" negotiations, nevertheless, the persistence of these reports from important quarters both in the West and in Central Europe point, in my opinion, to a conceivable postponement of what until recently threatened to be the commencement of a tense crisis period on the heels of the Pope's [Pius XII] coronation.

Considered in broad relief, it may be said that the past year has been characterized by a contest between Western and Eastern Europe to divert the course of the Axis cyclone in the other's direction. Until about six weeks ago, the West had succeeded in diverting the Nazi cyclone in an eastwardly direction. Thereupon, each state in the area northeast, east, and southeast of Berlin struggled to divert the course of Nazi attention from its own to another state's home front. Then, about six weeks ago, the main force of Axis diplomatic attention swung around towards the West, in turn reflecting itself in an evident sense of relief amongst the statesmen of those Eastern and Central European powers which had hitherto escaped subjugation to Nazi expansion. How long Axis attention will continue concentrating on the West depends upon the turn of nearby events.

Moreover, in my opinion, (a) the firmness of attitude manifested by President Roosevelt and other members of our Government, together with our armament program, and (b) the "gingering" effect thereof upon the official attitude of London and Paris, combined with Britain's subsequent armament program, served as a "stop-look-and-listen" sign to the dictators and drove them to cover to re-examine their respective and joint positions. They are now in a quandary, both as to their immediate objectives and as to the methods of approach thereto.

Past events indicate that, in preparing the ground for his expansion program, Hitler has made a scientific study of the potential weak spots in the European political arena. This indeed is an important factor in the technique of his political engineering. Considering, then, the situation of today with a view to estimating Hitler's next move, it may be said that he has already in the back of his mind an inventory of potential politico-economic-military weaknesses all along the line. He now faces the immediate future like the quarterback of a football team, who puts his play through the first opening he discerns. Moreover, such as in the case of the quarterback who has his team trained to the mechanics of each play applicable to a given potential opening, so Hitler has up his sleeve his formulae applicable to each potential opening in the international field. Hence, I believe we may look for him to approach his immediate objectives as a quarterback, ready to direct his play through whatever opening in the line he discerns.

As regards Mussolini's attitude, in terms of its bearing on France and the Mediterranean problem generally, it appears for the moment to be confused and often characterized by perplexing contradictions. On the one hand, he is manifesting an unusual self-restraint, vocally speaking; on the other hand, it is being stated in important quarters in Berlin that he is preparing to approach France, or to hint that he would like to be approached by her through discreet diplomatic channels for purpose of negotiations not conducted from councils [of the League of Nations] nor under the pressure of the extremist Fascist press.

One might perhaps ascribe Mussolini's self-restraint in part to his concern lest the formulation of Italy's demands in the open might land him in an awkward dilemma, since France would be certain to reject those demands, both in form and substance. Thus he would find it impossible to square any potentially "reasonable" demands which France might conceivably treat as a basis for negotiation with the shrill and impossible program of his extremists. Whatever form

Mussolini's next move in connection with Italy's claims might take, it is reasonable to look for the question of "timing" to play an important part; he will undoubtedly seek a moment which he considers psychologically favorable to his interests. (Beck has gained the impression that Rome, believing that Paris is already cognizant of Italy's claims, is now awaiting some form of response from Paris; moreover, Beck has gained the impression that important elements in Paris official circles are apprehensive lest Mussolini formulate an impossible list of claims deliberately aimed as a pretext for coming to grips with France. On the other hand, however, Beck gained the impression in his talks with Ciano that his attitude was non-aggressive vis-à-vis France when discussing Italian claims; furthermore, Ciano had implied Italy was not eager to go to war with France and hoped to settle Italo-French differences peacefully.)

In light of the foregoing, and in view of persistent reports from the Western and Axis capitals to effect that "behind-[the-]scenes" negotiations are in progress, I am now prompted to look for the immediate future to entail a period wherein Hitler and Mussolini will feel their way and will conduct soundings looking to potential negotiations. During the early stage of these soundings we may conceivably enjoy comparative quiet. In event, however, the Dictators gained an impression at any stage of these soundings [that] either the Western capitals were playing for time, or that little could be gained by potential negotiations, it would be reasonable to expect an immediate recrudescence of boisterousness and acute tension. It is, moreover, conceivable to my mind that if (a) an agreement to expunge the "guilt clause", and a recognition of Germany's right to colonies; and if (b) Italy's realization of the so-called "reasonable" items of her list of claims were to grow out of any possible negotiations, this might mark a prelude to boisterous chantages by both ends of the Axis, aimed at attaining the more substantial objectives of their respective and joint appetites, for I do not believe the Axis chiefs have abandoned hope of prying further concessions from the Western European powers, before the latter may have attained a higher degree of armament.

April 4, 1939

Subject: Observations on (a) Nazi-inspired campaign
of destructive propaganda in Poland, (b) Berlin's and
German minority's attitude, (c) Polish precautions
to protect German minority

I have the honor[1] to report that German machinations within
Poland aimed at spreading confusion and weakening the internal political-economic structure of the state, assumed a grave
aspect last week.

In part, Berlin's campaign consisted (a) of inspired tenden-
cious rumors regarding an acute conflict of opinions in Government circles, and (b) false telephone messages to the various Foreign missions, including our own. For example, one
German-inspired report which gained swift and wide-spread
circulation amongst the Polish population of Warsaw, as well as
diplomatic circles, was to the effect that due to disagreement
in policy, Marshal Śmigły-Rydz had shot Foreign Minister
Beck. On another occasion, our Embassy was telephoned at
9 P.M., Friday, March 24th, that pursuant a German ultimatum, Beck had refused to agree with his associates that
Poland surrender Bogumin to the Germans, and that Beck was
consequently resigning within two hours of the time of the
telephone call. Though I placed little if any credence in the
substance of this telephone message, I went immediately to
the Foreign Office for the purpose of making discreet observations for myself. As I expected, I found Beck and his Cabinet
members together with General Staff representatives, informally gathered, discussing various aspects of the "black out",

which at that time was in progress.[2] Upon their invitation, I "sat in" the conference for several hours, and having assured myself that all was in order, and that the telephone message was only another mendacious effort to create confusion, I returned home.

On a subsequent occasion, the telephone operator at our chancery telephoned me at 8:40 on the morning of March 27, stating that some one purporting to represent the Foreign Office had telephoned to announce that Polish troops had entered Danzig at 8:30 a.m. I immediately suspected a trick, characteristic of Nazi technic [sic!], and requested our operator to check back on the Foreign Office to verify the source and substance of the message. I was therefore not surprised when our operator telephoned me five minutes later to say that having conformed with my request, he ascertained that the Foreign Office knew nothing of the aforementioned message. Major Colbern, our Military Attaché, thereupon immediately notified the Second Bureau of the General Staff, while I apprised Beck, the Vice Premier, the Governor of Warsaw, and the Chief of Police, suggesting that some appropriate measures be adopted swiftly to curb what we considered a campaign deliberately aimed at causing confusion and general disturbance. That same day, the Government adopted emergency precautions aimed at arresting this wave of harmful propaganda.

As regards continued reports emanating from the Berlin broadcast stations and the German press accusing Poland of maltreating the German minority, I am aware that in anticipation of Polish mass anti-German feeling and in a determined effort to prevent acts which might provoke Germany, the Polish Government issued strict orders to the local police authorities throughout Poland to adopt strict measures to protect the German minority.[3] However, before these measures came into effect, there had taken place, according to my information from usually reliable sources, a few cases of "rough housing", mainly on part of exuberant Polish youths, expressing their feelings against the Germans, who, particularly in Bydgoszcz, had become overbearing and provocative in their attitude towards the local Poles. As an illustration of the extent of aforementioned police precaution, the Belgian Minister informed me that in the area industrialized by Belgian invested capital, the Polish police authorities had forbidden the German employees to leave the town without police visas. Moreover, the police were careful to point out that since they were responsible for the welfare and protection of each German in that area, the police could not afford to allow the Germans to "go wandering out of sight".

My further examination of subsequently reported incidents gives me more than an impression that the German minority has been deliberately attempting to provoke incidents. For example, a report came to my notice this morning to the effect that at Chorzów, a town of about 125,000 inhabitants and a nitrate industrial center in Upper Silesia, the Polish police apprehended a number of young German students deliberately in the act of smashing the windows of the German high school of which they were students. Under subsequent police examination the boys confessed their fathers had instructed them to commit these disorders.

The apparent determination both of Berlin and the German minority in Poland to keep Polish-German minority differences an almost daily "headline" issue, suggests that they aim to keep this an open question whereon to build a case for potential forceful intervention.

1. This report was prepared after Hitler had occupied Prague (March 12) and after Poland had accepted the British guarantee (March 31).

2. There was a partial mobilization in Poland at the time that Germany seized Memel, March 23–24.

3. The German minority in Poland had been a persistent thorn in the government's side throughout the interwar period, but had become especially virulent in its anti-Polish sentiments after Hitler's attainment of power in 1933. For a study of this problem, see Edward D. Wynot, Jr., "The Polish Germans, 1919–1939: National Minority in a Multinational State," *The Polish Review* 17, no. 1 (Winter, 1972): 23–64.

May 12, 1939

Subject: Potemkin's conversation with Beck
in Warsaw; further observations thereon

With reference to my cable No. 107 of May 10, 2 p.m.,[1] I have the honor to report that, after a lengthy talk with Beck and just before his departure from Warsaw, Potemkin[2] imparted the following to the Turkish Ambassador:

He was highly satisfied with his talk with Beck. Beck had been very friendly and had manifested marked comprehension in connection with all aspects covered in the discussion. While maintaining the characteristic Polish reserve in respect to a potential alliance with Russia, Beck had stressed Poland's desire for a mutual re-invigoration of all aspects of the Non-Aggression Agreement and emphasized Poland's desire for a broadening of the scope of the Commercial Agreement between Warsaw and Moscow. Moreover, Beck had assured Potemkin of the Polish Government's desire for friendly Polish-Russian relations.

Potemkin had assured Beck in turn that Moscow reciprocated Warsaw's desires on all points mentioned. Moreover, Potemkin explained to my informant that he clearly understood Poland's position *vis-à-vis* a potential alliance with Russia as characterized by Beck's reserve on the subject. Furthermore, Potemkin had assured Beck that Litvinov's replacement by Molotov did not entail a change in Moscow's foreign policy.

Judging from the above disclosures and from Beck's remarks subsequent to his conversation with Potemkin, the substance of which I reported in my cable under reference, I am inclined to believe that for Poland's part Poland desires: (a) mutual re-invigoration of Non-Aggression Agreement; (b) friendly relations along commercial but not political lines; (c) broadening of scope of existent Commercial Agreement to meet 1/ Poland's requirements of war *materiel* and supplies, and 2/ to provide Russian outlets for coal and industrial production of the Teschen district; (d) to avoid committing herself to an alliance with Russia whereby Poland, due to her strict principle of refusing to accept unilateral guarantees, might in turn find it necessary to guarantee the territorial integrity of Russia.

For Russia's part, Russia (a) desires to meet Poland's wishes regarding a non-aggression agreement, (b) understands and is willing to meet Poland's desires for friendly relations along commercial but not political lines, (c) is apparently willing to 1/ meet Poland's desire to broaden the scope of the existent Commercial Agreement to meet Poland's requirements of war *materiel* and supplies, and 2/ meet within reason Poland's requirement for a Russian outlet for coal and industrial production of the Teschen district.

Moreover, I perceive that Moscow not only understands Poland's position regarding a potential alliance with Russia, but perhaps welcomes [it], thus avoiding a closer tie-in to potential conflict whereby Russian troops might be involved beyond the Russian frontier.

1. This dispatch is not reproduced in this volume but is deposited in the Department of State Files of the National Archives, Washington, D.C.

2. Vladimir Potemkin (1878–1944), was the deputy commissar for foreign affairs of the Soviet Union. For Potemkin's report on this conversation, see *Dokumenty i Materialy* (Warsaw, 1973), 7:107–8.

May 20, 1939

Memorandum

   Today's conversations with official circles here reveal they
are aware of the following report: Berlin plans stirring up
trouble in Upper Silesia over a period of the next six weeks.
This is to serve partly as a diversion activity and partly as a
smoke screen for further machinations vis-à-vis Danzig,[1]
which are to be brought to a head at the end of the six-weeks
period. At that time, Berlin plans a bold stroke involving
Gdynia as well as Danzig. The German fleet is to take station
at a point vis-à-vis the two ports, and within gun range
thereof, while East Prussian troops are to enter the city by
the bridge at Marienburg and by the canal leading into the
city from the Vistula (This canal was deepened about one
and a half years ago with the idea of affording access to light
draught boats). Leading up to this point, a gradual accumula-
tion of German East Prussian troops will have taken place in
the city—under the guise, perhaps, of tourists. Already some
twenty truck loads of ammunition have been smuggled into
Danzig with a view to German occupation of some central
point within the confines of the city. (Polish authorities are
now in process of verifying this report and in ascertaining
the point whereat this ammunition is now allegedly stored.)
The plan, moreover, envisages an ultimatum stating that, if
the Poles did not surrender Danzig intact, the German fleet

would lay the port of Gdynia in ashes and the German troops (then envisagedly in the city) would synchronize their action with that of the fleet.

This plan has evidently been conceived as a means of circumventing the Polish plan to take over the city, in the event of a German threat thereto, before the East Prussian troops might have had time to cross the Vistula into Danzig. In this connection, it is well to bear in mind that there is but one bridge across the Vistula from East Prussia; while the Poles are afforded a comparatively speedy approach through a number of highways and several railways leading into Danzig. Moreover, the Polish batteries at Hel command the city. Furthermore, I am aware that the military authorities here, typifying the feelings of the Government and public opinion, would sooner lay Danzig in ashes than to permit its seizure and militarization by Germany. As several of the Polish High Command remarked to me: To lay Danzig in ashes would be exceedingly painful for the Poles but, after all, every Pole realizes that German militarization thereof would spell the eventual end of Poland's access to the Baltic. German artillery mounted in Danzig would be within easy range of Gdynia and would serve the Nazi agents as a threat to Polish interests and as a constant instrument of pressure on Polish shippers and shipping interests.

In discussing the aforementioned report of Berlin's plan to force the surrender of Danzig, I am aware that, while my informants are disinclined to attach a too great importance thereto, they are aware that such reports call for added calm consideration and vigilance. In fact, they are inclined to put these reports down to a Berlin-inspired "open secret", characteristic of Berlin's jitters-inspiring technique, and such might be aimed not only at racking Polish nerves but also at causing sufficient anxiety in foreign quarters as to draw further offers of mediation. Moreover, one official, at the conclusion of reading aloud to me the details of the envisaged plan as reported by a Polish Intelligence officer, calmly remarked, "So what?" He then went on to say that this scheme should not be considered in the light of action which could be localized, for a military conflict which would ensue from such action would rapidly spread to the proportions of a general conflagration. Berlin knew this only too well and realized that the putting into operation of such a scheme would spell nothing short of a European war. Of course, if Hitler wanted war, that was one thing; but my informant did not think Hitler was willing actually to risk war over Danzig within the next six weeks.

---

1. It should be noted that shortly before this document was written, the Danzig Nazis had cancelled the elections promised for the spring of 1939, and tension was mounting in Danzig.

June 9, 1939

Subject: Reactions of Polish Official
circles to Berlin's current attitude

I have the honor to report that my recent conversations with informed officials here reveal that their reactions to Berlin's current attitude assume in effect the following line:

Notwithstanding (A) a noticeable *détente* in general tone of German press *vis-à-vis* Poland; (B) Berlin officialdom's suggestion that Warsaw and Berlin agree to soft-pedal their respective press campaigns; and (C) Wilhelmstrasse's having recently "taken to sending word" to Warsaw, 1/ indirectly through League High Commissioner Burckhardt and others, and 2/ through German Ambassador to Poland von Moltke, that Berlin would welcome re-opening of Warsaw-Berlin negotiations when times were quieter; Berlin (a) continues to "hack away" at the Danzig problem both in press and through other forms of propaganda, as well as through inspiration of provocative activities in Danzig; and (b) appears to be deliberately heaping coals on smoldering fires by further irritating Warsaw with attempt to deport to Poland Jews of Polish origin living in Germany.*

From the foregoing disclosures, I gained the impression my informants feel that the discrepancy between Berlin's words and actions cautions against attaching too much credence to Berlin's "smiles". Moreover, they are frank to admit that the aforementioned discrepancy serves further to diminish confidence in any expression of intention or policy on part either of Hitler or his associates.

* In this connection, Jewish leaders here inform me that during the past three days 80 Jews have been chased from Germany over the German-Polish border. Although most of them had no papers, the Polish authorities at Zbąszyn took pity and permitted them to enter Poland. According to my aforementioned informants, about 4,000 Jews of Polish origin living in Germany recently received orders to evacuate Germany. My informants understood that the Polish Government had warned Berlin that it would have recourse to retaliatory measures should mass expulsion of Jews of Polish origin take place in Germany. My informants added their estimate that there were about 20,000 Jews of Polish origin currently inhabiting Germany. Some of these had passports in order; others had no papers. [Biddle's own footnote—Eds.]

June 9, 1939

Subject: Current propaganda campaign of German
Ambassador and his staff amongst their colleagues,
aimed at weakening anti-aggression front

I have the honor to report the following observations upon
current propaganda activities of the German Ambassador and
his staff: They have for the past several weeks been actively
engaged in propagandizing among the Chiefs and staffs of
Missions representing a number of the links in the chain of
anti-aggression forces.* The Ambassador's program has
thus far entailed a series of luncheons and dinners whereat
he arranges that the particular colleague whom he wishes to
impress joins him in after-luncheon or after-dinner conversation in a salon apart from the other guests. During the past
two weeks he has thus conducted lengthy talks with the
Rumanian Ambassador, the Yugoslav Minister, the Greek
Minister, the Swiss Minister, the Swedish Minister, the
Finnish Minister, and the Netherlands Minister.

I learn that Moltke usually adopts the following "line":
Both the moral and armed strength of the Axis is far superior
to that of the democracies. He thereupon cites statistics on
comparative air strengths and motorized equipment, heavy
artillery, etc. Moreover, he makes it a point to emphasize
that, in case of war, the anti-aggression forces east of the Axis
would have to look for aid from Russia, for neither Britain
nor France could help them directly either in terms of troops
or equipment. This would mean that the anti-aggression

forces of the aforementioned category would be forced to run the risk of encountering eventual Russian pressure. Realizing the dependence of certain states upon her aid, Russia might thus be in position to impose conditions to the disadvantage of states concerned.

Moltke, moreover, points out that, should London and Paris come to terms with Berlin, the other anti-aggression forces, having served London and Paris usefully as "scenery in a big show", would be left to shift for themselves. They should therefore be mindful of their potential subsequent position vis-à-vis a Berlin which had a limit to its patience (This is clearly a warning that, in event Britain, France, and Germany came to terms, the "little fellows" had better be careful lest they be left at the mercy of Germany's potential vindictiveness).

Regarding Poland, Moltke points out that now, given an opportunity to count Poland among the anti-aggression forces, Britain and France had thus far given little, if any, tangible evidence of their confidence and serious intention. Indeed, their combined attitude had been characterized by delay in extending Poland accommodation in terms of equipment and finance. This example could hardly prove encouraging for other links in the anti-aggression chain (This remark indicates Berlin is keeping close watch over London-Warsaw negotiations).[1]

In further attempt to engage his listeners' concern over London and Paris, and particularly London, Moltke significantly intimates that reports reaching Berlin indicate that certain important elements in both capitals are only awaiting a psychological moment to invite the Axis powers to a peace conference. In this connection, Moltke intimates in effect that, for purposes of home consumption, London might conceivably resort to a pretext that, in terms of peace gestures, it was necessary to leave no stone unturned, in order to place the blame for a possible conflict at Hitler's door. Judging, however, from current delays in implementing the present form of the Anglo-Polish Pact with moves of practical value, it would appear London was hesitating, and giving serious consideration to the risk of involvement in a war over such questions as Danzig and a Corridor passageway.

In cases where Moltke's listeners have subsequently imparted in confidence the substance of his remarks, I have been careful to study my informants' reactions. Accordingly, I discerned that, with but few exception, they were greatly impressed and concerned—in some cases obviously dismayed. As I have pointed out in previous writings, Moltke is intelligent and possesses a charming, convincing manner.

* The newly appointed Soviet Ambassador here [Nicholas Sharonov] confidentially volunteered the information that Moscow was aware that the German Mission Chiefs in all capitals throughout Europe were, pursuant [to the] Wilhelmstrasse's instructions, conducting a propaganda campaign among their colleagues with a view to weakening, if not breaking up, the anti-aggression front. [Biddle's own footnote—Eds.]

1. On the London-Warsaw negotiations, see Raczynski, *In Allied London*, pp. 17–18, and Szembek, *Diariusz i Teki*, vol. 4, passim.

June 27, 1939

Memorandum

In a recent informal but confidential conversation with a group of informed, high-ranking Government officials and military authorities, I enjoyed the opportunity of "listening in" to their "thinking out loud" in a several hours' *tour d'horizon*. I thus gained an insight to their trend of thought in relation to the chances of current European developments' coming to a war.[1]

The following in effect represents the substance of my informants' discussion:

To their minds, it would be difficult to liquidate the current conflict of forces in Europe through statesmanship and diplomacy in that the differences at stake did not wholly constitute material problems. Indeed, underlying the conflict were two discernible, basically different conceptions. The Nazi regime of Germany were determined to impose their will upon states which they envisaged as a part of an eventual pan-Germanic area under Hitler's sovereignty. Moreover, Berlin wanted no outside interference, either with its methods of acquiring control over that area or with the form of control it might wish subsequently to exercise thereover. In this connection, the matter of recognized principles governing international relationships counted for naught in Berlin's view. Ethical principles had little to do with the conception of the power politicians of current-day Germany. Their mentality was attuned to the conception of ruthless, strong-armed methods to gain and subsequently maintain control over their objectives.

On the other hand, the forces in conflict with this conception based their international relations upon the principles of ethics and justice. It might even be said that they looked upon disputes arising out of international differences as a business man looked upon problems arising out of differences in the business field, and in this light upheld the method of conference and negotiation as a means of settlement of disputes. Hitler might be expected to participate in a conference only if he were amply assured in advance that the "cards were stacked" in his favor.

Moreover, acceptance of the thought that the conflict between the totalitarian and democratic states found its roots in the fundamental difference between two divergent conceptions led one in turn to consider the question as to whether these two conceptions could live alongside of each other in the same world. Did it not, therefore, boil down to a question as to whether the democracies were willing and capable of tolerating the existence of the totalitarian regimes, and all they implied, and whether the democracies, in the interests of humanity, international law and order, and "good business", might eventually decide to put an end to them.

In line with this thought, and in attempting to estimate in what direction Europe was heading, it seemed that one of the following three eventualities might be expected to prove the case: either appeasement (of the "Munich" type), or revolution in Germany (envisaging the downfall of the Nazi regime), or war, or prevention of war by no relaxation in the anti-aggression front, and principally in a three-cornered nucleus thereof, London, Paris, and Warsaw.

So far as appeasement was concerned, the results of "Munich" had shown the flaws in such a course, and the disastrous results served as a warning against returning to such a means of settlement.

As regards a revolution in Germany, there were important elements, particularly in the "City" of London (some connected with no less an institution than the Bank of England), whose "wish-thinking" gave rise to political dreams devoid of realism, and envisaging the Nazi regime's downfall in consequence of mounting internal economic discomfort. Too much importance was apt to be attached to this possibility by these "stay-at-home" British elements. They were over-inclined, moreover, to think of Europe in terms of pre-War considerations, and were unfortunately given to "ostriching" their way through the "sunset years" of their lives. They failed to realize, however, that while Hitler's star went into a tailspin after the pogroms, and again immediately after Germany's occupation of Czecho-Slovakia, nevertheless his star later regained ascendency when the German masses awoke to a realization that their Fuehrer had "gotten away" with a major *coup* without spilling German blood. It gained added ascendent momentum, moreover, when Hitler, feeling around for some slogan to rally mass support again, seized upon "encirclement" as a "battle cry."

Meanwhile Hitler's having "gotten away" with his Czech *coup* strengthened his hand with the General Staff. Moreover, it should not be overlooked that during the interval between the end of the Great War and the Nazi regime, the Army played a minor role, and that Hitler's advent to power marked the commencement of an era characterized by the re-establishment of the German Army as a formidable factor —indeed, in German eyes, the Army's re-glorification. The officers' corps were aware of this fact. In other words, it was useless to allow wish-thinking to overcome a necessarily realistic consideration of Hitler's current position. There were sufficient stores of food-stuffs to cover at least the requirements of the coming year; there was also the present harvest, which should cover about 90 per cent of Germany's next eleven months' requirements—besides, the masses were capable of further tightening their belts. Moreover, the internal political forces opposed to Hitler were not organized and lacked leadership. Hence, in terms of the next year at least, revolution in Germany was more likely *after* than *before* the commencement of a war.

If, therefore, one were to admit the impracticability of appeasement in the "Munich" sense, and that a pre-war revolution in Germany were unlikely, then one was confronted with the questions as to whether war might be the only solution and whether war might be prevented and by what means.

In this connection, my informants remarked that Hitler, whose political power depended on employment, bread and circuses, could hardly be expected to stop now—for to draw back at this point would spell industrial shutdowns resulting in unemployment, which would eventually prove a monkey wrench in the machinery propelling the momentum of Nazi policy. Indeed, employment formed one of the chief planks in Hitler's platform. The fact that employment in the Greater Reich was based mainly on the armament industry and construction of fortifications meant that Hitler would necessarily encounter serious social and economic problems were he to agree to participate in a program of disarmament. This was a picture wherefrom Hitler and, even to no less degree, the extremists constituting the "Mafia" (currently surrounding him) would be apt to recoil. Rather than face such a prospect, the extremists might press Hitler to gamble "the works" for "big stakes"—this crowd still believed they could win in a campaign of lightning destruction. From the standpoint of logic, Hitler might be expected to recognize that the forces were mounting against him with the passing of each month, and in the same light one might expect that if Europe "got by" early November without war the chances of war during this generation would be almost nil. However, it was difficult to appraise the situation from the standpoint of logic when the situation rested solely upon the whims of a cyclothymic, Austrian mentality such as Hitler's. Meanwhile Hitler must go on providing his public with employment, bread and circuses.

At this point my informants emphasized their unanimous opinion that the only way to prevent war would be constant vigilance of a strong London-Paris-Warsaw front, which after all represented the nucleus of what had subsequently become known as the anti-aggression front. Accordingly, London and Paris must avoid giving Berlin the slightest impression of doubt as to their determination to support Poland in relation to Danzig. My informants then pointed out that Poland stood as the cornerstone of strength in Eastern Europe, and, if anything happened to Poland, Eastern and Central Europe would undoubtedly collapse. Up to this point, Hitler had been halted and might possibly be prevented from bursting out, provided the anti-aggression front were maintained in vigor.

The strengthening and maintenance of the anti-aggression front might prove an expensive operation, but if it succeeded, as was its cardinal policy in preventing war, it would prove far cheaper than a conflagration. Besides, it should be borne in mind that since Hitler alone would decide the issue of war or peace, Hitler had an Austrian mentality, traditionally formidable vis-à-vis weakness but inclined to confusion and even retreat in the face of strength.

1. This memorandum is especially important because of the accurate picture it presents of the way the international situation was then seen in Warsaw. Indeed, it shows how well informed Biddle's informants—high government officials—were about the thinking going on in London and how well they understood Berlin.

July 26, 1939

Subject: Substance of Marshal Śmigły-Rydz's additional confidential observations on: (a) the pace and extent of Polish and German mobilization vis-à-vis one another; (b) time necessary for Germany to mobilize for conflict with Poland; (c) dates in connection with German maneuvers; (d) general aspects of military-political picture in making; (e) estimate as to chances of war—60%; (f) clarification thereof (supplementing his former observations); (g) best means of war prevention

I have the honor to supplement my cable No. 139 of July 6, 1 p.m., and my despatches Nos. 1104 of June 20 and 1115 of June 24, 1939,[1] and to report in the following paragraphs the substance of Marshal Śmigły-Rydz's additional confidential observations.

Several days ago Marshal Śmigły-Rydz confidentially characterized the course of military activities on both sides of the Polish-German fence between March and the present as successive efforts on the part of each side to match the other in terms of mobilized strength; for example, when Poland had concentrated two divisions in vicinity of the Polish-German frontier, the Germans thereupon concentrated three on their side; immediately following this Poland increased her strength to five; shortly thereafter the Germans replied by equalling this amount in their side; thus each side had successively stepped up its strength gradually over a period of four months. However, the amount of German force now in the field vis-à-vis the Polish frontier could not as yet be regarded as an intensive mobilization. German troops were now gradually concentrating in the area vis-à-vis Poznan—but to date not to an alarming degree. Moreover, very recent reports indicated a slight increase in troop movement in the Breslau-Oppeln area—but not to an alarming extent thus far.

The Marshal then imparted that according to his own and his military experts' estimate it would take the Germans two weeks to mobilize forces sufficient to come to grips with Poland.* He then stated that his intelligence reports indicated that: (a) all leaves of absence granted on large scale to German officers corps during this month would terminate July 28 and (b) that the student corps now engaged in harvesting would have returned to their respective home centers by August 10 and, as these students were reservists, they would be ready thereupon to engage in maneuvers.

Commenting then upon the more general aspects of the military-political picture in the making, the Marshal estimated that chances were 60% in favor of war and 40% in favor of the prevention of war this year. By way of clarification he pointed out that this represented Germany's strategic year; at the moment it was only reasonable to admit that despite declarations of firmness and public utterances regarding mounting strength of the anti-aggression front, the Axis still had the edge. Time, however, was working against Germany and a year hence would have found the military strength of the anti-aggression forces pretty well in balance with Axis strength; two years hence it would undoubtedly have surpassed Axis strength.

I am aware, moreover, that the Marshal is in accord with Beck's conviction that solidity on part of the anti-aggression front in a firm stand would prove the most effective antidote to Germany's expansion aspirations. They both share the belief that this is the only language which might succeed in halting Hitler, who had thus far employed his armed force more as a blackmailing instrument than as a factor intended to come actually to grips with formidable strength. However, they both feel that Hitler, alert for openings, would seize immediate advantage of any sign of weakness at any point along the anti-aggression front.

1. These dispatches are not reproduced in this volume but are deposited in the Department of State Files of the National Archives, Washington, D.C.

* According to information from other competent sources, however, the German air force is in constant readiness for action either to the west or east, a consideration which, to my mind, might have important bearing, for example, in [the] event Berlin might suddenly decide to present Warsaw with an ultimatum. [Biddle's own footnote—Eds.]

[*Washington*]

August 9, 1939

Memorandum of Conversation

Subject: General European situation
Participants: Count Jerzy Potocki, Polish Ambassador;
the Under Secretary [Sumner Welles]

The Polish Ambassador called to see me this afternoon upon his return to the United States after a month's stay in Poland.

The Ambassador stated, first of all, that he was gratified to be able to tell me that the morale in Poland was admirable, and that he had not detected the slightest sign of hysteria nor of nervousness in any section of public opinion. He said that the attitude unanimously assumed by the Polish people was that if Germany forced a war upon them by threatening the autonomy and independence of Poland by the taking over of Danzig or by jeopardizing the integrity of the Corridor, the Poles would fight to the last ditch to preserve their independence. He stated that this feeling was eminently strengthened by the intimate knowledge which the Poles had, through their familiarity with what was going on within Bohemia and Moravia, of the treatment being accorded to the Czechs by the German authorities. He said that it was notorious in Poland that the Czech male population had been classified by the Germans according to categories, and that many of these categories of Czechs had already been removed from the occupied provinces and had been taken to Germany, where they were being subjected to forced labor in the construction of fortifications, roads, etc.

The Ambassador stated that he had been equally impressed in the visits which he had made to England and France with the great change which had taken place within those two countries since last year. He said that in England particularly the morale was now magnificent and the rearmament program had reached a point of the greatest efficiency.

The Ambassador stated that the Germans were pursuing a policy along the Polish frontier of attempting to break down Polish nerves by continued concentrations of German divisions. He said on one day German divisions would be concentrated at one point on the frontier and a couple of days later there would be a similar concentration on another point of the frontier, but he said that the significant thing about this was that they were practically always the same German divisions. The Ambassador said that his Government was aware that in Slovakia the Germans were exceedingly active in the way of military preparations. These preparations, he said, consisted primarily of the widening of existing roads, strengthening of bridges, and the construction of new feeder roads leading towards the Polish frontier. Within Poland itself, he said there was little evidence of military activity to the average observer. He said that most of the maneuvers were carried out at night, and that these operations were conducted with complete efficiency. He said that in the event of war the Polish General Staff had determined that they would not limit themselves to a defensive war, but would undertake an offensive campaign in order to penetrate into Germany, and that, with their highly mobilized forces, particularly the cavalry, the Polish General Staff believed that they had a reasonable prospect for success in such an endeavor.[2]

With regard to the prospects during the next few weeks, the Ambassador said that Colonel Beck was inclined to believe that war would not break out. He said it was Beck's impression that Hitler was becoming gradually convinced that the risks of a general war were too great for Germany to force the issue and that, while Ribbentrop was still continually telling Hitler that England and France would not fight over Danzig, the Polish Government knew that the German generals had informed Hitler two weeks ago that, while if the war could be limited to a war between Poland and Germany Germany would win easily, if the war involved England and France the German generals could give no assurances of any kind to Hitler as to the outcome. He said that Hitler was beginning to get information from sources other than Ribbentrop which was leading him to feel that England and France would fight with Poland should Poland fight on the Danzig issue.

Beck believed that Germany would probably not risk war over Danzig but would continue for an indefinite period its present policy of constant provocation of Poland without going to the extreme limit. Beck believed it was far more likely that Hitler before the middle of September would bring about the downfall of the Hungarian Government, replacing it with a government completely subservient to Germany, and then spend the next six months in amalgamating the position so obtained in order to make it easier for Germany to attack Poland when the time came through Hungary and Slovakia and in the same manner obtain a more preponderant position in southeastern Europe.

I asked the Ambassador what solution his Government saw to the present situation since it would clearly seem incredible that mobilization and military preparations could continue at the existing rate and that the entire world be kept at its present state of extreme uncertainty and of anxiety for any protracted period. To this the Ambassador made the singularly unconvincing reply that he thought that if no war broke out this autumn, the internal situation in Germany would become so serious by midwinter that Hitler would be overthrown by the spring and some more reasonable regime would come into power in Germany before next summer. I asked him if he had any reason to think that public opinion in Germany showed any signs of extreme dissatisfaction with the present regime, and he stated that he had no specific information to that effect but that he knew the internal economy of Germany was so precarious that the utmost measure of dissatisfaction was inevitable before many months had passed.

The Ambassador stated that on his return to the United States he had stopped off for a few hours in Berlin to talk with his colleague the Polish Ambassador, [Józef] Lipski. He said that Lipski had told him that the refusal of the American Congress to revise the neutrality legislation had had an eminently encouraging effect upon the German authorities, both civil and military, but that fortunately this had been counteracted completely by the announcement made by the Government of the United States of its termination of the commercial treaty with Japan. Ambassador Lipski had said that no one could exaggerate the consternation which this step by the United States had created in Berlin.

I asked the Ambassador if he had any information, or what the opinion of his Government might be, with regard to the success of the negotiations now in progress in Moscow between the British and French and the Soviets for a political and military agreement. The Ambassador replied that Colonel Beck believed that a political agreement was improbable, but that he thought a military agreement would be concluded. In reply to a further inquiry from me, the Ambassador said that the Polish Government was informed that the Italian Government was continually counseling moderation on the German Government, but that no representations of any kind had been made to Poland by Italy with regard to the Polish-German situation.

The Ambassador told me explicitly that there had been no conversations and no negotiations of any character whatever between Germany and Poland with regard to the Danzig issue. He said that the Polish Government had deliberately refrained from making any approach at all to Germany because of its conviction that if any such approach were made, Germany would construe it as a sign of fear and of weakness and would adopt a far more vigorous attitude.

The Ambassador stated in conclusion that Poland expected to get a cash loan from Great Britain and France in addition to the credits already arranged. He said that Poland's great need at this time was pursuit planes and raw materials, particularly cotton and copper. He said that a certain amount of the latter commodities could be obtained from Russia but that Russia was not in a position to supply very much, and that it was the most earnest hope of the Polish Government that some arrangements could be made in the United States for obtaining these raw materials. He said that his Government fully understood its situation in this country on account of the Johnson Act,[3] but it hoped, nevertheless, that some way could be found whereby credits might be obtained for the purchase of these supplies. I told the Ambassador that if he had any definite suggestions to make, I should be glad to consider them. He told me that he would talk with me again about this matter.

In general the Ambassador seemed to feel that war was not imminent and that, while undoubtedly a very serious crisis would arise before the end of August, it would probably pass off for the time being.

1. This document has been partially published in *Foreign Relations of the United States, 1939* (Washington, D.C., 1956), 1:206–8.

2. This information was incorrect. The Polish plan was a defensive one, aimed at holding up the German forces as much as possible, until the French army launched the great offensive against Germany promised in the Polish-French military agreement of May, 1939. See above, Part 2, footnote 9, for details of the defense plan. Potocki probably did not know of this plan, since it was known only to the commander in chief and the chief of staff. He may have been thinking of terms of the old Foch plan of 1923, whereby if France were attacked, Poland was to penetrate into Germany.

3. The Johnson Act of April 13, 1934, initiated by Congress, forbade Americans to make loans to nations that had not paid their war debts. The Federal government could, however, grant credits in certain cases through the Export-Import Bank.

Warsaw

August 25, 1939

Telegram

Supplementing my number 191, August 24, 3 p.m.[1] Further conversation with Beck and associates discloses that while it is difficult for them to stomach Danzig Senate's decree nevertheless after careful consideration all aspects Government thereupon decided to exercise further restraint.[2]

Accordingly Government adopted an official attitude along following lines: while substance of decree represented open violation of Danzig statutes its bearing was mainly internal and in such light a matter of consideration and action of Committee of Three and League of Nations. For Poland, Danzig's internal structure was of secondary importance. Poland was mainly interested in full respect of Polish rights in Free City, accordingly Poland would interpret any one of following actions as violation of these rights: (a) attempt to annex Danzig to Reich; (b) exclusion of Danzig from Polish customs zone; (c) subjection of Polish rights in Danzig to control of third state; (d) withdrawal of Polish rights covering national development of Poles in Danzig. Moreover Polish Government would carefully observe development of conditions in Danzig inasmuch as Danzig had failed to manifest good will in the matter of customs inspectors.

In connection with foregoing Beck confidentially imparted his Government would declare its attitude toward Danzig governmental alteration when the real aims of the revision become clear.

Meanwhile 24 railway men arrested in Danzig yesterday were released and Polish courier detained early yesterday in Breslau was released and diplomatic pouch restored to him.

Schoolship SCHLESWIG HOLSTEIN came to anchor as per schedule 7:40 this morning Danzig harbor.[3] Early morning atmosphere in Danzig increasingly electric as evidenced among other factors by (a) overnight augmentation of military cars and trucks (b) yesterday's evacuation of many school children and (c) today's closing of schools.

Either Hitler has decided to act and not talk or else the absence of some statement after his last night's conference with Nazi bigwigs (for which all press wires had been kept open until dawn) indicates Hitler is still undecided as to definite plan of action.[4]

1. This document is not reproduced in this volume but is deposited in the Department of State Files of the National Archives, Washington, D.C.

2. Biddle's reference here to a "decree" is unclear. The Danzig Senate issued no major decrees immediately preceding this telegram, except for the proclamation recognizing the installment of Forster as chief (*Stadtoberhaupt*) of the Free City on August 23, in express violation of its statutes. But the Senate and the Polish government had been waging an undeclared war since March, 1939, when the Senate arbitrarily decreed that elections to it would not be held as scheduled that Spring, but instead would be postponed four years; since Polish and anti-Nazi candidates expected to gain considerably in the elections, this unconstitutional act upset Warsaw. Moreover, when Polish customs officers tried to perform their assigned tasks in July and August in the face of a new high of illegal weapons smuggling from Germany into Danzig, local officials applied every imaginable device to obstruct them, even resorting to violence.

3. Biddle's use of the term "schoolship" to describe the German vessel *Schleswig Holstein* is misleading. In reality, it was a modern warship used for practical training in the arts of advanced naval warfare provided to German line naval personnel, and possessed a full complement of the latest naval weaponry. When the Nazi forces assaulted Poland on September 1, the *Schleswig Holstein* played a key role in subduing Danzig with the firepower from its cannon, situated so advantageously in the harbor.

4. Hitler originally had set August 26 as the date for the opening campaign against Poland, but the signing of a formal Anglo-Polish Mutual Assistance Pact on the August 25 forced him to postpone his plans for nearly a week. This accounts for the unexplained absence of activity that so puzzled Biddle.

INDEX